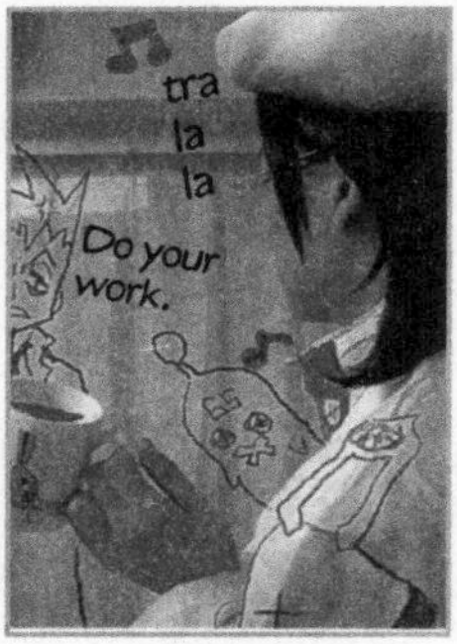
tra
la
la
Do your work.

I received a fan mail that said the kanji character for "Katsura" also means moon. So my full name – Hoshino Katsura – could mean "star's moon" (because *hoshi* means star and *no* is a possessive particle). It's so romantic... It's a bit *too* romantic; it's kind of embarrassing.

—Katsura Hoshino

Shiga Prefecture native Katsura Hoshino's hit manga series *D.Gray-man* has been serialized in *Weekly Shonen Jump* since 2004. Katsura's first series "Continue" first appeared in *Weekly Shonen Jump* in 2003.

Katsura adores cats.

D.GRAY-MAN

VOL. 3

SHONEN JUMP ADVANCED
Manga Edition

STORY AND ART BY
KATSURA HOSHINO

English Adaptation/Lance Caselman
Translation/Toshifumi Yoshida
Touch-up Art & Lettering/Elizabeth Watasin
Design/Yukiko Whitley
Editor/Urian Brown

D.GRAY-MAN © 2004 by Katsura Hoshino. All rights reserved.
First published in Japan in 2004 by SHUEISHA Inc., Tokyo.
English translation rights arranged by SHUEISHA Inc.

The rights of the author(s) of the work(s) in this publication to be so identified have
been asserted in accordance with the Copyright, Designs and Patents Act 1988. A CIP
catalogue record for this book is available from the British Library.

The stories, characters and incidents mentioned in this publication are entirely fictional.

Printed in the U.S.A.

Published by VIZ Media, LLC
P.O. Box 77010
San Francisco, CA 94107

10 9 8 7 6
First printing, November 2006
Sixth printing, December 2010

THE WORLD'S MOST
CUTTING-EDGE MANGA

SHONEN JUMP
ADVANCED
www.shonenjump.com

www.viz.com

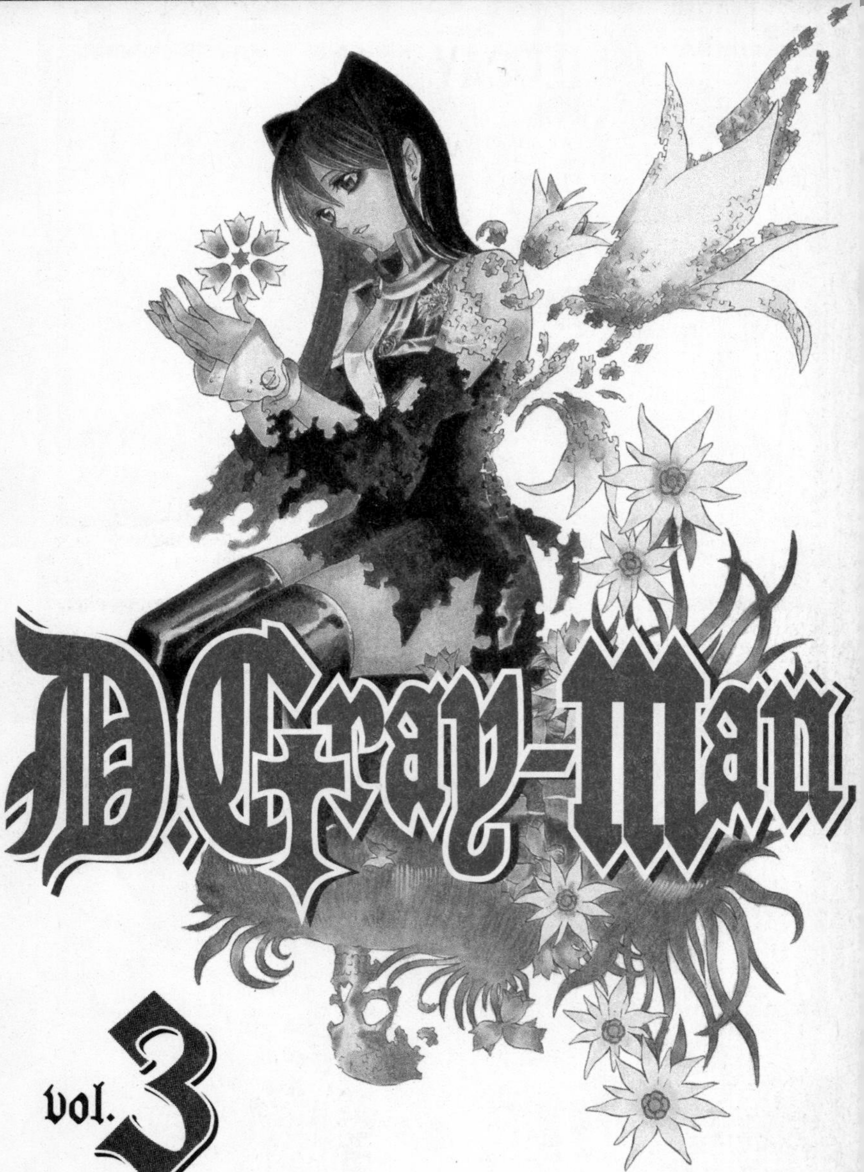

D.Gray-man

vol. 3

STORY & ART BY
Katsura Hoshino

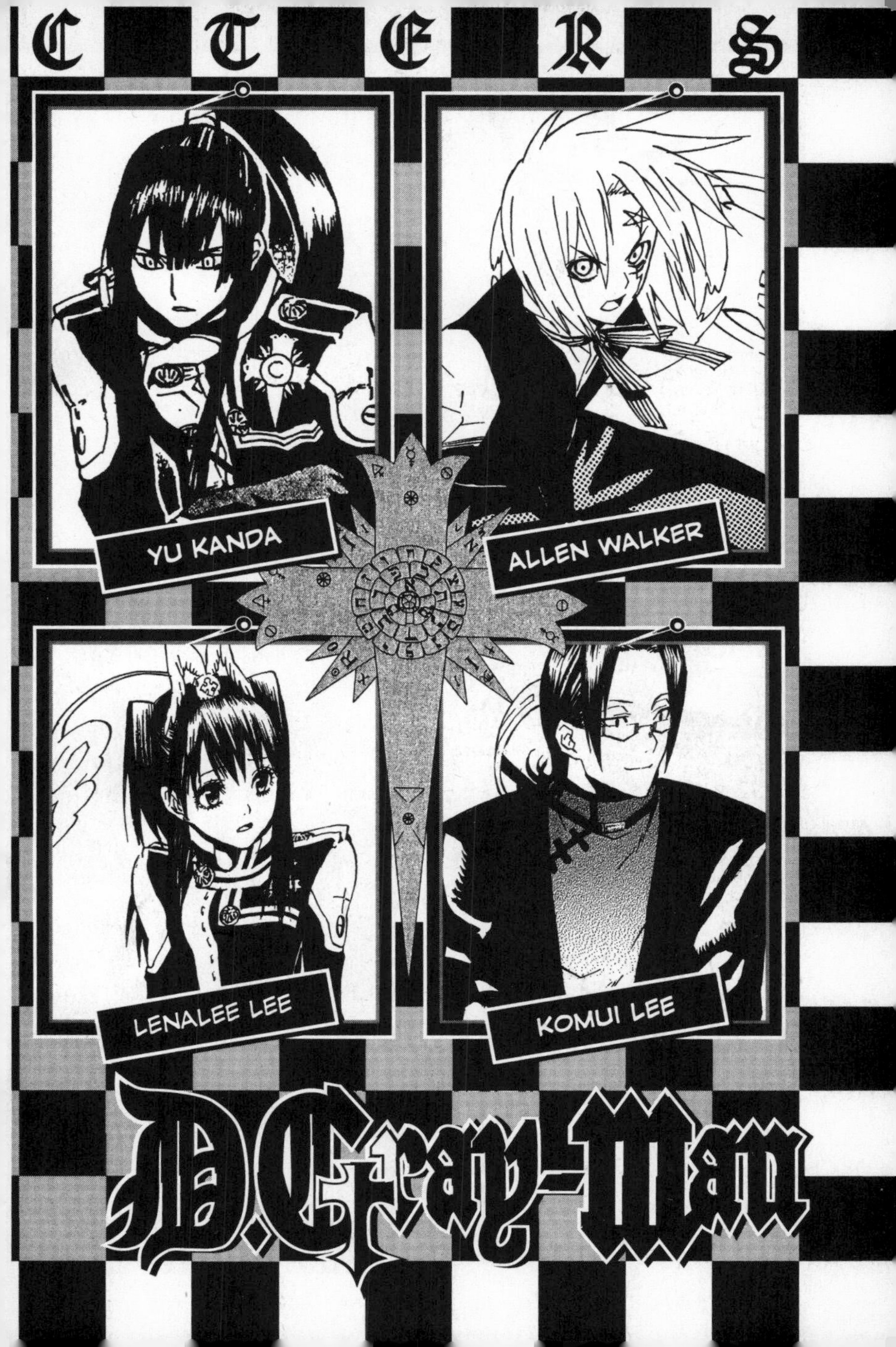
C T E R S
YU KANDA
ALLEN WALKER
LENALEE LEE
KOMUI LEE
D.Gray-man

C H A R A

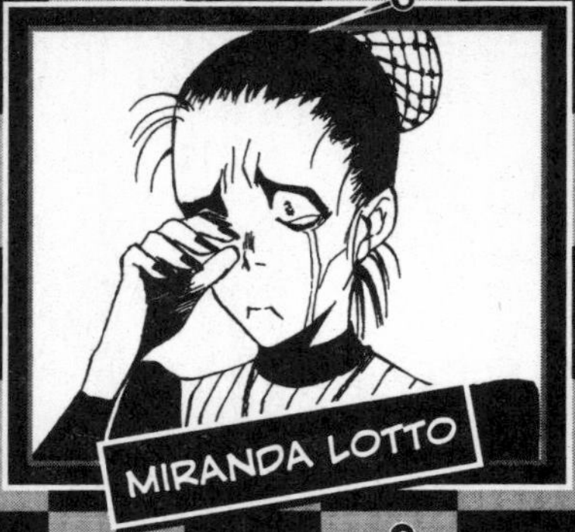
MIRANDA LOTTO

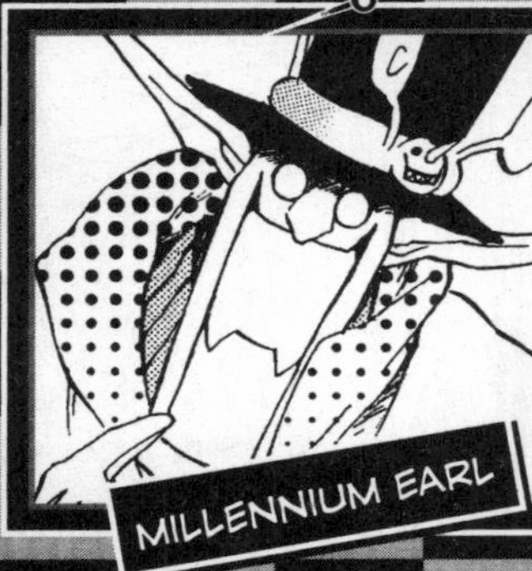
MILLENNIUM EARL

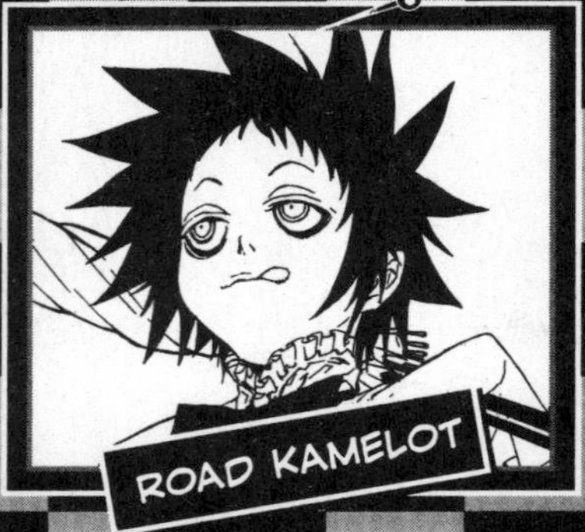
ROAD KAMELOT

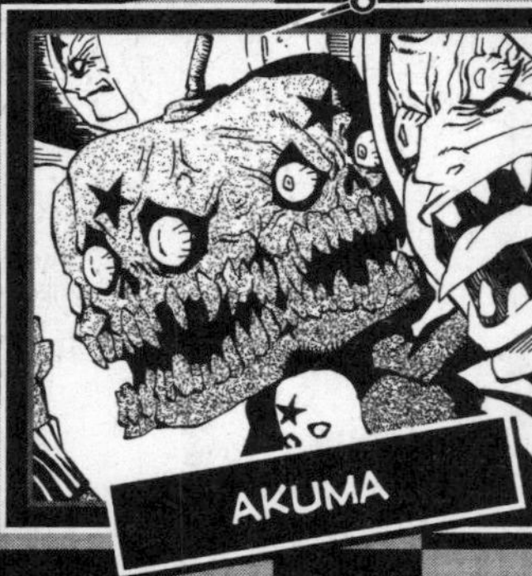
AKUMA

S T O R Y

...AFTER ARRIVING AT THE EXORCIST HEADQUARTERS, "THE BLACK ORDER," ALLEN OFFICIALLY BECAME AN EXORCIST. HE SUCCESSFULLY ACCOMPLISHED HIS FIRST MISSION WITH THE HELP OF FELLOW EXORCIST, KANDA. WHAT MISSION AWAITS ALLEN NEXT, AS HE DELIVERS THE RETRIEVED INNOCENCE?

D.GRAY-MAN
Vol. 3

CONTENTS

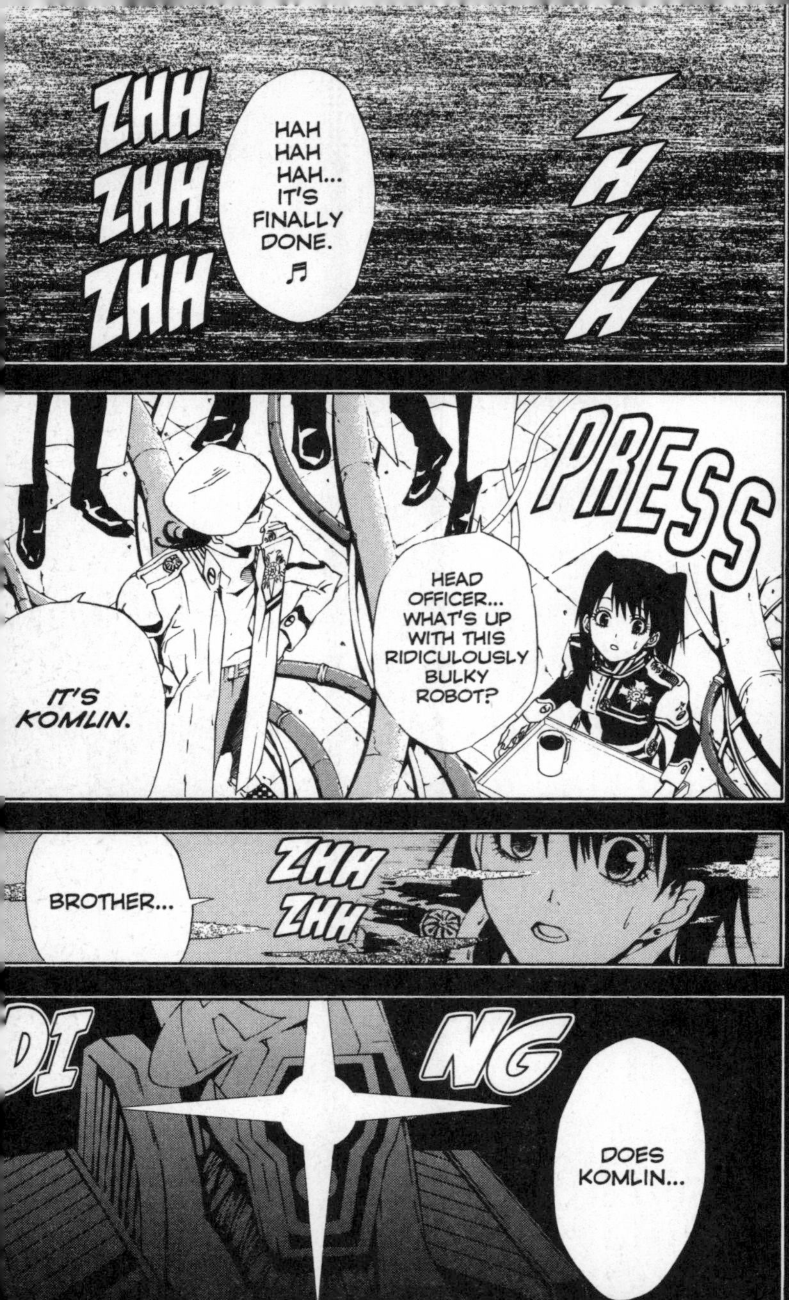
ZHHHH
HAH HAH HAH... IT'S FINALLY DONE. ♬
ZHH ZHH ZHH
PRESS
HEAD OFFICER... WHAT'S UP WITH THIS RIDICULOUSLY BULKY ROBOT?
IT'S KOMLIN.
ZHH ZHH
BROTHER...
DOES KOMLIN...
DING

HE 17TH NIGHT: THE BLACK ORDER ANNIHILATION INCIDENT

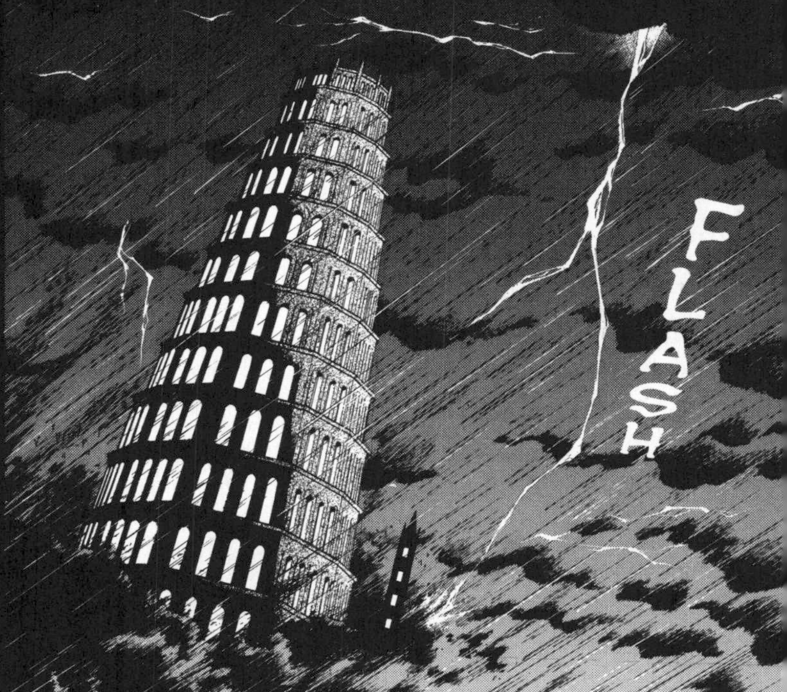
FLASH

THE 17TH NIGHT: THE BLACK ORDER ANNIHILATION INCIDENT

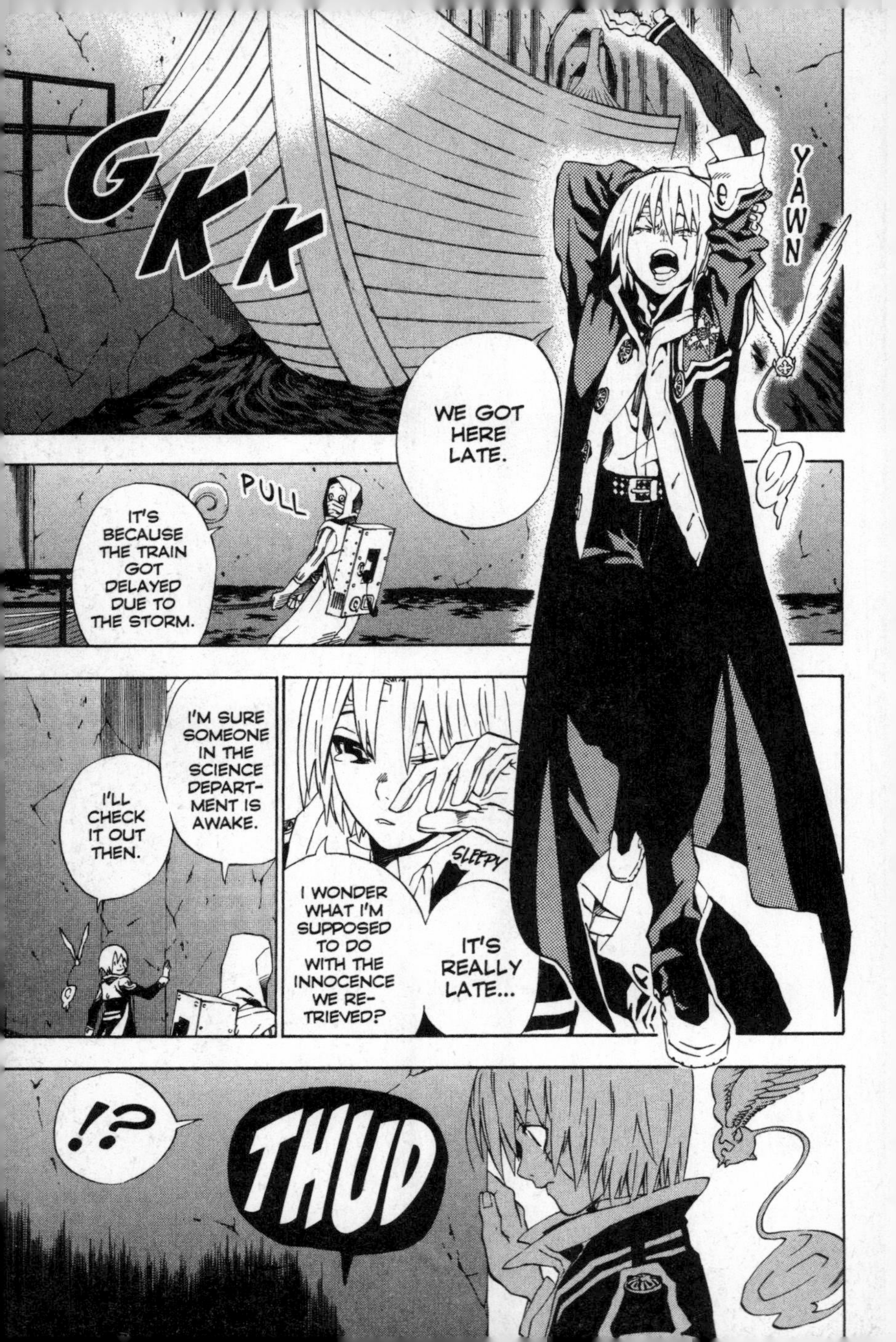
YAWN
WE GOT HERE LATE.
GKK
PULL
IT'S BECAUSE THE TRAIN GOT DELAYED DUE TO THE STORM.
SLEEPY
IT'S REALLY LATE...
I WONDER WHAT I'M SUPPOSED TO DO WITH THE INNOCENCE WE RE-TRIEVED?
I'M SURE SOMEONE IN THE SCIENCE DEPART-MENT IS AWAKE.
I'LL CHECK IT OUT THEN.
THUD
!?

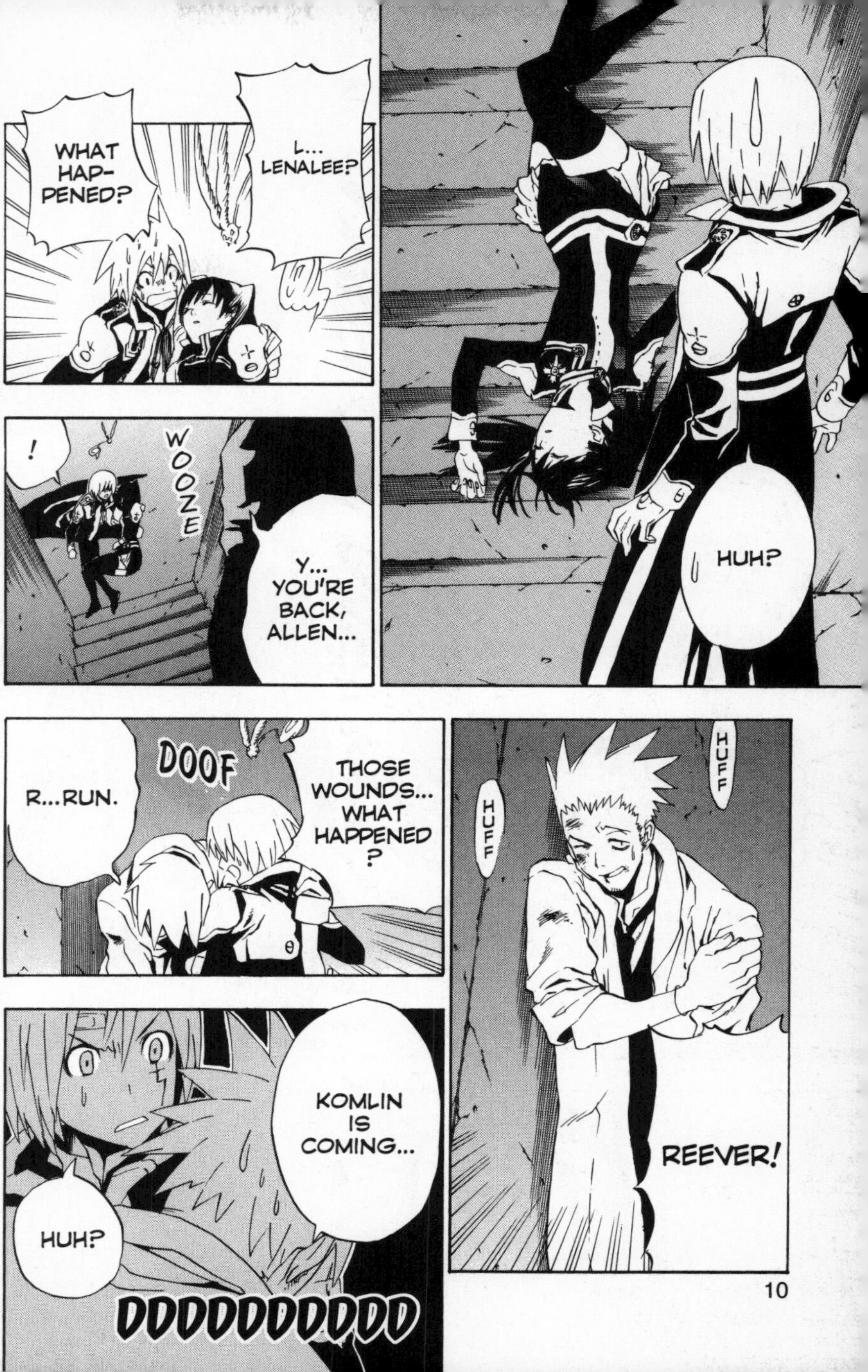
HUH?
L... LENALEE?
WHAT HAP-PENED?
WOOZE
!
Y... YOU'RE BACK, ALLEN...
HUFF
HUFF
REEVER!
THOSE WOUNDS... WHAT HAPPENED?
DOOF
R...RUN.
KOMLIN IS COMING...
HUH?
DDDDDDDDDDD

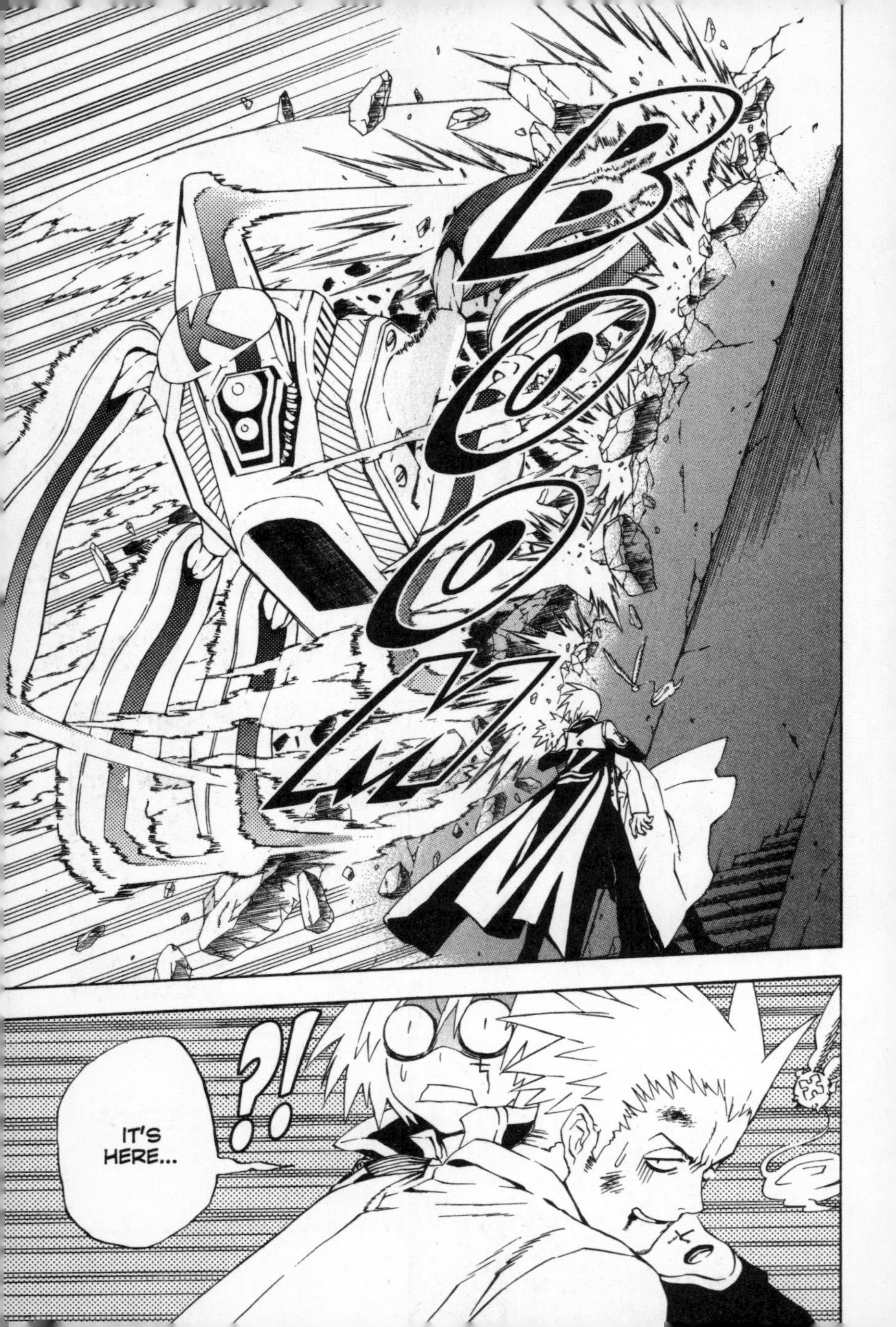
BOOOM
?!
IT'S HERE...

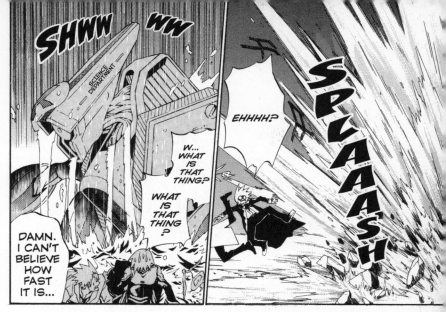

SHWWWW

SPLAAAASH

W... WHAT IS THAT THING?

WHAT IS THAT THING?

EHHHH?

DAMN. I CAN'T BELIEVE HOW FAST IT IS...

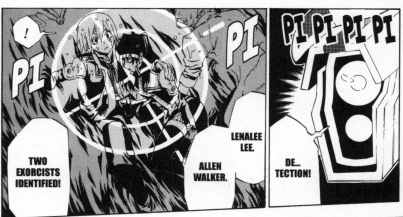

PI

PI

PI PI PI PI

!

TWO EXORCISTS IDENTIFIED!

LENALEE LEE.

ALLEN WALKER.

DE... TECTION!

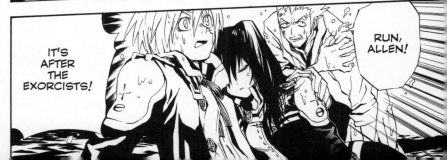

IT'S AFTER THE EXORCISTS!

RUN, ALLEN!

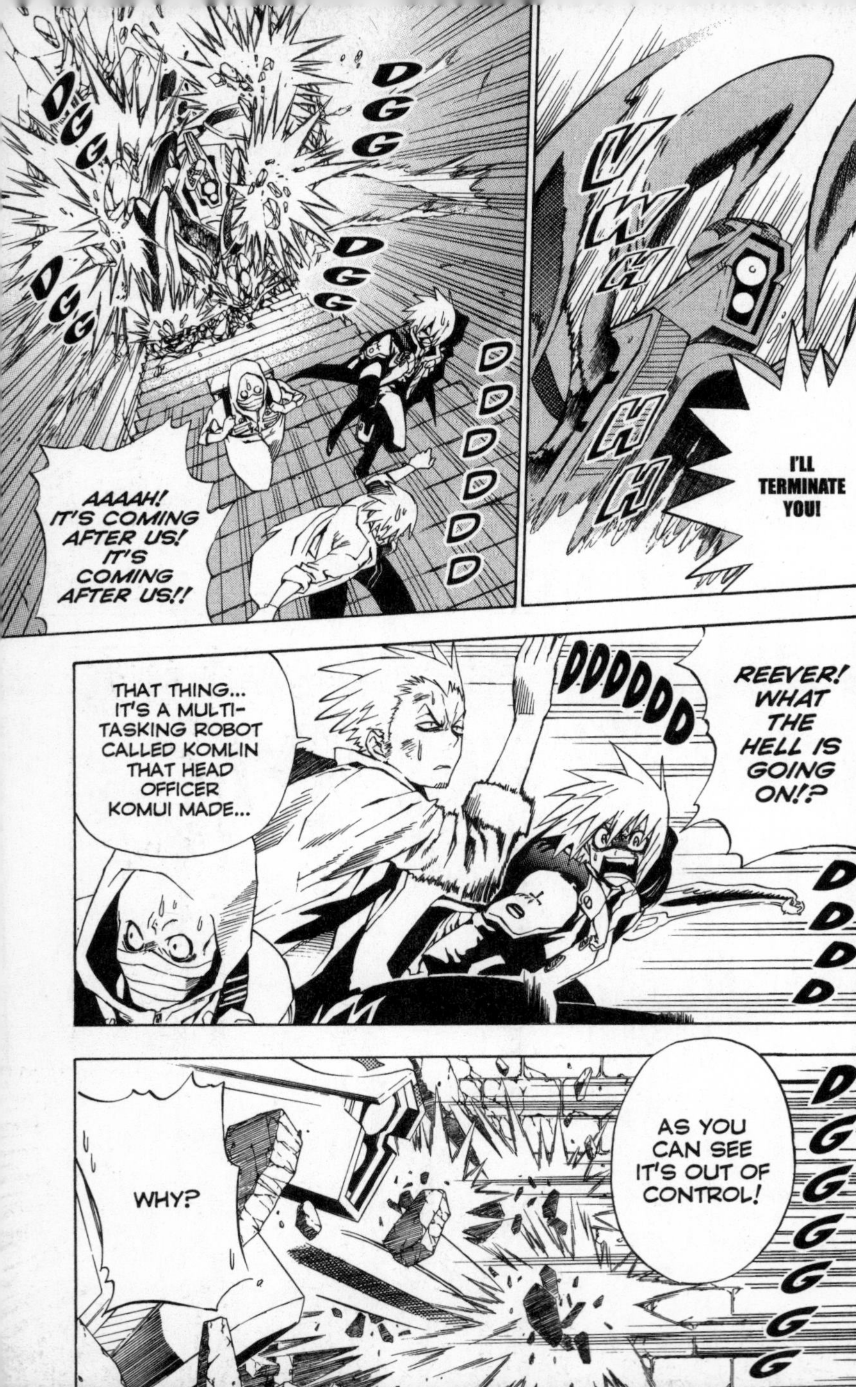
I'LL TERMINATE YOU!
DGG
DGG
DGG
DGG
DDDDDDDD
AAAAH! IT'S COMING AFTER US! IT'S COMING AFTER US!!
REEVER! WHAT THE HELL IS GOING ON!?
DDDDDDD
THAT THING... IT'S A MULTI-TASKING ROBOT CALLED KOMLIN THAT HEAD OFFICER KOMUI MADE...
DDDD
DGGGGGGGG
AS YOU CAN SEE IT'S OUT OF CONTROL!
WHY?

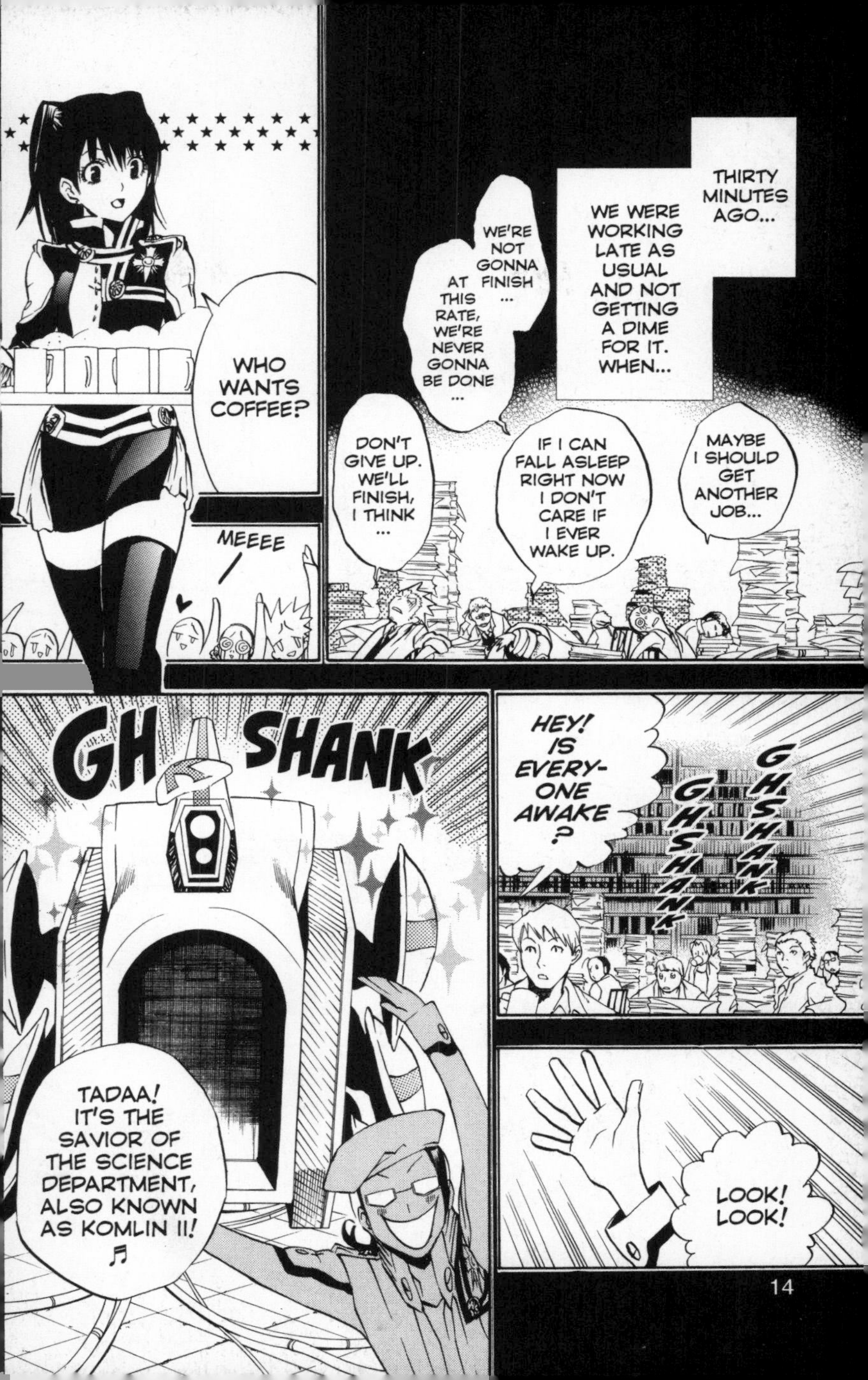
THIRTY MINUTES AGO...
WE WERE WORKING LATE AS USUAL AND NOT GETTING A DIME FOR IT. WHEN...
WE'RE NOT GONNA FINISH... AT THIS RATE, WE'RE NEVER GONNA BE DONE...
MAYBE I SHOULD GET ANOTHER JOB...
IF I CAN FALL ASLEEP RIGHT NOW I DON'T CARE IF I EVER WAKE UP.
DON'T GIVE UP. WE'LL FINISH, I THINK...
WHO WANTS COFFEE?
MEEEE
HEY! IS EVERY-ONE AWAKE?
GHSHANK
GHSHANK
LOOK! LOOK!
GH SHANK
TADAA! IT'S THE SAVIOR OF THE SCIENCE DEPARTMENT, ALSO KNOWN AS KOMLIN II! ♪

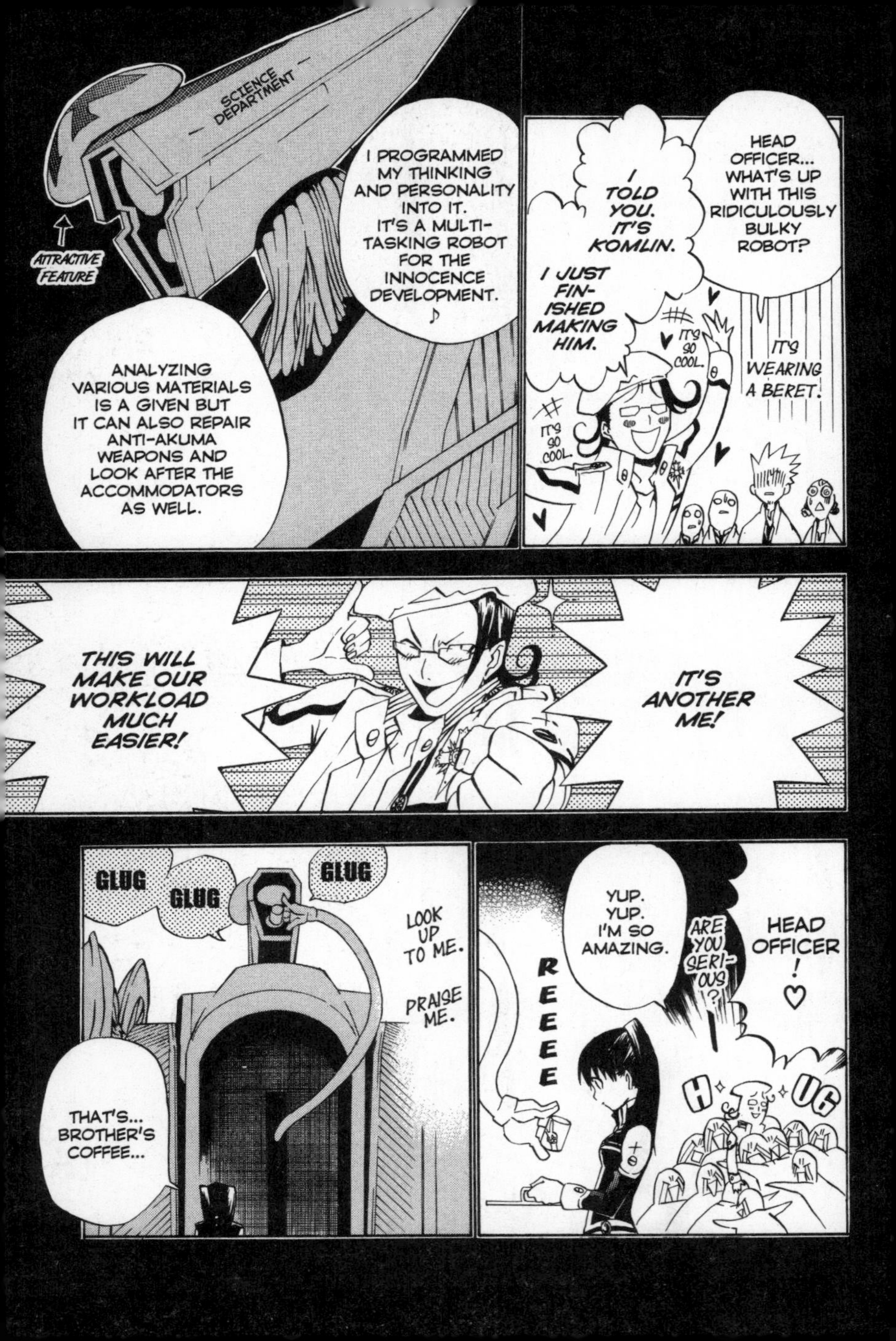
HEAD OFFICER... WHAT'S UP WITH THIS RIDICULOUSLY BULKY ROBOT?
I TOLD YOU. IT'S KOMLIN.
I JUST FIN-ISHED MAKING HIM.
IT'S SO COOL.
IT'S SO COOL.
IT'S WEARING A BERET.
SCIENCE DEPARTMENT
I PROGRAMMED MY THINKING AND PERSONALITY INTO IT. IT'S A MULTI-TASKING ROBOT FOR THE INNOCENCE DEVELOPMENT. ♪
ATTRACTIVE FEATURE
ANALYZING VARIOUS MATERIALS IS A GIVEN BUT IT CAN ALSO REPAIR ANTI-AKUMA WEAPONS AND LOOK AFTER THE ACCOMMODATORS AS WELL.
IT'S ANOTHER ME!
THIS WILL MAKE OUR WORKLOAD MUCH EASIER!
HEAD OFFICER! ♡
ARE YOU SERI-OUS?!
YUP. YUP. I'M SO AMAZING.
REEEEE
HUG
GLUG
GLUG
GLUG
LOOK UP TO ME.
PRAISE ME.
THAT'S... BROTHER'S COFFEE...

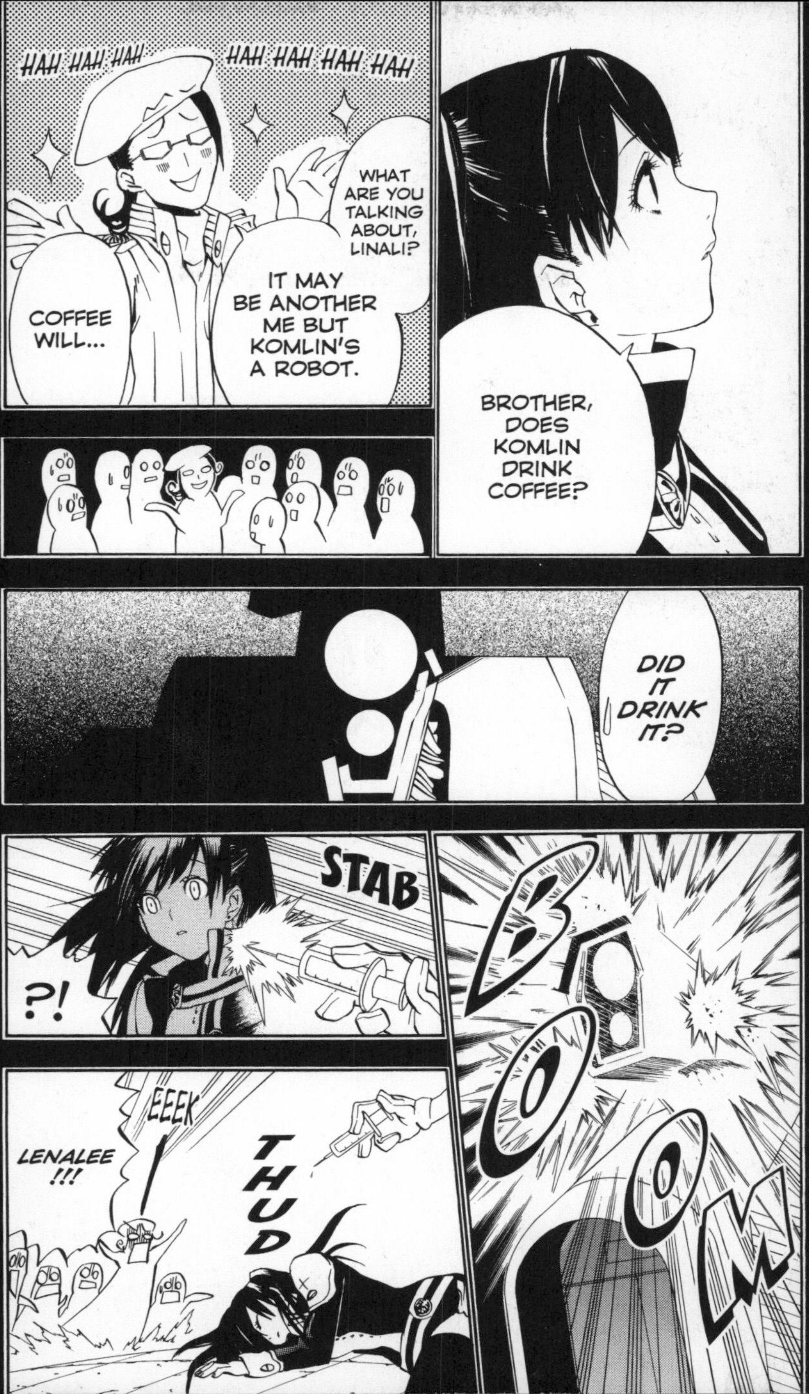
BROTHER, DOES KOMLIN DRINK COFFEE?
HAH HAH HAH HAH
HAH HAH HAH
WHAT ARE YOU TALKING ABOUT, LINALI?
IT MAY BE ANOTHER ME BUT KOMLIN'S A ROBOT.
COFFEE WILL...
DID IT DRINK IT?
BOOOM
STAB
?!
EEEK
THUD
LENALEE !!!

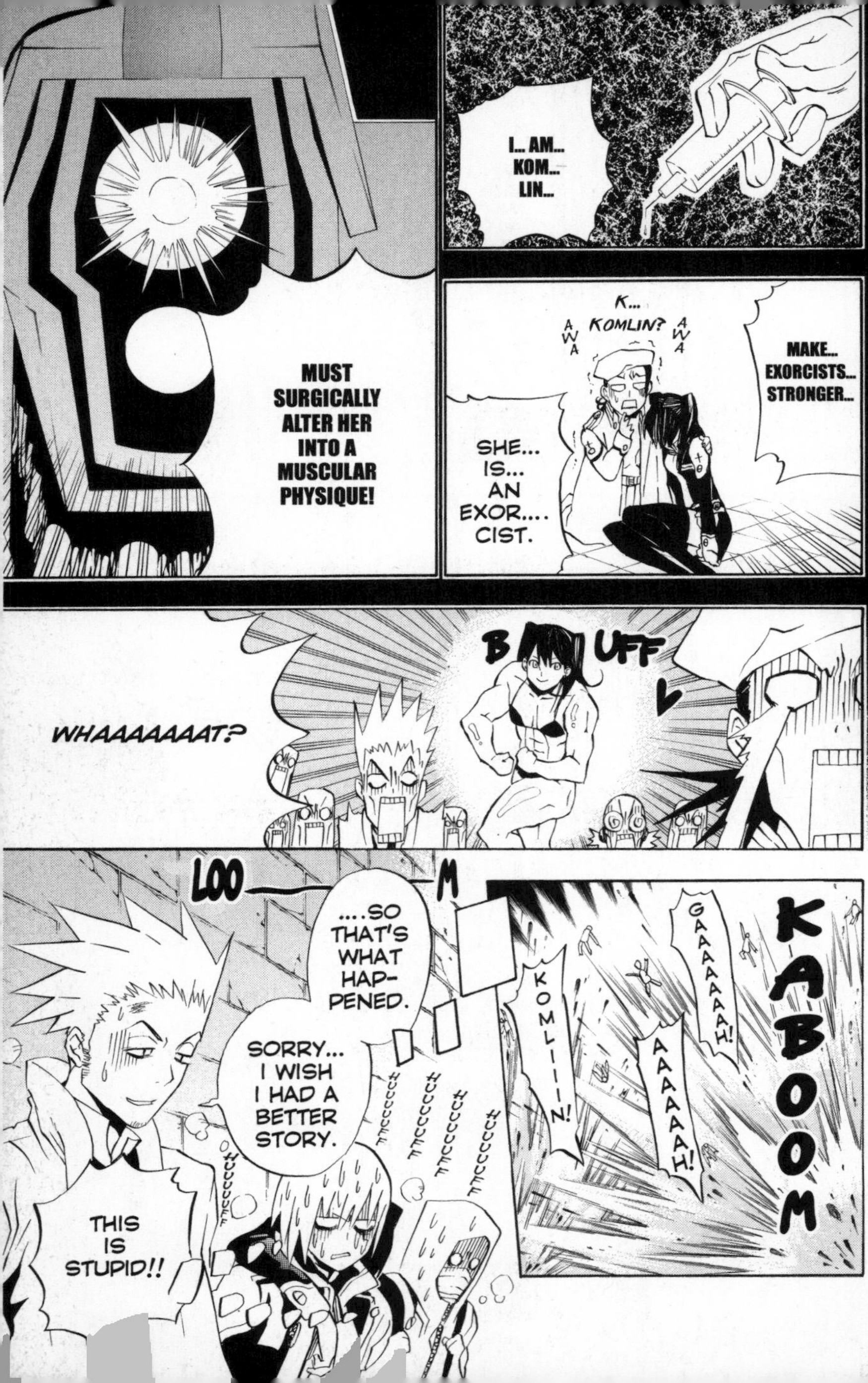
I... AM... KOM... LIN...
MAKE... EXORCISTS... STRONGER...
K... KOMLIN?
AWA AWA
SHE... IS... AN EXOR.... CIST.
MUST SURGICALLY ALTER HER INTO A MUSCULAR PHYSIQUE!
BUFF
WHAAAAAAAT?
KABOOM
GAAAAAAAH!
AAAAAAAH!
KOMLIIIN!
LOOM
....SO THAT'S WHAT HAP-PENED.
SORRY... I WISH I HAD A BETTER STORY.
HUUUUUFF
HUUUUUFF
HUUUUUFF
HUUUUUFF
HUUUUUFF
THIS IS STUPID!!

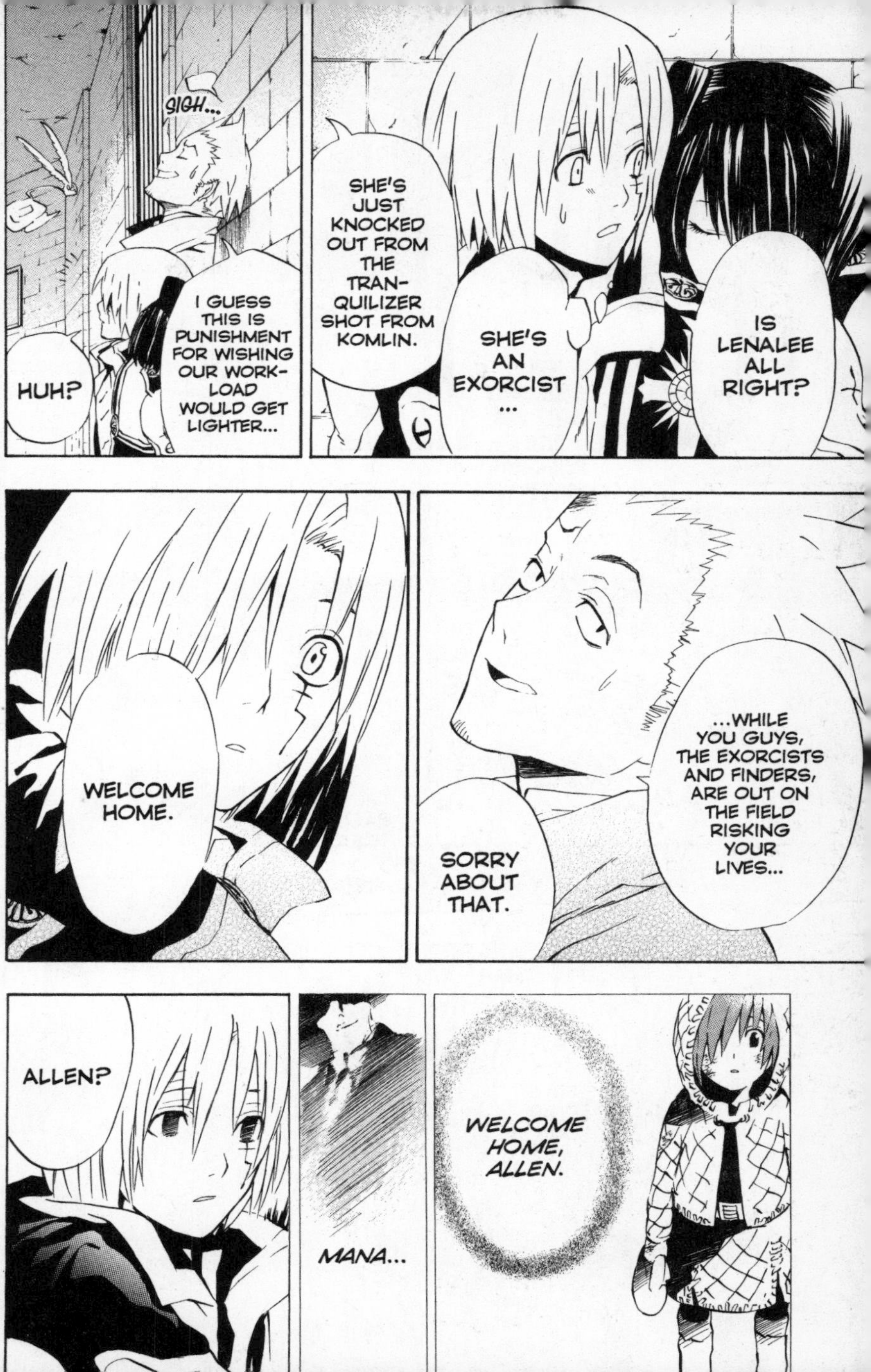
IS LENALEE ALL RIGHT?
SHE'S JUST KNOCKED OUT FROM THE TRANQUILIZER SHOT FROM KOMLIN.
SHE'S AN EXORCIST ...
SIGH...
I GUESS THIS IS PUNISHMENT FOR WISHING OUR WORKLOAD WOULD GET LIGHTER...
HUH?
...WHILE YOU GUYS, THE EXORCISTS AND FINDERS, ARE OUT ON THE FIELD RISKING YOUR LIVES...
SORRY ABOUT THAT.
WELCOME HOME.
WELCOME HOME, ALLEN.
MANA...
ALLEN?

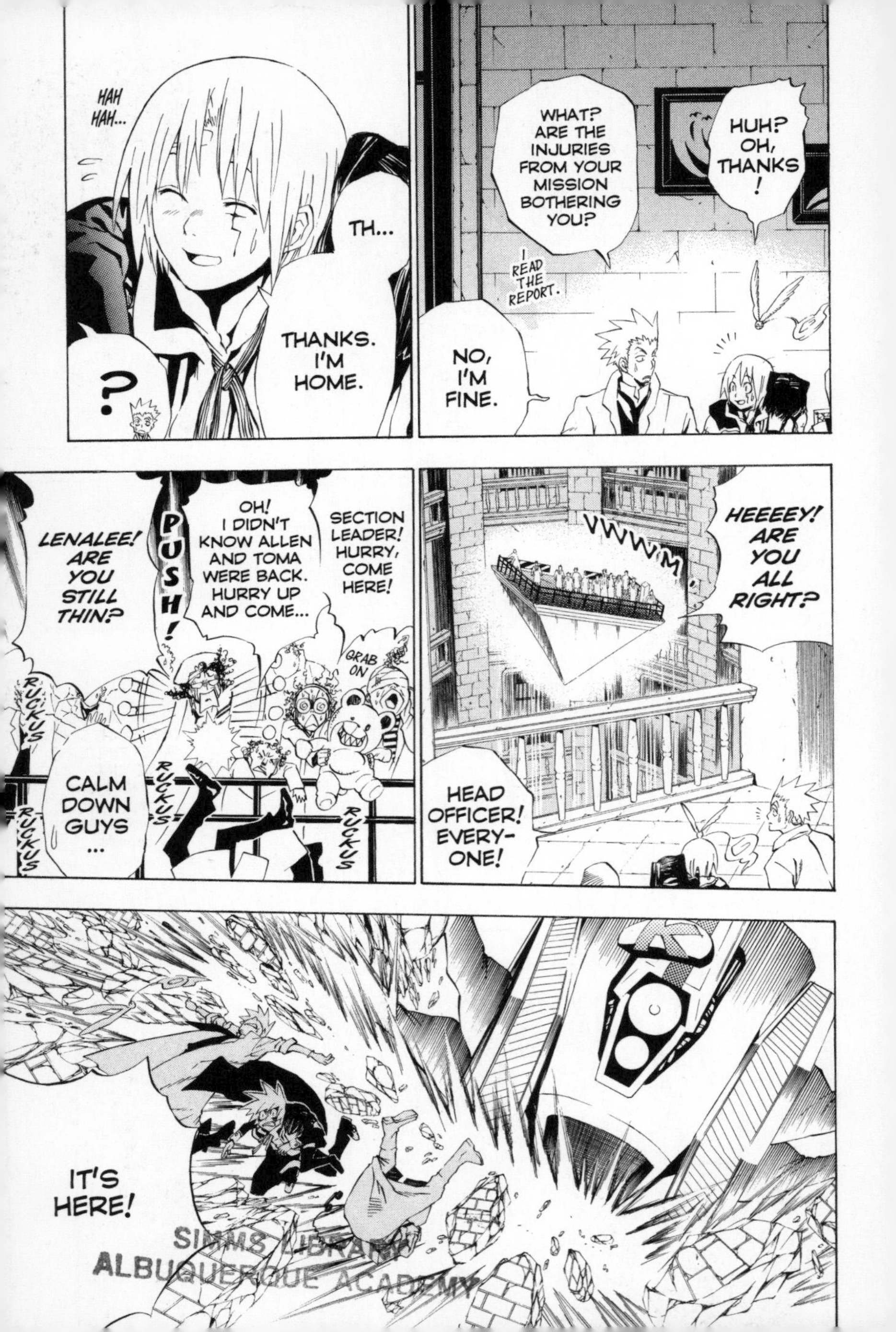
HUH? OH, THANKS!
WHAT? ARE THE INJURIES FROM YOUR MISSION BOTHERING YOU?
I READ THE REPORT.
NO, I'M FINE.
HAH HAH...
TH...
THANKS. I'M HOME.
?
HEEEEY! ARE YOU ALL RIGHT?
VWWM
HEAD OFFICER! EVERYONE!
SECTION LEADER! HURRY, COME HERE!
OH! I DIDN'T KNOW ALLEN AND TOMA WERE BACK. HURRY UP AND COME...
PUSH!
LENALEE! ARE YOU STILL THIN?
GRAB ON
RUCKUS
RUCKUS
RUCKUS
RUCKUS
CALM DOWN GUYS ...
IT'S HERE!

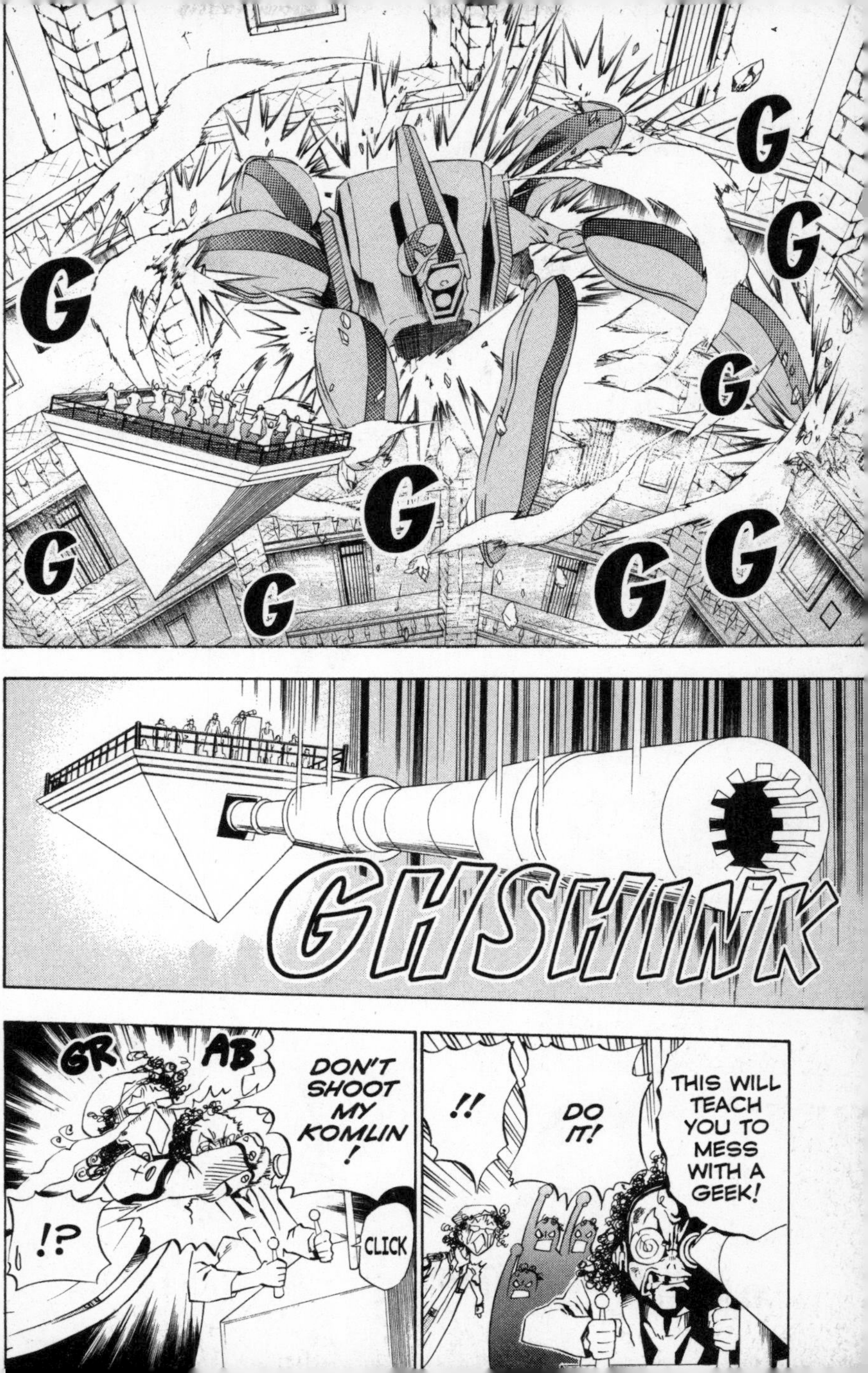
G
G
G
G
G
G
G
G
G
G
GHSHINK
THIS WILL TEACH YOU TO MESS WITH A GEEK!
DO IT!
!!
DON'T SHOOT MY KOMLIN!
GR AB
CLICK
!?

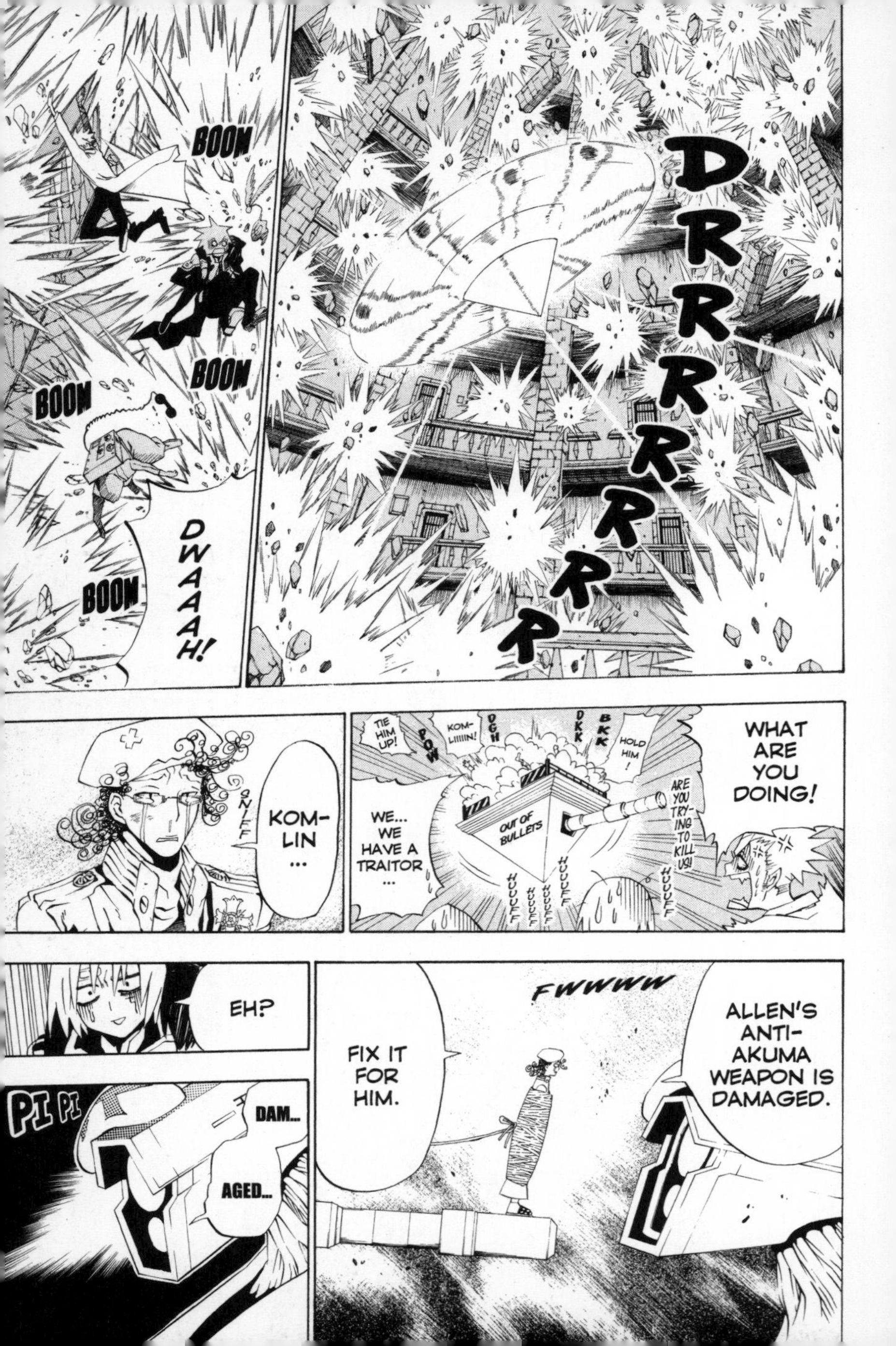
DRRRRRRR
BOOM
BOOM
BOOM
BOOM
DWAAAAH!
WHAT ARE YOU DOING!
ARE YOU TRYING TO KILL US!
HOLD HIM!
BKK
DKK
KOM-LIIIIIN!
DGH
TIE HIM UP!
POW
WE... WE HAVE A TRAITOR...
OUT OF BULLETS
HUUUFF
HUUUFF
HUUUFF
HUUUFF
HUUUFF
KOM-LIN...
SNIFF
ALLEN'S ANTI-AKUMA WEAPON IS DAMAGED.
FWWWW
FIX IT FOR HIM.
EH?
PI PI
DAM...
AGED...

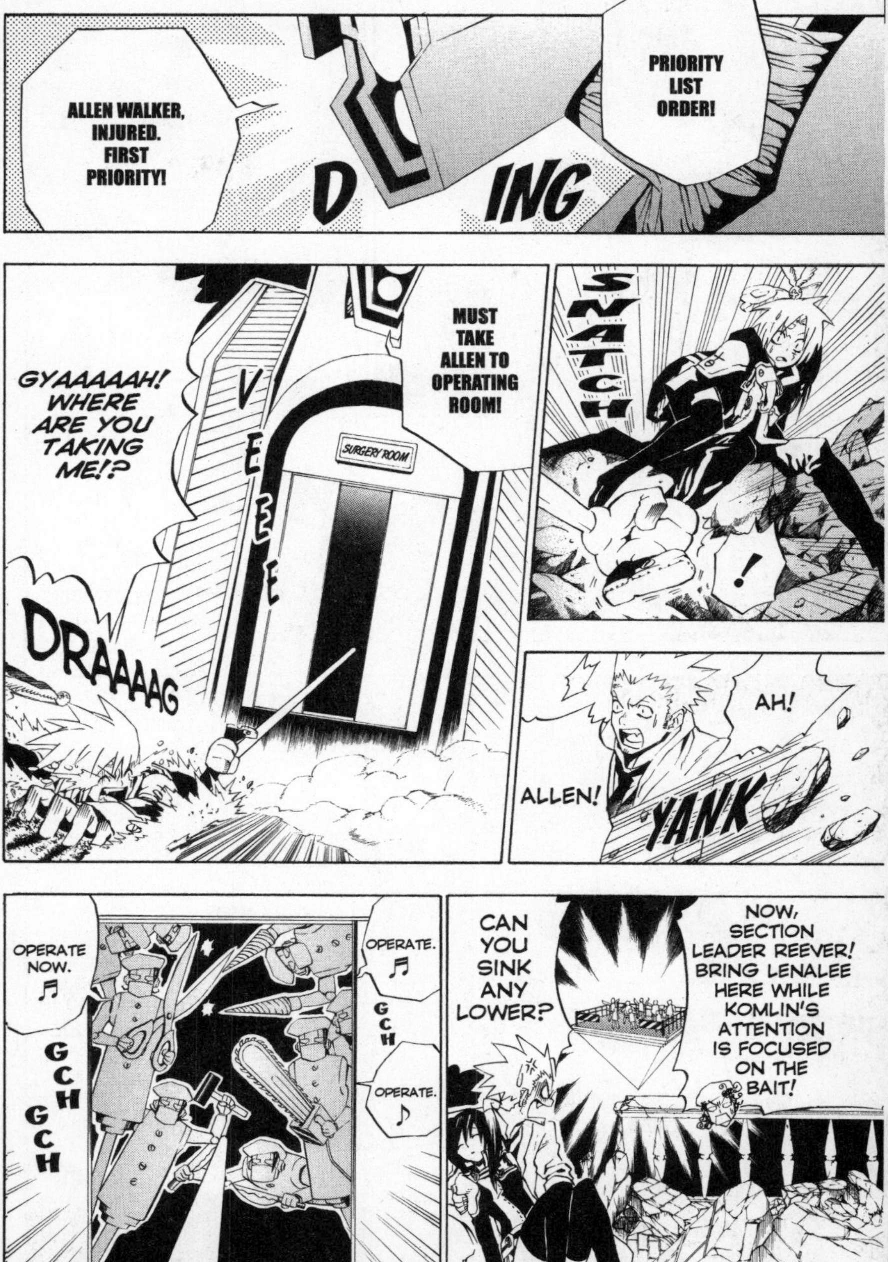
PRIORITY LIST ORDER!
ALLEN WALKER, INJURED. FIRST PRIORITY!
DING
SNATCH
!
AH!
ALLEN!
YANK
MUST TAKE ALLEN TO OPERATING ROOM!
SURGERY ROOM
GYAAAAAH! WHERE ARE YOU TAKING ME!?
VEEE
DRAAAAG
NOW, SECTION LEADER REEVER! BRING LENALEE HERE WHILE KOMLIN'S ATTENTION IS FOCUSED ON THE BAIT!
CAN YOU SINK ANY LOWER?
OPERATE. ♬
GCH
OPERATE. ♪
OPERATE NOW. ♬
GCH
GCH

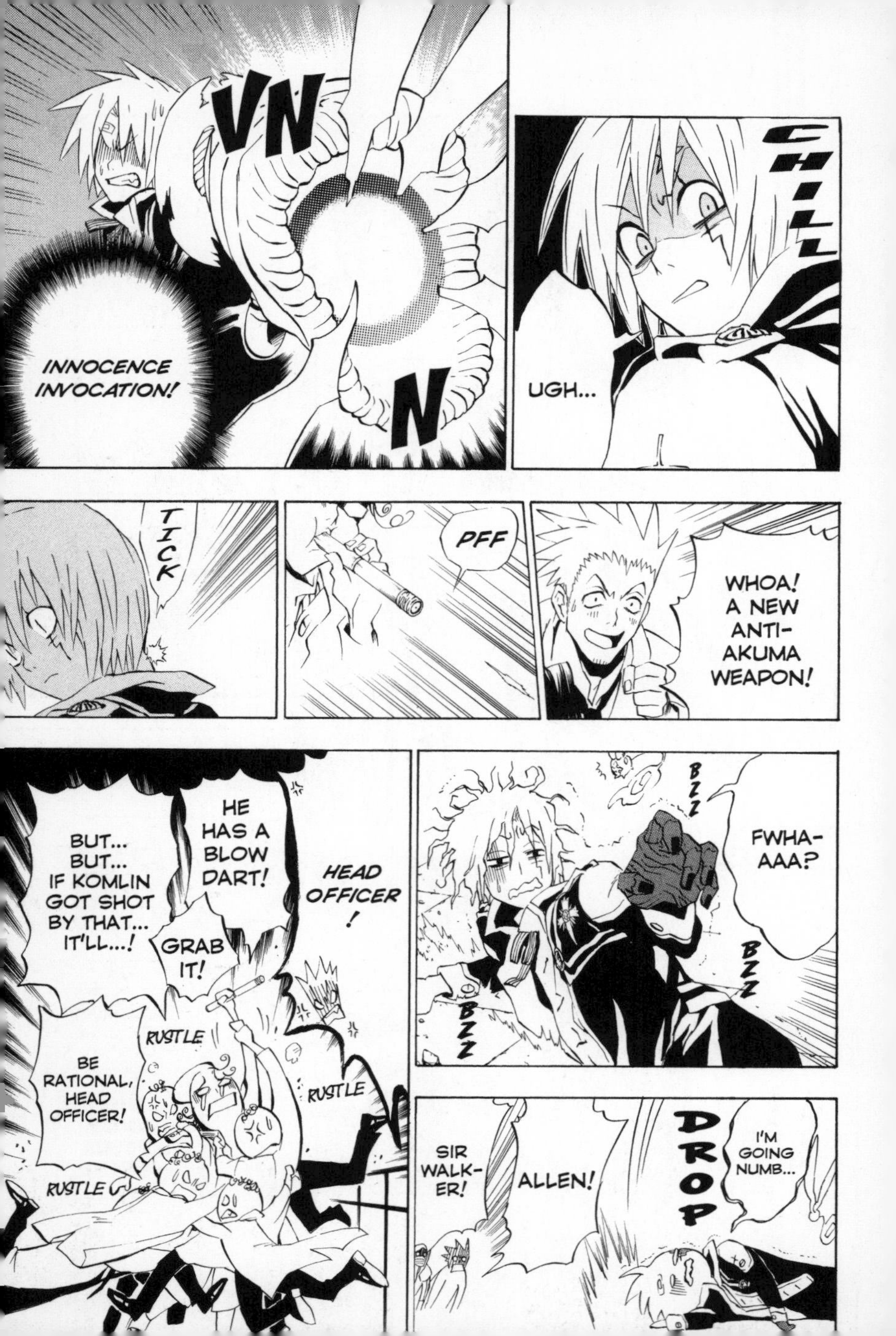
CHILL
UGH...
VN
N
INNOCENCE INVOCATION!
WHOA! A NEW ANTI-AKUMA WEAPON!
PFF
TICK
BZZ
FWHA-AAA?
BZZ
BZZ
I'M GOING NUMB...
DROP
ALLEN!
SIR WALKER!
HEAD OFFICER!
HE HAS A BLOW DART!
BUT... BUT... IF KOMLIN GOT SHOT BY THAT... IT'LL...!
GRAB IT!
RUSTLE
RUSTLE
BE RATIONAL, HEAD OFFICER!
RUSTLE

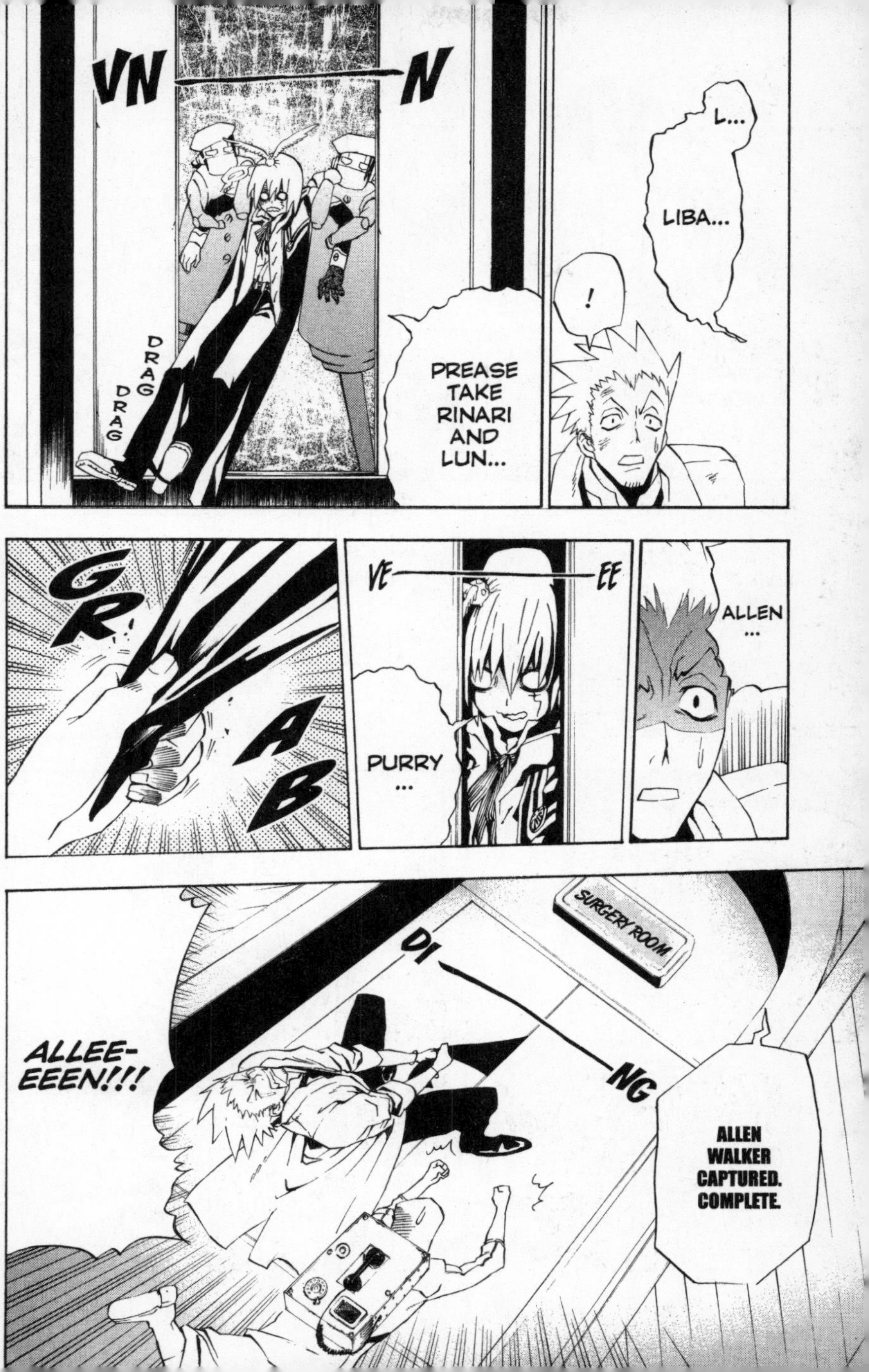
L...
LIBA...
!
VN—N
PREASE TAKE RINARI AND LUN...
DRAG DRAG
ALLEN ...
VE—EE
PURRY ...
GRAB
SURGERY ROOM
DI—NG
ALLEN WALKER CAPTURED. COMPLETE.
ALLEE-EEEN!!!

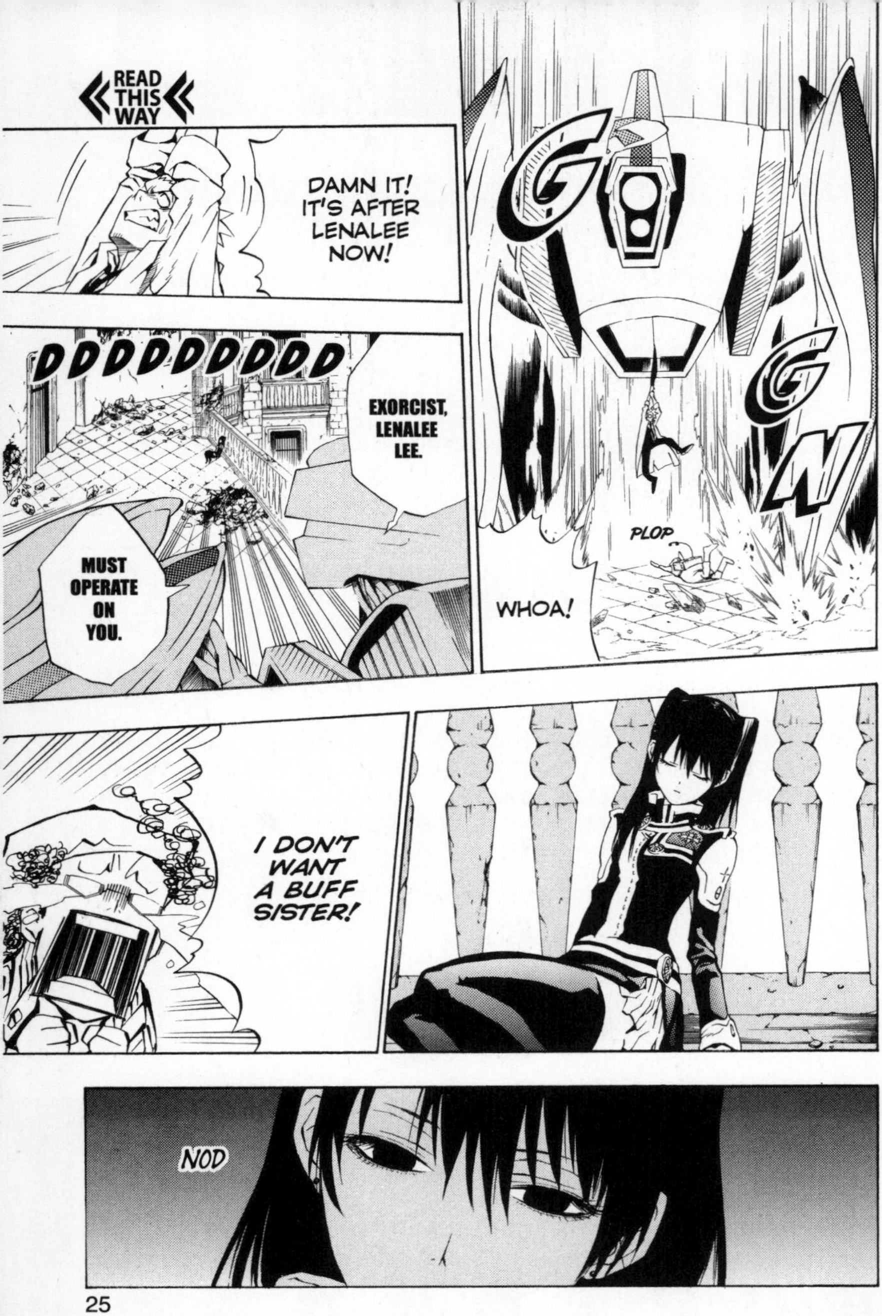

READ THIS WAY
GOGGN
PLOP
WHOA!
DAMN IT! IT'S AFTER LENALEE NOW!
DDDDDDDDDD
EXORCIST, LENALEE LEE.
MUST OPERATE ON YOU.
I DON'T WANT A BUFF SISTER!
NOD

KOMUI'S EXPERIMENT ROOM DISCUSSION ROOM VOL. 1

Q 1. THE CHARACTERS COME FROM VARIOUS COUNTRIES. WHAT'S THEIR COMMON LANGUAGE?

A. THEY SPEAK ENGLISH, THE UNIVERSAL LANGUAGE. EVEN KANDA SPEAKS IN ENGLISH.

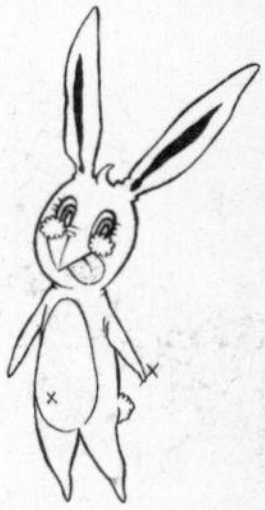

Q 2. WHAT'S THAT RABBIT THAT APPEARS FROM TIME TO TIME? DOES IT HAVE A NAME?

A. I MADE MY EDITOR Y INTO AN ANIMAL. ITS NAME IS YOSHI. YOSHI APPEARED IN A ONE-SHOT MANGA BUT I LIKED IT SO MUCH I KEPT USING IT (JUST TO TICK HIM OFF). MAYBE ONE DAY I'LL HAVE AN AKUMA THAT LOOKS LIKE HIM... JUST MAYBE... (LOOKS OFF INTO THE DISTANCE).

Q 3. WHAT DOES THE TITLE, D.GRAY-MAN MEAN?

A. IT'S A WORD THAT I MADE UP AND HAS VARIOUS MEANINGS. IT COULD APPLY TO ALLEN AND THE OTHER CHARACTERS AS WELL... ON A SEPARATE NOTE, I WAS THINKING "DOLLS" FOR THE TITLE BEFORE I CAME UP WITH "D.GRAY-MAN." OTHER TITLES I CAME UP BEFORE THAT WERE "CHRONOA" AND "ZONE."

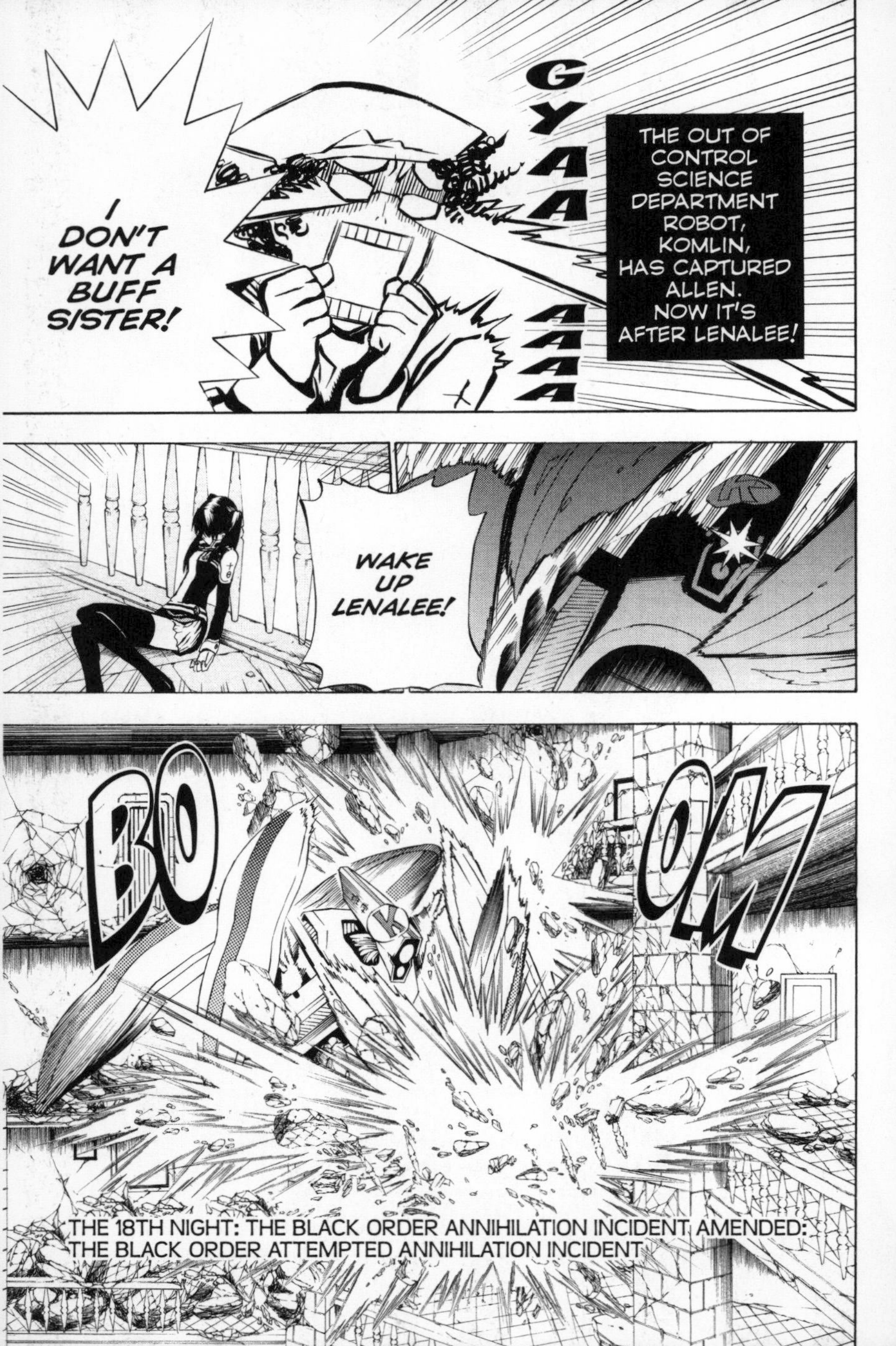
THE OUT OF CONTROL SCIENCE DEPARTMENT ROBOT, KOMLIN, HAS CAPTURED ALLEN. NOW IT'S AFTER LENALEE!
GYAAAAAA
I DON'T WANT A BUFF SISTER!
WAKE UP LENALEE!
BOOM
THE 18TH NIGHT: THE BLACK ORDER ANNIHILATION INCIDENT AMENDED: THE BLACK ORDER ATTEMPTED ANNIHILATION INCIDENT

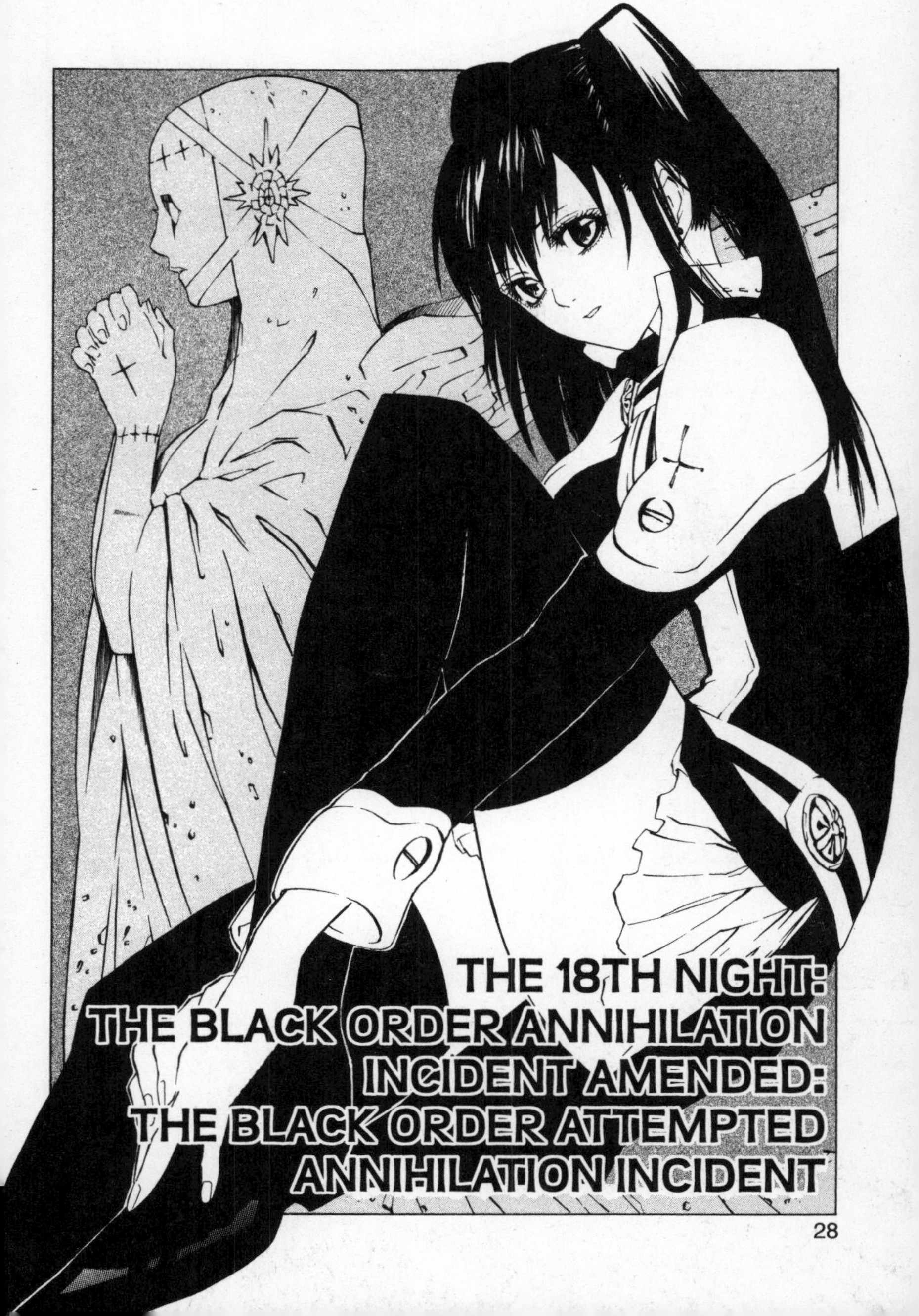
THE 18TH NIGHT:
THE BLACK ORDER ANNIHILATION
INCIDENT AMENDED:
THE BLACK ORDER ATTEMPTED
ANNIHILATION INCIDENT

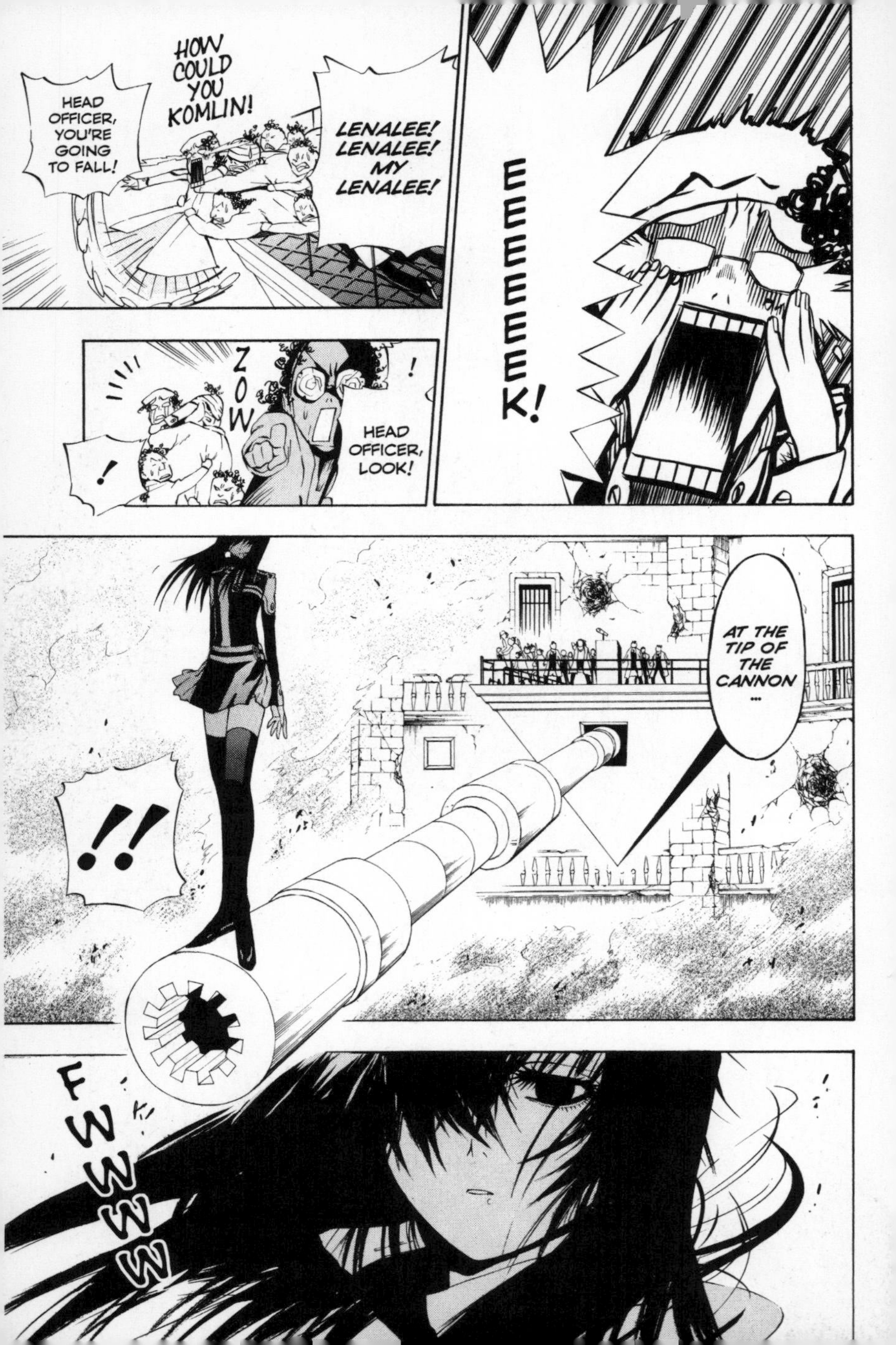
EEEEEEEK!
LENALEE! LENALEE! MY LENALEE!
HOW COULD YOU KOMLIN!
HEAD OFFICER, YOU'RE GOING TO FALL!
HEAD OFFICER, LOOK!
ZOW
!
AT THE TIP OF THE CANNON ...
!!
FWWWW

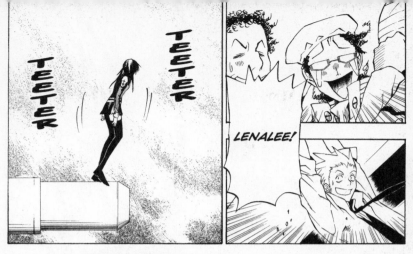

TEETER TEETER

LENALEE!

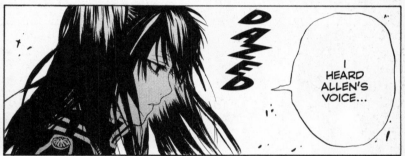

DAZED

I HEARD ALLEN'S VOICE...

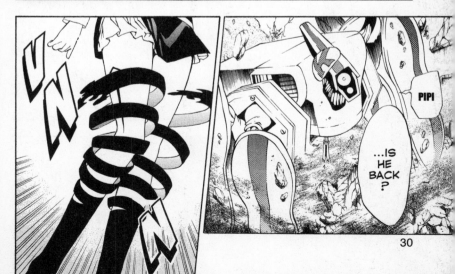

UN

PIPI

...IS HE BACK?

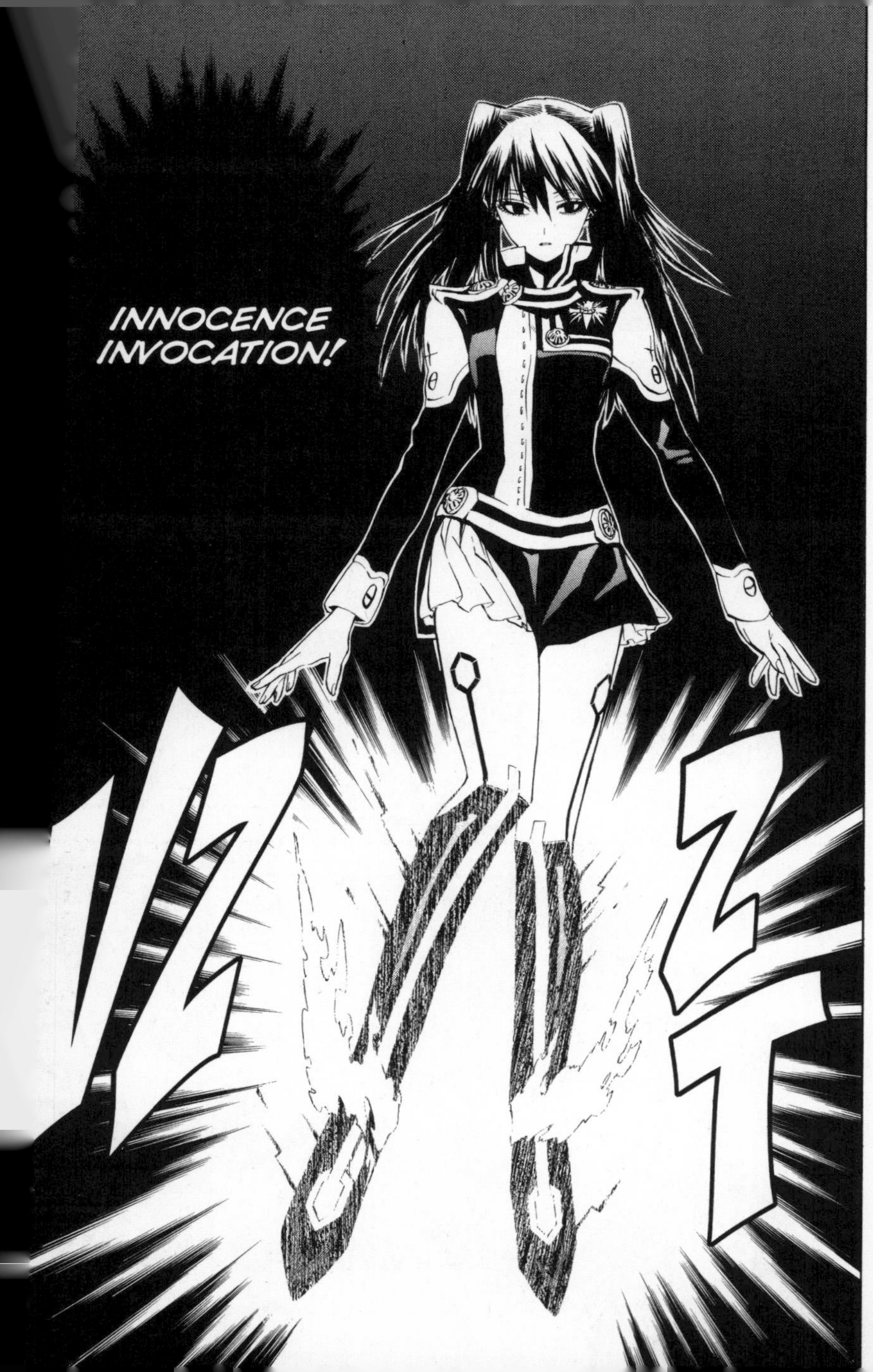
INNOCENCE INVOCATION!

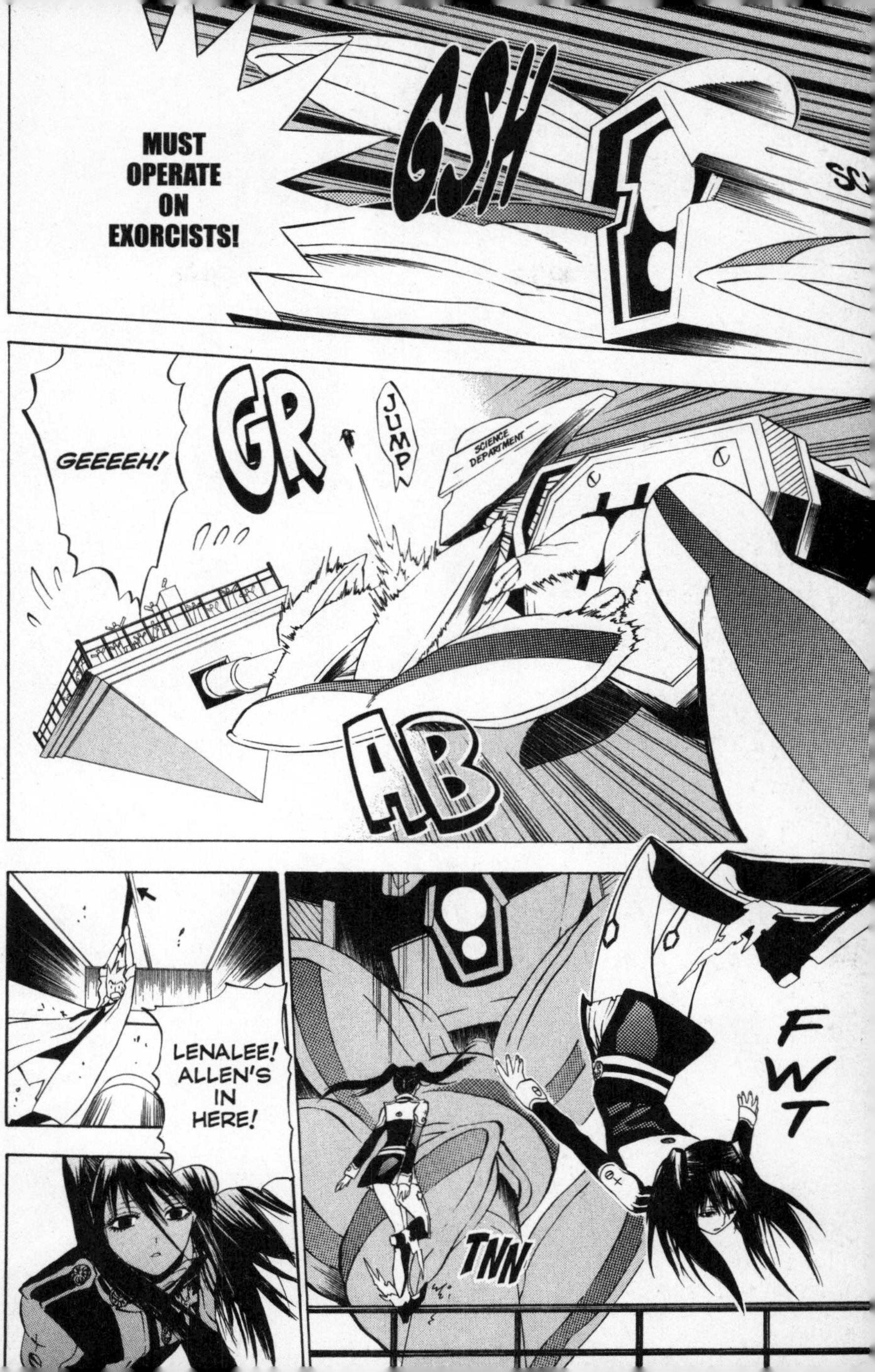
GSH
MUST OPERATE ON EXORCISTS!
SCIENCE DEPARTMENT
JUMP
GR
GEEEEH!
AB
FWT
TNN
LENALEE! ALLEN'S IN HERE!

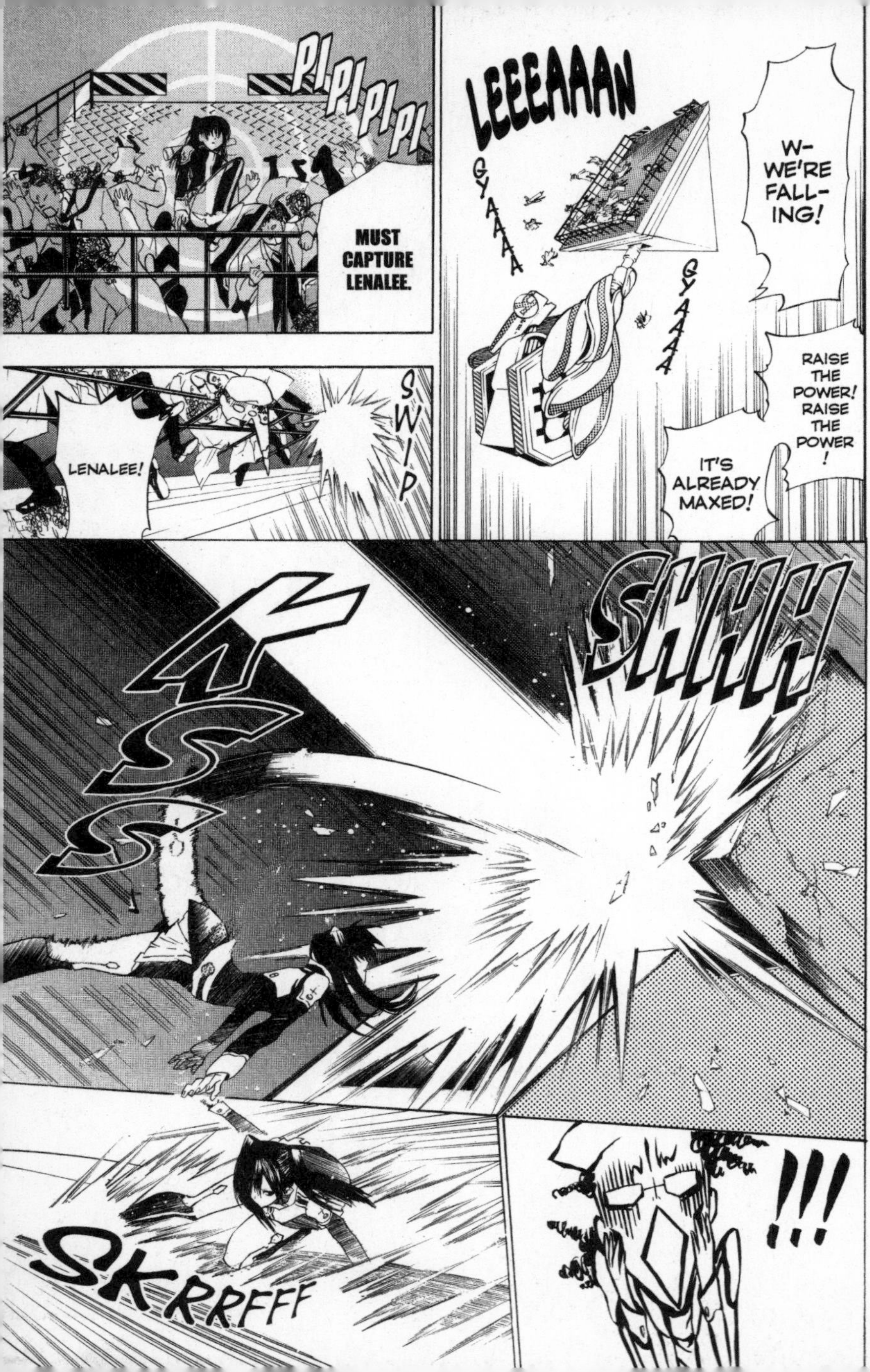

W-WE'RE FALLING!
LEEEAAAN
GYAAAA
GYAAAA
RAISE THE POWER! RAISE THE POWER!
IT'S ALREADY MAXED!
PIPIPIPI
MUST CAPTURE LENALEE.
SWIP
LENALEE!
SHHHH
KSSS
!!!
SKRRFFF

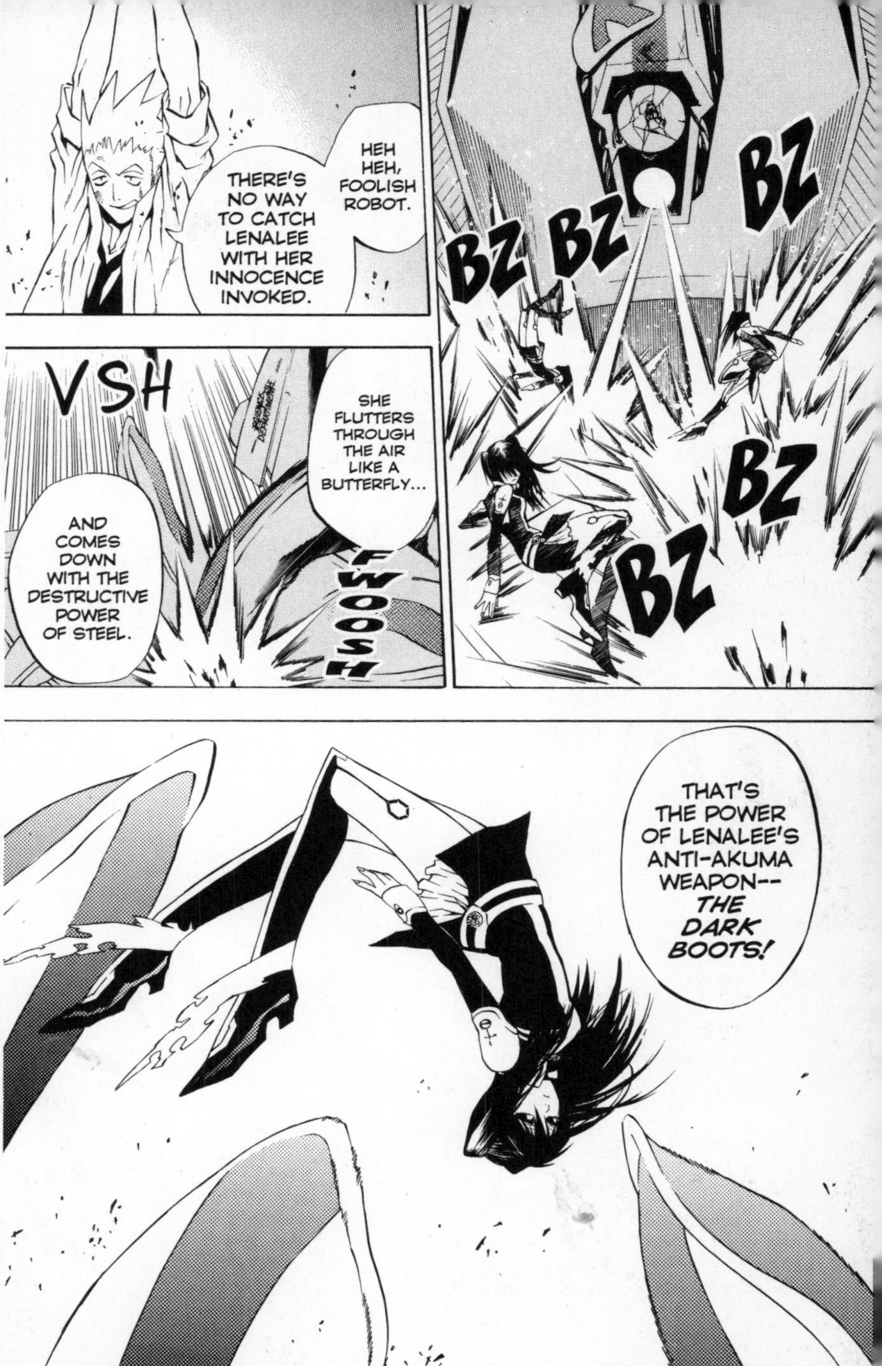
BZ BZ BZ
BZ BZ BZ
HEH HEH, FOOLISH ROBOT.
THERE'S NO WAY TO CATCH LENALEE WITH HER INNOCENCE INVOKED.
SHE FLUTTERS THROUGH THE AIR LIKE A BUTTERFLY...
FWOOSH
VSH
AND COMES DOWN WITH THE DESTRUCTIVE POWER OF STEEL.
THAT'S THE POWER OF LENALEE'S ANTI-AKUMA WEAPON-- *THE DARK BOOTS!*

READ THIS WAY

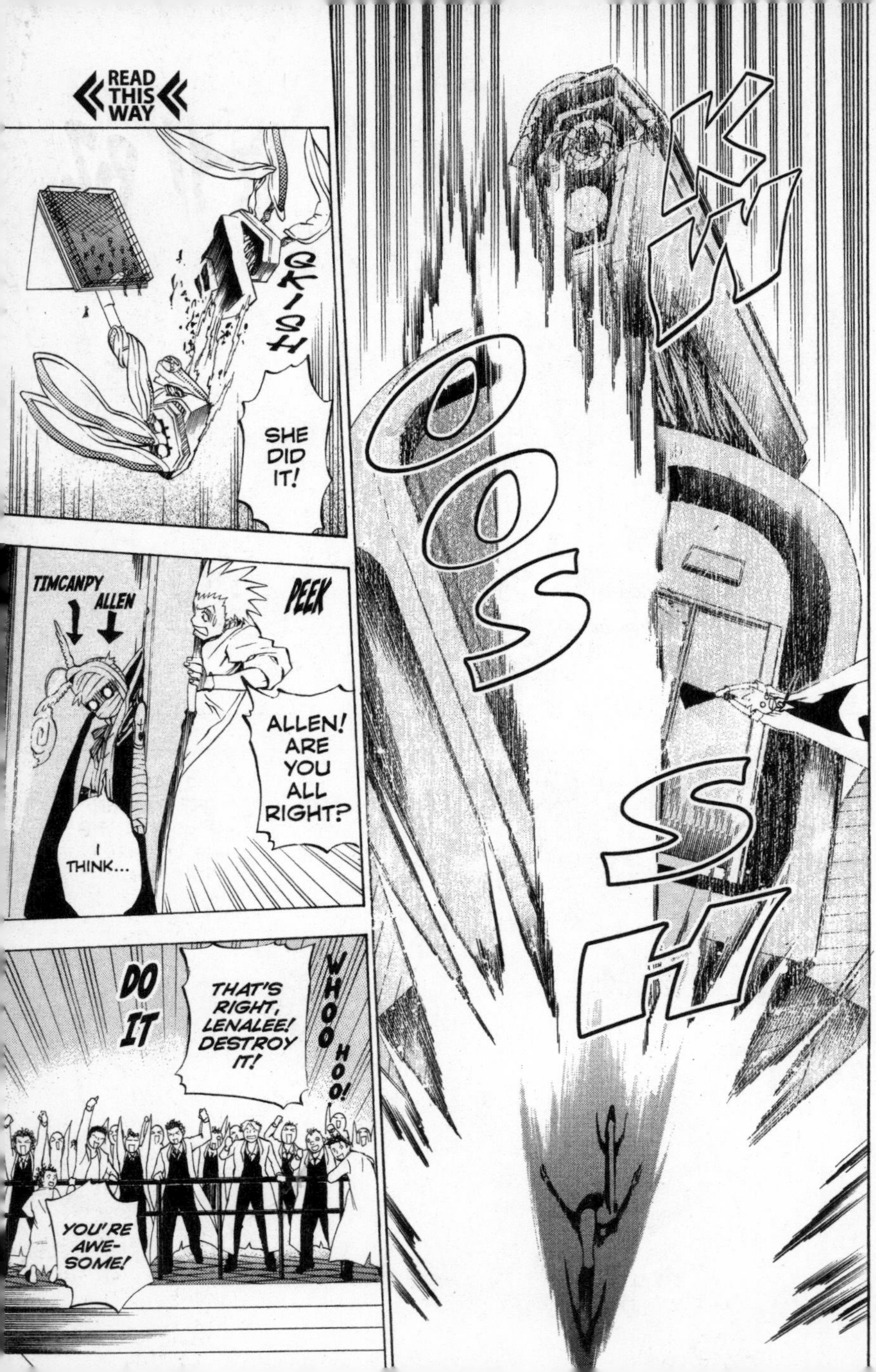
KWOOSSH
QKISH
SHE DID IT!
PEEK
ALLEN! ARE YOU ALL RIGHT?
TIMCANPY
ALLEN
I THINK...
WHOO HOO!
THAT'S RIGHT, LENALEE! DESTROY IT!
DO IT
YOU'RE AWESOME!

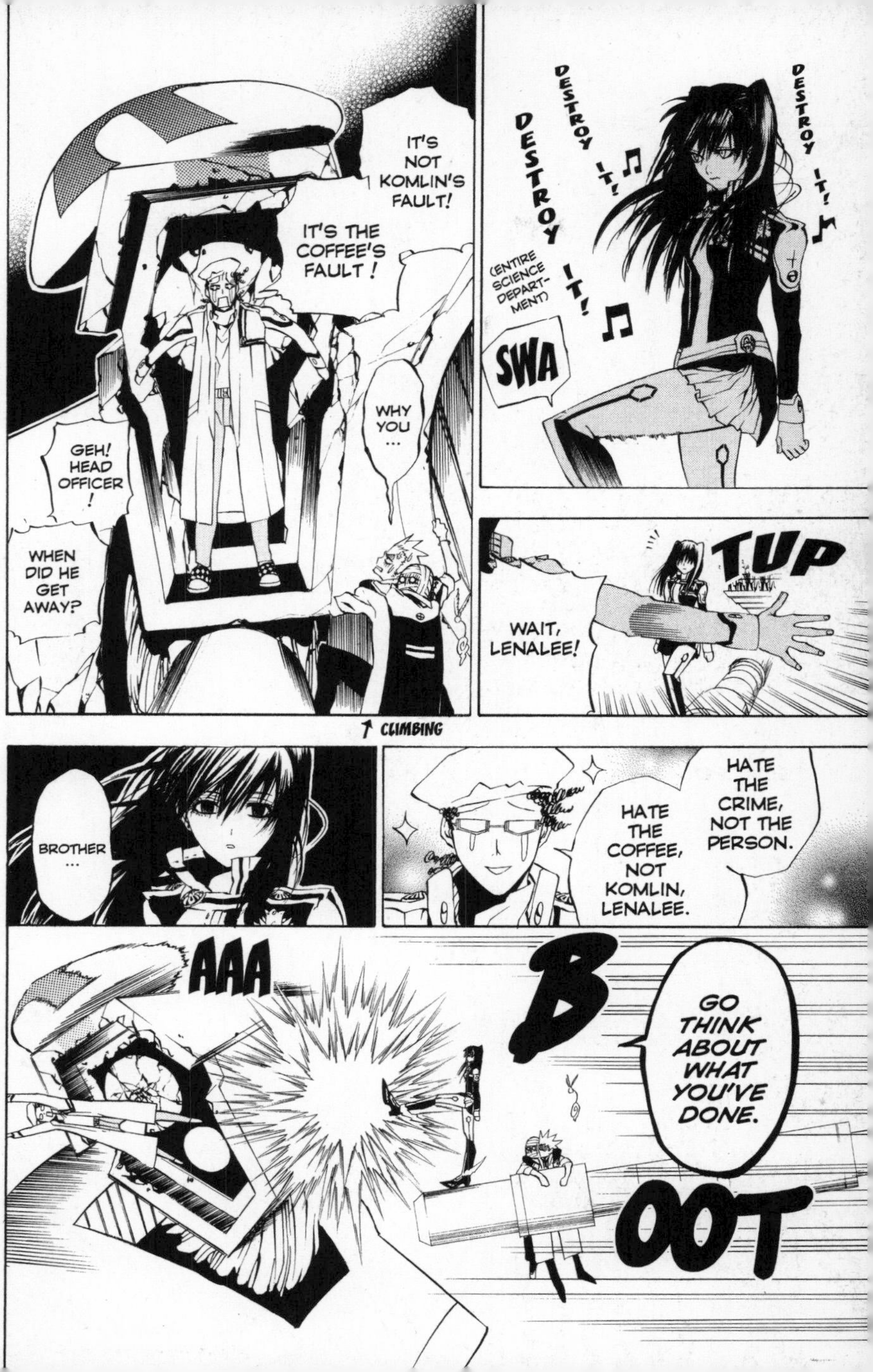
DESTROY IT! ♪
DESTROY IT! ♪
DESTROY IT! ♪
(ENTIRE SCIENCE DEPARTMENT)
SWA
TUP
WAIT, LENALEE!
IT'S NOT KOMLIN'S FAULT!
IT'S THE COFFEE'S FAULT!
WHY YOU ...
GEH! HEAD OFFICER!
WHEN DID HE GET AWAY?
↑ CLIMBING
HATE THE CRIME, NOT THE PERSON.
HATE THE COFFEE, NOT KOMLIN, LENALEE.
BROTHER ...
GO THINK ABOUT WHAT YOU'VE DONE.
B
AAA
OOT

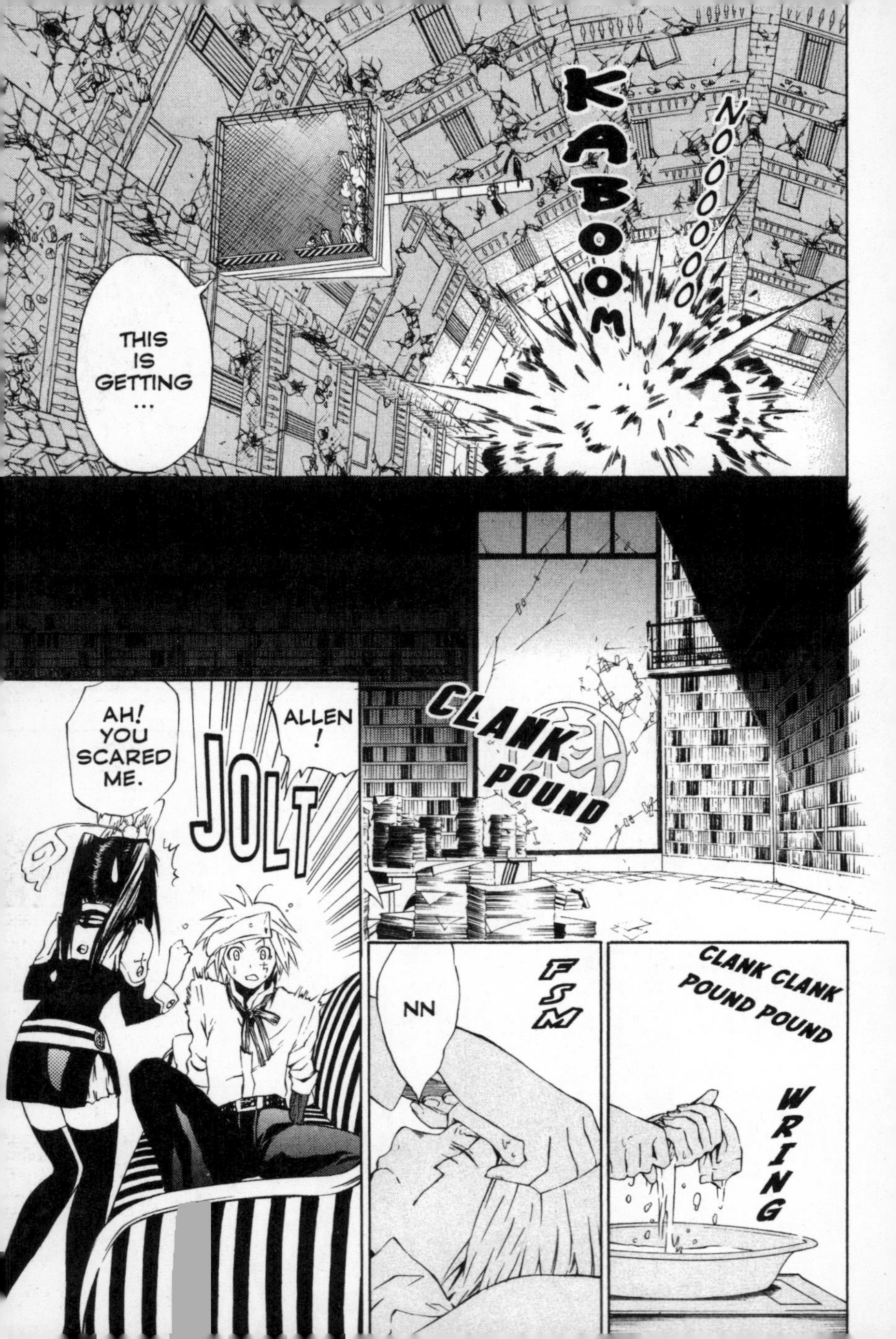
NOOOOOOO
KABOOM
THIS IS GETTING ...
CLANK POUND
CLANK CLANK POUND POUND
WRING
FSM
NN
ALLEN!
JOLT
AH! YOU SCARED ME.

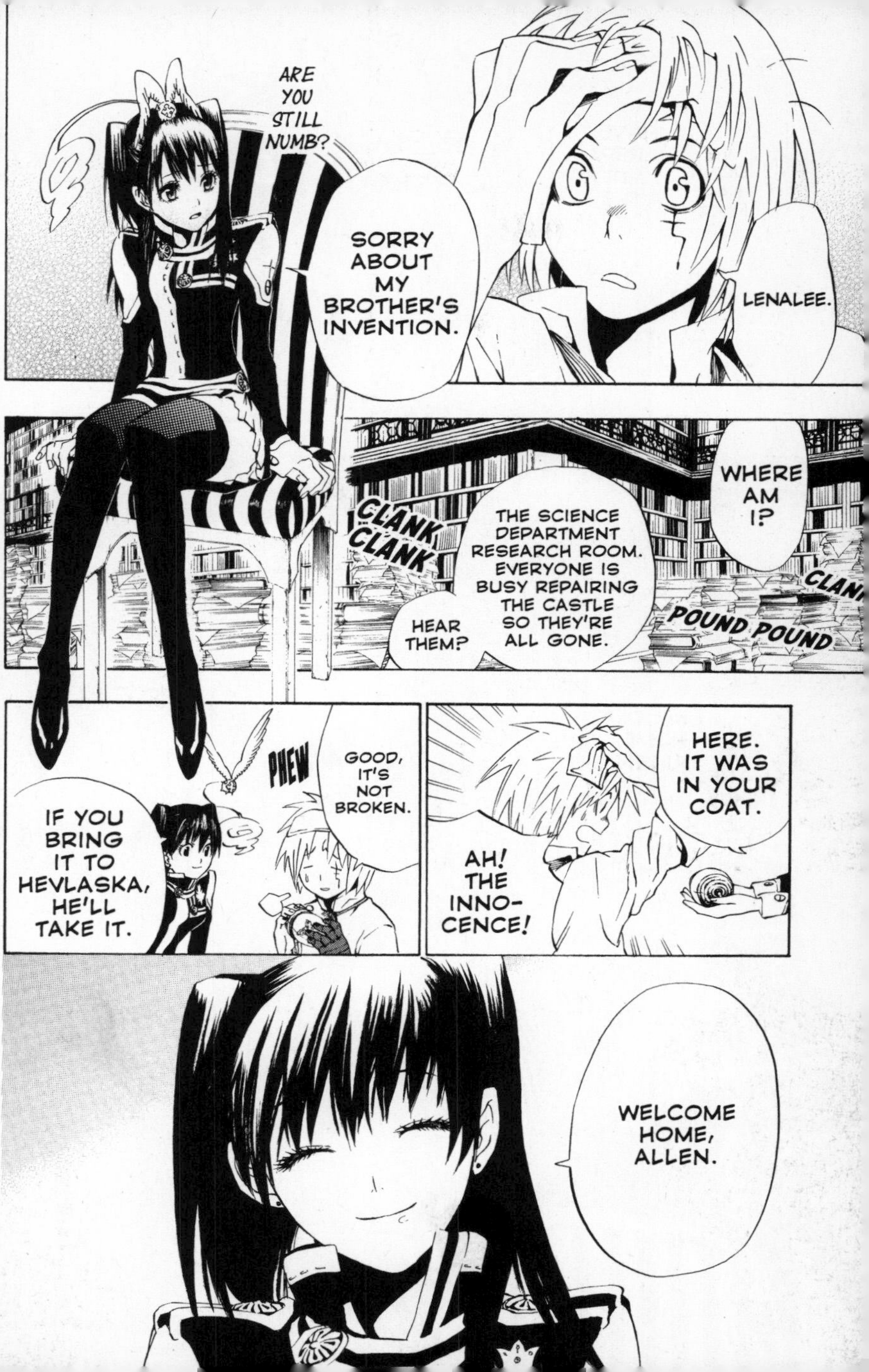
LENALEE.
ARE YOU STILL NUMB?
SORRY ABOUT MY BROTHER'S INVENTION.
WHERE AM I?
CLAN
POUND POUND
THE SCIENCE DEPARTMENT RESEARCH ROOM. EVERYONE IS BUSY REPAIRING THE CASTLE SO THEY'RE ALL GONE.
HEAR THEM?
CLANK CLANK
HERE. IT WAS IN YOUR COAT.
AH! THE INNO-CENCE!
GOOD, IT'S NOT BROKEN.
PHEW
IF YOU BRING IT TO HEVLASKA, HE'LL TAKE IT.
WELCOME HOME, ALLEN.

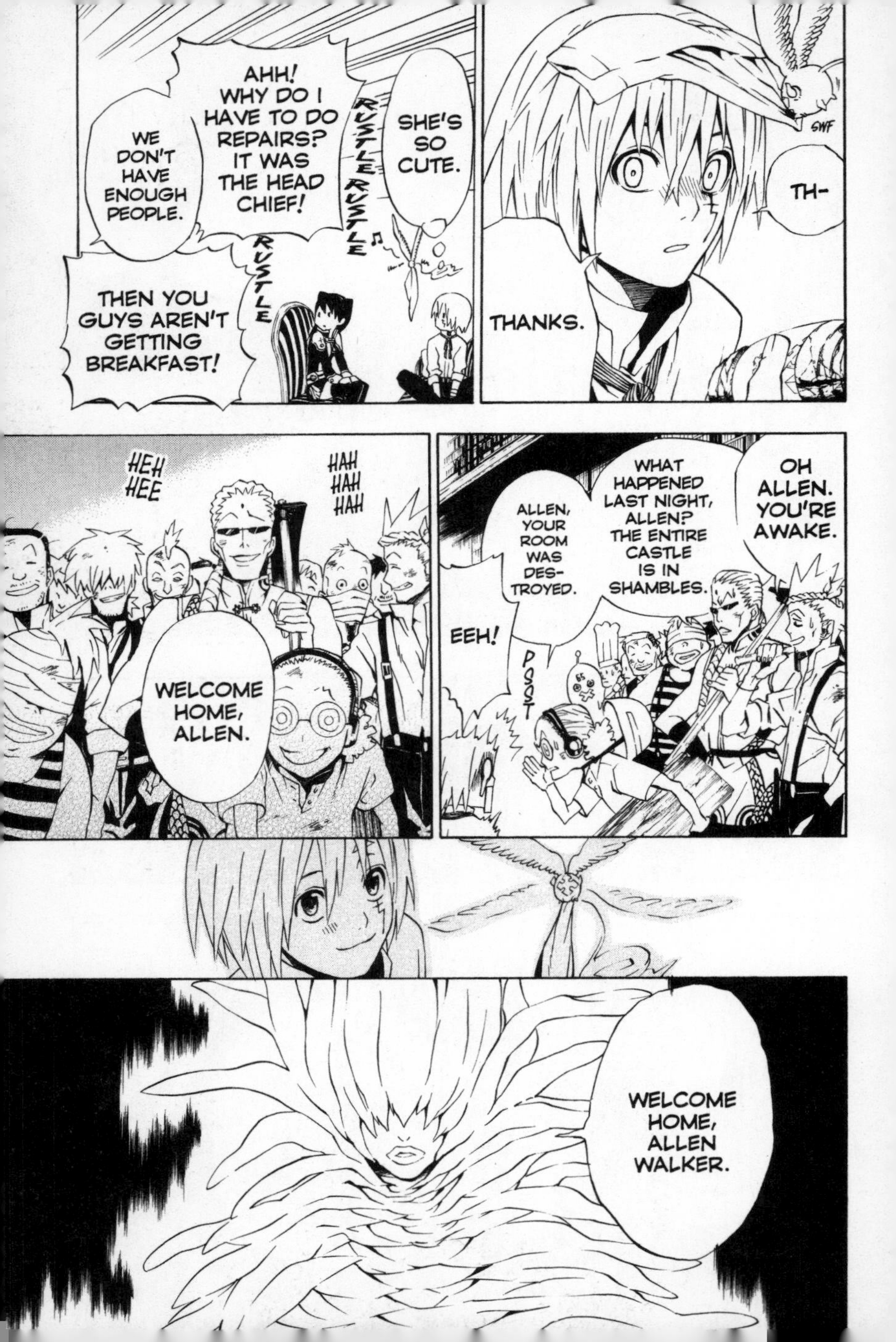
SWF
TH-
THANKS.
SHE'S SO CUTE.
RUSTLE RUSTLE
AHH! WHY DO I HAVE TO DO REPAIRS? IT WAS THE HEAD CHIEF!
WE DON'T HAVE ENOUGH PEOPLE.
RUSTLE
THEN YOU GUYS AREN'T GETTING BREAKFAST!
OH ALLEN. YOU'RE AWAKE.
WHAT HAPPENED LAST NIGHT, ALLEN? THE ENTIRE CASTLE IS IN SHAMBLES.
ALLEN, YOUR ROOM WAS DES-TROYED.
EEH!
PSST
HAH HAH HAH
HEH HEE
WELCOME HOME, ALLEN.
WELCOME HOME, ALLEN WALKER.

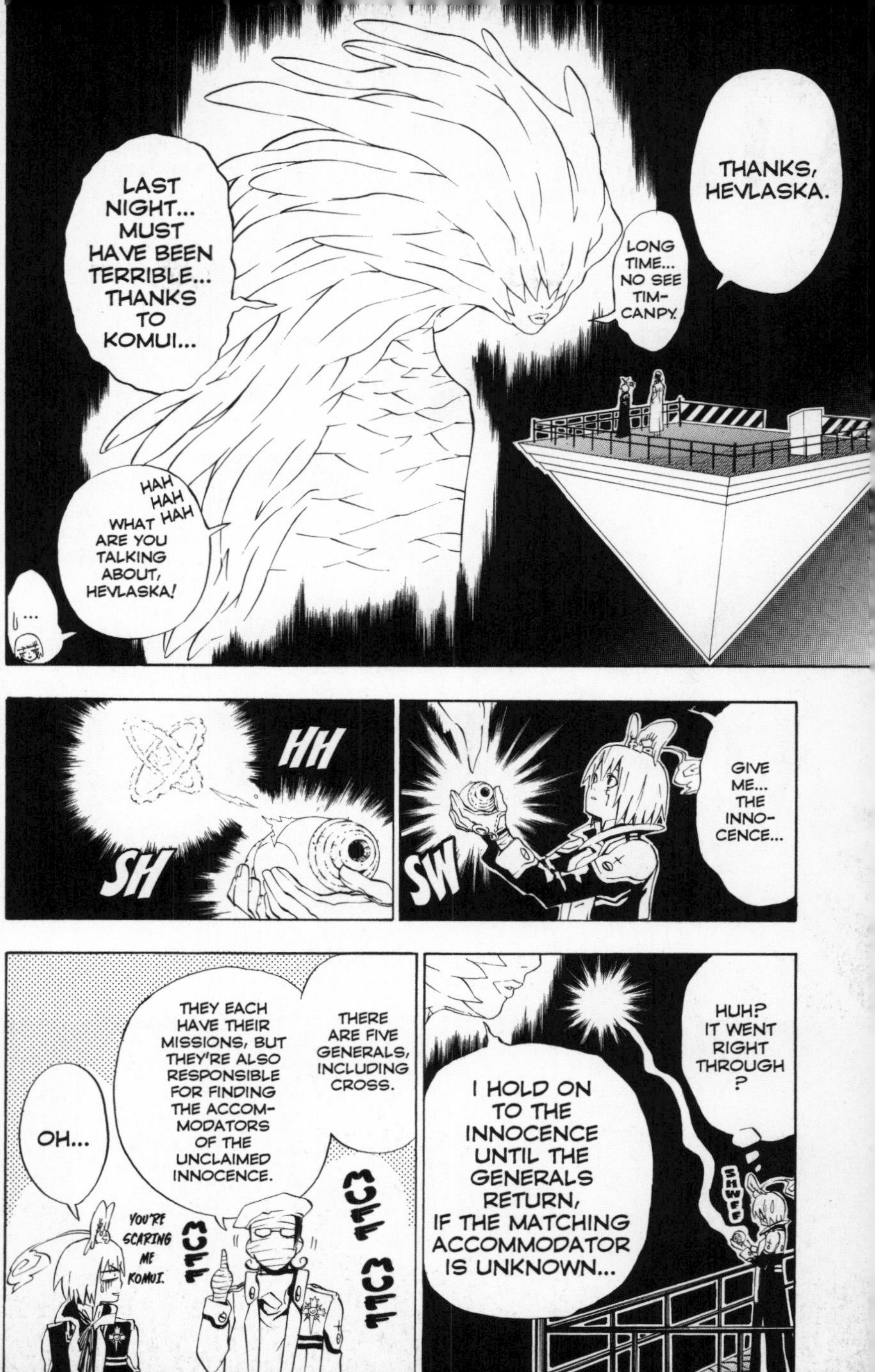
THANKS, HEVLASKA.
LONG TIME... NO SEE TIM-CANPY.
LAST NIGHT... MUST HAVE BEEN TERRIBLE... THANKS TO KOMUI...
HAH HAH HAH WHAT ARE YOU TALKING ABOUT, HEVLASKA!
...
GIVE ME... THE INNO-CENCE...
SW
HH
SH
HUH? IT WENT RIGHT THROUGH?
SHWFF
I HOLD ON TO THE INNOCENCE UNTIL THE GENERALS RETURN, IF THE MATCHING ACCOMMODATOR IS UNKNOWN...
THERE ARE FIVE GENERALS, INCLUDING CROSS.
THEY EACH HAVE THEIR MISSIONS, BUT THEY'RE ALSO RESPONSIBLE FOR FINDING THE ACCOM-MODATORS OF THE UNCLAIMED INNOCENCE.
MUFF MUFF
MUFF
OH...
YOU'RE SCARING ME KOMUI.
MUFF

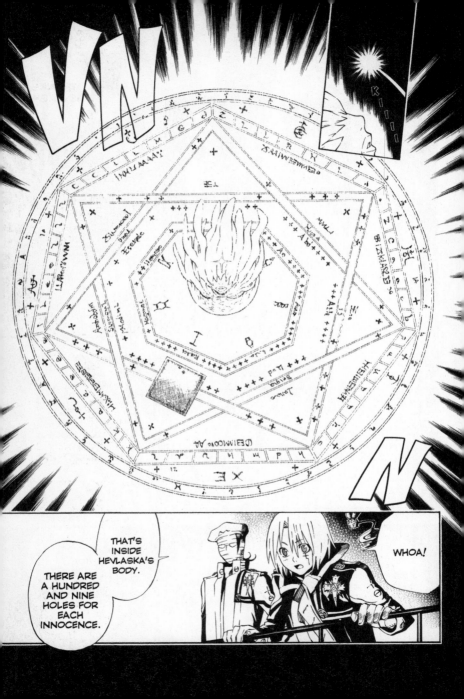

THAT'S INSIDE HEVLASKA'S BODY.

THERE ARE A HUNDRED AND NINE HOLES FOR EACH INNOCENCE.

WHOA!

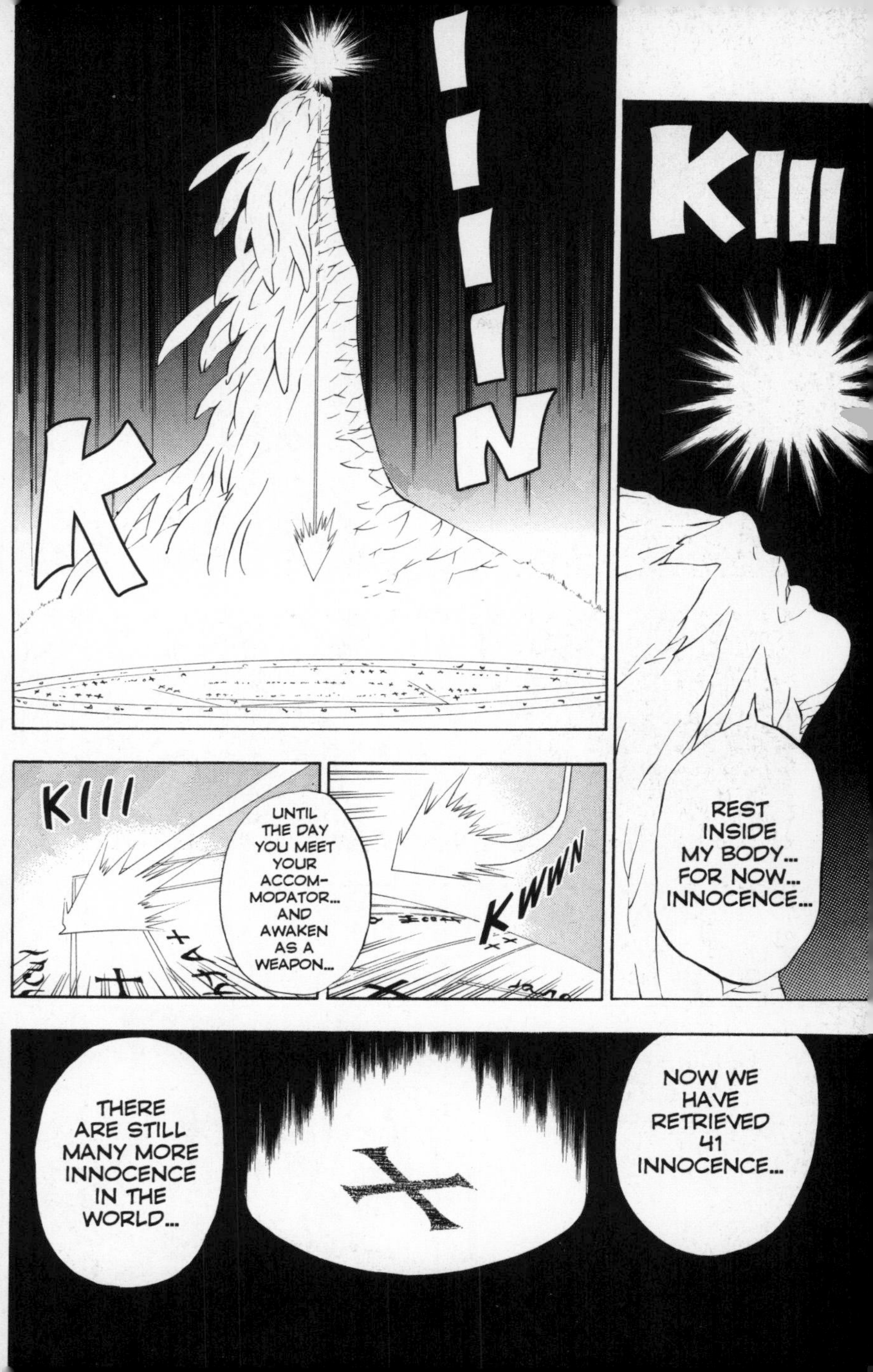
KIII
REST INSIDE MY BODY... FOR NOW... INNOCENCE...
KIIIIN
UNTIL THE DAY YOU MEET YOUR ACCOM-MODATOR... AND AWAKEN AS A WEAPON...
KWWN
KIII
NOW WE HAVE RETRIEVED 41 INNOCENCE...
THERE ARE STILL MANY MORE INNOCENCE IN THE WORLD...

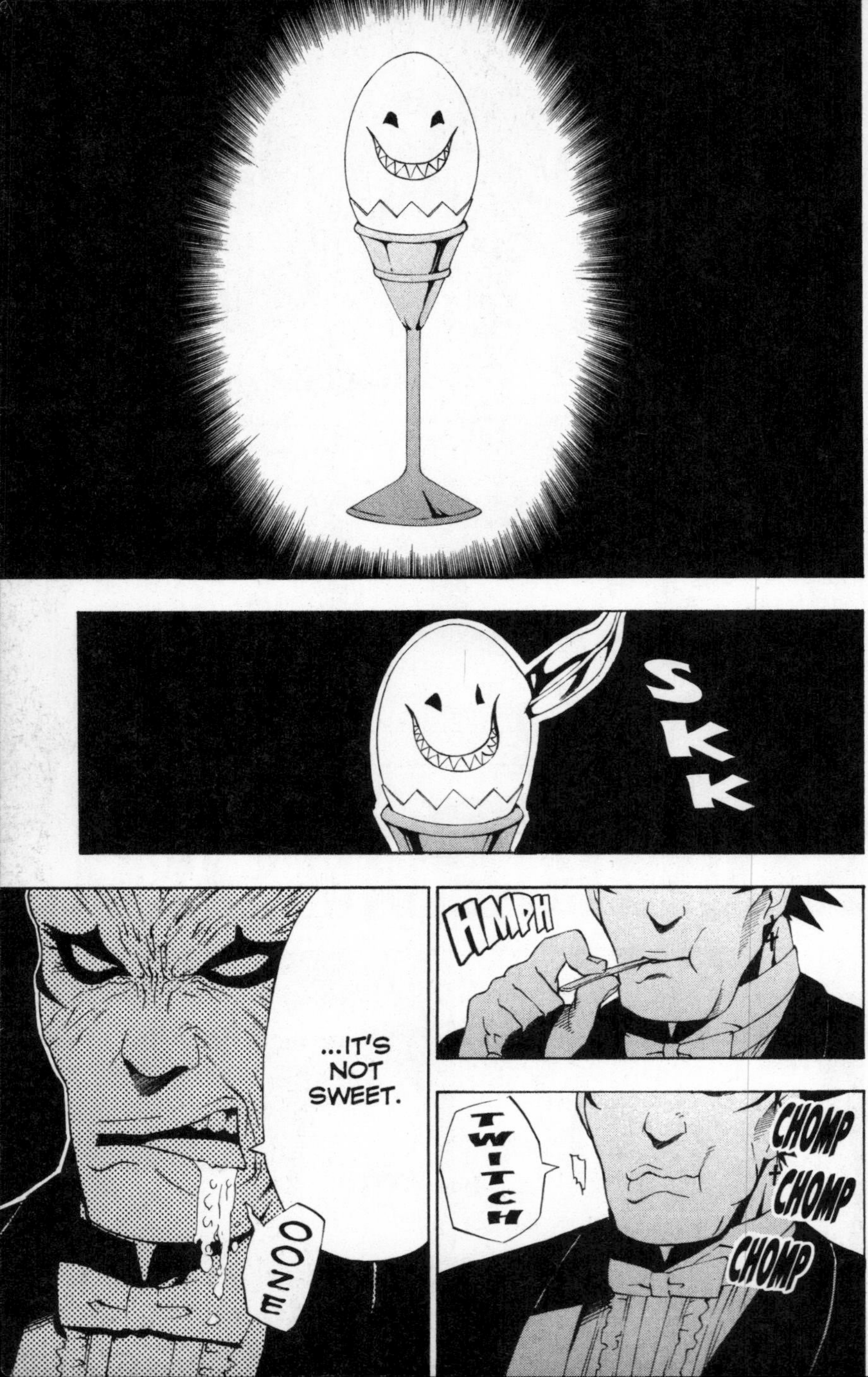

SKK
HMPH
TWITCH
CHOMP
CHOMP
CHOMP
...IT'S NOT SWEET.
OONE

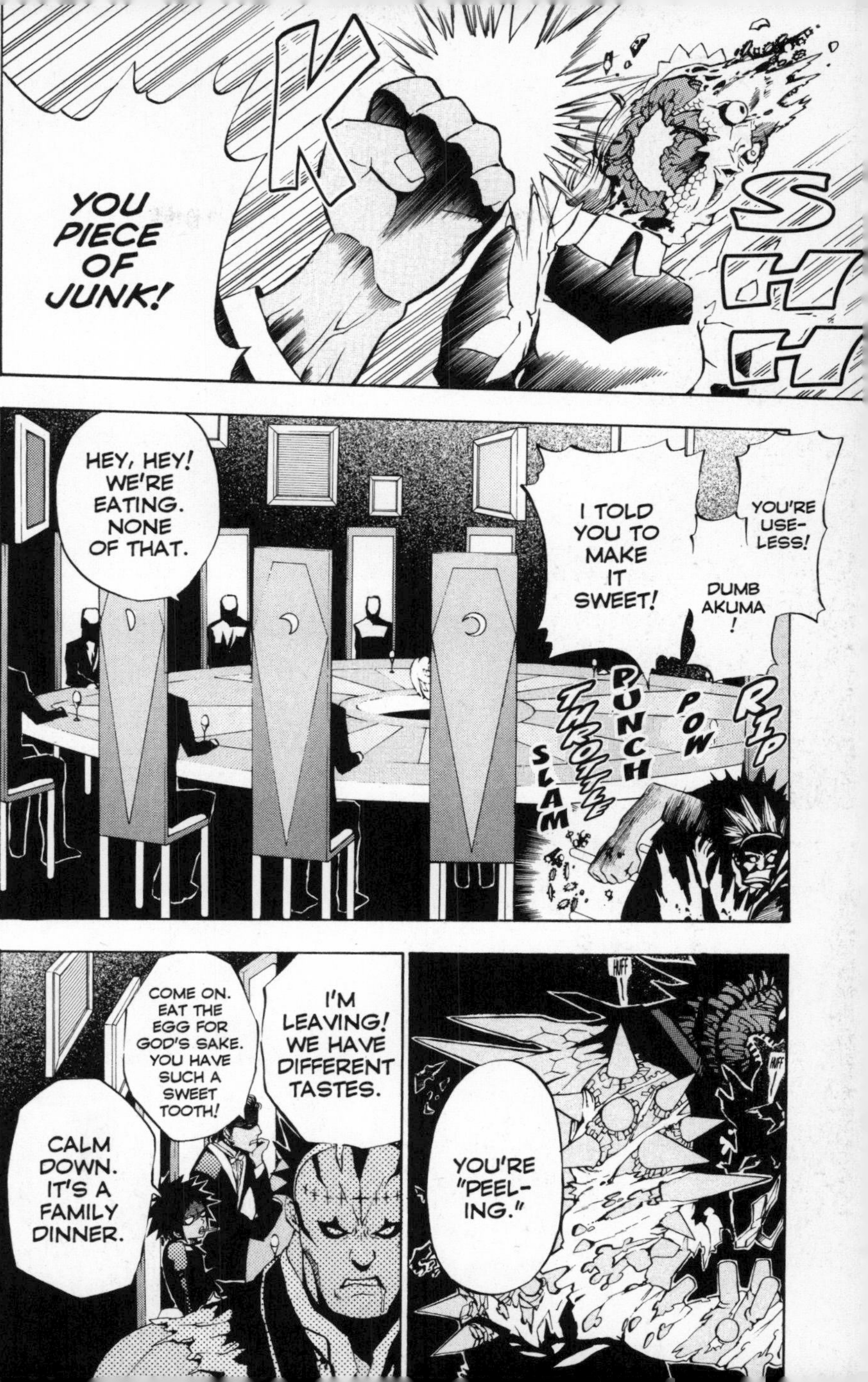
YOU PIECE OF JUNK!
YOU'RE USE-LESS!
I TOLD YOU TO MAKE IT SWEET!
DUMB AKUMA!
RIP
POW
PUNCH
THROWW
SLAM
HEY, HEY! WE'RE EATING. NONE OF THAT.
HUFF
HUFF
YOU'RE "PEEL-ING."
I'M LEAVING! WE HAVE DIFFERENT TASTES.
COME ON. EAT THE EGG FOR GOD'S SAKE. YOU HAVE SUCH A SWEET TOOTH!
CALM DOWN. IT'S A FAMILY DINNER.

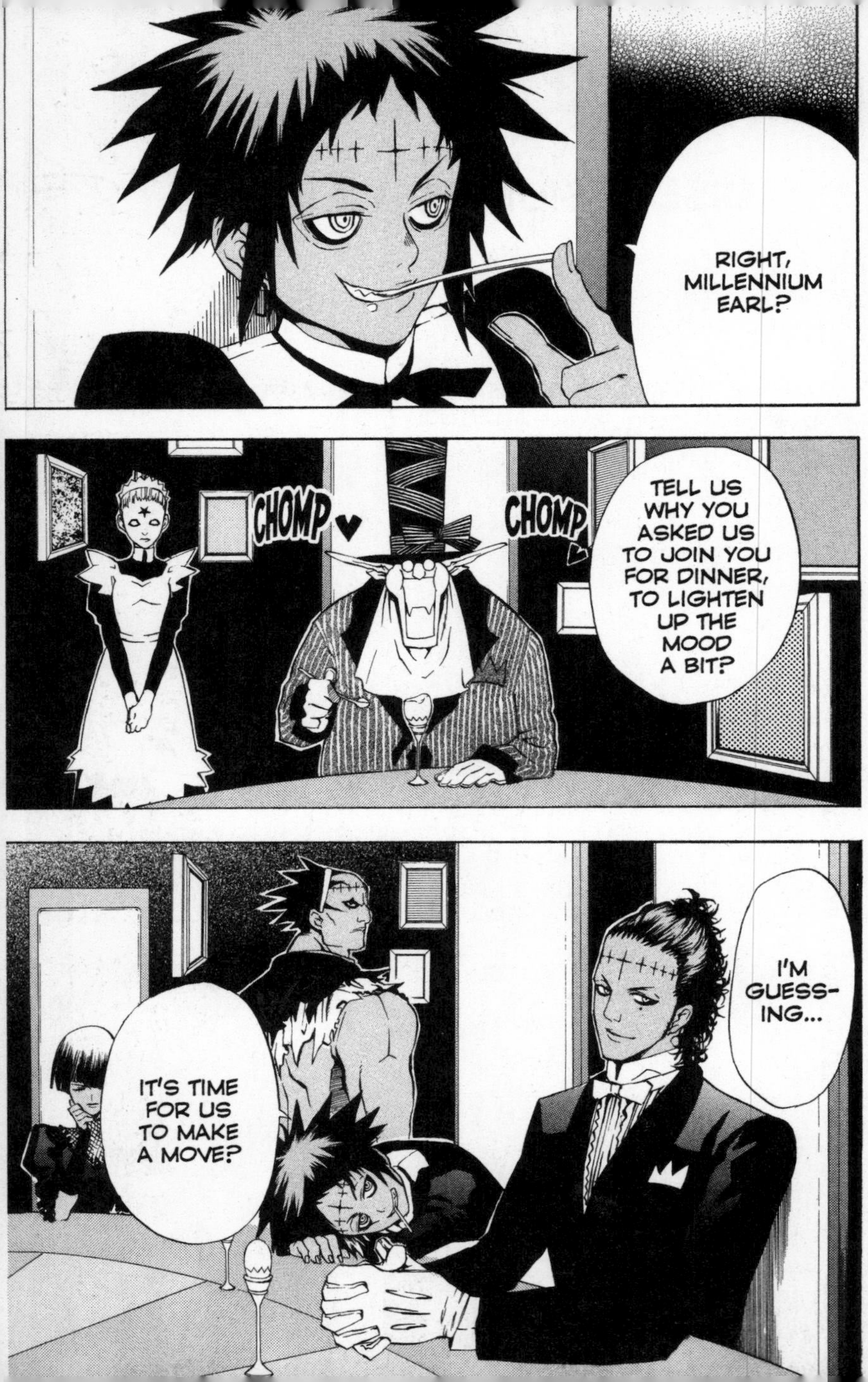
RIGHT, MILLENNIUM EARL?
TELL US WHY YOU ASKED US TO JOIN YOU FOR DINNER, TO LIGHTEN UP THE MOOD A BIT?
CHOMP
CHOMP
I'M GUESS-ING...
IT'S TIME FOR US TO MAKE A MOVE?

DISCUSSION ROOM VOL. 2

Q 1. IS THE TIMCANPY THAT WAS ON MASTER CROSS'S HEAD THE SAME ONE THAT'S WITH ALLEN NOW?

A.   THEY'RE BOTH TIMCANPY.

Q 2. TIMCANPY LOOKS LIKE IT'S GETTING BIGGER.

A.   HE'S GROWING BIGGER EVERY DAY (I THINK?). I GOT EDITOR Y'S APPROVAL SO I'M GOING TO START MAKING HIM BIGGER STILL!!

Q 3. DOES THE EARL REALLY HAVE RABBIT EARS?

A... I WONDER... HEH HEH HEH.

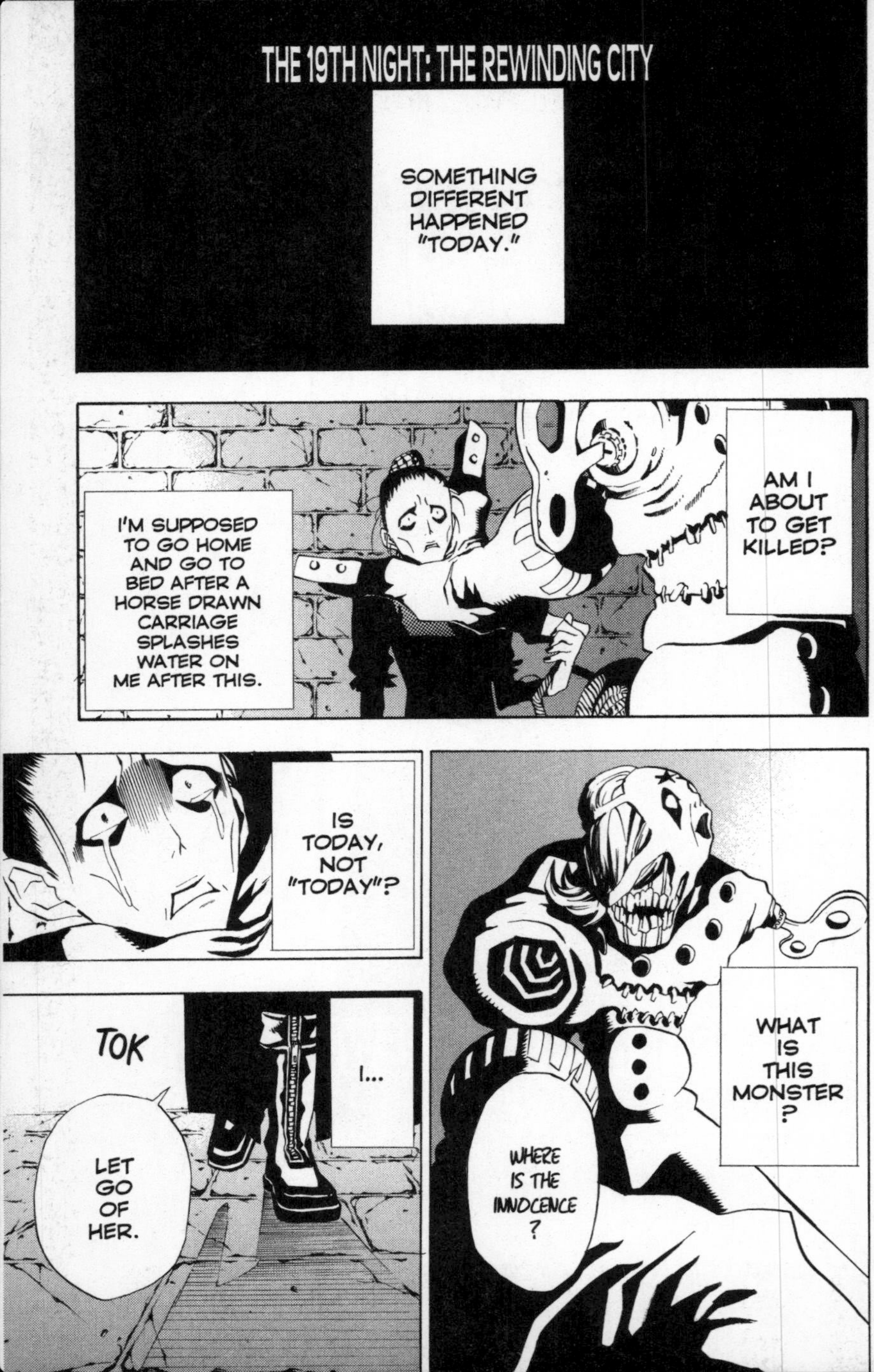
THE 19TH NIGHT: THE REWINDING CITY
SOMETHING DIFFERENT HAPPENED "TODAY."
AM I ABOUT TO GET KILLED?
I'M SUPPOSED TO GO HOME AND GO TO BED AFTER A HORSE DRAWN CARRIAGE SPLASHES WATER ON ME AFTER THIS.
WHAT IS THIS MONSTER?
WHERE IS THE INNOCENCE?
IS TODAY, NOT "TODAY"?
I...
TOK
LET GO OF HER.

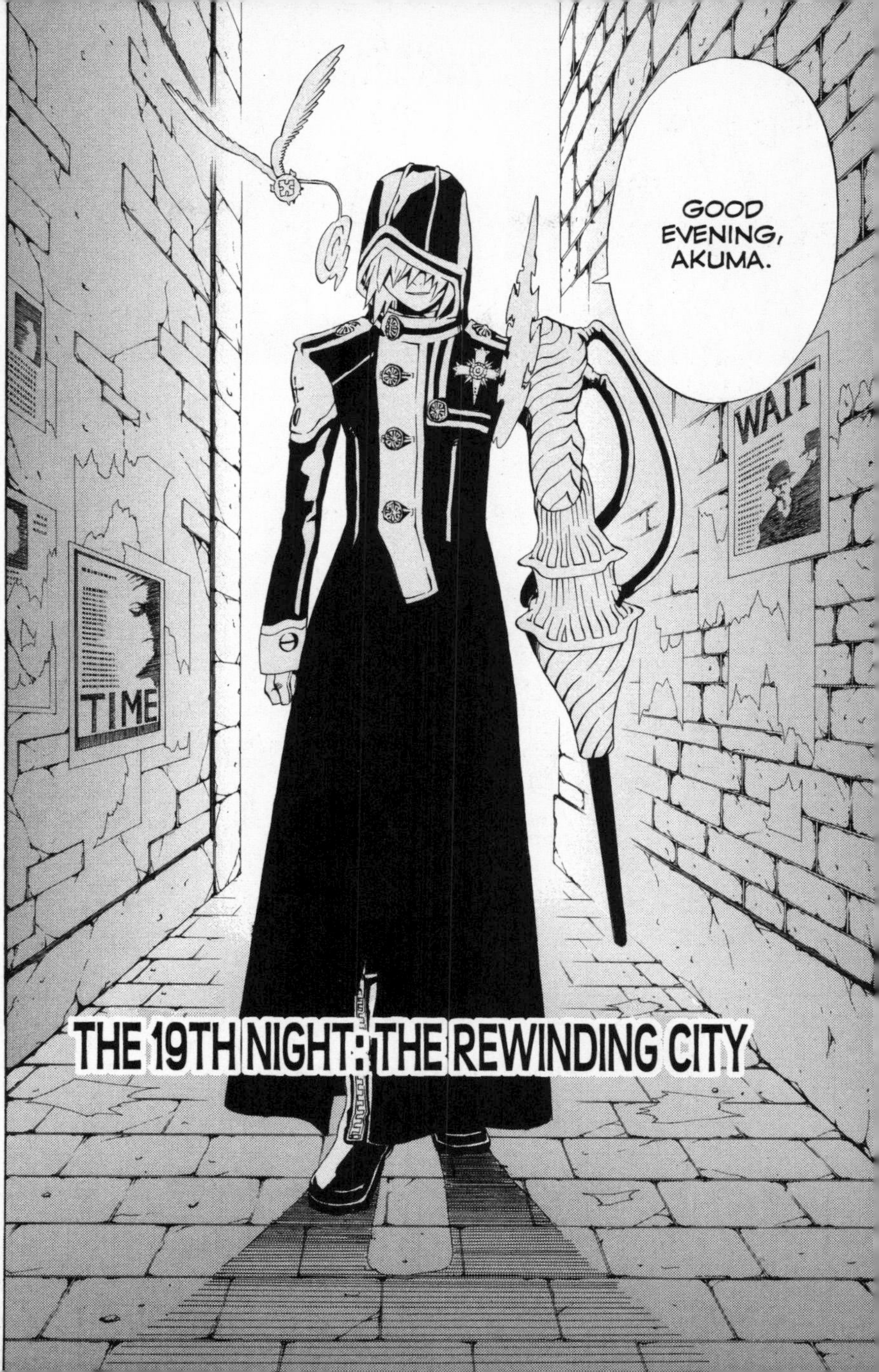
GOOD EVENING, AKUMA.
WAIT
TIME
THE 19TH NIGHT: THE REWINDING CITY

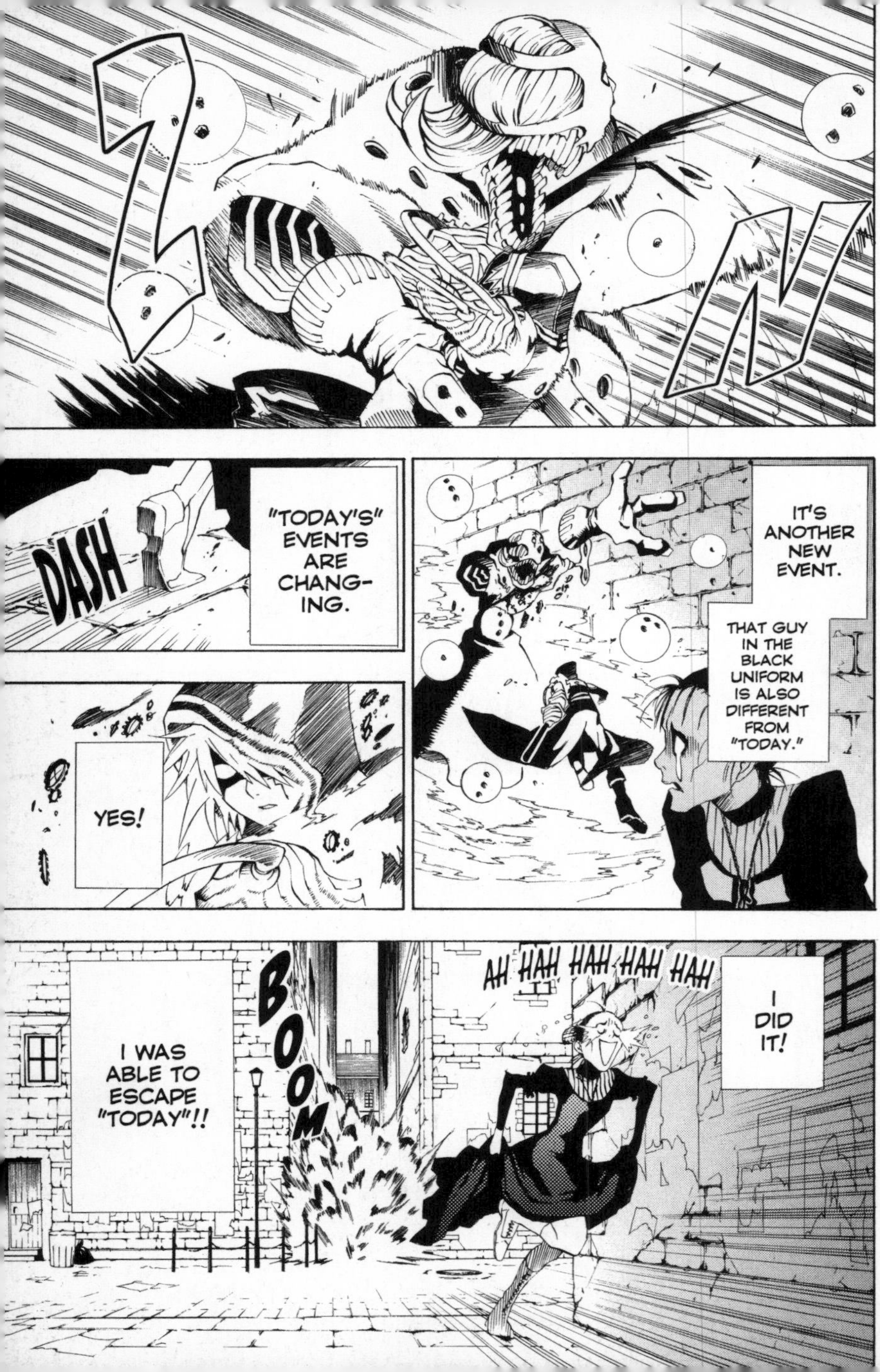
ZN
IT'S ANOTHER NEW EVENT.
THAT GUY IN THE BLACK UNIFORM IS ALSO DIFFERENT FROM "TODAY."
"TODAY'S" EVENTS ARE CHANG-ING.
DASH
YES!
I DID IT!
AH HAH HAH HAH HAH
BOOM
I WAS ABLE TO ESCAPE "TODAY"!!

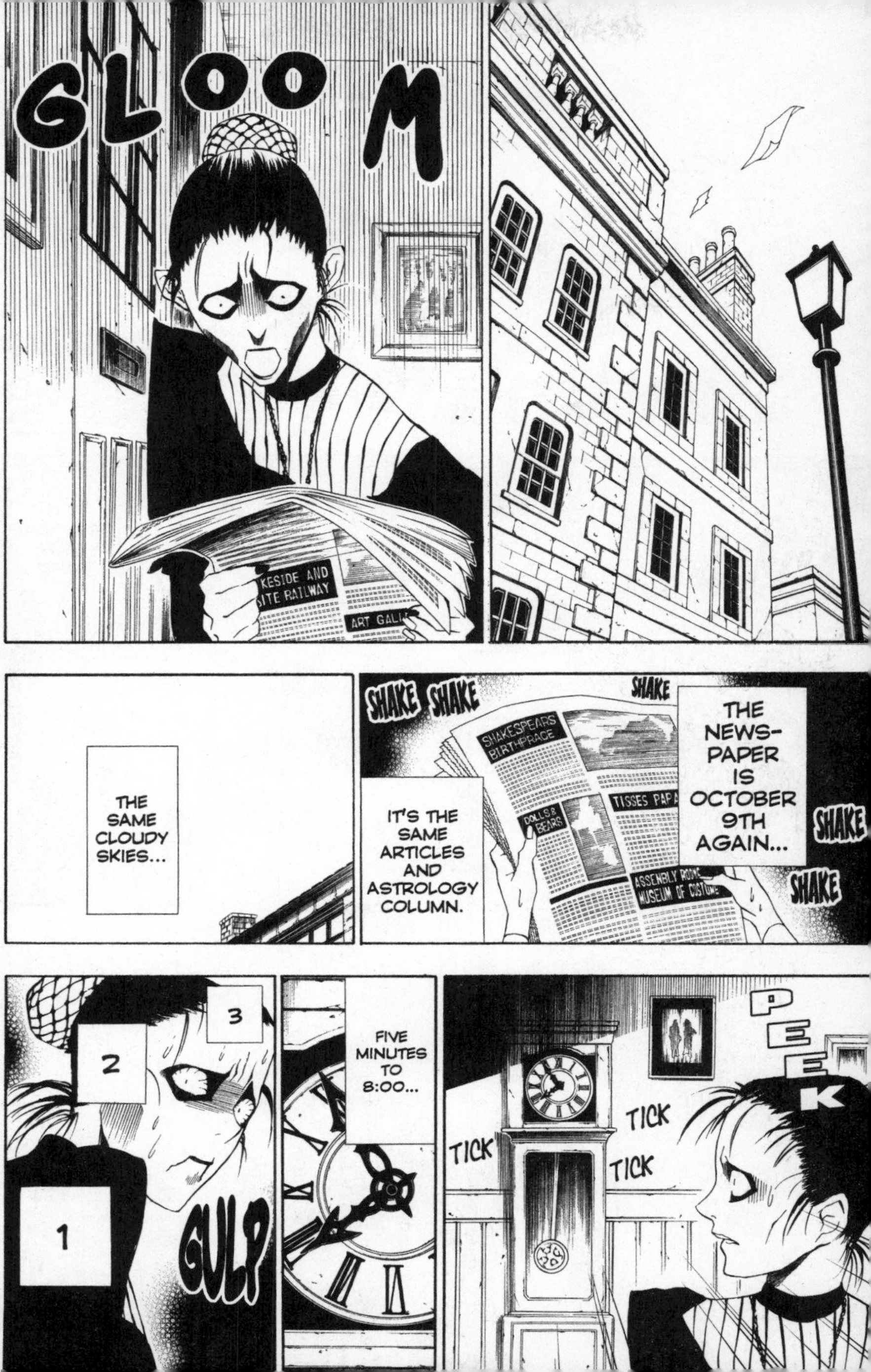
GLOOM
KESIDE AND
SITE RAILWAY
ART GALL
SHAKE
THE NEWS-PAPER IS OCTOBER 9TH AGAIN...
SHAKE
SHAKE
SHAKE SHAKE
SHAKESPEARS BIRTHPRACE
TISSES PAPA
DOLLS & BEARS
ASSENBLY ROOMS MUSEUM OF COSTUME
IT'S THE SAME ARTICLES AND ASTROLOGY COLUMN.
THE SAME CLOUDY SKIES...
PEEK
TICK
TICK
TICK
FIVE MINUTES TO 8:00...
3
2
GULP
1

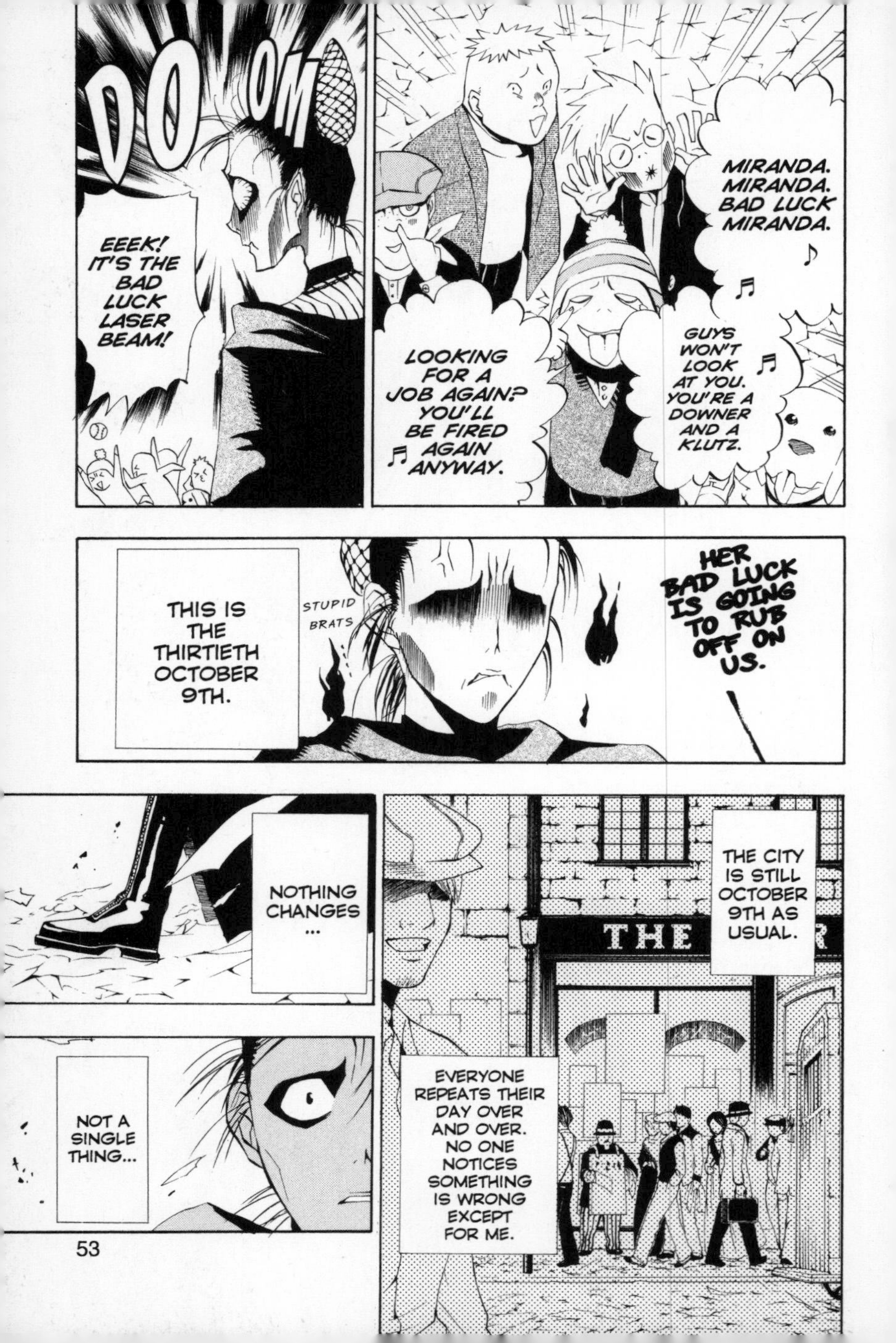
MIRANDA. MIRANDA. BAD LUCK MIRANDA.
GUYS WON'T LOOK AT YOU. YOU'RE A DOWNER AND A KLUTZ.
LOOKING FOR A JOB AGAIN? YOU'LL BE FIRED AGAIN ANYWAY.
DOOM
EEEK! IT'S THE BAD LUCK LASER BEAM!
HER BAD LUCK IS GOING TO RUB OFF ON US.
STUPID BRATS
THIS IS THE THIRTIETH OCTOBER 9TH.
THE CITY IS STILL OCTOBER 9TH AS USUAL.
THE
EVERYONE REPEATS THEIR DAY OVER AND OVER. NO ONE NOTICES SOMETHING IS WRONG EXCEPT FOR ME.
NOTHING CHANGES...
NOT A SINGLE THING...

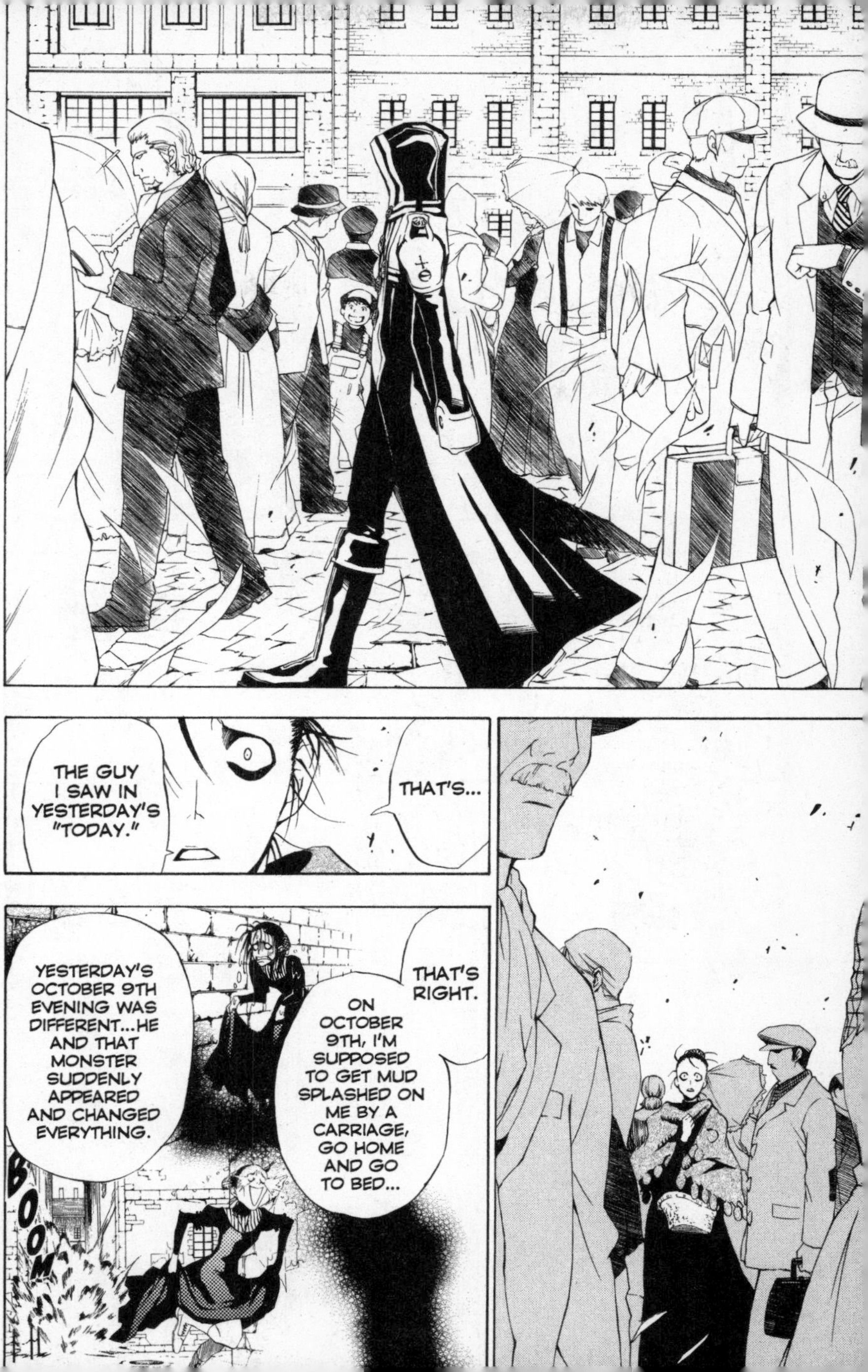
THAT'S...
THE GUY I SAW IN YESTERDAY'S "TODAY."
THAT'S RIGHT.
ON OCTOBER 9TH, I'M SUPPOSED TO GET MUD SPLASHED ON ME BY A CARRIAGE, GO HOME AND GO TO BED...
YESTERDAY'S OCTOBER 9TH EVENING WAS DIFFERENT...HE AND THAT MONSTER SUDDENLY APPEARED AND CHANGED EVERYTHING.
BOOM

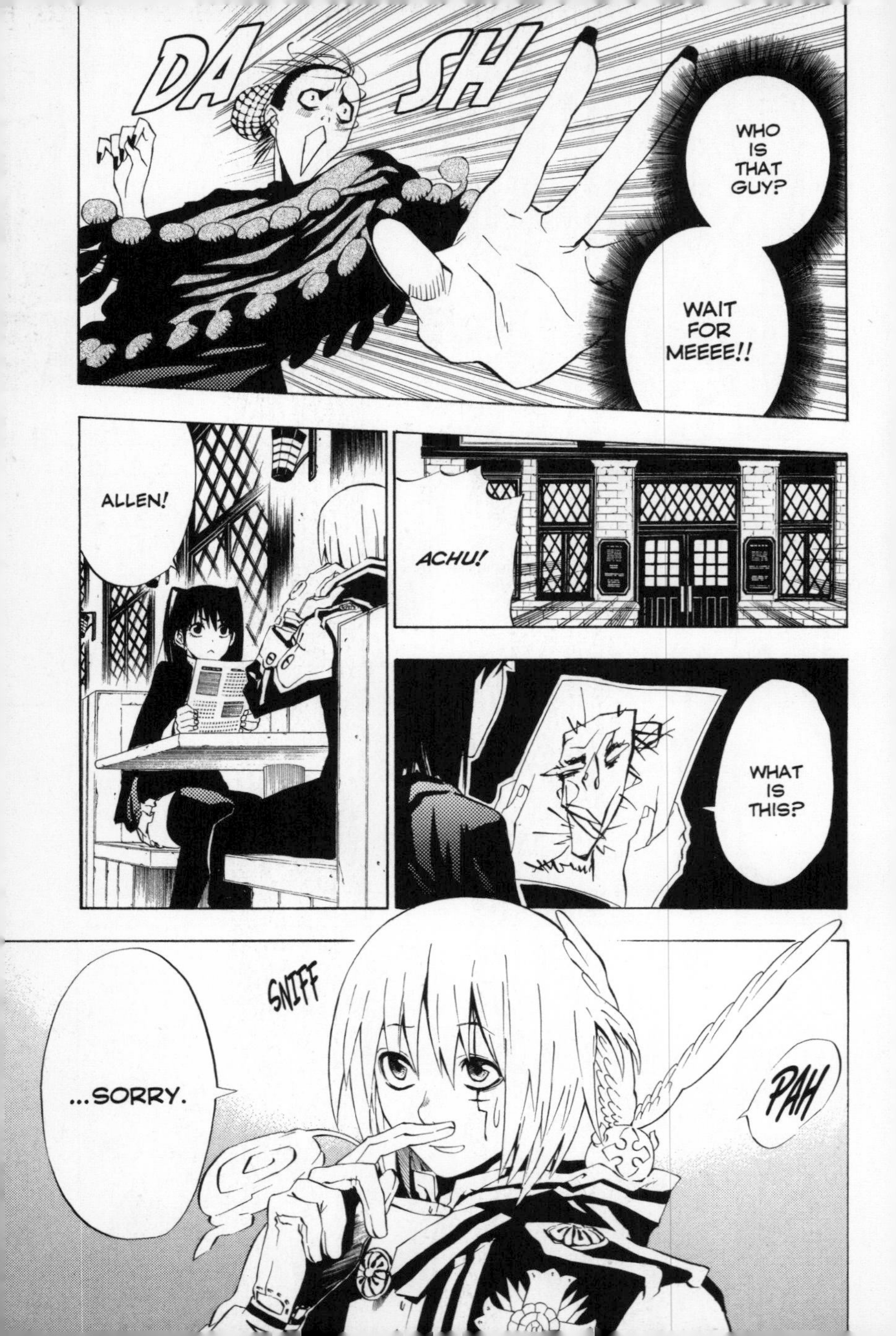
WHO IS THAT GUY?
WAIT FOR MEEEE!!
DA SH
ACHU!
WHAT IS THIS?
ALLEN!
PAH
SNIFF
...SORRY.

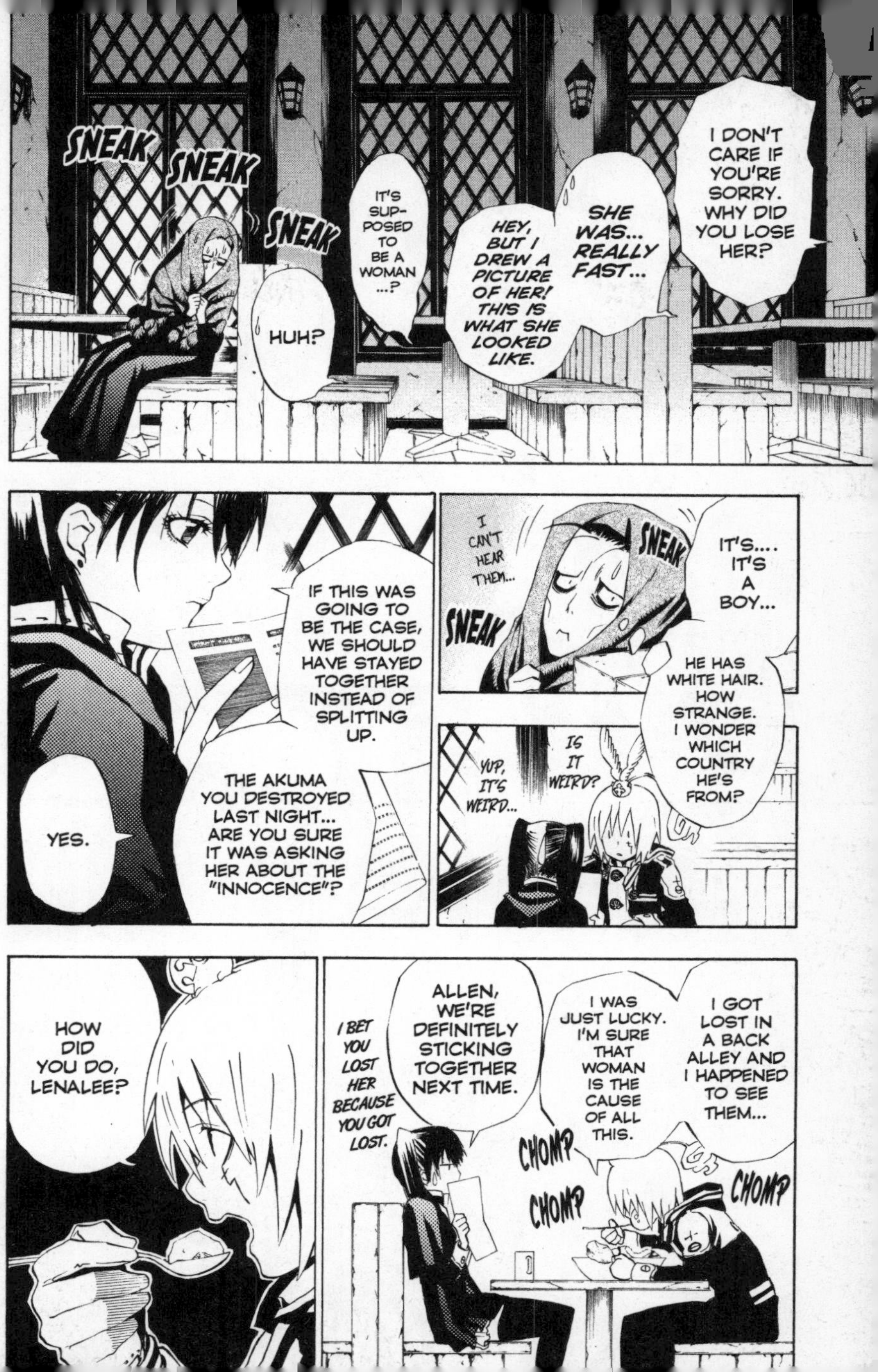
I DON'T CARE IF YOU'RE SORRY. WHY DID YOU LOSE HER?
SHE WAS... REALLY FAST...
HEY, BUT I DREW A PICTURE OF HER! THIS IS WHAT SHE LOOKED LIKE.
IT'S SUP-POSED TO BE A WOMAN ...?
HUH?
SNEAK
SNEAK
SNEAK
IT'S.... IT'S A BOY...
SNEAK
I CAN'T HEAR THEM...
SNEAK
HE HAS WHITE HAIR. HOW STRANGE. I WONDER WHICH COUNTRY HE'S FROM?
IS IT WEIRD?
YUP, IT'S WEIRD...
IF THIS WAS GOING TO BE THE CASE, WE SHOULD HAVE STAYED TOGETHER INSTEAD OF SPLITTING UP.
THE AKUMA YOU DESTROYED LAST NIGHT... ARE YOU SURE IT WAS ASKING HER ABOUT THE "INNOCENCE"?
YES.
I GOT LOST IN A BACK ALLEY AND I HAPPENED TO SEE THEM...
I WAS JUST LUCKY. I'M SURE THAT WOMAN IS THE CAUSE OF ALL THIS.
ALLEN, WE'RE DEFINITELY STICKING TOGETHER NEXT TIME.
I BET YOU LOST HER BECAUSE YOU GOT LOST.
CHOMP
CHOMP
CHOMP
HOW DID YOU DO, LENALEE?

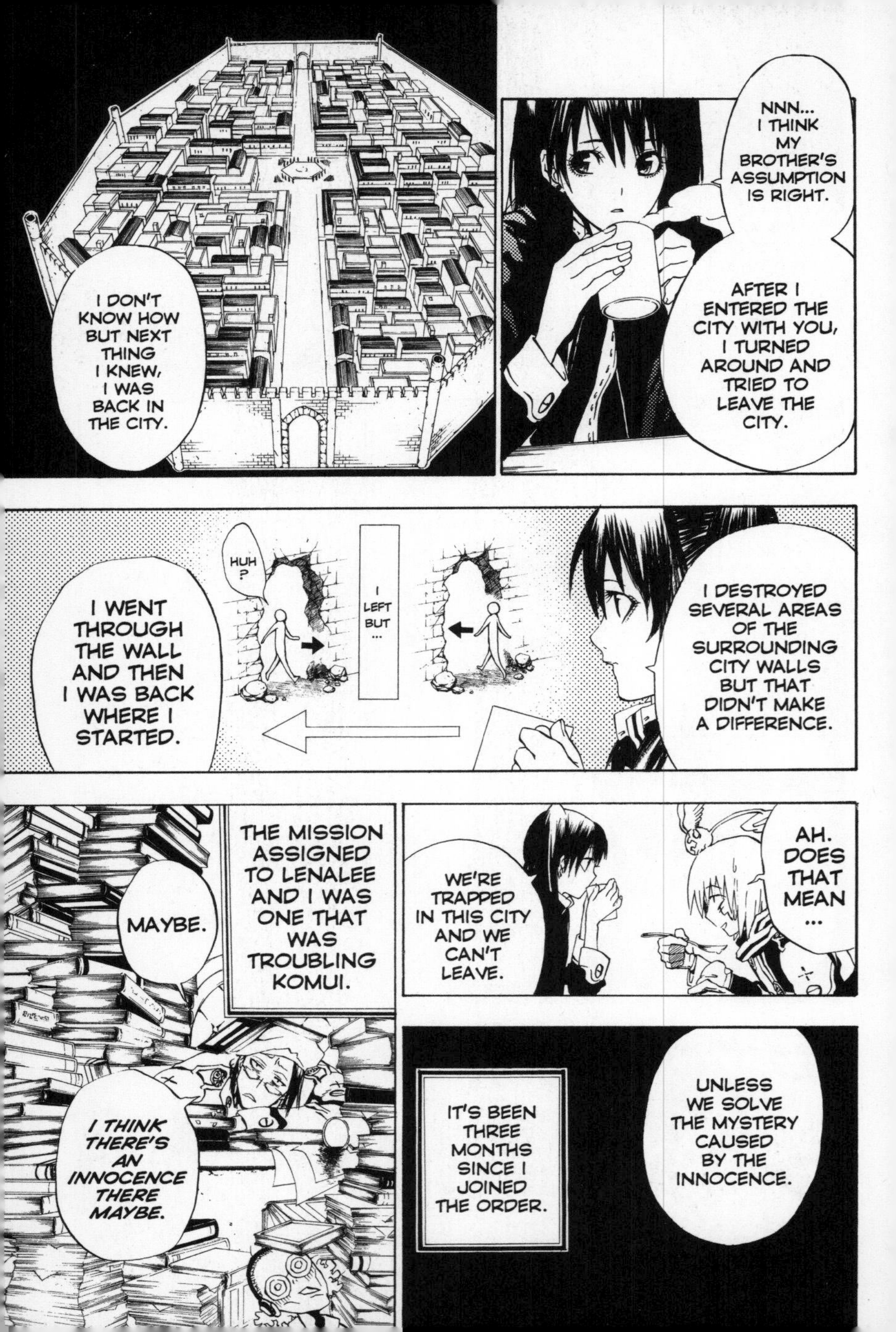
NNN... I THINK MY BROTHER'S ASSUMPTION IS RIGHT.
AFTER I ENTERED THE CITY WITH YOU, I TURNED AROUND AND TRIED TO LEAVE THE CITY.
I DON'T KNOW HOW BUT NEXT THING I KNEW, I WAS BACK IN THE CITY.
I DESTROYED SEVERAL AREAS OF THE SURROUNDING CITY WALLS BUT THAT DIDN'T MAKE A DIFFERENCE.
I LEFT BUT ...
HUH ?
I WENT THROUGH THE WALL AND THEN I WAS BACK WHERE I STARTED.
AH. DOES THAT MEAN ...
WE'RE TRAPPED IN THIS CITY AND WE CAN'T LEAVE.
UNLESS WE SOLVE THE MYSTERY CAUSED BY THE INNOCENCE.
IT'S BEEN THREE MONTHS SINCE I JOINED THE ORDER.
THE MISSION ASSIGNED TO LENALEE AND I WAS ONE THAT WAS TROUBLING KOMUI.
MAYBE.
I THINK THERE'S AN INNOCENCE THERE MAYBE.

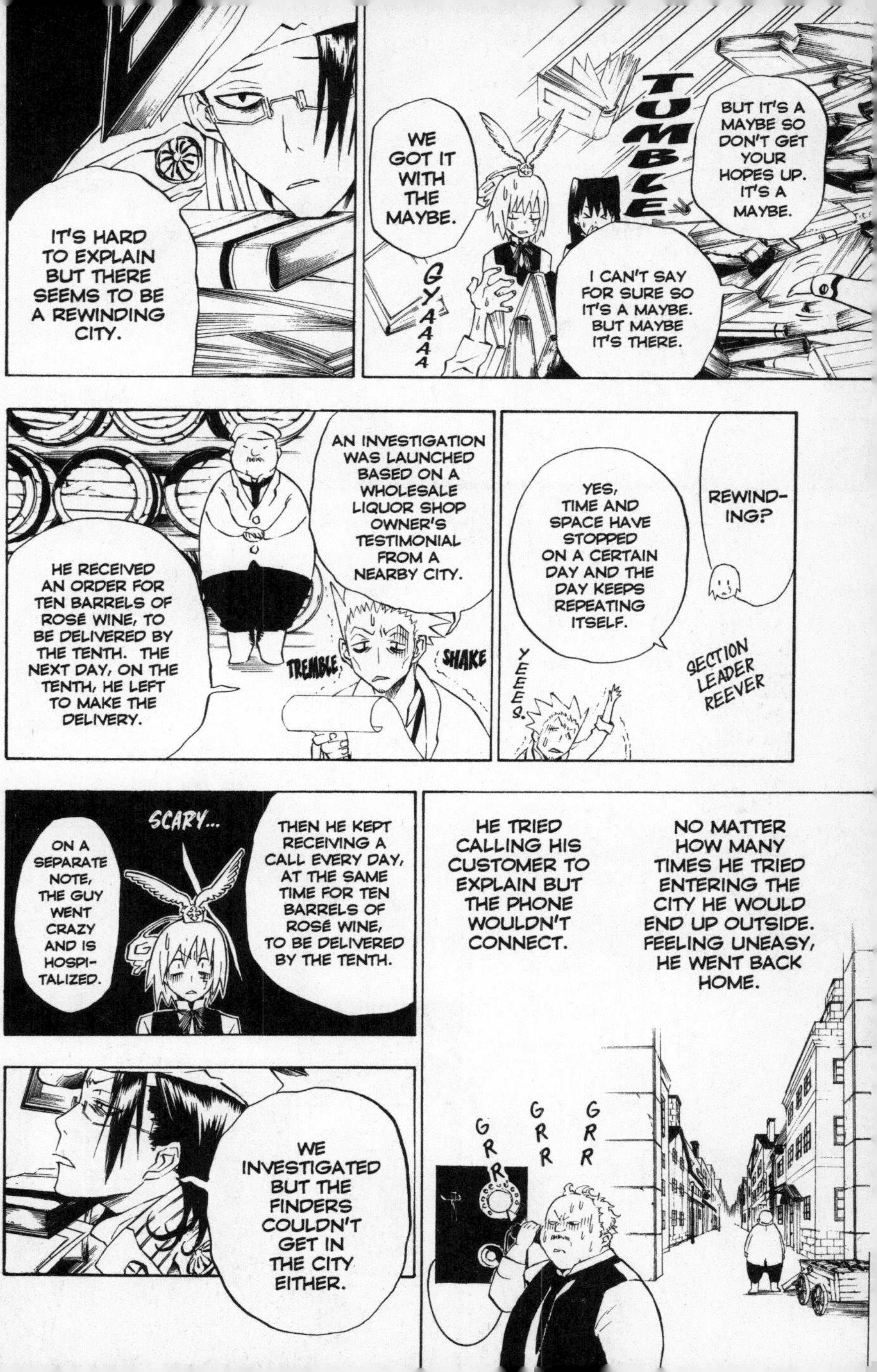
BUT IT'S A MAYBE SO DON'T GET YOUR HOPES UP. IT'S A MAYBE.
TUMBLE
WE GOT IT WITH THE MAYBE.
I CAN'T SAY FOR SURE SO IT'S A MAYBE. BUT MAYBE IT'S THERE.
GYAAAAA
IT'S HARD TO EXPLAIN BUT THERE SEEMS TO BE A REWINDING CITY.
REWINDING?
YES, TIME AND SPACE HAVE STOPPED ON A CERTAIN DAY AND THE DAY KEEPS REPEATING ITSELF.
SECTION LEADER REEVER
YEEES.
AN INVESTIGATION WAS LAUNCHED BASED ON A WHOLESALE LIQUOR SHOP OWNER'S TESTIMONIAL FROM A NEARBY CITY.
HE RECEIVED AN ORDER FOR TEN BARRELS OF ROSÉ WINE, TO BE DELIVERED BY THE TENTH. THE NEXT DAY, ON THE TENTH, HE LEFT TO MAKE THE DELIVERY.
SHAKE
TREMBLE
NO MATTER HOW MANY TIMES HE TRIED ENTERING THE CITY HE WOULD END UP OUTSIDE. FEELING UNEASY, HE WENT BACK HOME.
HE TRIED CALLING HIS CUSTOMER TO EXPLAIN BUT THE PHONE WOULDN'T CONNECT.
GRR GRR GRR
THEN HE KEPT RECEIVING A CALL EVERY DAY, AT THE SAME TIME FOR TEN BARRELS OF ROSÉ WINE, TO BE DELIVERED BY THE TENTH.
SCARY...
ON A SEPARATE NOTE, THE GUY WENT CRAZY AND IS HOSPI-TALIZED.
WE INVESTIGATED BUT THE FINDERS COULDN'T GET IN THE CITY EITHER.

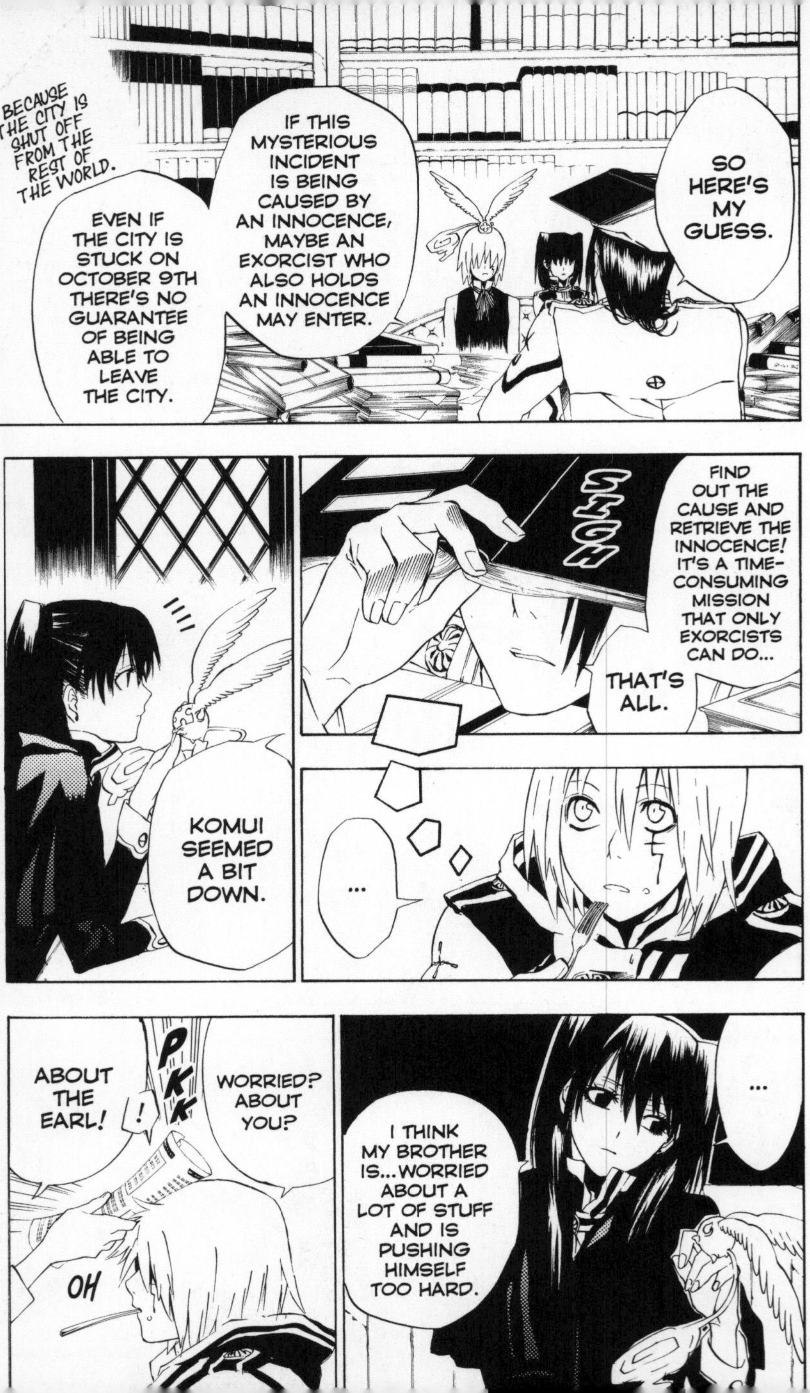
SO HERE'S MY GUESS.
IF THIS MYSTERIOUS INCIDENT IS BEING CAUSED BY AN INNOCENCE, MAYBE AN EXORCIST WHO ALSO HOLDS AN INNOCENCE MAY ENTER.
EVEN IF THE CITY IS STUCK ON OCTOBER 9TH THERE'S NO GUARANTEE OF BEING ABLE TO LEAVE THE CITY.
BECAUSE THE CITY IS SHUT OFF FROM THE REST OF THE WORLD.
SIGH
FIND OUT THE CAUSE AND RETRIEVE THE INNOCENCE! IT'S A TIME-CONSUMING MISSION THAT ONLY EXORCISTS CAN DO...
THAT'S ALL.
...
KOMUI SEEMED A BIT DOWN.
...
I THINK MY BROTHER IS...WORRIED ABOUT A LOT OF STUFF AND IS PUSHING HIMSELF TOO HARD.
WORRIED? ABOUT YOU?
PKK
!
ABOUT THE EARL!
OH

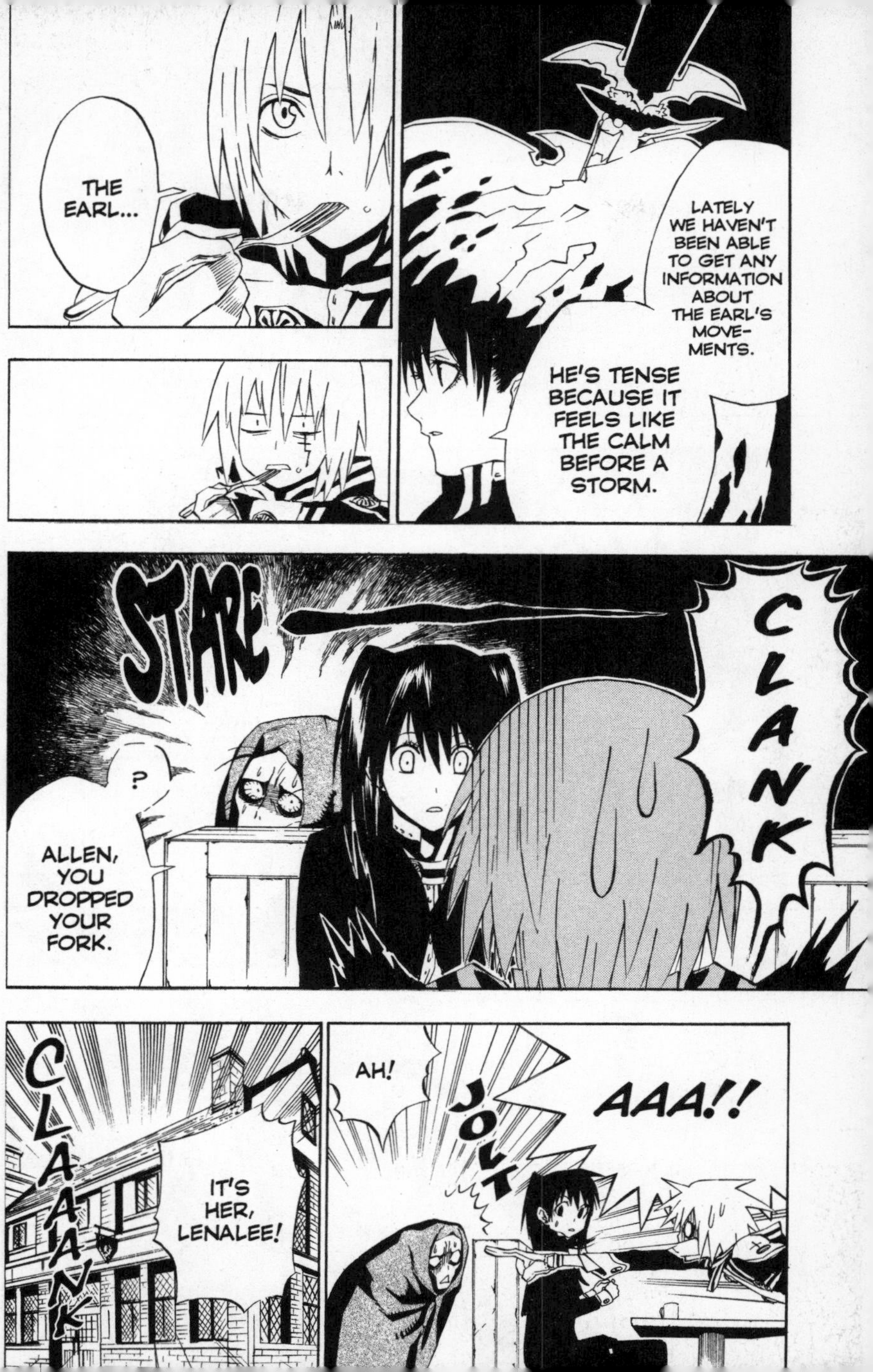

LATELY WE HAVEN'T BEEN ABLE TO GET ANY INFORMATION ABOUT THE EARL'S MOVE-MENTS.
HE'S TENSE BECAUSE IT FEELS LIKE THE CALM BEFORE A STORM.
THE EARL...
CLANK
STARE
?
ALLEN, YOU DROPPED YOUR FORK.
AAA!!
JOLT
AH!
IT'S HER, LENALEE!
CLAAANK

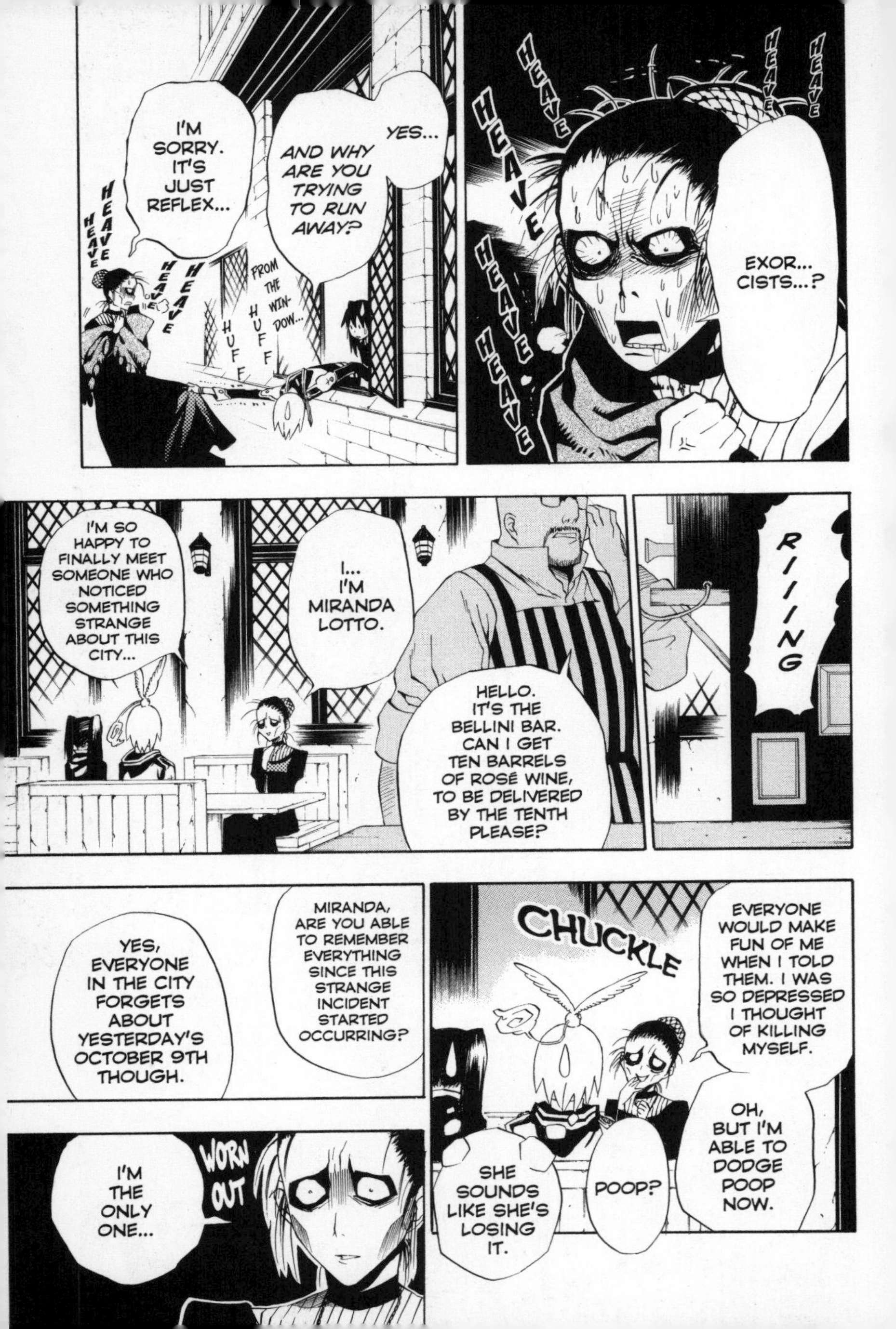
HEAVE HEAVE HEAVE HEAVE HEAVE HEAVE
EXOR... CISTS...?
YES...
AND WHY ARE YOU TRYING TO RUN AWAY?
FROM THE WIN-DOW...
HUFF HUFF
I'M SORRY. IT'S JUST REFLEX...
HEAVE HEAVE HEAVE HEAVE
RIIIING
HELLO. IT'S THE BELLINI BAR. CAN I GET TEN BARRELS OF ROSÉ WINE, TO BE DELIVERED BY THE TENTH PLEASE?
I... I'M MIRANDA LOTTO.
I'M SO HAPPY TO FINALLY MEET SOMEONE WHO NOTICED SOMETHING STRANGE ABOUT THIS CITY...
CHUCKLE
EVERYONE WOULD MAKE FUN OF ME WHEN I TOLD THEM. I WAS SO DEPRESSED I THOUGHT OF KILLING MYSELF.
OH, BUT I'M ABLE TO DODGE POOP NOW.
POOP?
SHE SOUNDS LIKE SHE'S LOSING IT.
MIRANDA, ARE YOU ABLE TO REMEMBER EVERYTHING SINCE THIS STRANGE INCIDENT STARTED OCCURRING?
YES, EVERYONE IN THE CITY FORGETS ABOUT YESTERDAY'S OCTOBER 9TH THOUGH.
WORN OUT
I'M THE ONLY ONE...

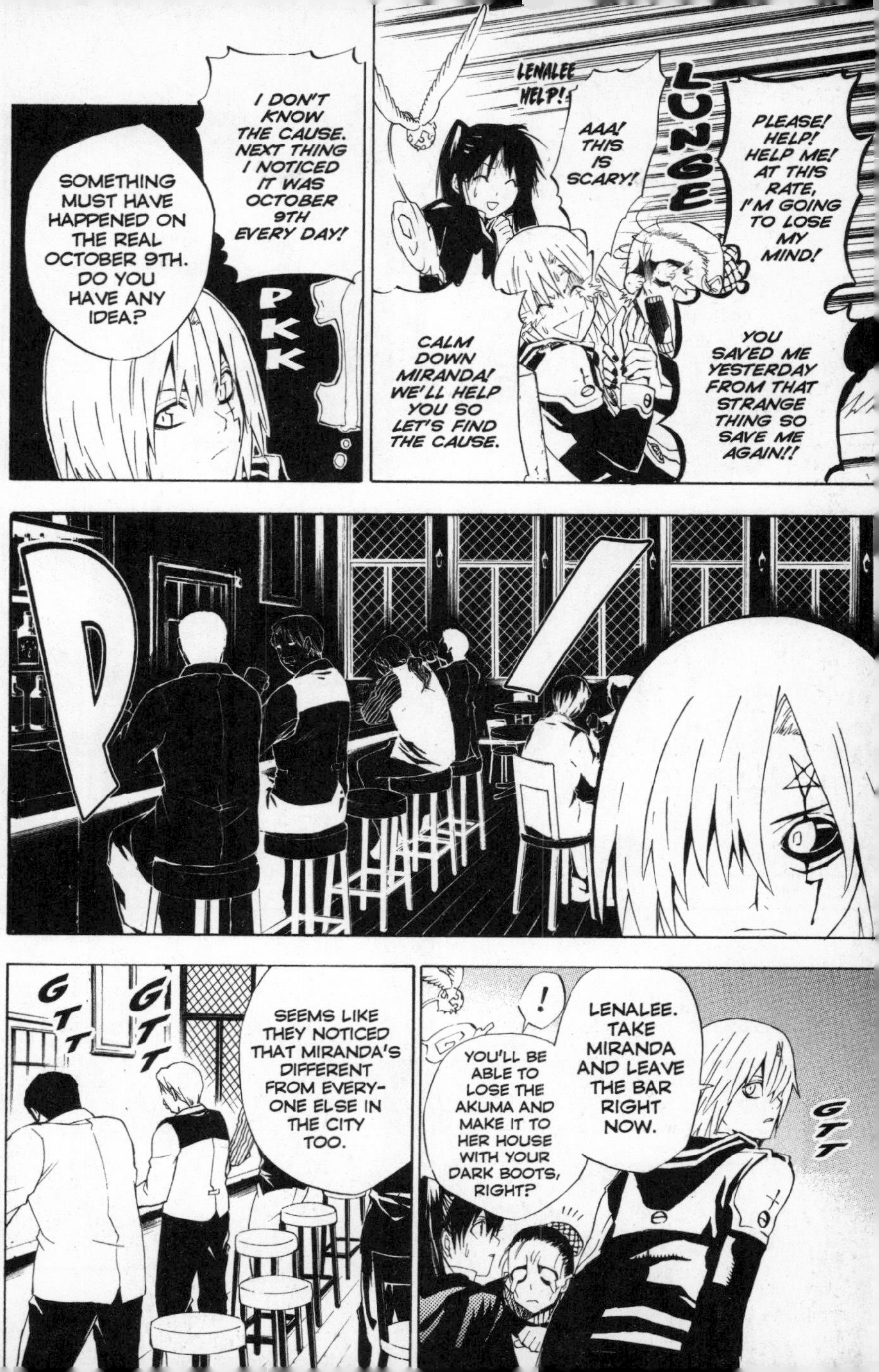
PLEASE! HELP! HELP ME! AT THIS RATE, I'M GOING TO LOSE MY MIND!
LUNGE
AAA! THIS IS SCARY!
LENALEE HELP!
YOU SAVED ME YESTERDAY FROM THAT STRANGE THING SO SAVE ME AGAIN!!
CALM DOWN MIRANDA! WE'LL HELP YOU SO LET'S FIND THE CAUSE.
I DON'T KNOW THE CAUSE. NEXT THING I NOTICED IT WAS OCTOBER 9TH EVERY DAY!
SOMETHING MUST HAVE HAPPENED ON THE REAL OCTOBER 9TH. DO YOU HAVE ANY IDEA?
PKK
!
LENALEE. TAKE MIRANDA AND LEAVE THE BAR RIGHT NOW.
YOU'LL BE ABLE TO LOSE THE AKUMA AND MAKE IT TO HER HOUSE WITH YOUR DARK BOOTS, RIGHT?
GTT
SEEMS LIKE THEY NOTICED THAT MIRANDA'S DIFFERENT FROM EVERY-ONE ELSE IN THE CITY TOO.
GTT
GTT

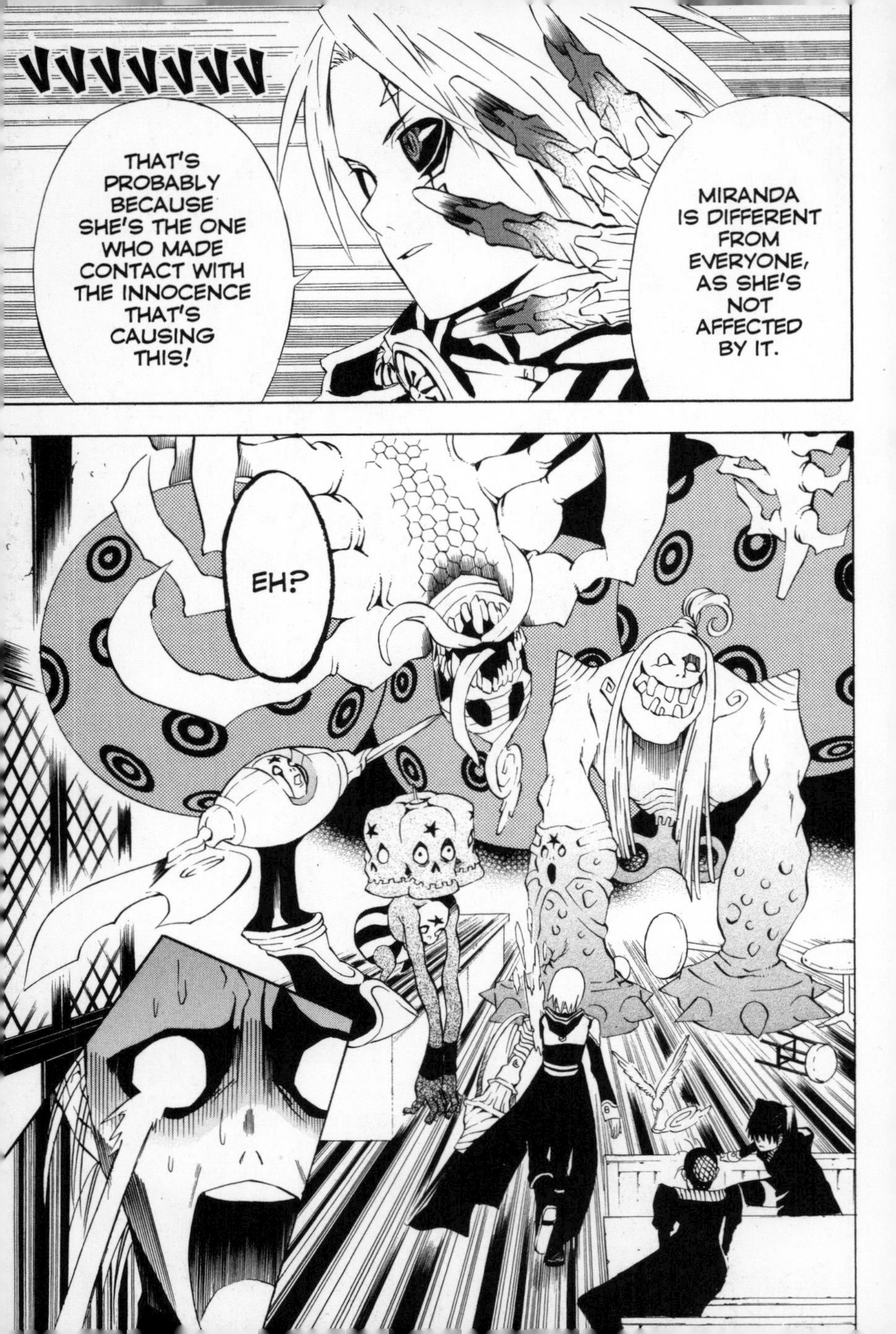
MIRANDA IS DIFFERENT FROM EVERYONE, AS SHE'S NOT AFFECTED BY IT.
VVVVVVVV
THAT'S PROBABLY BECAUSE SHE'S THE ONE WHO MADE CONTACT WITH THE INNOCENCE THAT'S CAUSING THIS!
EH?

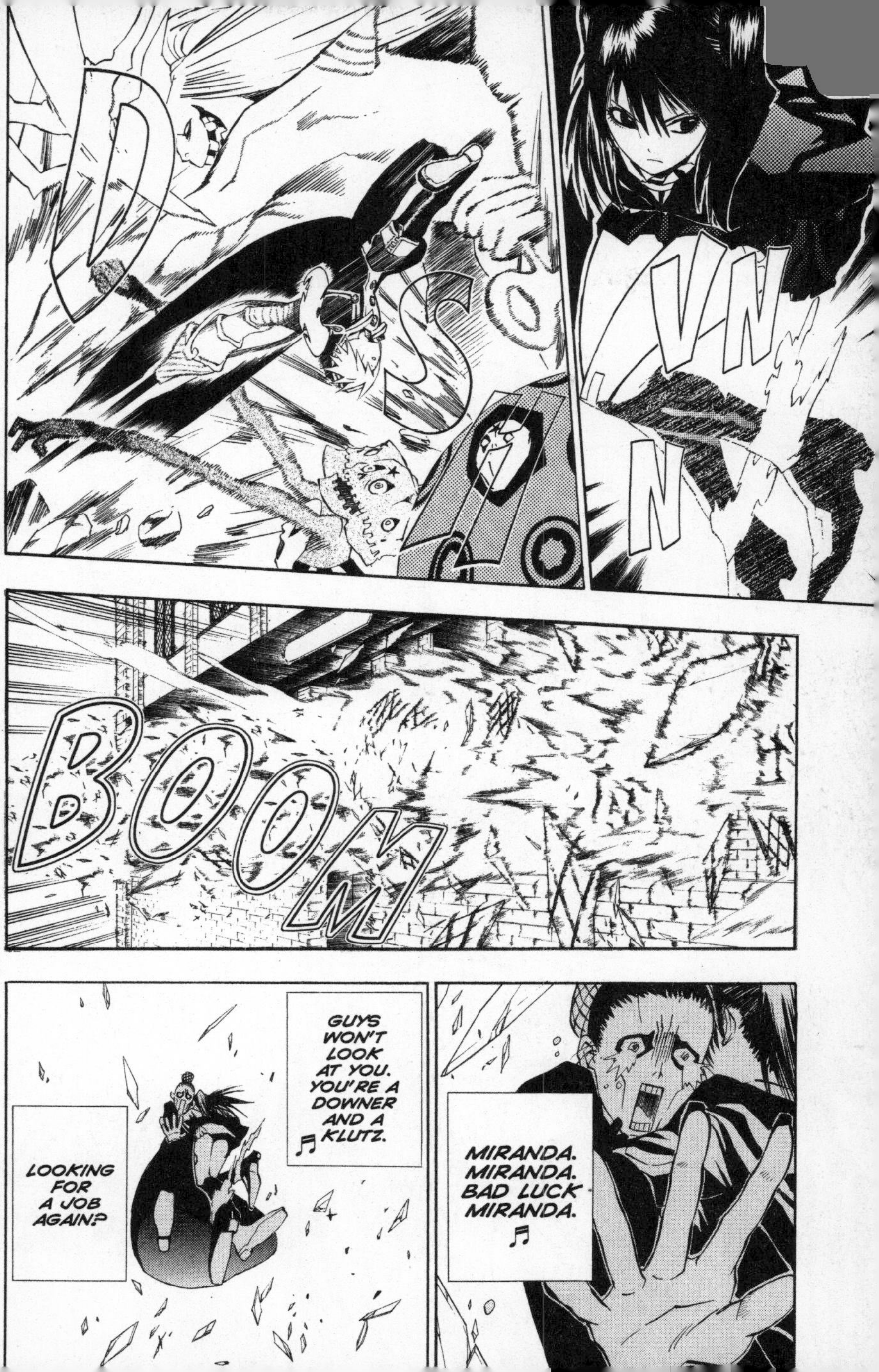
BOOM
MIRANDA. MIRANDA. BAD LUCK MIRANDA. ♪
GUYS WON'T LOOK AT YOU. YOU'RE A DOWNER AND A KLUTZ. ♪
LOOKING FOR A JOB AGAIN?

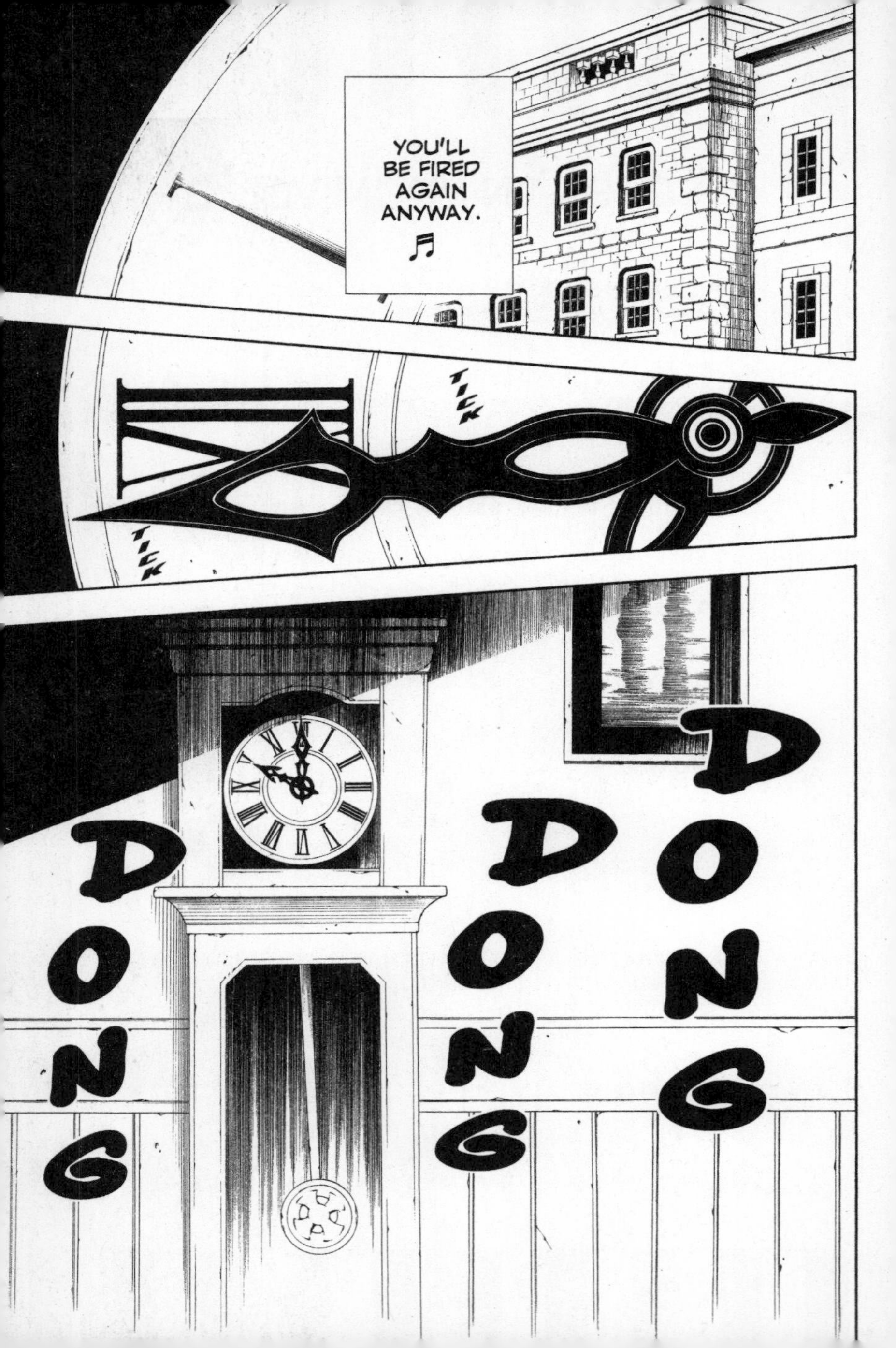
YOU'LL BE FIRED AGAIN ANYWAY. ♬
TICK
TICK
DONG
DONG
DONG

DISCUSSION ROOM VOL. 3

★THERE WERE QUITE A FEW NON-D.GRAY-MAN-
RELATED QUESTIONS SO...

Q 1.   WHAT KIND OF CONVERSATIONS DO YOU HAVE WITH YOUR STAFF
MEMBERS, LIKE OI-CHAN? WHO DO YOU HANG OUT WITH THE
MOST?

A.   WE SHOW EACH OTHER OUR EARLIER MANGA CREATIONS AND
LAUGH ABOUT IT. I THINK I HANG OUT WITH OI-CHAN AND
MIYAZAKI THE MOST. WE'RE ALWAYS PLAYING AROUND AND
IMITATING GHIBLI AND GUNDAM CHARACTERS WHEN WE'RE
WORKING.

Q 2.   IS YOUR ASSISTANT OI-CHAN YOUR NEPHEW?

A.   NO, HE'S MY BUDDY.

Q 3.   DO YOU WEAR A TOUPEE?

A.   WHAAAAAAA!!? (SLAMS DESK!) I DO NOT! I USED TO GET TEASED
ABOUT THAT WHEN I WAS YOUNG...

Q 4.   WHAT KIND OF MUSIC DO YOU LISTEN TO WHILE WORKING?

A.   FINAL FANTASY SOUNDTRACK AND DRAGONBALL CDS, ETC.

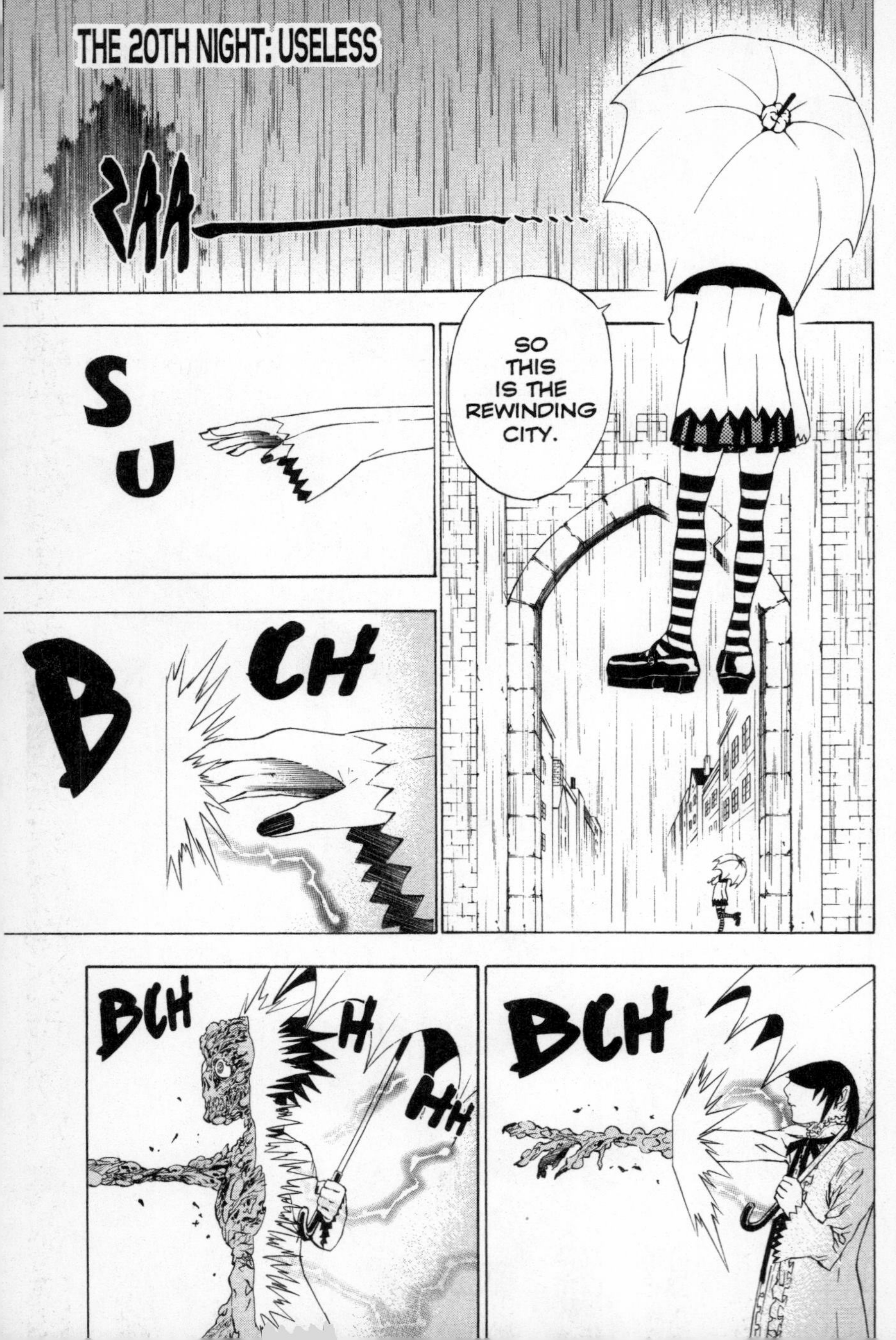
THE 20TH NIGHT: USELESS
ZAA
SO THIS IS THE REWINDING CITY.
SU
BCH
BCH
BCH
HHH

THE 20TH NIGHT: USELESS

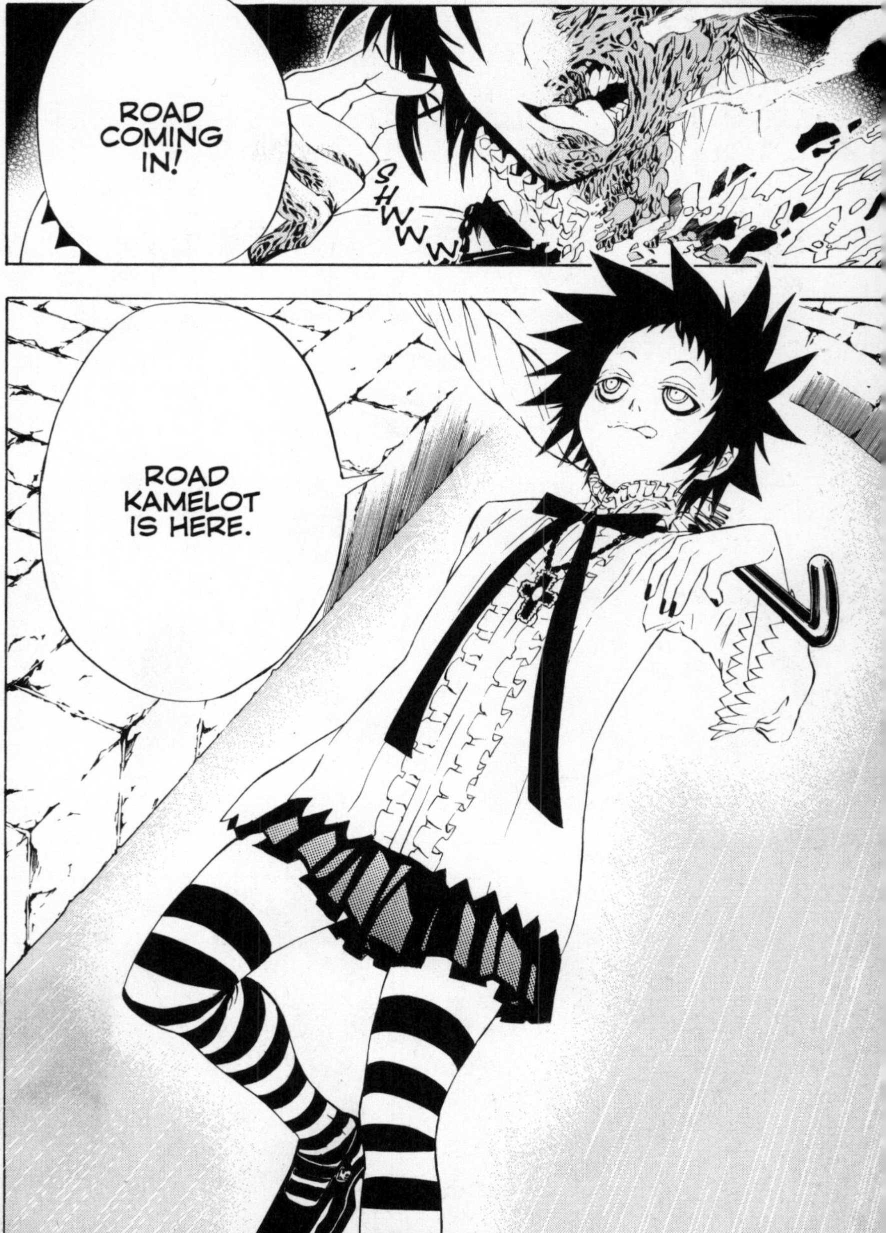
ROAD COMING IN!
SHWWW
ROAD KAMELOT IS HERE.

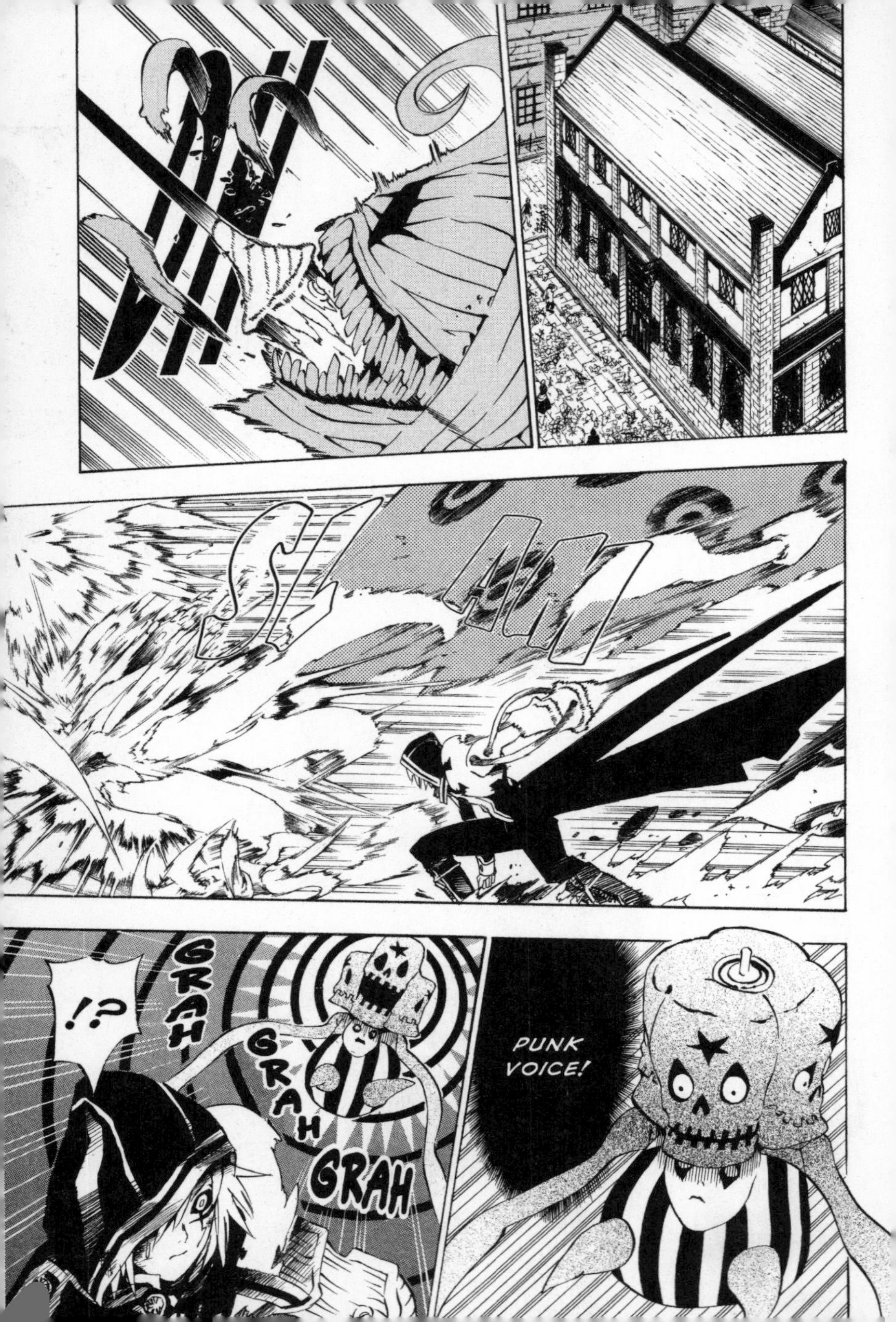
SLAM
PUNK VOICE!
!?
GRAH
GRAH
GRAH
GRAH

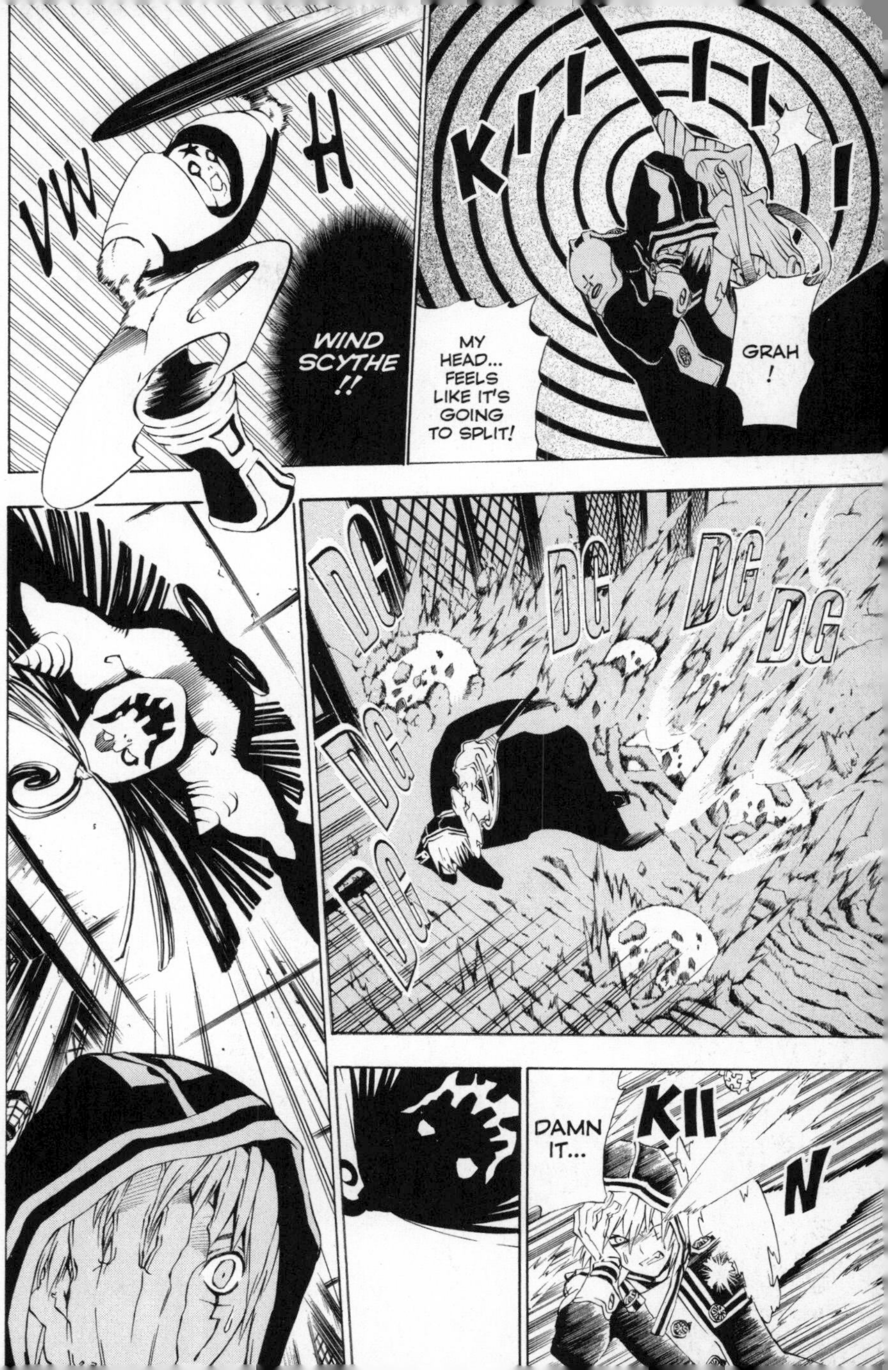
KIIIIII
GRAH!
MY HEAD... FEELS LIKE IT'S GOING TO SPLIT!
VWH
WIND SCYTHE!!
DG DG DG
DG DG DG DG
DAMN IT...
KIIN

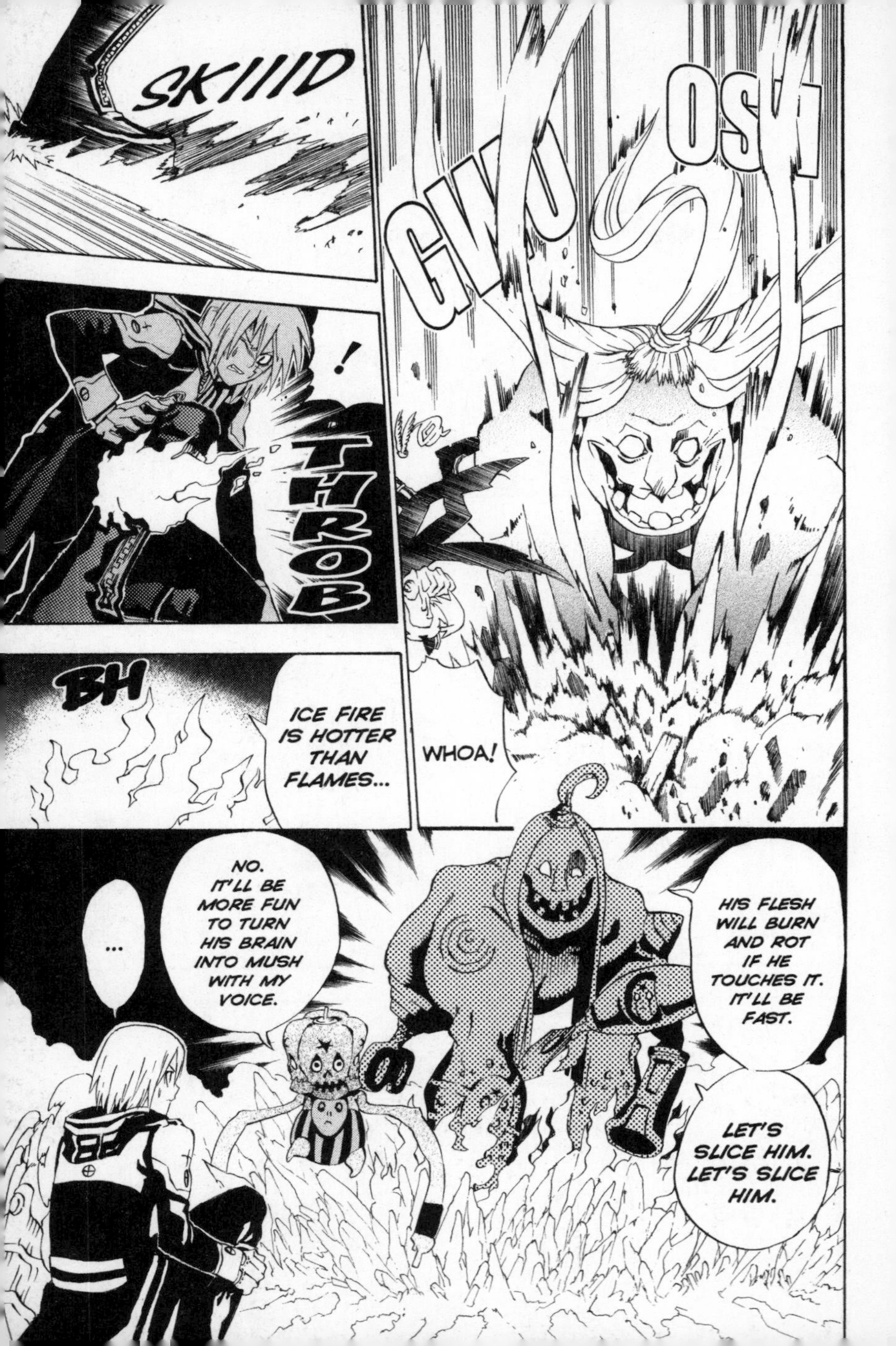

GWOOSH
WHOA!
SKIIID
!
THROB
BH
ICE FIRE IS HOTTER THAN FLAMES...
HIS FLESH WILL BURN AND ROT IF HE TOUCHES IT. IT'LL BE FAST.
LET'S SLICE HIM. LET'S SLICE HIM.
NO. IT'LL BE MORE FUN TO TURN HIS BRAIN INTO MUSH WITH MY VOICE.
...

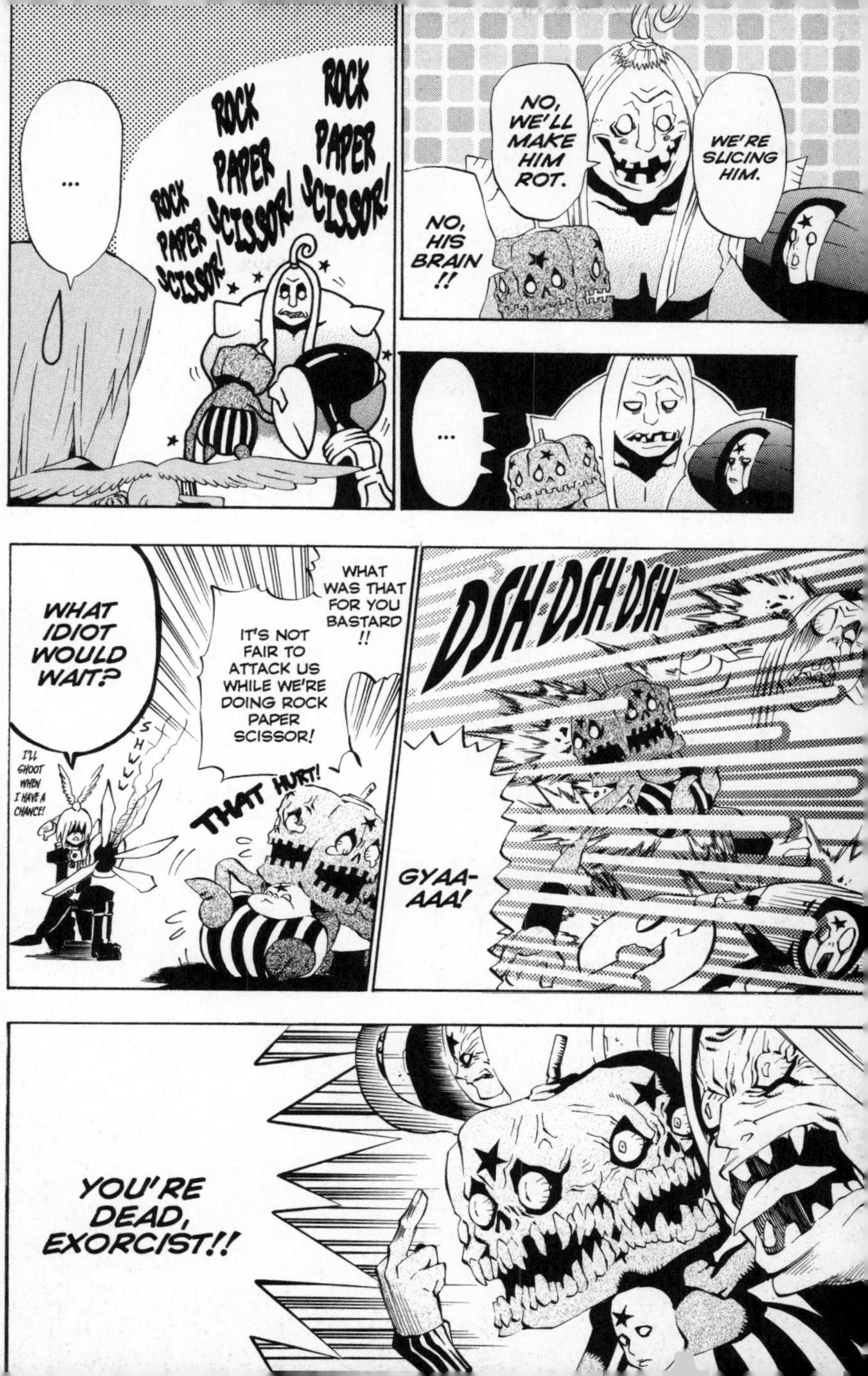
WE'RE SLICING HIM.
NO, WE'LL MAKE HIM ROT.
NO, HIS BRAIN!!
...
ROCK PAPER SCISSOR!
ROCK PAPER SCISSOR!
ROCK PAPER SCISSOR!
...
DSH DSH DSH
GYAA-AAA!
WHAT WAS THAT FOR YOU BASTARD!!
IT'S NOT FAIR TO ATTACK US WHILE WE'RE DOING ROCK PAPER SCISSOR!
WHAT IDIOT WOULD WAIT?
THAT HURT!
SHWWW
I'LL SHOOT WHEN I HAVE A CHANCE!
YOU'RE DEAD, EXORCIST!!

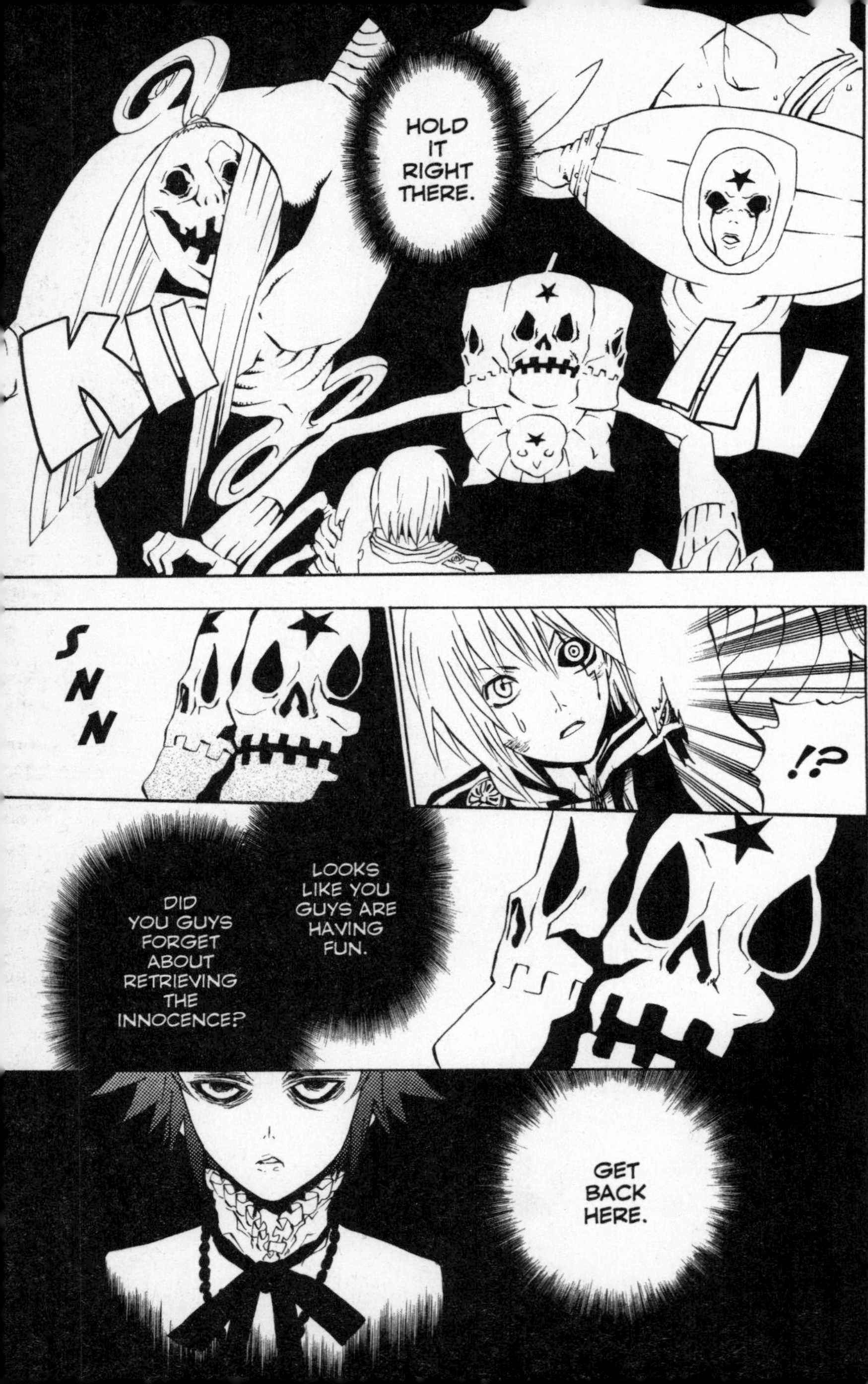
HOLD IT RIGHT THERE.
KII
IN
!?
SNN
LOOKS LIKE YOU GUYS ARE HAVING FUN.
DID YOU GUYS FORGET ABOUT RETRIEVING THE INNOCENCE?
GET BACK HERE.

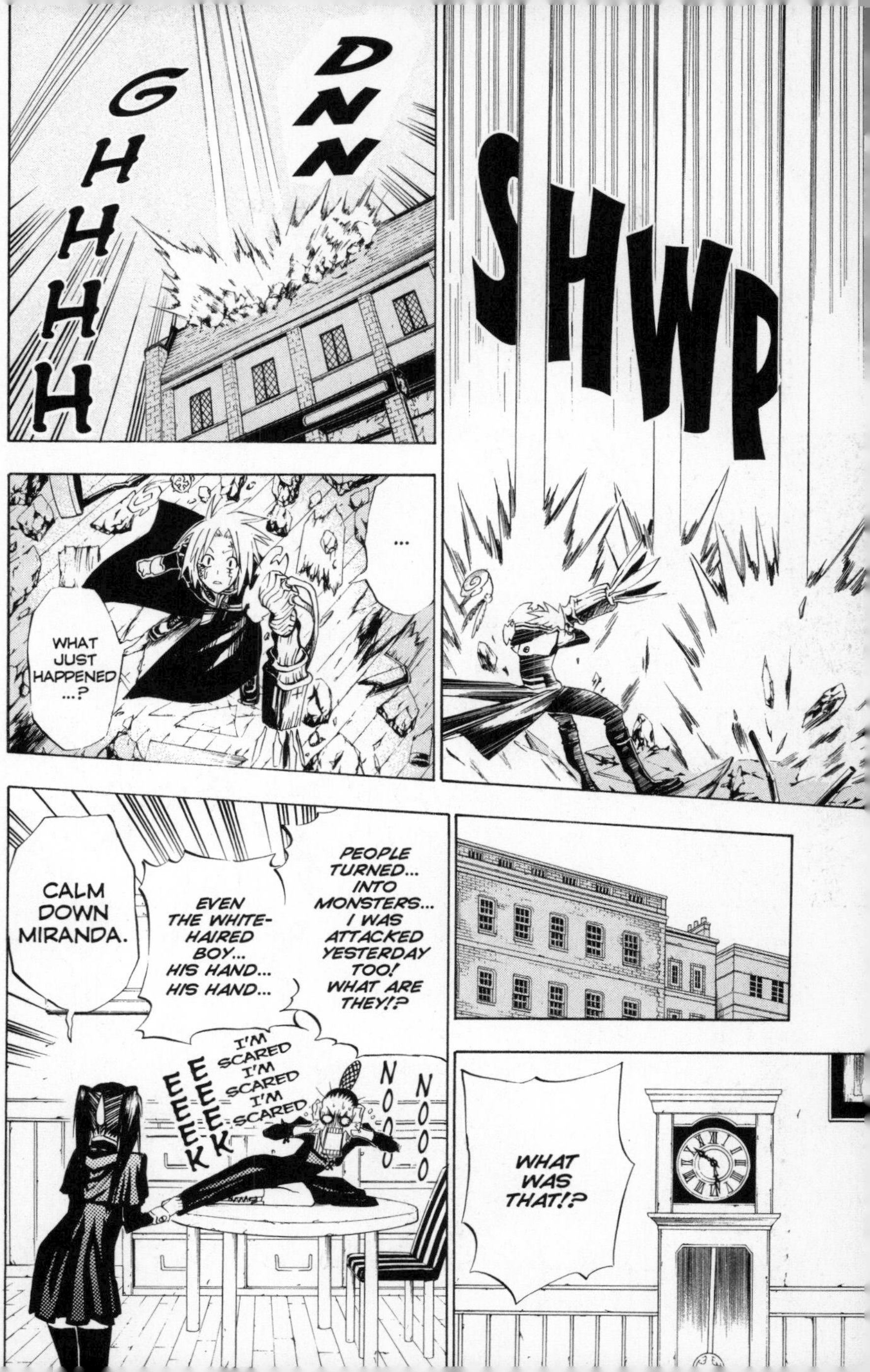
SHWP
DNN
GHHHH
...
WHAT JUST HAPPENED ...?
WHAT WAS THAT!?
PEOPLE TURNED... INTO MONSTERS... I WAS ATTACKED YESTERDAY TOO! WHAT ARE THEY!?
EVEN THE WHITE-HAIRED BOY... HIS HAND... HIS HAND...
CALM DOWN MIRANDA.
NOOO
NOOO
I'M SCARED I'M SCARED I'M SCARED
EEEK
EEEK

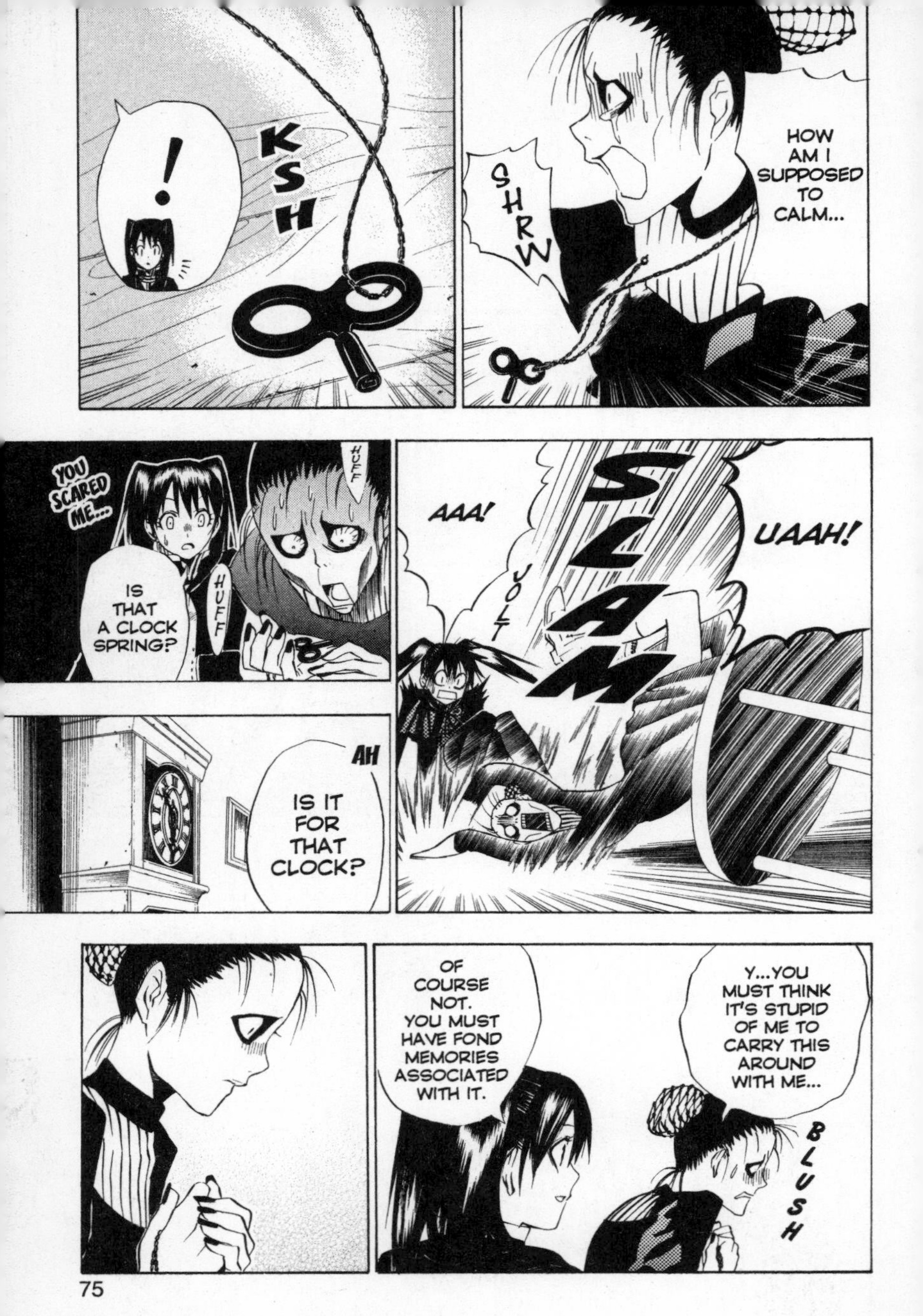
HOW AM I SUPPOSED TO CALM...
SHRW
KSH
!
SLAM
UAAH!
AAA!
JOLT
HUFF
YOU SCARED ME...
HUFF
IS THAT A CLOCK SPRING?
AH
IS IT FOR THAT CLOCK?
Y...YOU MUST THINK IT'S STUPID OF ME TO CARRY THIS AROUND WITH ME...
BLUSH
OF COURSE NOT. YOU MUST HAVE FOND MEMORIES ASSOCIATED WITH IT.

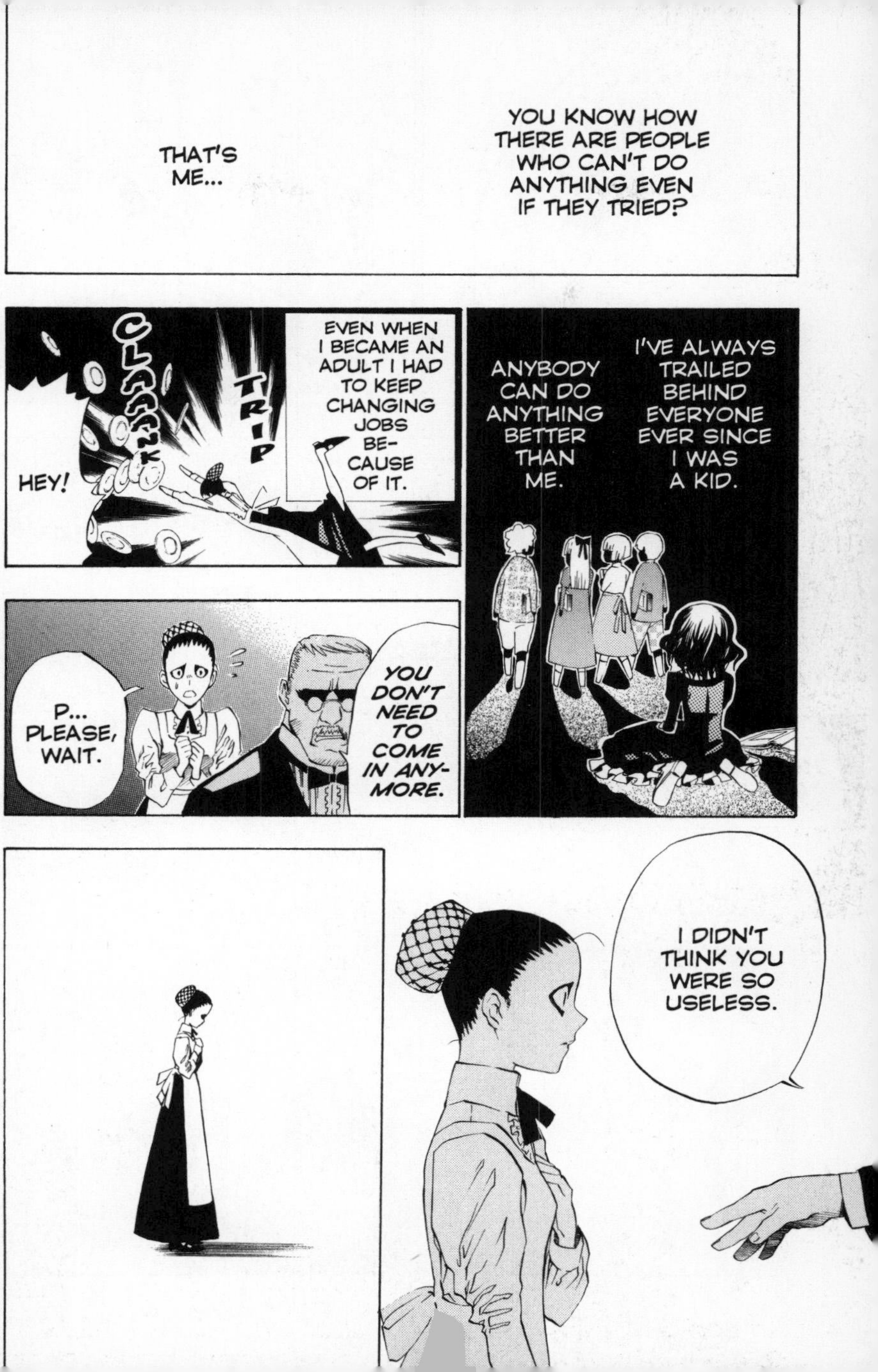
YOU KNOW HOW THERE ARE PEOPLE WHO CAN'T DO ANYTHING EVEN IF THEY TRIED?
THAT'S ME...
I'VE ALWAYS TRAILED BEHIND EVERYONE EVER SINCE I WAS A KID.
ANYBODY CAN DO ANYTHING BETTER THAN ME.
EVEN WHEN I BECAME AN ADULT I HAD TO KEEP CHANGING JOBS BE-CAUSE OF IT.
TRIP
CLAAANK
HEY!
YOU DON'T NEED TO COME IN ANY-MORE.
P... PLEASE, WAIT.
I DIDN'T THINK YOU WERE SO USELESS.

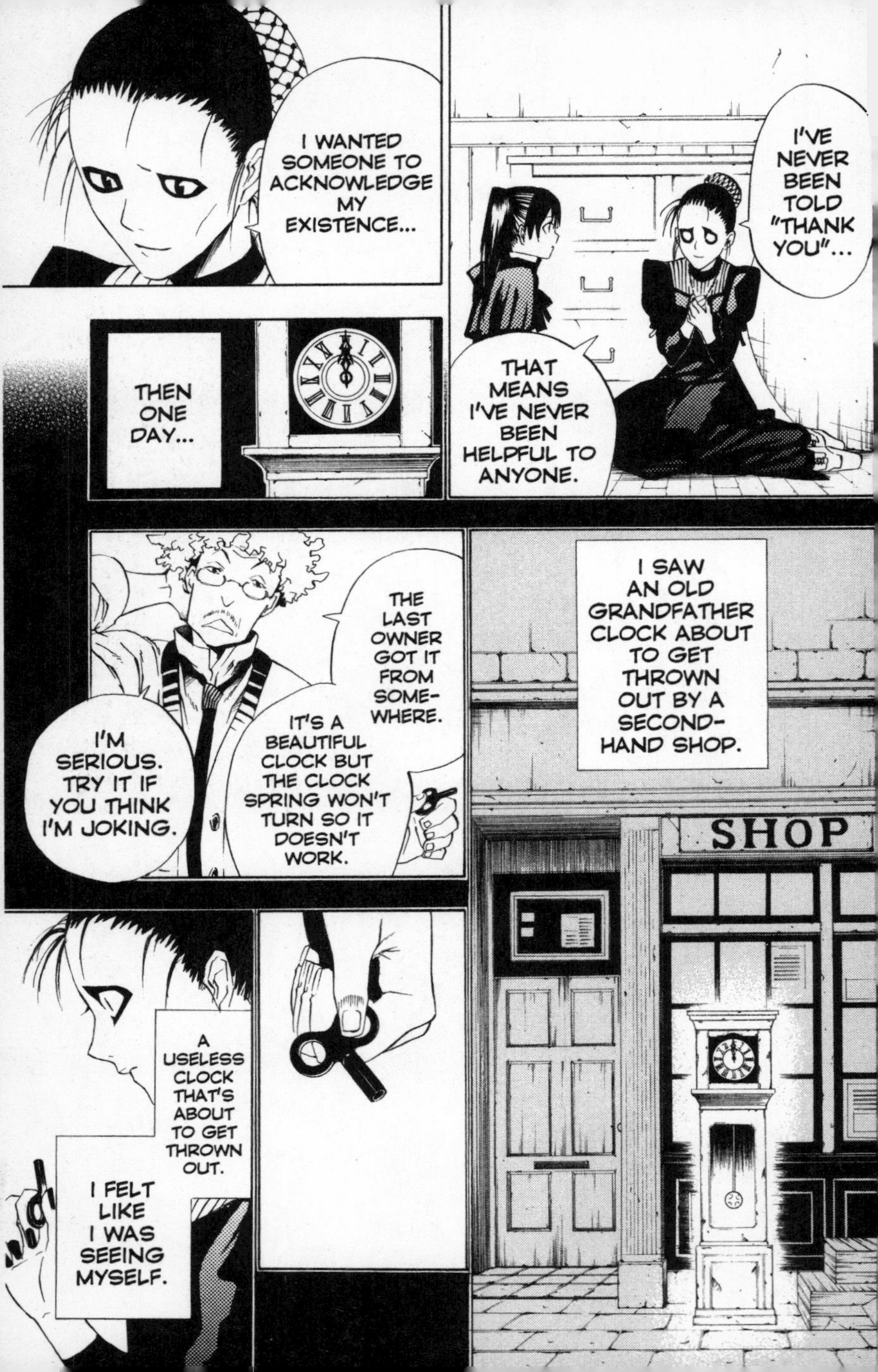
I'VE NEVER BEEN TOLD "THANK YOU"...
THAT MEANS I'VE NEVER BEEN HELPFUL TO ANYONE.
I WANTED SOMEONE TO ACKNOWLEDGE MY EXISTENCE...
THEN ONE DAY...
I SAW AN OLD GRANDFATHER CLOCK ABOUT TO GET THROWN OUT BY A SECOND-HAND SHOP.
SHOP
THE LAST OWNER GOT IT FROM SOME-WHERE.
IT'S A BEAUTIFUL CLOCK BUT THE CLOCK SPRING WON'T TURN SO IT DOESN'T WORK.
I'M SERIOUS. TRY IT IF YOU THINK I'M JOKING.
A USELESS CLOCK THAT'S ABOUT TO GET THROWN OUT.
I FELT LIKE I WAS SEEING MYSELF.

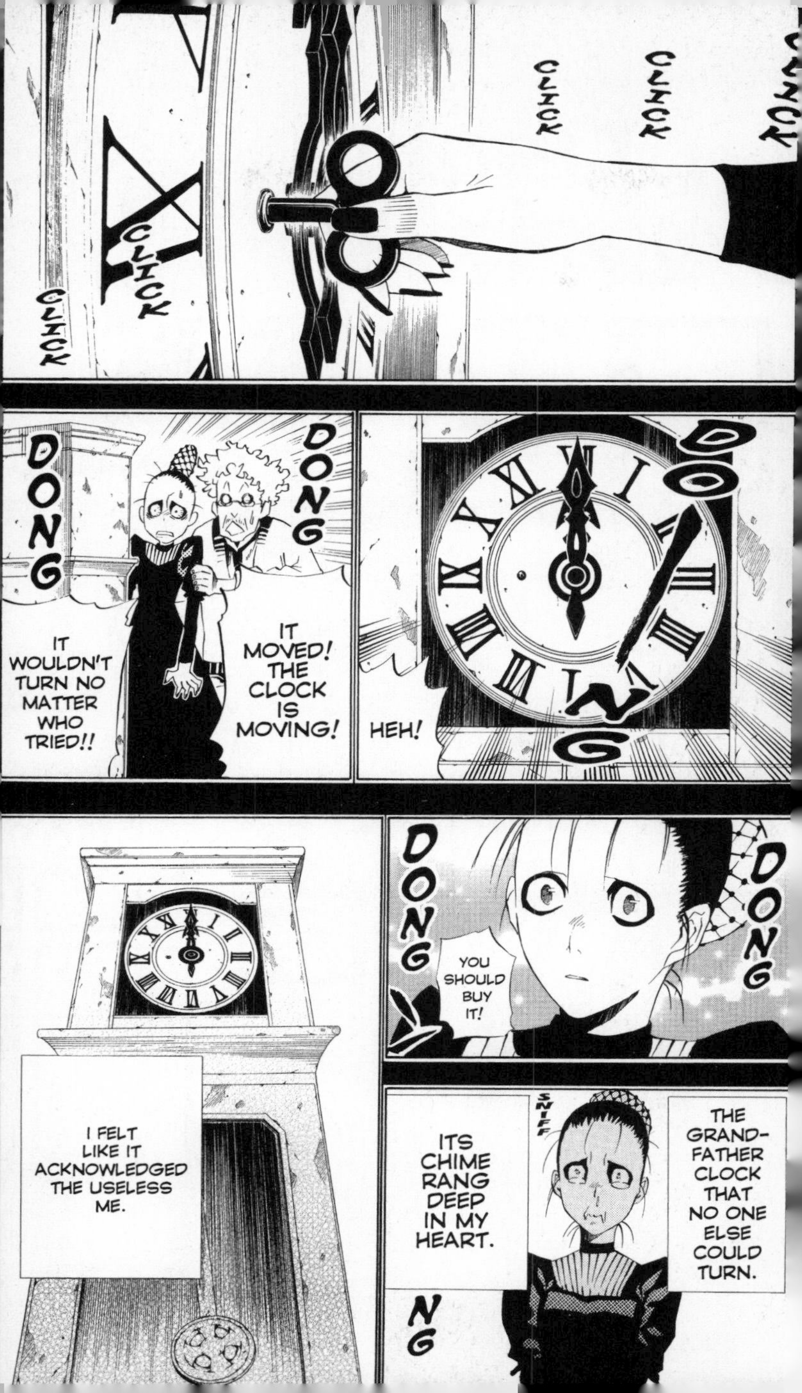
CLICK
CLICK
CLICK
CLICK
CLICK
DONG
HEH!
DONG
DONG
IT MOVED! THE CLOCK IS MOVING!
IT WOULDN'T TURN NO MATTER WHO TRIED!!
DONG
DONG
YOU SHOULD BUY IT!
THE GRAND-FATHER CLOCK THAT NO ONE ELSE COULD TURN.
SNIFF
ITS CHIME RANG DEEP IN MY HEART.
NG
I FELT LIKE IT ACKNOWLEDGED THE USELESS ME.

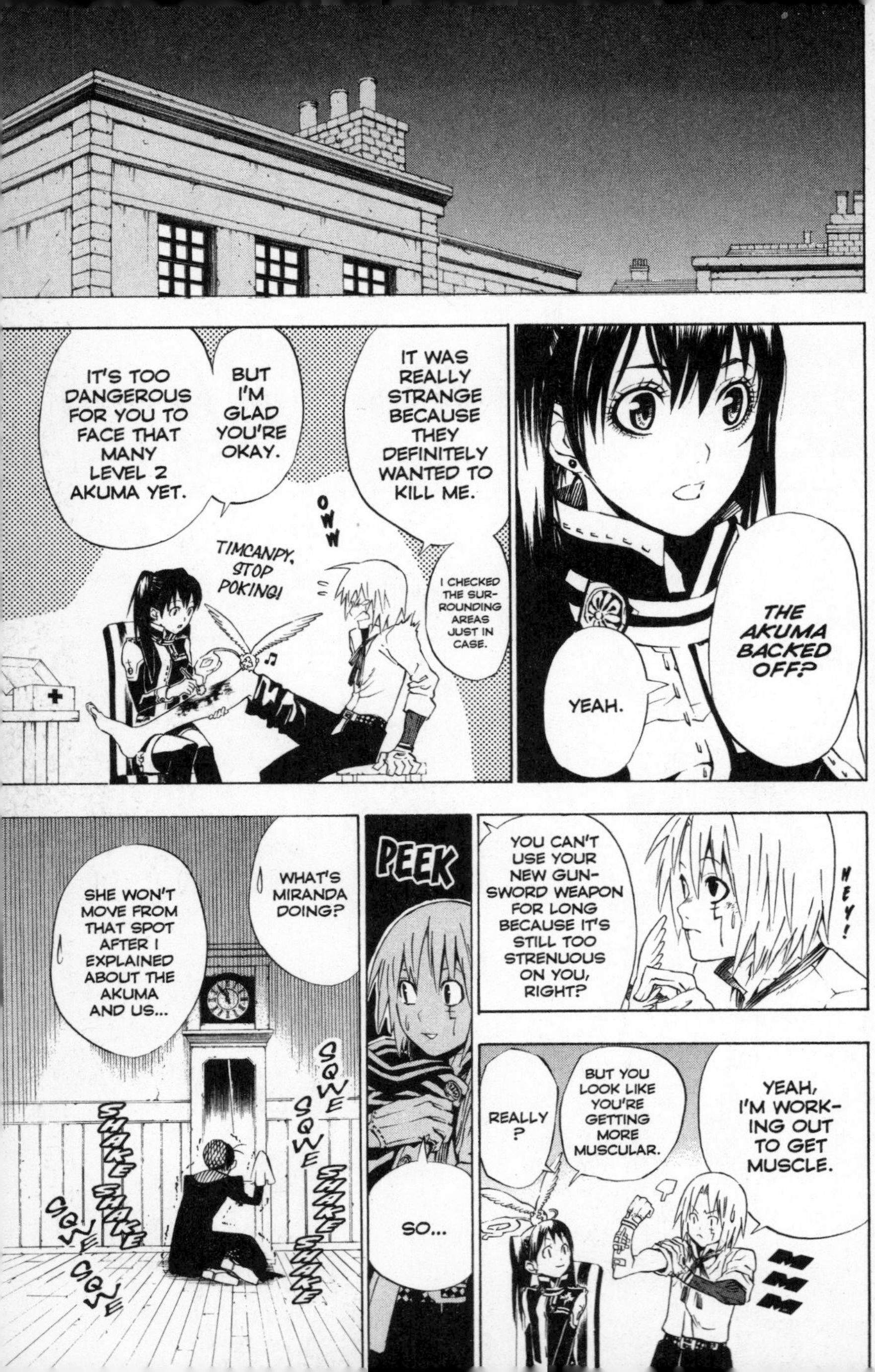
THE AKUMA BACKED OFF?
YEAH.
IT WAS REALLY STRANGE BECAUSE THEY DEFINITELY WANTED TO KILL ME.
I CHECKED THE SURROUNDING AREAS JUST IN CASE.
BUT I'M GLAD YOU'RE OKAY.
IT'S TOO DANGEROUS FOR YOU TO FACE THAT MANY LEVEL 2 AKUMA YET.
OWW
TIMCANPY, STOP POKING!
HEY!
YOU CAN'T USE YOUR NEW GUN-SWORD WEAPON FOR LONG BECAUSE IT'S STILL TOO STRENUOUS ON YOU, RIGHT?
YEAH, I'M WORKING OUT TO GET MUSCLE.
BUT YOU LOOK LIKE YOU'RE GETTING MORE MUSCULAR.
REALLY?
MMM
PEEK
SO...
WHAT'S MIRANDA DOING?
SHE WON'T MOVE FROM THAT SPOT AFTER I EXPLAINED ABOUT THE AKUMA AND US...
SQWE SQWE
SHAKE SHAKE
SQWE SQWE
SHAKE SHAKE

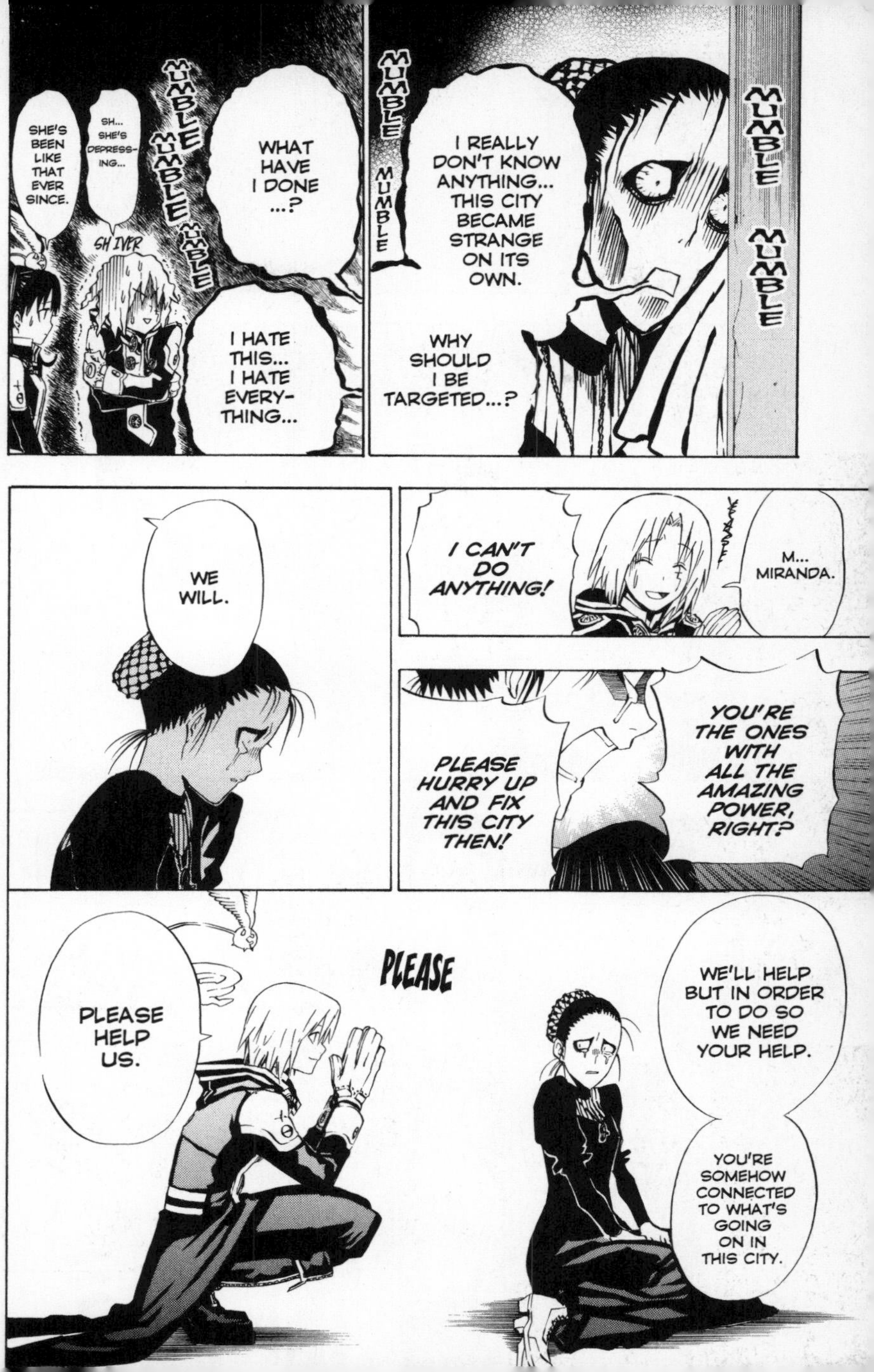
MUMBLE MUMBLE
I REALLY DON'T KNOW ANYTHING... THIS CITY BECAME STRANGE ON ITS OWN.
WHY SHOULD I BE TARGETED...?
MUMBLE MUMBLE
WHAT HAVE I DONE ...?
I HATE THIS... I HATE EVERYTHING...
MUMBLE MUMBLE MUMBLE
SH... SHE'S DEPRESSING...
SHIVER
SHE'S BEEN LIKE THAT EVER SINCE.
M... MIRANDA.
I CAN'T DO ANYTHING!
YOU'RE THE ONES WITH ALL THE AMAZING POWER, RIGHT?
PLEASE HURRY UP AND FIX THIS CITY THEN!
WE WILL.
WE'LL HELP BUT IN ORDER TO DO SO WE NEED YOUR HELP.
YOU'RE SOMEHOW CONNECTED TO WHAT'S GOING ON IN THIS CITY.
PLEASE
PLEASE HELP US.

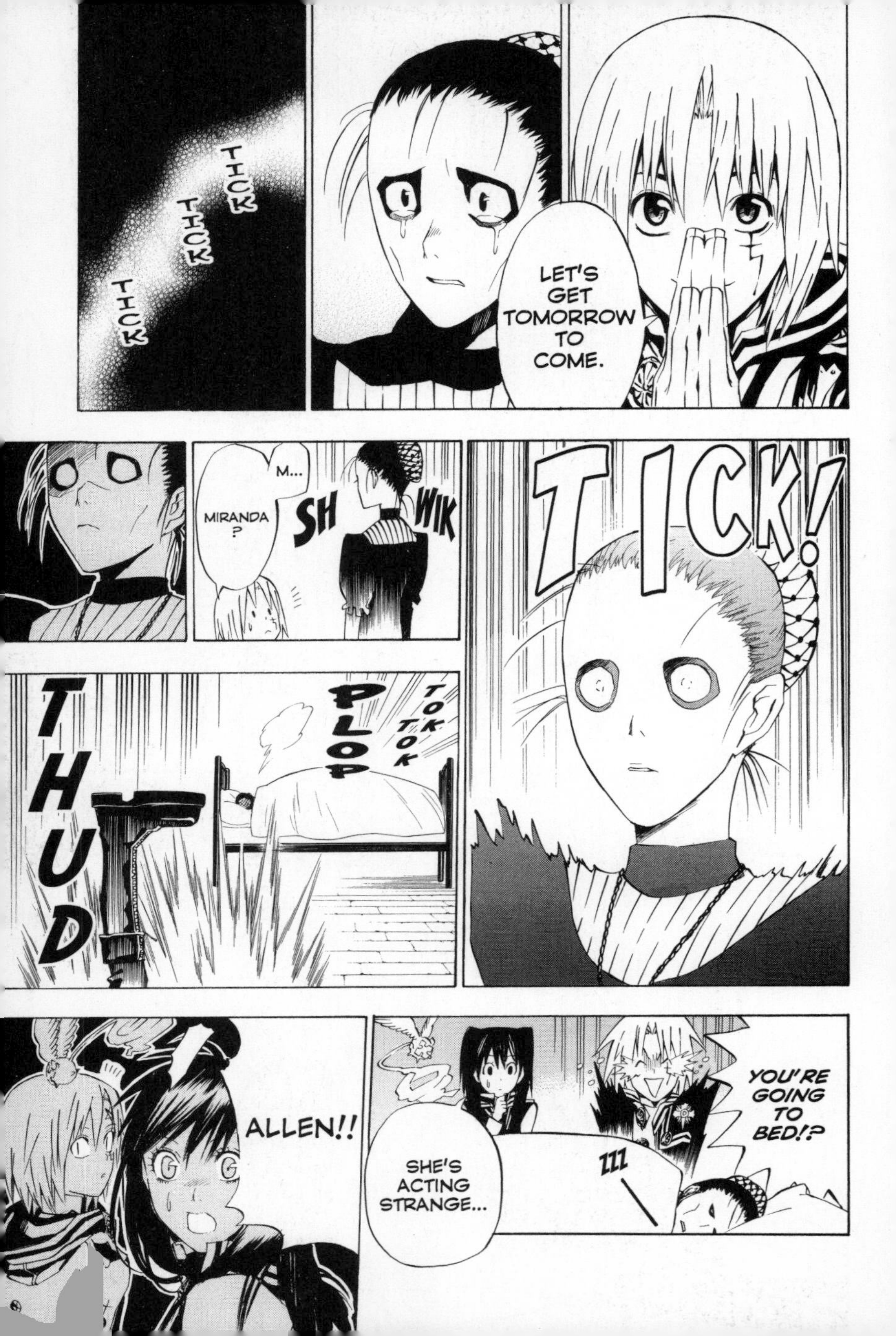
LET'S GET TOMORROW TO COME.
TICK
TICK
TICK
TICK!
M...
MIRANDA?
SHWIK
THUD
PLOP
TOK TOK
YOU'RE GOING TO BED!?
ZZZ
SHE'S ACTING STRANGE...
ALLEN!!

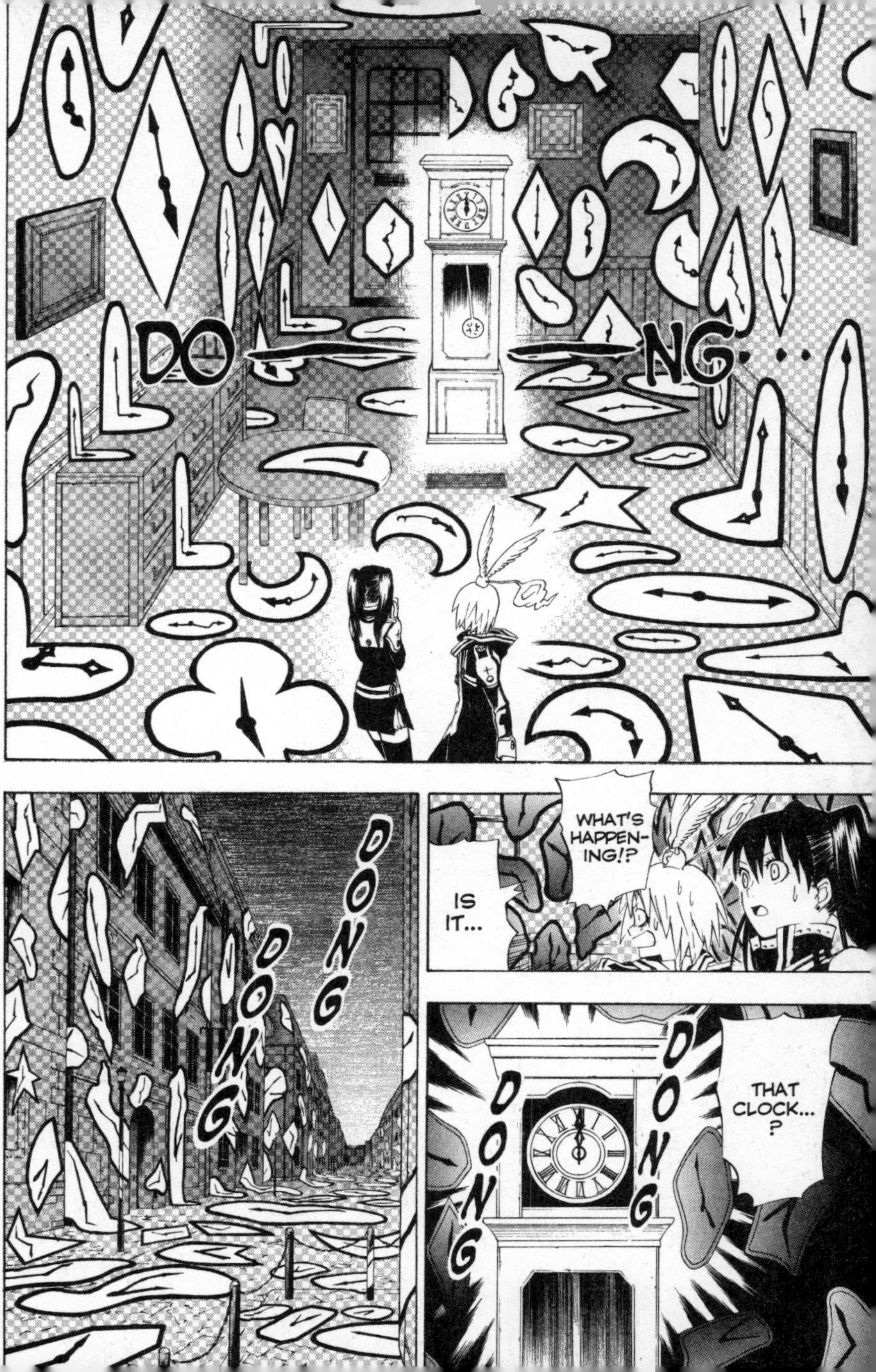
DO——NG...
WHAT'S HAPPENING!?
IS IT...
DOONG
DOONG
THAT CLOCK...?
DOONG
DOONG

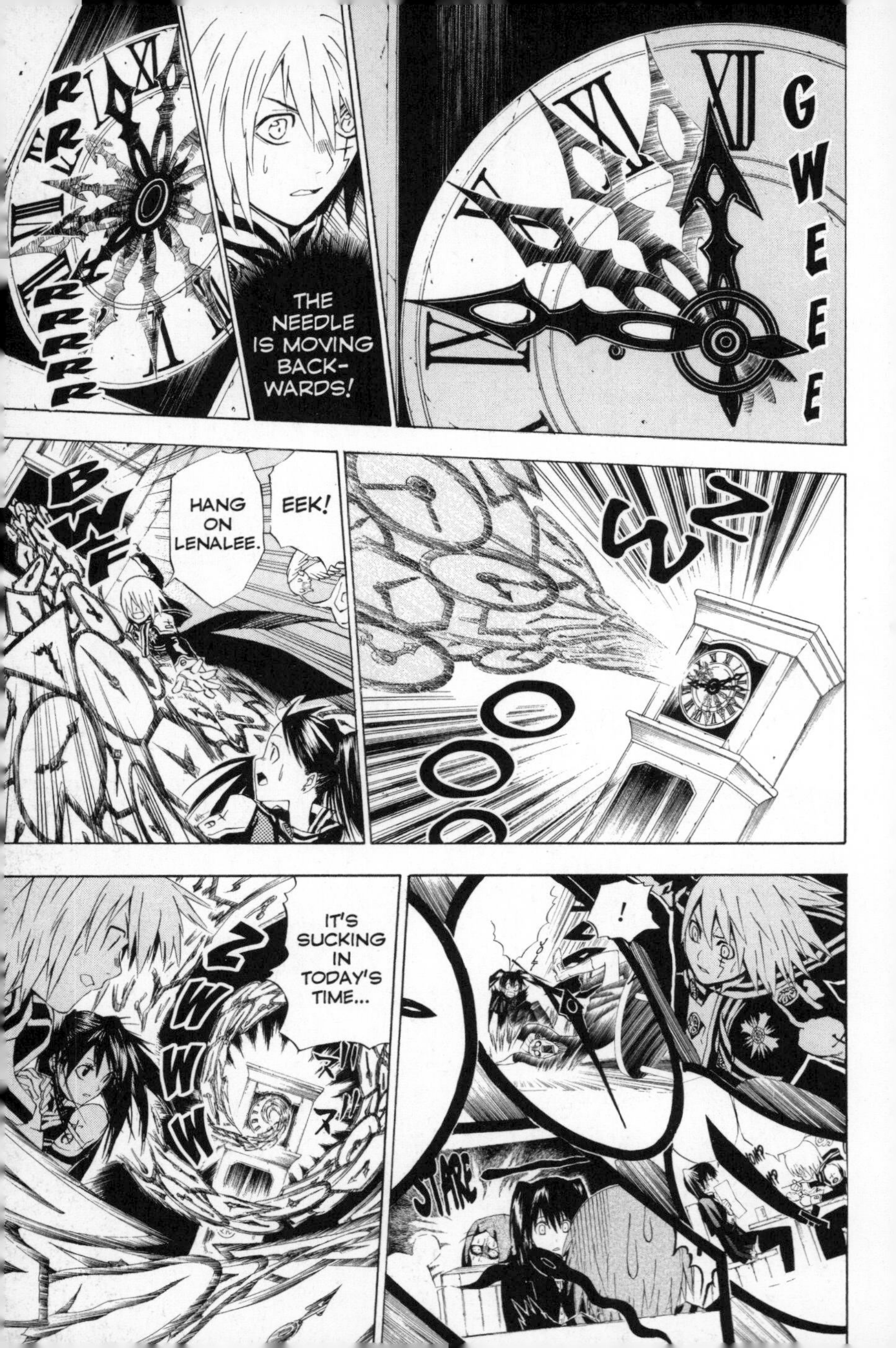
GWEEE
THE NEEDLE IS MOVING BACKWARDS!
RRRRRRRR
ZW
OOOO
EEK!
HANG ON LENALEE.
BWF
!
STARE
IT'S SUCKING IN TODAY'S TIME...
ZWWWWW

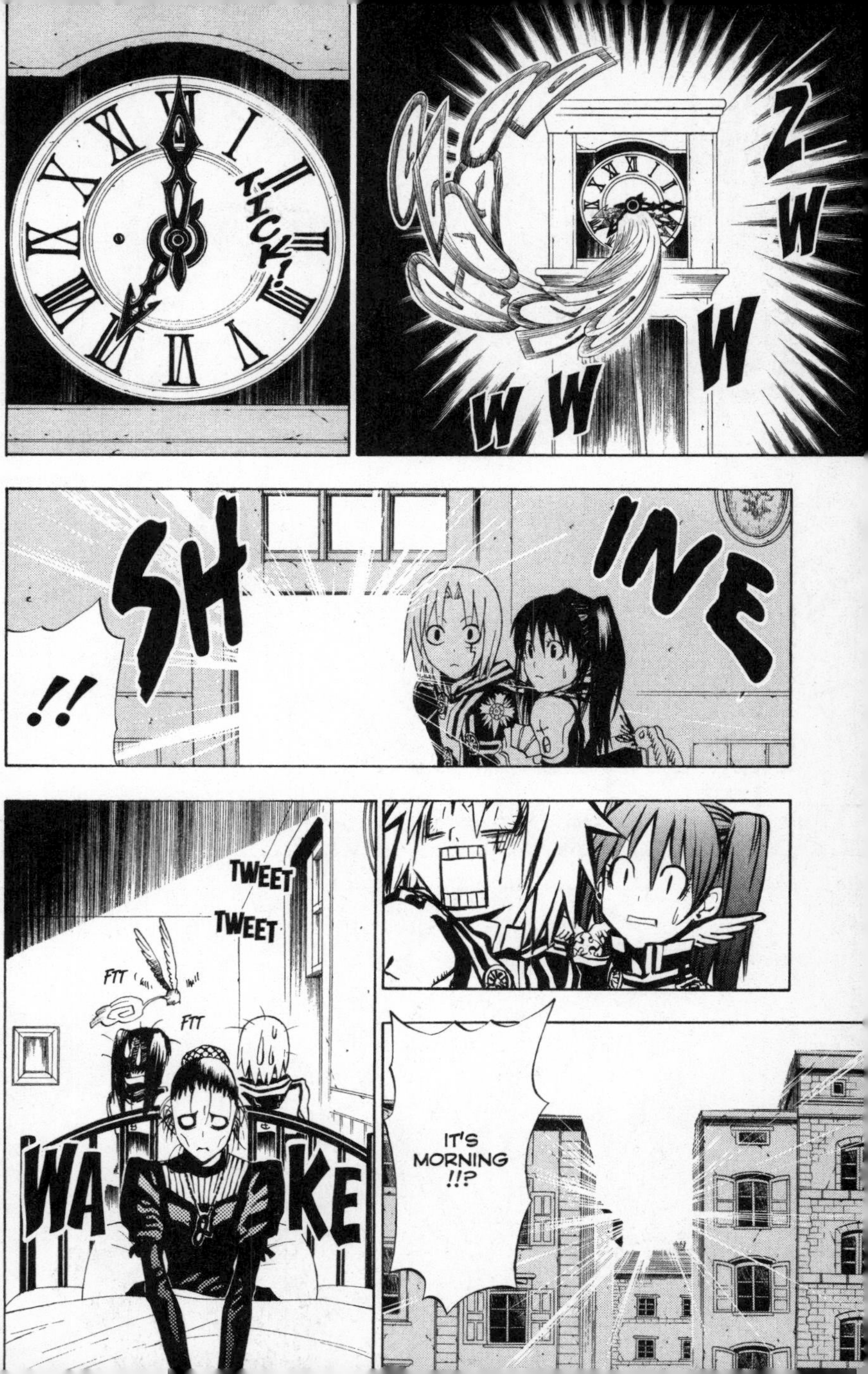
ZWWWWW
TICK!
SHINE
!!
IT'S MORNING !!?
TWEET
TWEET
FTT
FTT
WAKE

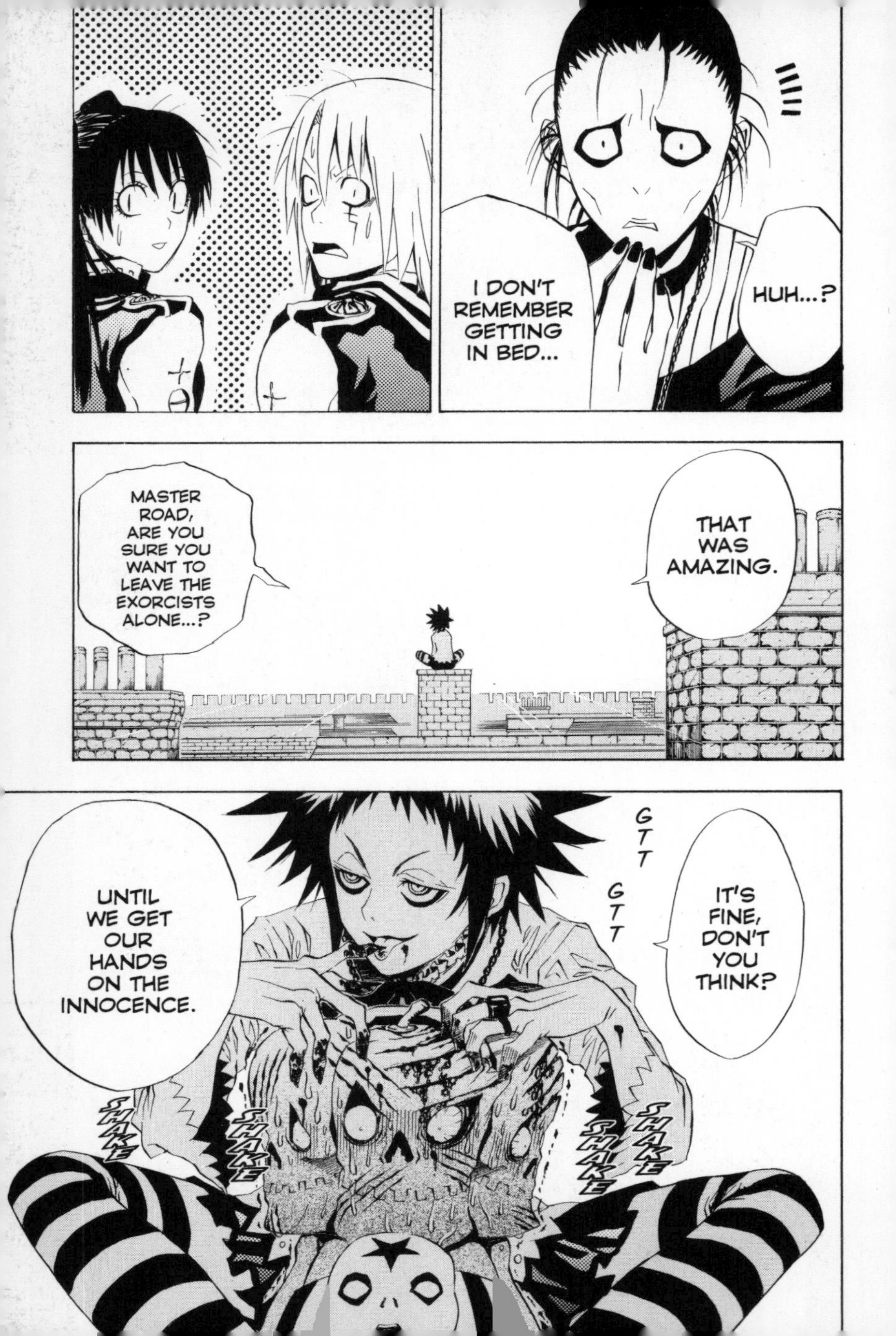
HUH...?
I DON'T REMEMBER GETTING IN BED...
THAT WAS AMAZING.
MASTER ROAD, ARE YOU SURE YOU WANT TO LEAVE THE EXORCISTS ALONE...?
GTT GTT
GTT GTT
IT'S FINE, DON'T YOU THINK?
UNTIL WE GET OUR HANDS ON THE INNOCENCE.
SHAKE SHAKE
SHAKE SHAKE

DISCUSSION ROOM VOL. 4

Q 1.   PLEASE TELL US YOUR PROFILE.

A.   I WAS BORN IN SHIGA PREFECTURE ON APRIL 21ST. I'M A TAURUS
AND MY BLOOD TYPE IS O. I LIKE CURRY, BATHS, THE COLOR
BLACK AND CURLING UP IN BED. I HATE BANANAS, MILK AND
MISO SOUP. I HATE BANANAS SO MUCH I'LL SCREAM AND TOSS IT
SOMEWHERE IF I SEE ONE. I LISTEN TO PORNO GRAFITTI, L'ARC
EN CIEL AND JAZZ. I'M FANTASTIC AT DOING A GHIBLI IMITATION.
IT'S GOTTEN A LOT MORE FUN SINCE MY ASSISTANTS OI-CHAN
AND MIYAZAKI JOINED IN. I DREW MY FIRST MANGA WHEN I WAS
TWENTY ONE.

Q 2.   WHICH CHARACTER IS EASIEST TO DRAW?

A.   THE EARL AND HEVLASKA. THE ONES THAT ARE HARD ARE ALLEN,
KANDA AND MASTER CROSS... (LOTS OF MAIN CHARACTERS)

Q 3.   WHERE DO YOU COME UP WITH IDEAS FOR D.GRAY-MAN?

A.   WHILE TAKING A BATH. I HAVE A TENDENCY TO FALL ASLEEP FOR
SIX HOURS IN THE TUB. MY EDITOR Y TOLD ME TO STOP THE
OTHER DAY.

Q 4.   WHICH PEN DO YOU USE TO DRAW?

A.   I USE THE ZEBRA G-PEN AND CIRCLE PEN. I USE THEIR STANDARD
MODELS.

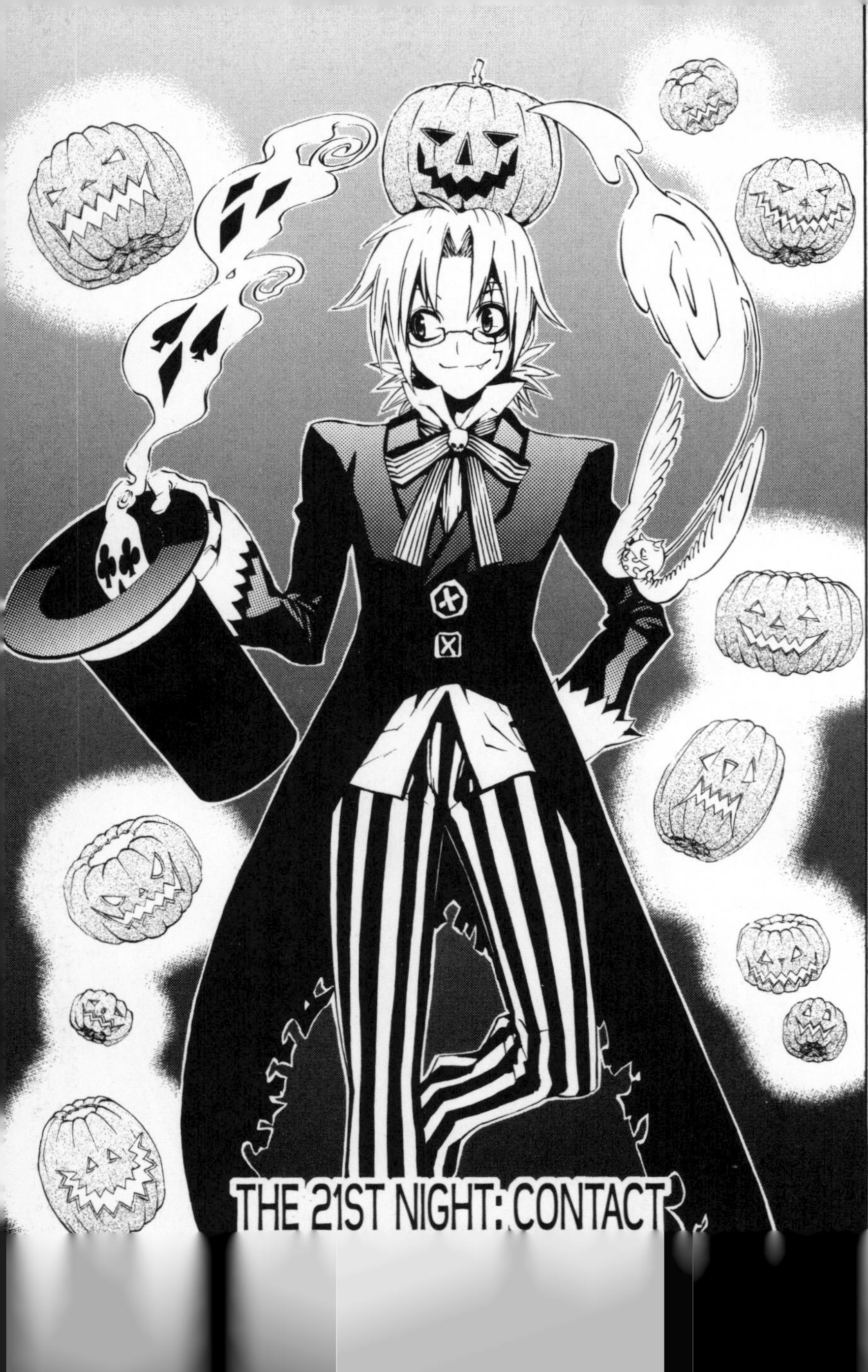
THE 21ST NIGHT: CONTACT

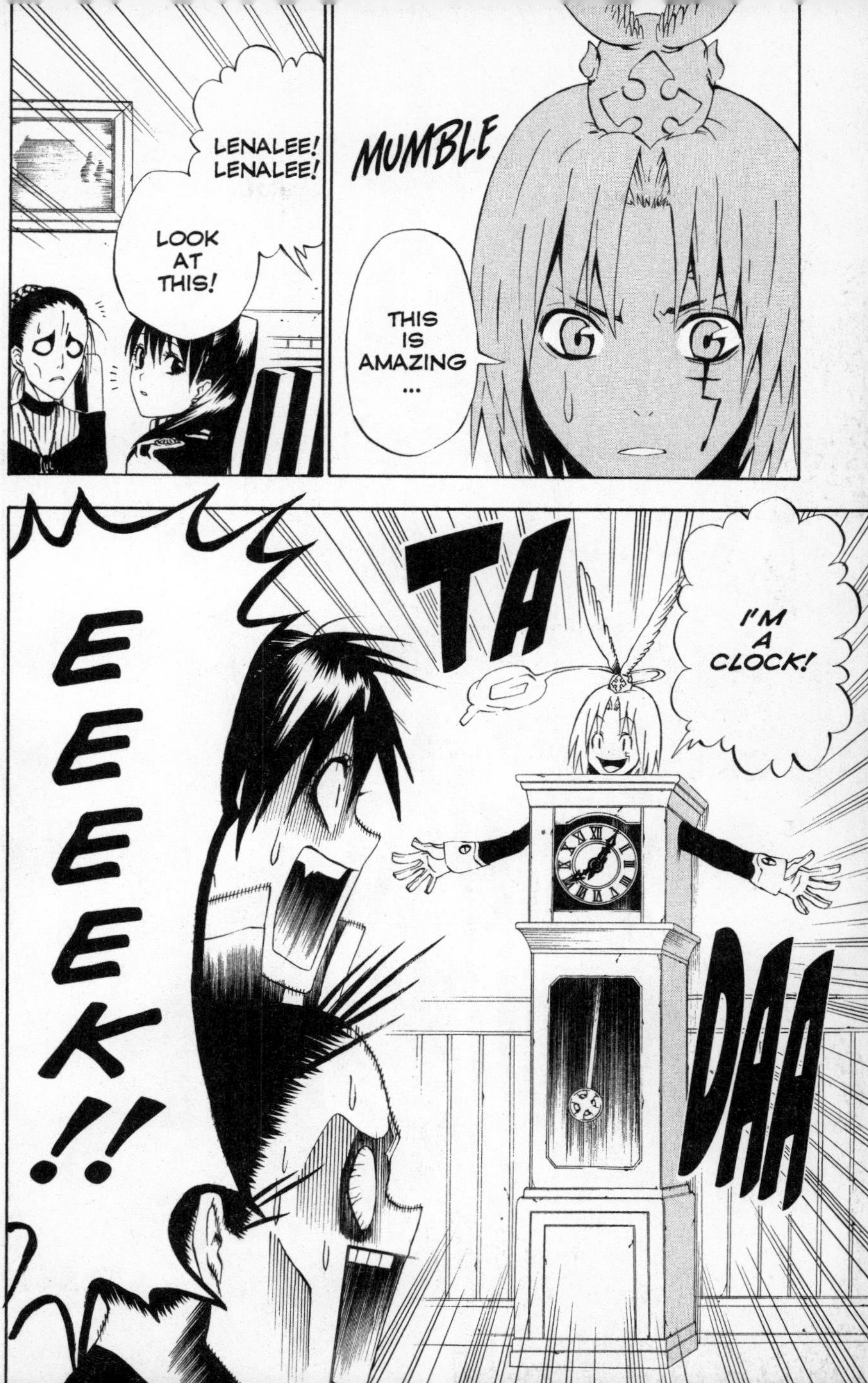
MUMBLE
THIS IS AMAZING ...
LENALEE! LENALEE!
LOOK AT THIS!
I'M A CLOCK!
TA
DAA
EEEEK!!

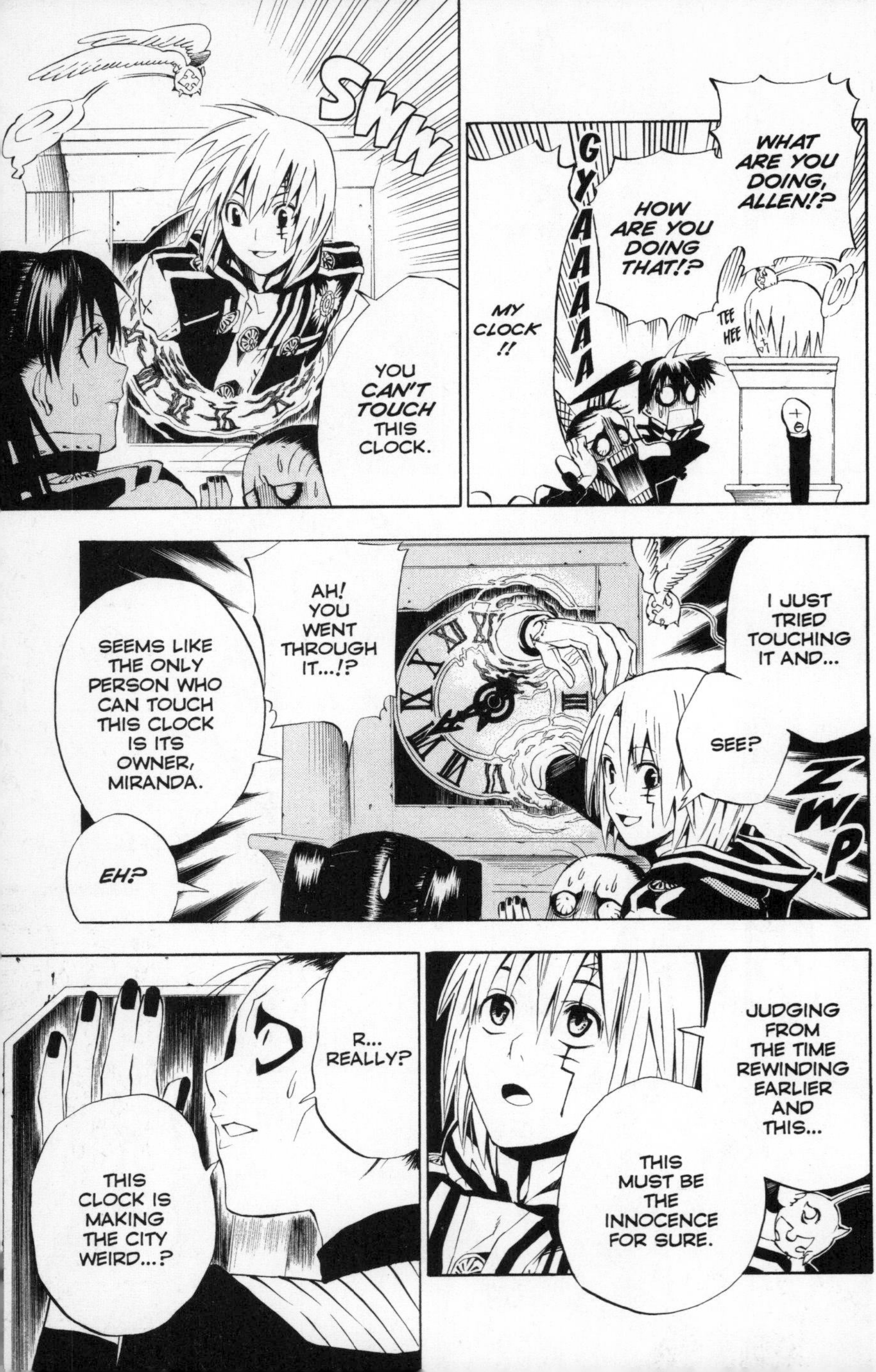
WHAT ARE YOU DOING, ALLEN!?
HOW ARE YOU DOING THAT!?
GYAAAAA
TEE HEE
MY CLOCK!!
SWW
YOU CAN'T TOUCH THIS CLOCK.
I JUST TRIED TOUCHING IT AND...
SEE?
ZWP
AH! YOU WENT THROUGH IT...!?
SEEMS LIKE THE ONLY PERSON WHO CAN TOUCH THIS CLOCK IS ITS OWNER, MIRANDA.
EH?
JUDGING FROM THE TIME REWINDING EARLIER AND THIS...
THIS MUST BE THE INNOCENCE FOR SURE.
R... REALLY?
THIS CLOCK IS MAKING THE CITY WEIRD...?

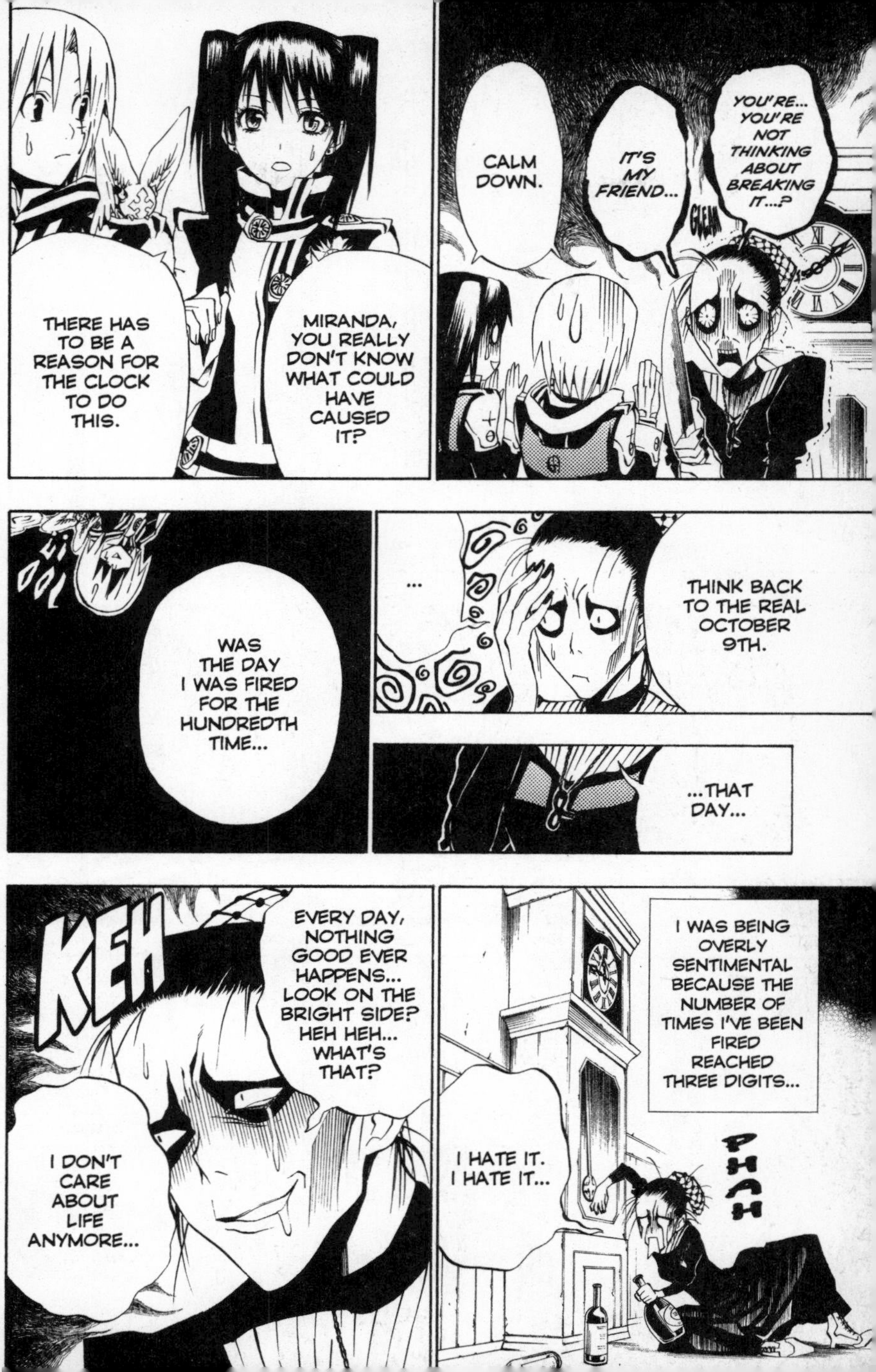
YOU'RE... YOU'RE NOT THINKING ABOUT BREAKING IT...?
GLEAM
IT'S MY FRIEND...
CALM DOWN.
MIRANDA, YOU REALLY DON'T KNOW WHAT COULD HAVE CAUSED IT?
THERE HAS TO BE A REASON FOR THE CLOCK TO DO THIS.
THINK BACK TO THE REAL OCTOBER 9TH.
...
...THAT DAY...
WAS THE DAY I WAS FIRED FOR THE HUNDREDTH TIME...
I WAS BEING OVERLY SENTIMENTAL BECAUSE THE NUMBER OF TIMES I'VE BEEN FIRED REACHED THREE DIGITS...
PHAH
I HATE IT. I HATE IT...
EVERY DAY, NOTHING GOOD EVER HAPPENS... LOOK ON THE BRIGHT SIDE? HEH HEH... WHAT'S THAT?
KEH
I DON'T CARE ABOUT LIFE ANYMORE...

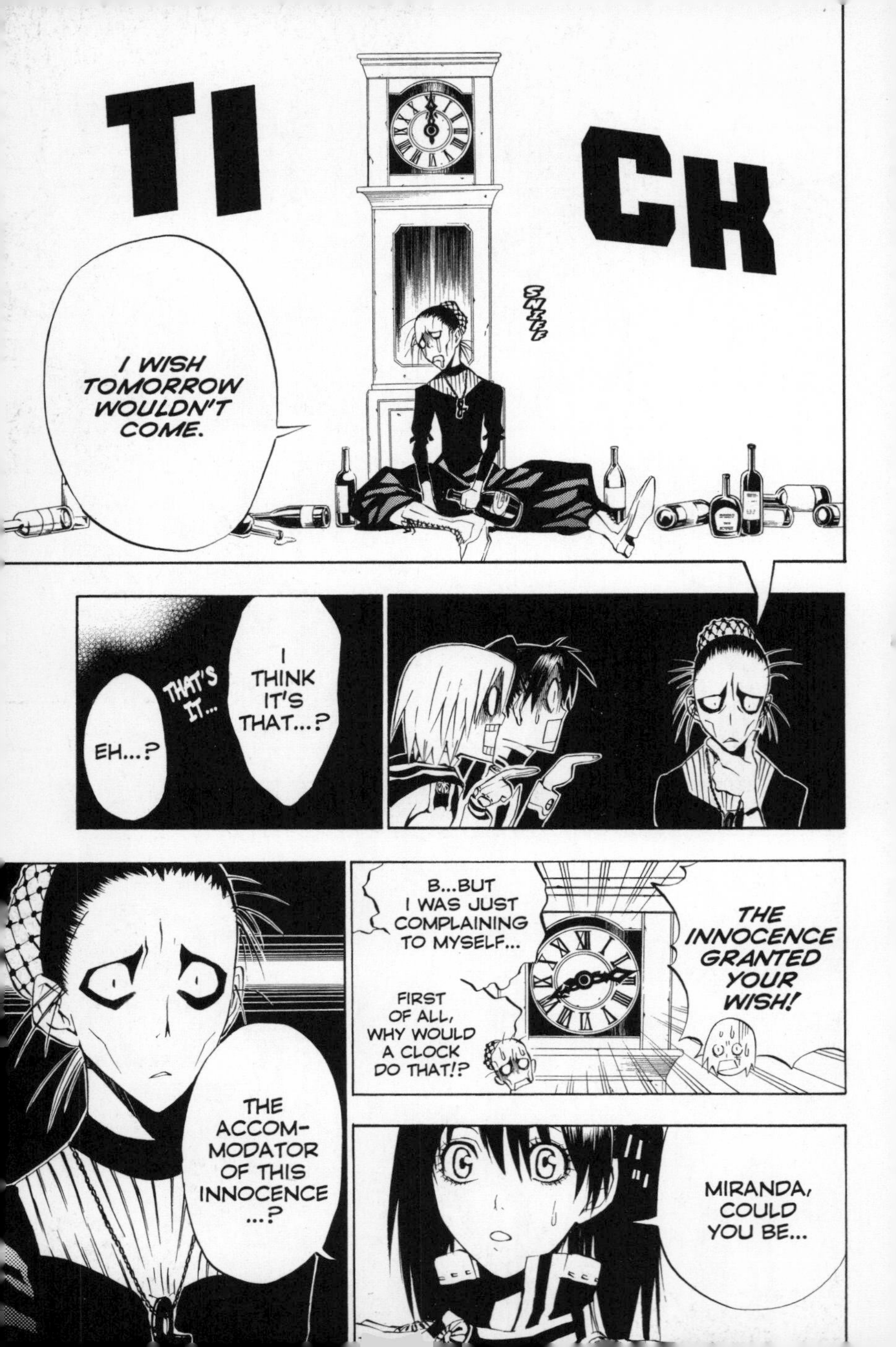
TI
CK
I WISH TOMORROW WOULDN'T COME.
SNIFF
I THINK IT'S THAT...?
THAT'S IT...
EH...?
THE INNOCENCE GRANTED YOUR WISH!
B...BUT I WAS JUST COMPLAINING TO MYSELF...
FIRST OF ALL, WHY WOULD A CLOCK DO THAT!?
MIRANDA, COULD YOU BE...
THE ACCOM-MODATOR OF THIS INNOCENCE ...?

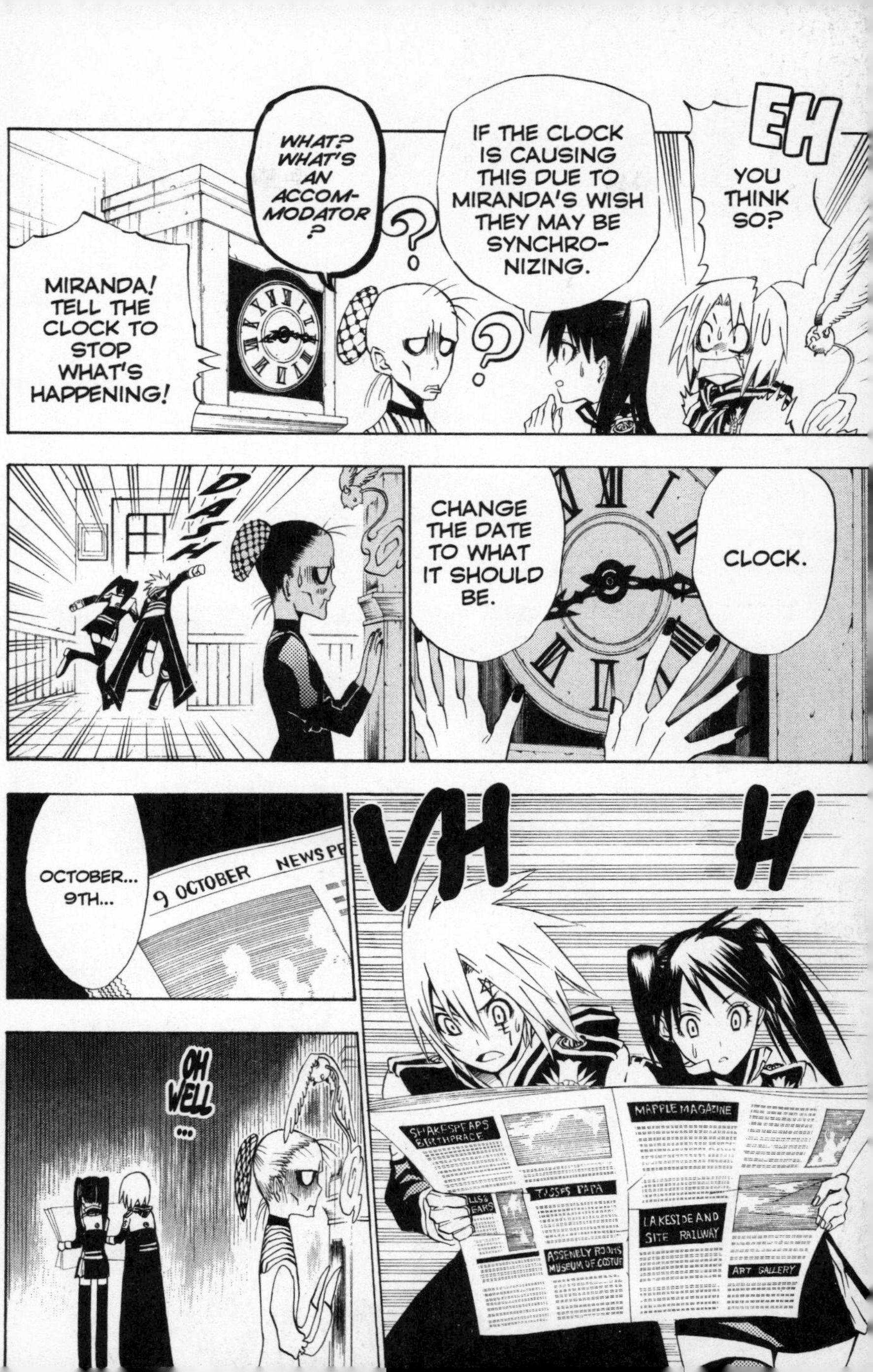
EH
YOU THINK SO?
IF THE CLOCK IS CAUSING THIS DUE TO MIRANDA'S WISH THEY MAY BE SYNCHRO-NIZING.
WHAT? WHAT'S AN ACCOM-MODATOR?
MIRANDA! TELL THE CLOCK TO STOP WHAT'S HAPPENING!
CLOCK.
CHANGE THE DATE TO WHAT IT SHOULD BE.
DASH
VH H
MAPPLE MAGAZINE
SHAKESPEAPS BIRTHPRACE
TUSSES PAPA
LAKESIDE AND SITE RAILWAY
ASSENBLY ROOMS MUSEUM OF COSTUE
ART GALLERY
9 OCTOBER
OCTOBER... 9TH...
OH WELL ...

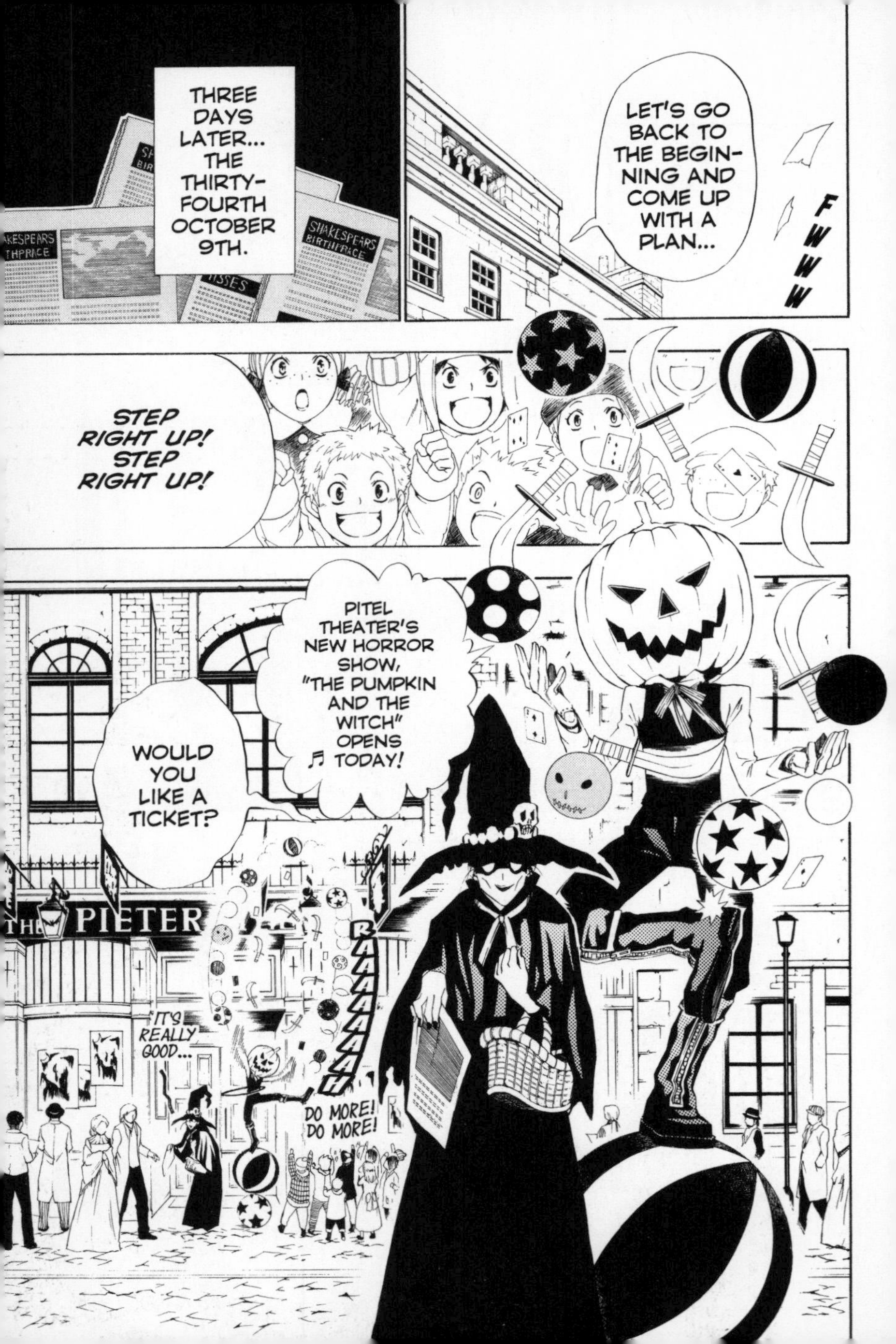
LET'S GO BACK TO THE BEGIN-NING AND COME UP WITH A PLAN...
FWWW
THREE DAYS LATER... THE THIRTY-FOURTH OCTOBER 9TH.
SHAKESPEARS BIRTHPRACE
STEP RIGHT UP! STEP RIGHT UP!
PITEL THEATER'S NEW HORROR SHOW, "THE PUMPKIN AND THE WITCH" OPENS ♫ TODAY!
WOULD YOU LIKE A TICKET?
RAAAAAAAAH
IT'S REALLY GOOD...
DO MORE! DO MORE!
THE PIETER

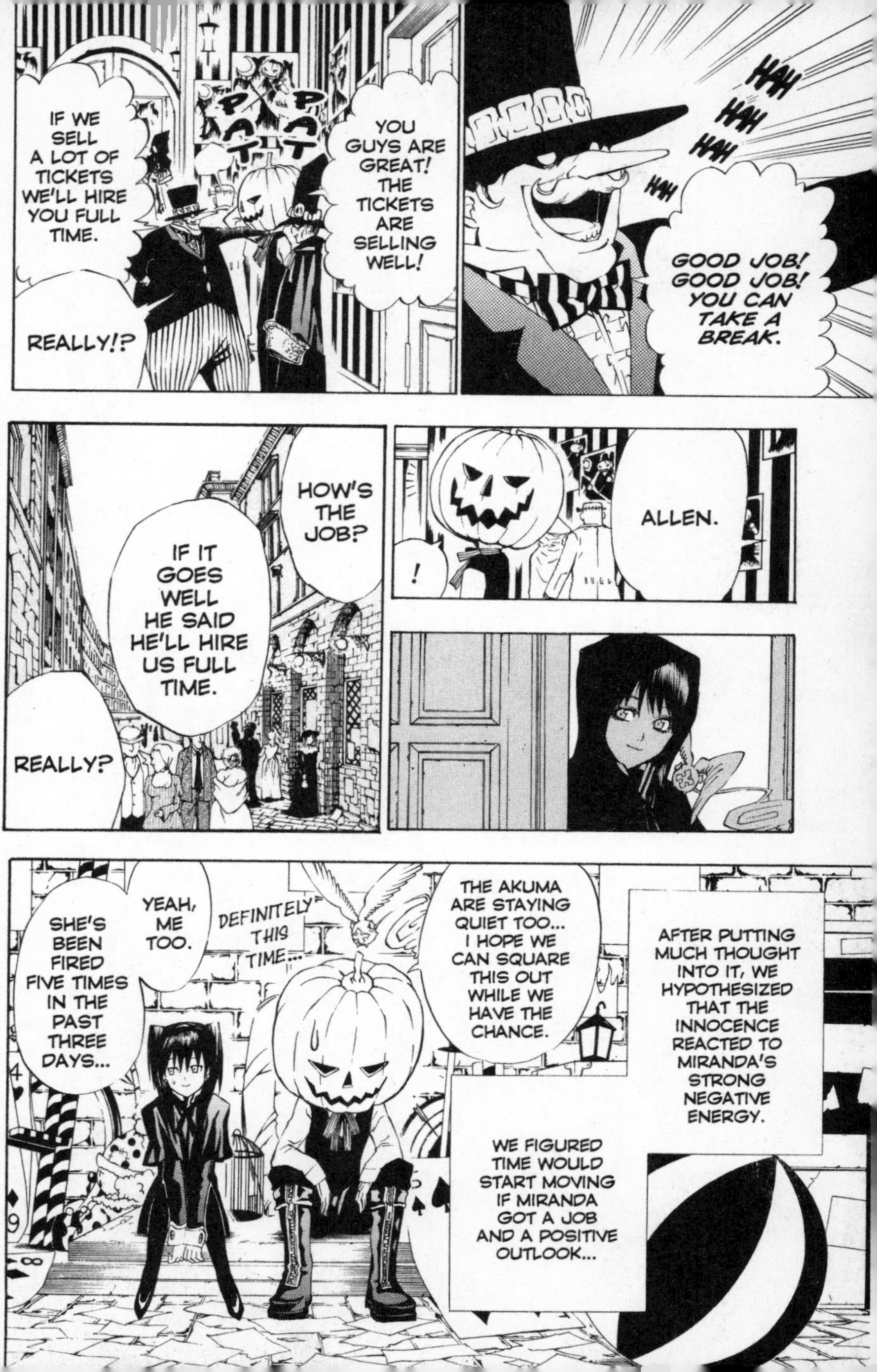
HAH HAH HAH HAH
GOOD JOB! GOOD JOB! YOU CAN TAKE A BREAK.
YOU GUYS ARE GREAT! THE TICKETS ARE SELLING WELL!
IF WE SELL A LOT OF TICKETS WE'LL HIRE YOU FULL TIME.
REALLY!?
ALLEN.
!
HOW'S THE JOB?
IF IT GOES WELL HE SAID HE'LL HIRE US FULL TIME.
REALLY?
AFTER PUTTING MUCH THOUGHT INTO IT, WE HYPOTHESIZED THAT THE INNOCENCE REACTED TO MIRANDA'S STRONG NEGATIVE ENERGY.
THE AKUMA ARE STAYING QUIET TOO... I HOPE WE CAN SQUARE THIS OUT WHILE WE HAVE THE CHANCE.
DEFINITELY THIS TIME...
YEAH, ME TOO.
SHE'S BEEN FIRED FIVE TIMES IN THE PAST THREE DAYS...
WE FIGURED TIME WOULD START MOVING IF MIRANDA GOT A JOB AND A POSITIVE OUTLOOK...

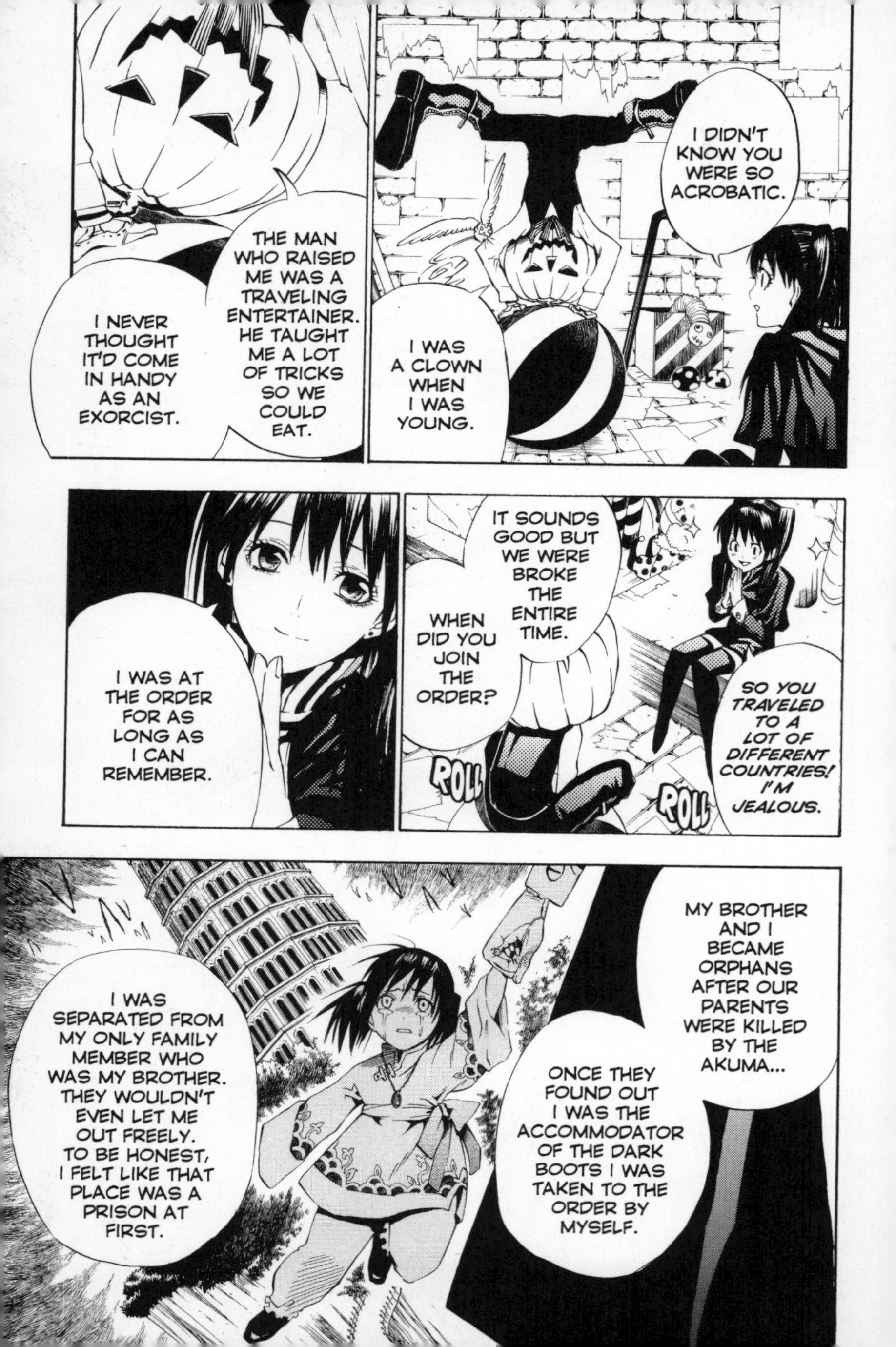
I DIDN'T KNOW YOU WERE SO ACROBATIC.
I WAS A CLOWN WHEN I WAS YOUNG.
THE MAN WHO RAISED ME WAS A TRAVELING ENTERTAINER. HE TAUGHT ME A LOT OF TRICKS SO WE COULD EAT.
I NEVER THOUGHT IT'D COME IN HANDY AS AN EXORCIST.
SO YOU TRAVELED TO A LOT OF DIFFERENT COUNTRIES! I'M JEALOUS.
IT SOUNDS GOOD BUT WE WERE BROKE THE ENTIRE TIME.
WHEN DID YOU JOIN THE ORDER?
ROLL
ROLL
I WAS AT THE ORDER FOR AS LONG AS I CAN REMEMBER.
MY BROTHER AND I BECAME ORPHANS AFTER OUR PARENTS WERE KILLED BY THE AKUMA...
ONCE THEY FOUND OUT I WAS THE ACCOMMODATOR OF THE DARK BOOTS I WAS TAKEN TO THE ORDER BY MYSELF.
I WAS SEPARATED FROM MY ONLY FAMILY MEMBER WHO WAS MY BROTHER. THEY WOULDN'T EVEN LET ME OUT FREELY. TO BE HONEST, I FELT LIKE THAT PLACE WAS A PRISON AT FIRST.

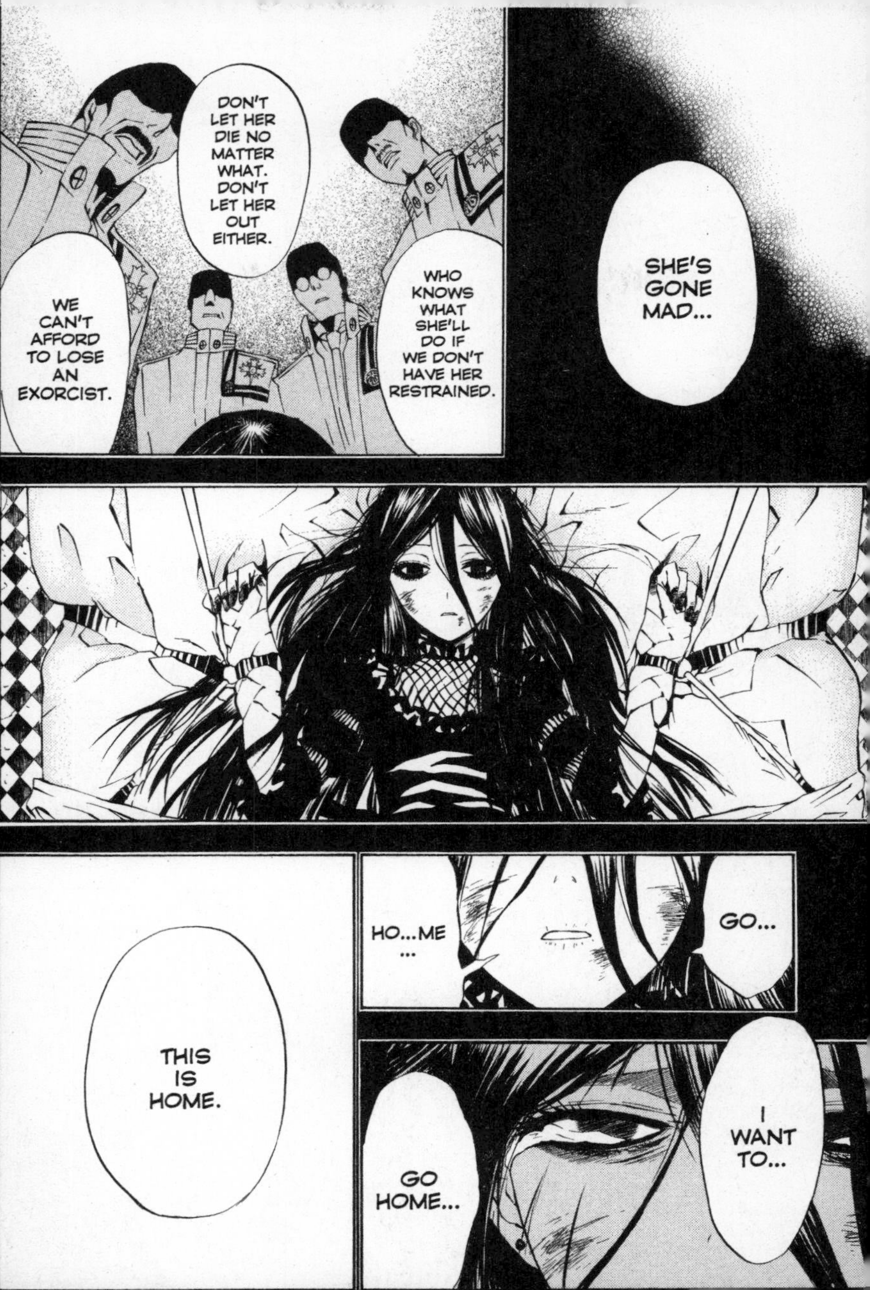
SHE'S GONE MAD...
DON'T LET HER DIE NO MATTER WHAT. DON'T LET HER OUT EITHER.
WHO KNOWS WHAT SHE'LL DO IF WE DON'T HAVE HER RESTRAINED.
WE CAN'T AFFORD TO LOSE AN EXORCIST.
GO...
HO...ME ...
I WANT TO...
GO HOME...
THIS IS HOME.

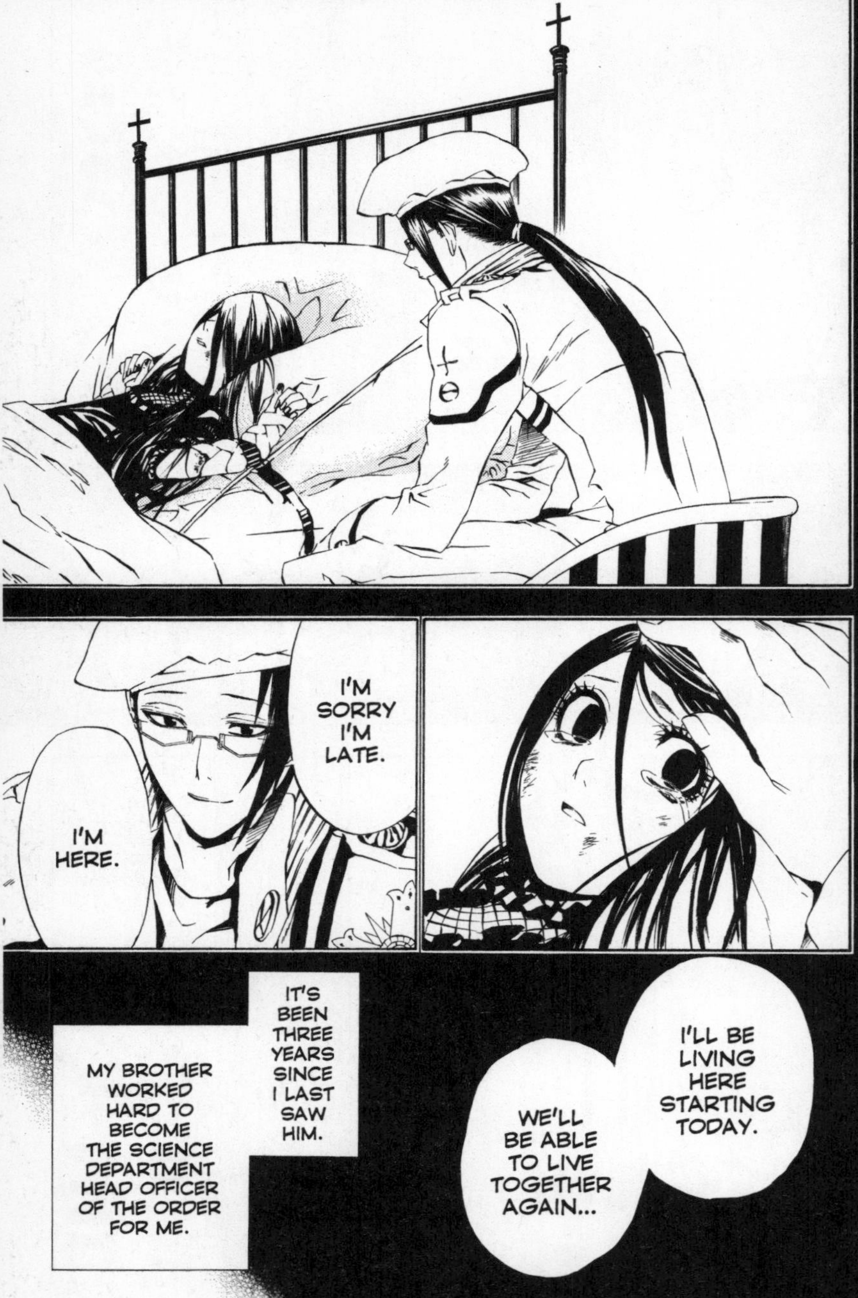
I'M SORRY I'M LATE.
I'M HERE.
I'LL BE LIVING HERE STARTING TODAY.
WE'LL BE ABLE TO LIVE TOGETHER AGAIN...
IT'S BEEN THREE YEARS SINCE I LAST SAW HIM.
MY BROTHER WORKED HARD TO BECOME THE SCIENCE DEPARTMENT HEAD OFFICER OF THE ORDER FOR ME.

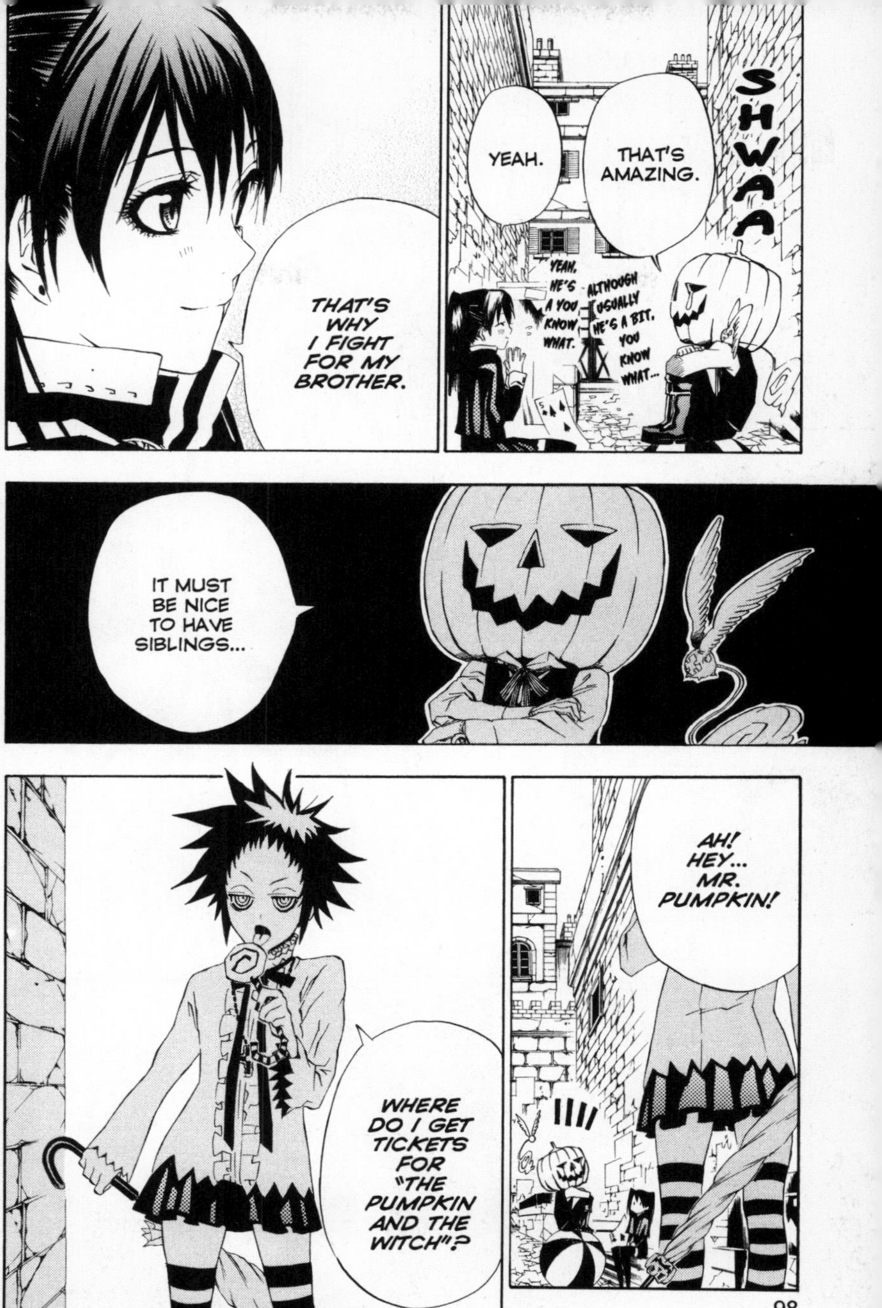
SHWAA
THAT'S AMAZING.
YEAH.
ALTHOUGH USUALLY HE'S A BIT, YOU KNOW WHAT...
YEAH, HE'S A YOU KNOW WHAT.
THAT'S WHY I FIGHT FOR MY BROTHER.
IT MUST BE NICE TO HAVE SIBLINGS...
AH! HEY... MR. PUMPKIN!
WHERE DO I GET TICKETS FOR "THE PUMPKIN AND THE WITCH"?

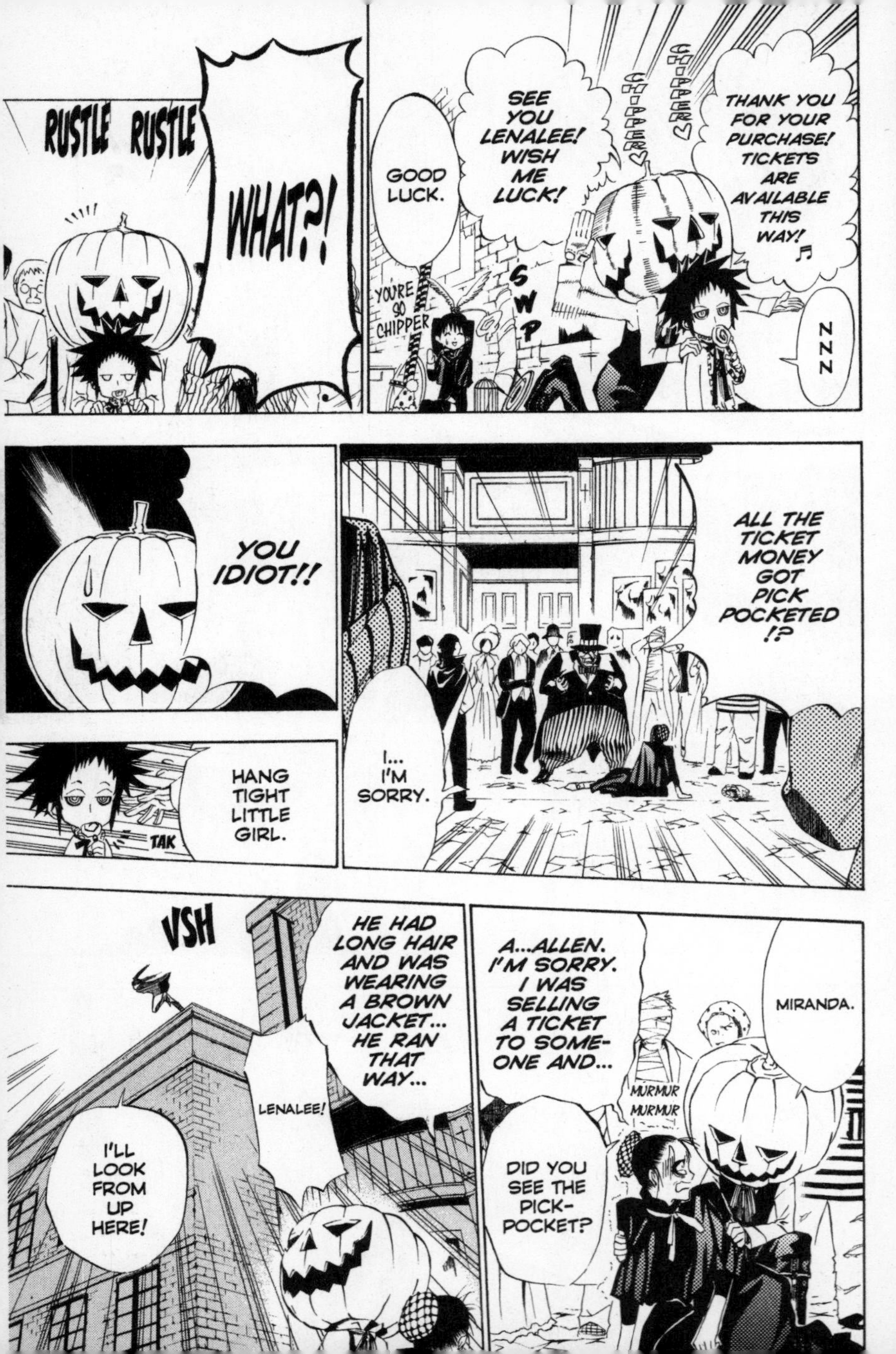
THANK YOU FOR YOUR PURCHASE! TICKETS ARE AVAILABLE THIS WAY! ♪
NNN
CHIPPER CHIPPER♡
SEE YOU LENALEE! WISH ME LUCK!
SWP
GOOD LUCK.
YOU'RE SO CHIPPER
WHAT?!
RUSTLE RUSTLE
ALL THE TICKET MONEY GOT PICK POCKETED !?
I... I'M SORRY.
YOU IDIOT!!
HANG TIGHT LITTLE GIRL.
TAK
MIRANDA.
A...ALLEN. I'M SORRY. I WAS SELLING A TICKET TO SOME-ONE AND...
MURMUR MURMUR
DID YOU SEE THE PICK-POCKET?
HE HAD LONG HAIR AND WAS WEARING A BROWN JACKET... HE RAN THAT WAY...
LENALEE!
VSH
I'LL LOOK FROM UP HERE!

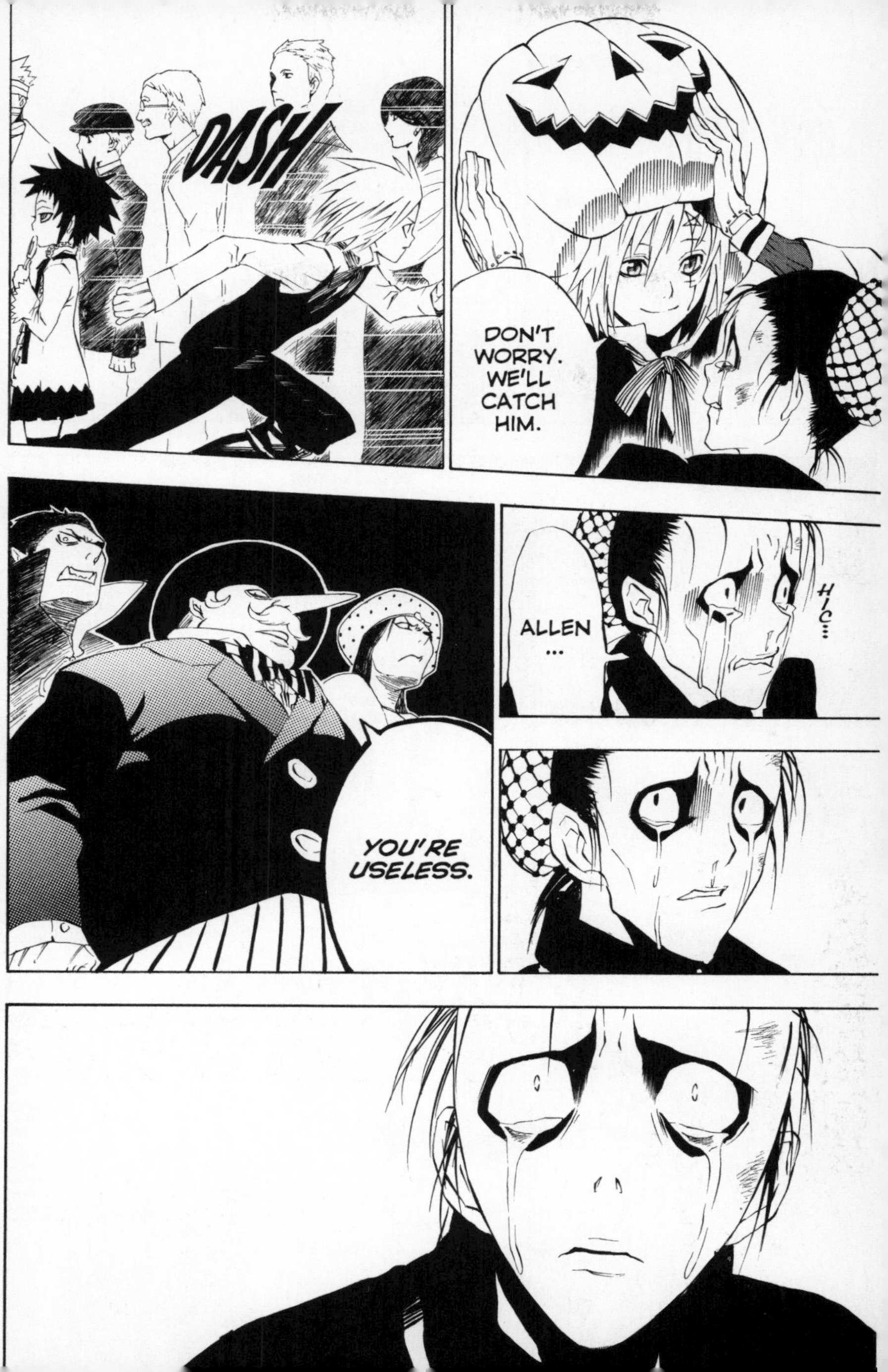
DON'T WORRY. WE'LL CATCH HIM.
DASH
ALLEN ...
HIC...
YOU'RE USELESS.

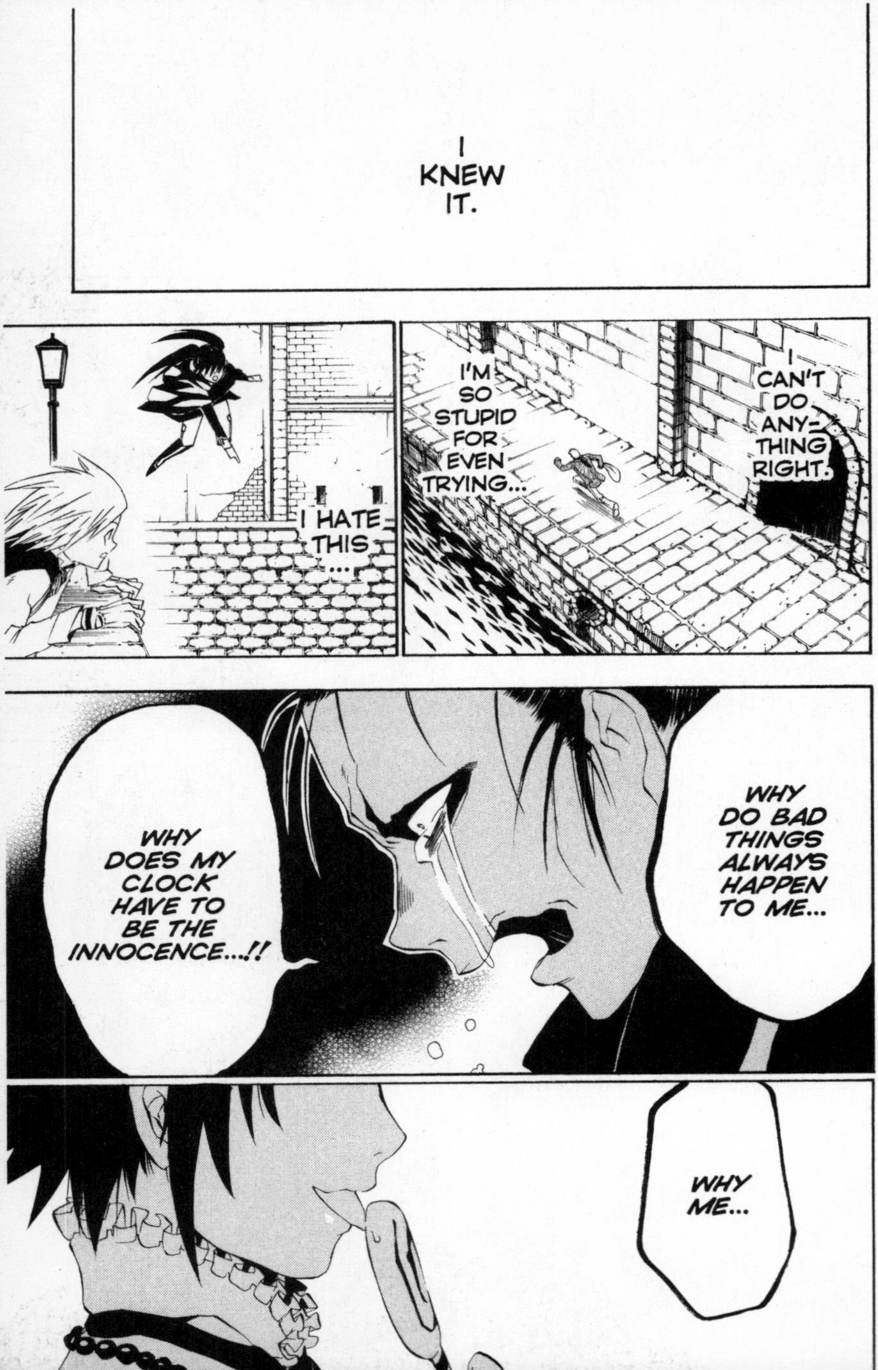
I KNEW IT.
I CAN'T DO ANY-THING RIGHT.
I'M SO STUPID FOR EVEN TRYING...
I HATE THIS...
WHY DO BAD THINGS ALWAYS HAPPEN TO ME...
WHY DOES MY CLOCK HAVE TO BE THE INNOCENCE...!!
WHY ME...

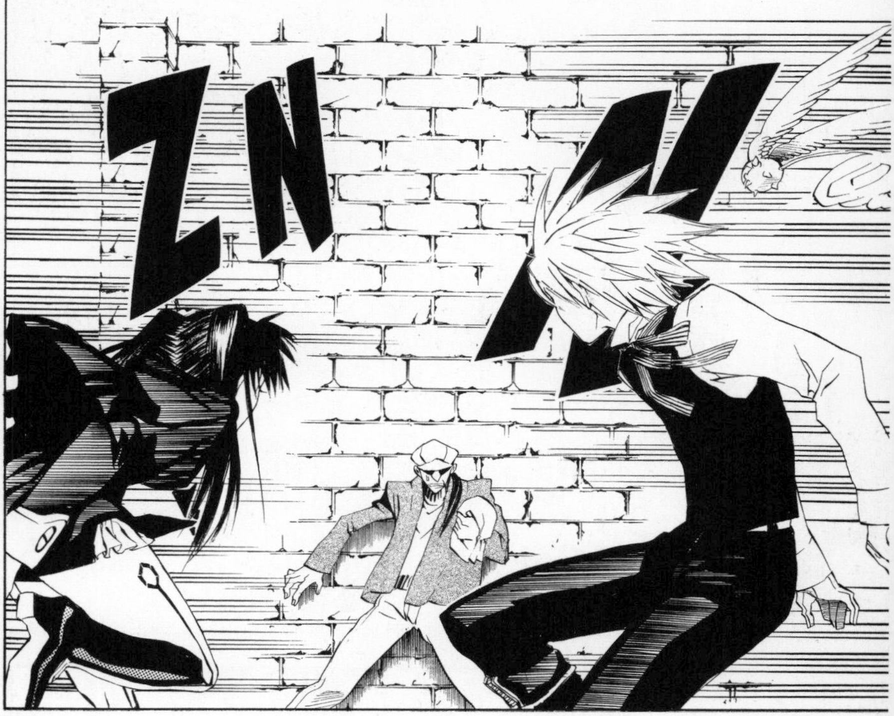
ZN
ZN
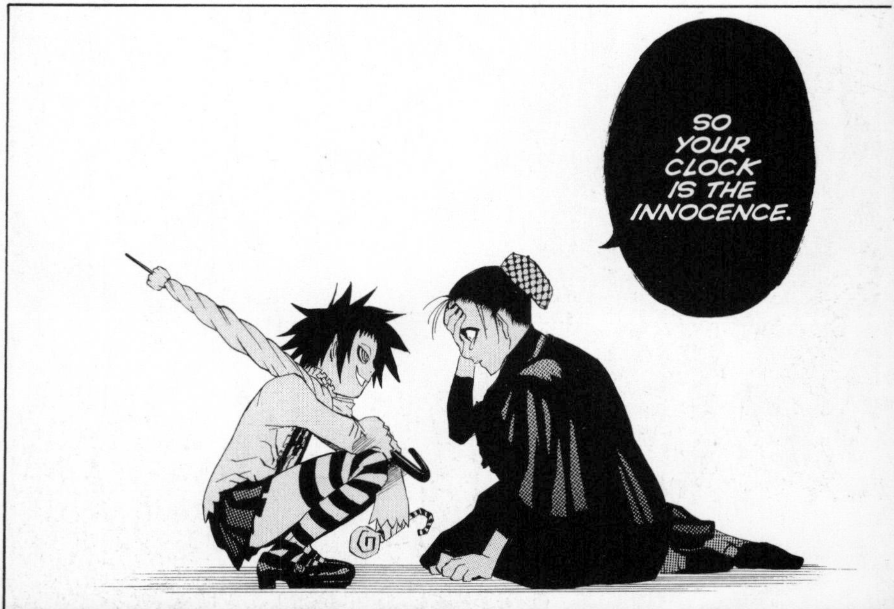
SO YOUR CLOCK IS THE INNOCENCE.

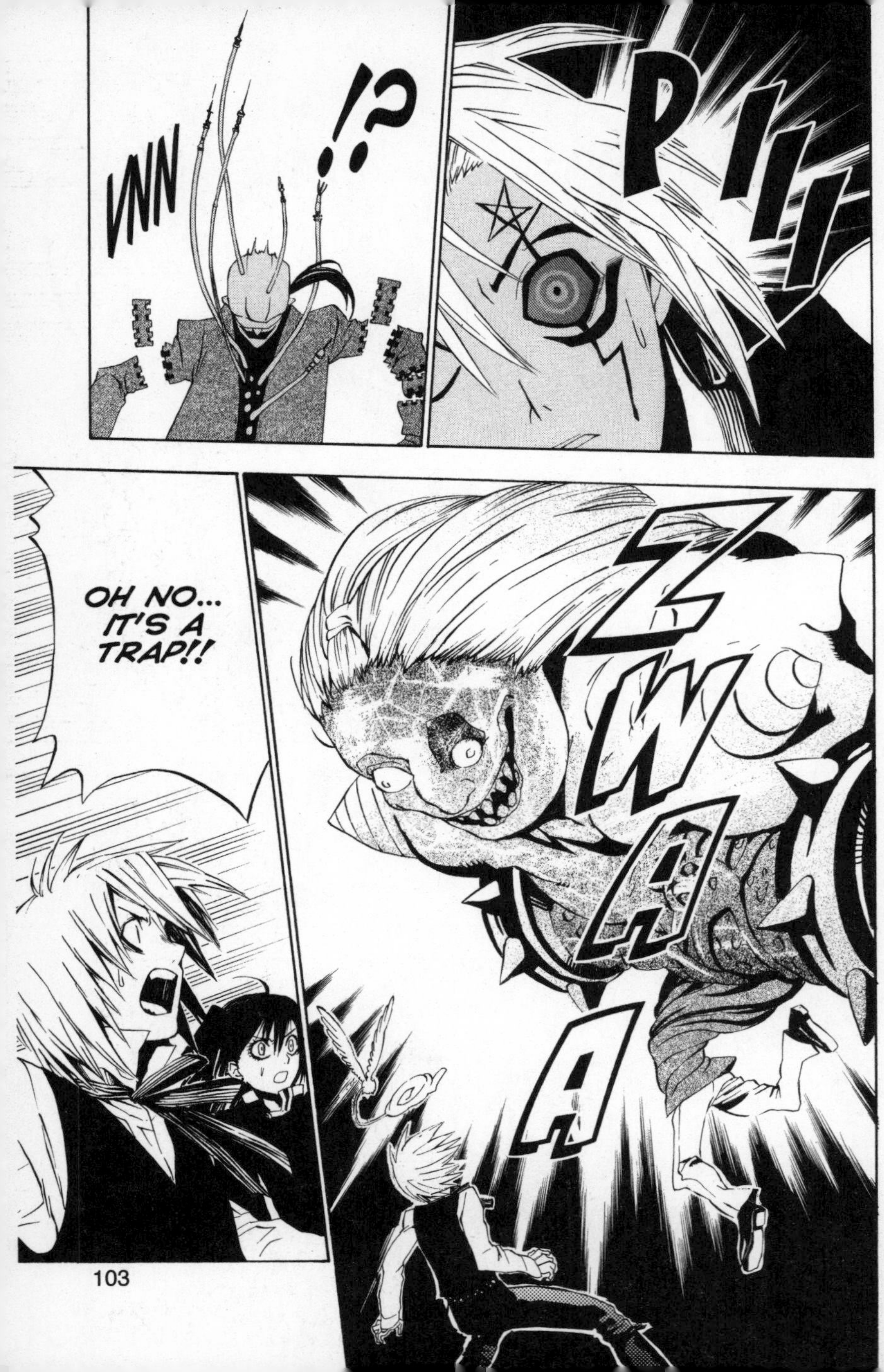
PIII
!?
VNN
ZWAAA
OH NO... IT'S A TRAP!!

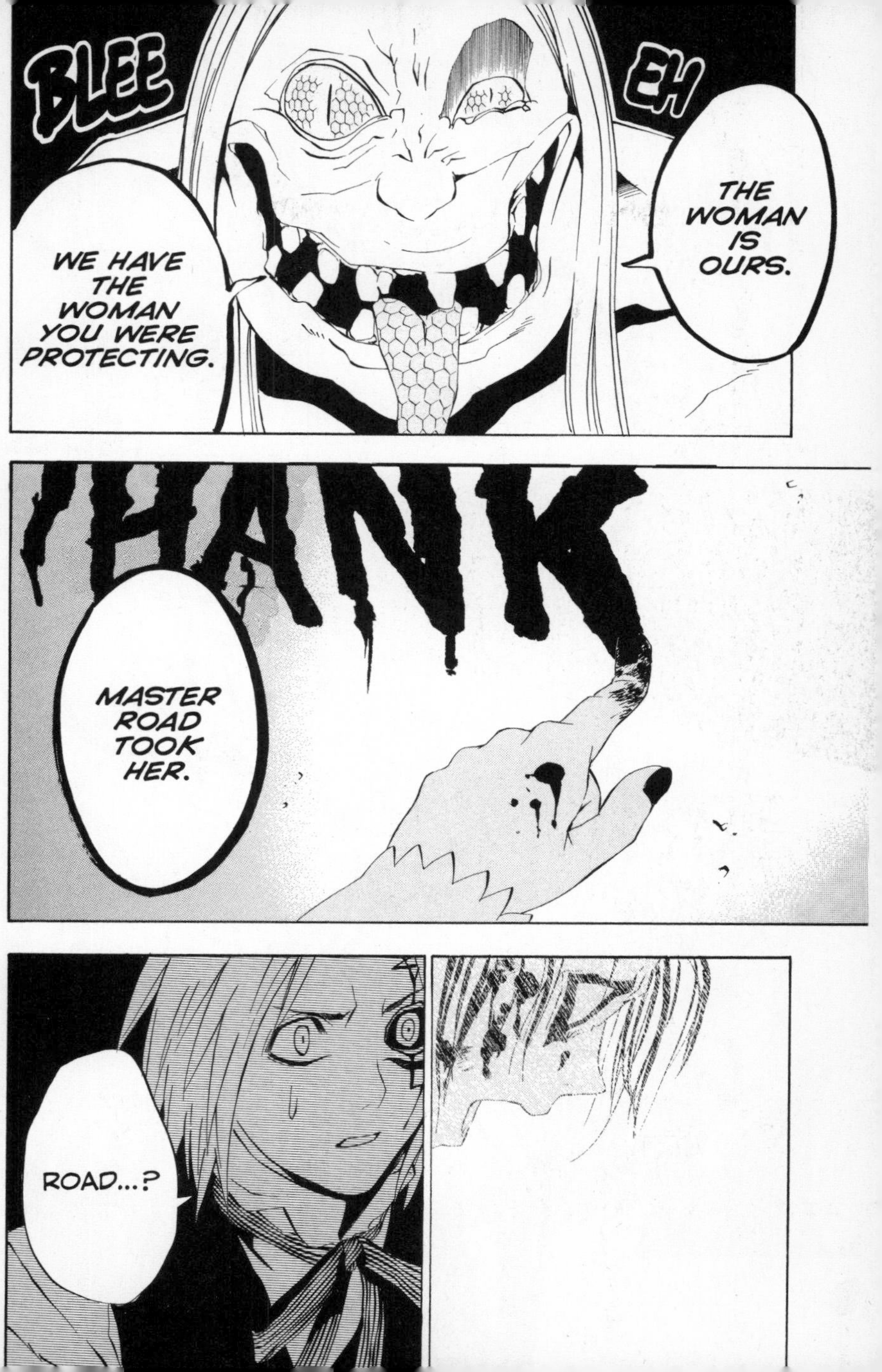
BLEE EH
THE WOMAN IS OURS.
WE HAVE THE WOMAN YOU WERE PROTECTING.
HANK
MASTER ROAD TOOK HER.
ROAD...?

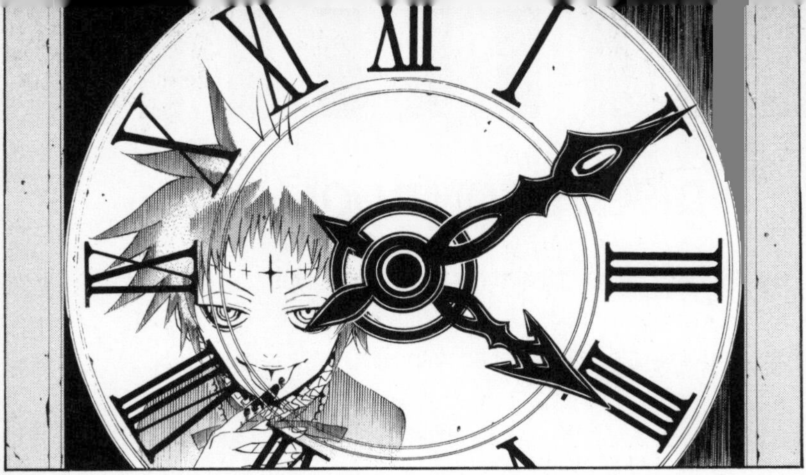

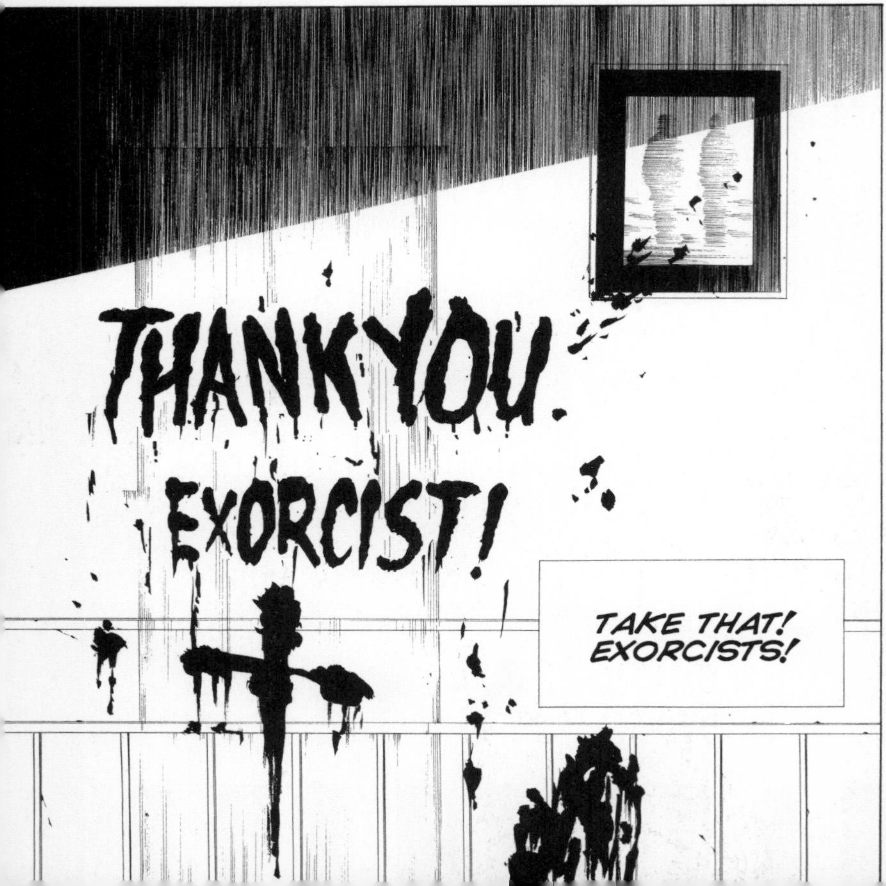
THANK YOU.
EXORCIST!
TAKE THAT! EXORCISTS!

DISCUSSION ROOM VOL. 5

Q 1. WHAT KIND OF TEMPURA DOES KANDA LIKE?

A.   PUMPKIN, SWEET PEPPER AND LOTUS ROOT TEMPURA.

Q 2. OUT OF A 100%, HOW MUST TRUST DOES KOMUI COMMAND FROM HIS STAFF?

A.   99% TRUST AND 1% MURDEROUS HATE.

Q 3. IS KOMUI A COFFEE SNOB OR DOES HE DRINK INSTANT COFFEE? PLEASE TELL US WHAT KIND HE DRINKS.

A.   HE'S A COFFEE SNOB. HE DRINKS BLUE MOUNTAIN COFFEE.

Q 4. WHO'S THE DUMBEST AND SMARTEST OUT OF KANDA, ALLEN, RABI AND LENALEE?

A.   (DUMBEST) KANDA -> ALLEN -> RABI -> LENALEE (SMARTEST)

Q 5. HOW MUCH DOES THE MILLENNIUM EARL WEIGH?

A.   85KG.

Q 6. WHAT'S THE GATEKEEPER'S NAME?

A.   ALESTINA DROW JOANASON P. ROBATHAN GIA AMADEUS NO. 5. HE'S THE FIFTH GATEKEEPER.

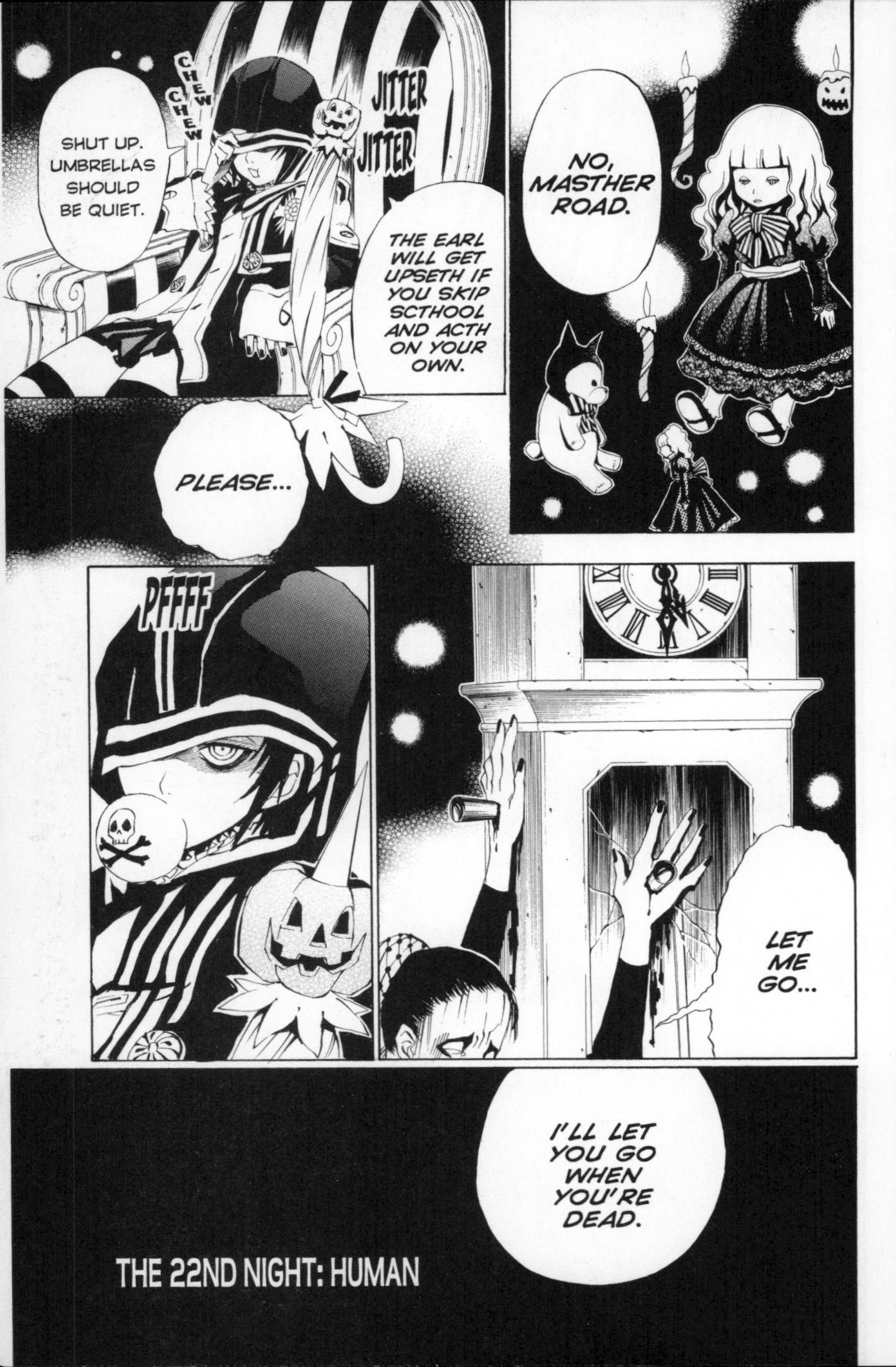

NO, MASTHER ROAD.
THE EARL WILL GET UPSETH IF YOU SKIP SCTHOOL AND ACTH ON YOUR OWN.
JITTER JITTER
CHEW CHEW
SHUT UP. UMBRELLAS SHOULD BE QUIET.
PLEASE...
LET ME GO...
PFFFF
I'LL LET YOU GO WHEN YOU'RE DEAD.
THE 22ND NIGHT: HUMAN

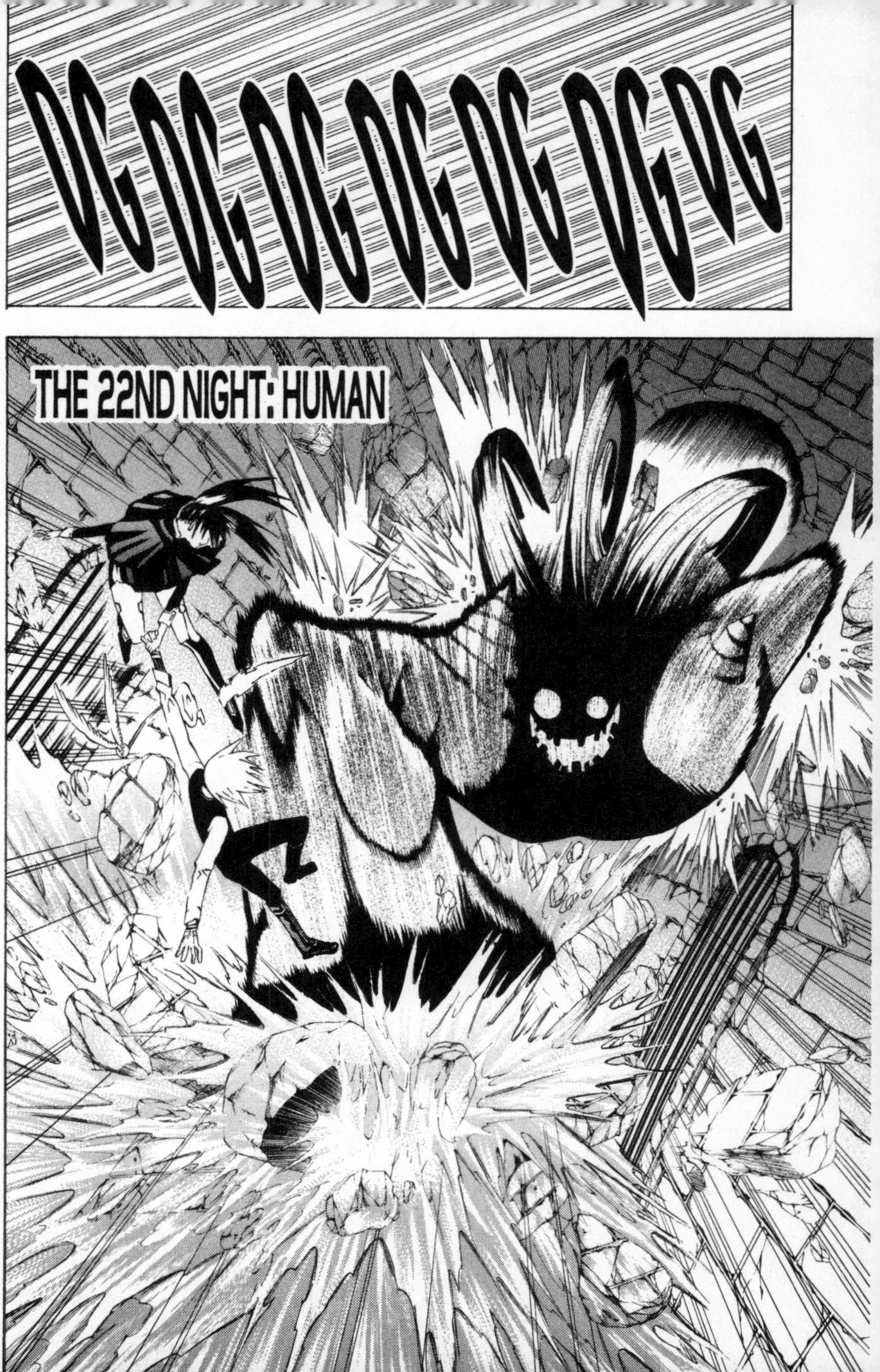
DG DG DG DG DG DG DG DG
THE 22ND NIGHT: HUMAN

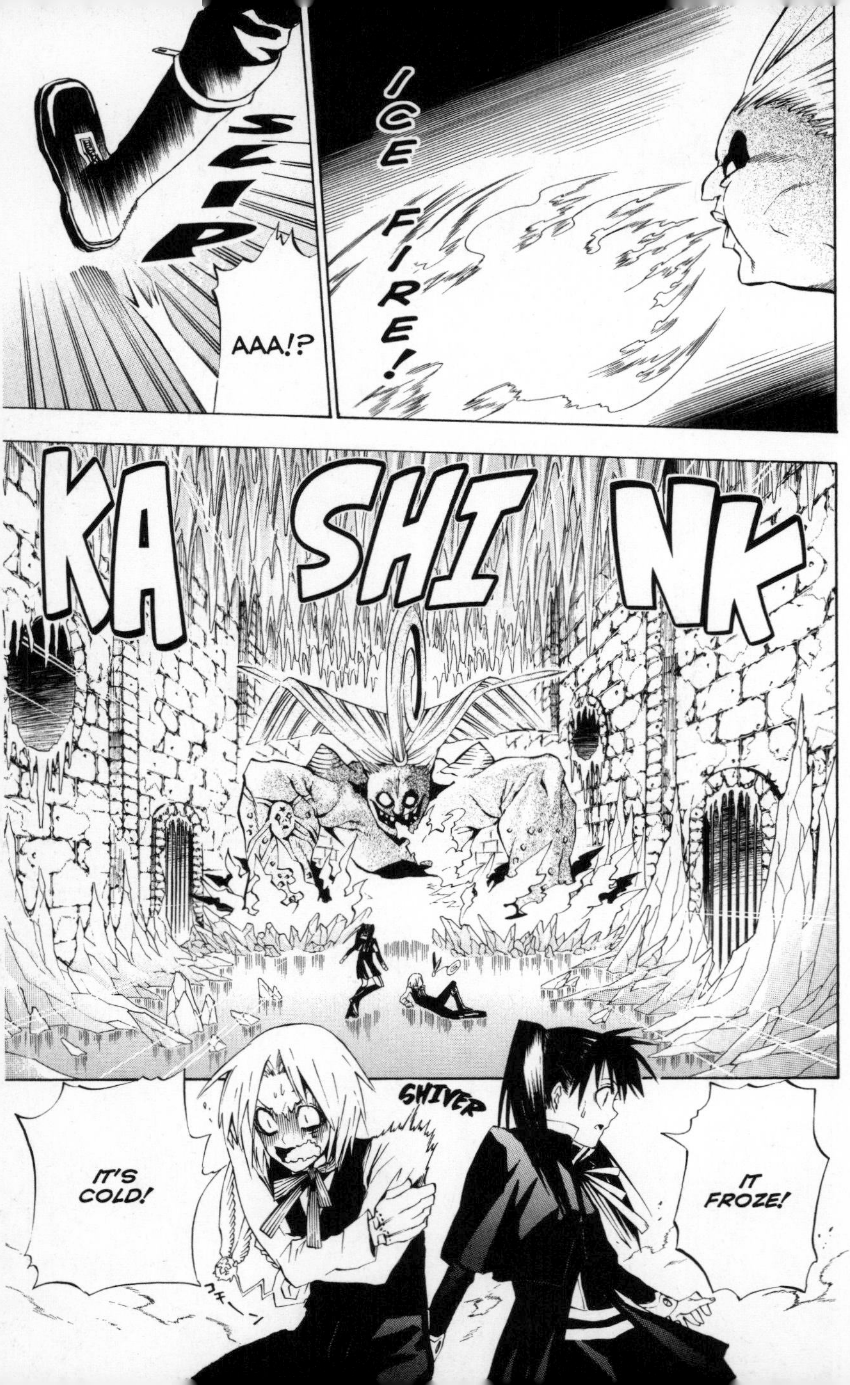
ICE FIRE!
SLIP
AAA!?
KA SHI NK
IT FROZE!
SHIVER
IT'S COLD!
コチーン

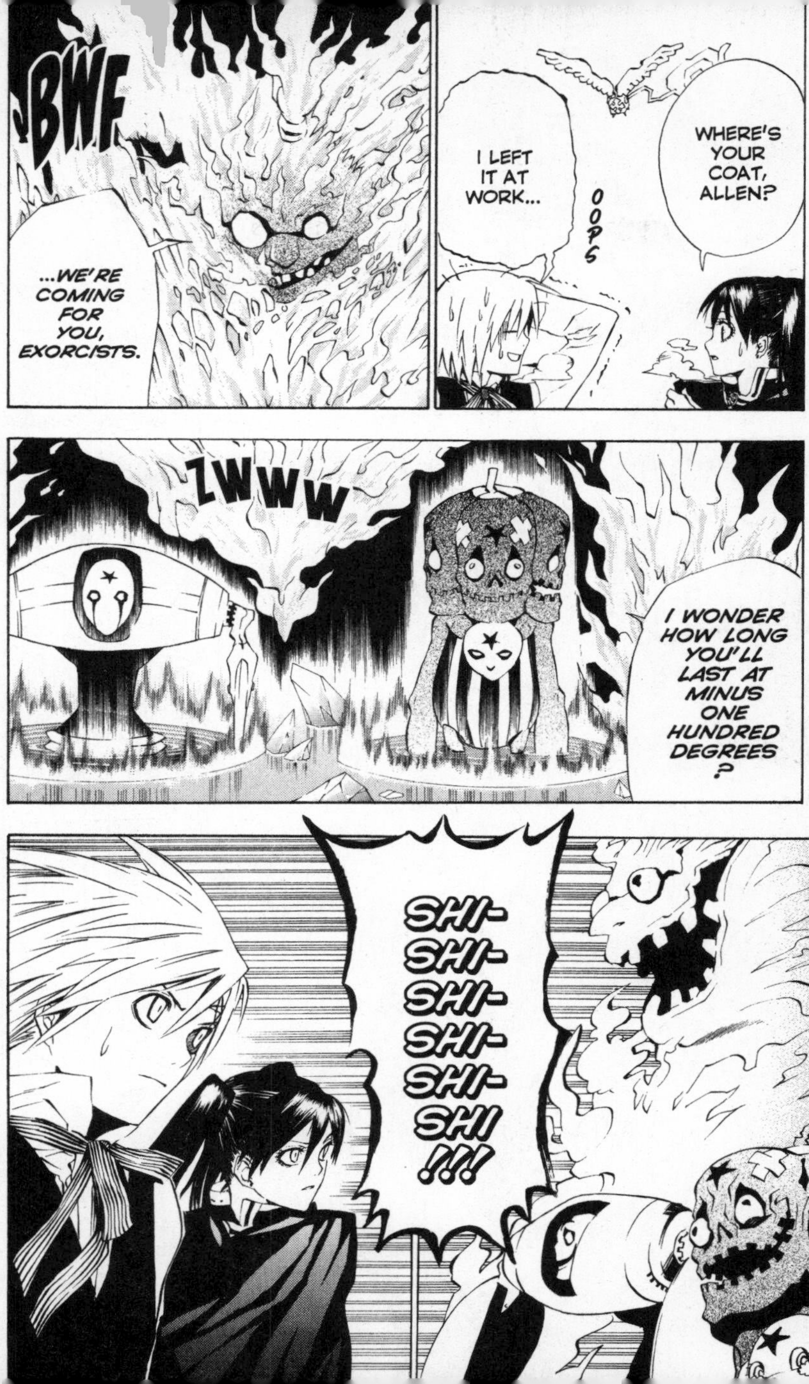
WHERE'S YOUR COAT, ALLEN?
OOPS
I LEFT IT AT WORK...
BWF
...WE'RE COMING FOR YOU, EXORCISTS.
ZWWW
I WONDER HOW LONG YOU'LL LAST AT MINUS ONE HUNDRED DEGREES?
SHI-SHI-SHI-SHI-SHI-SHI!!!

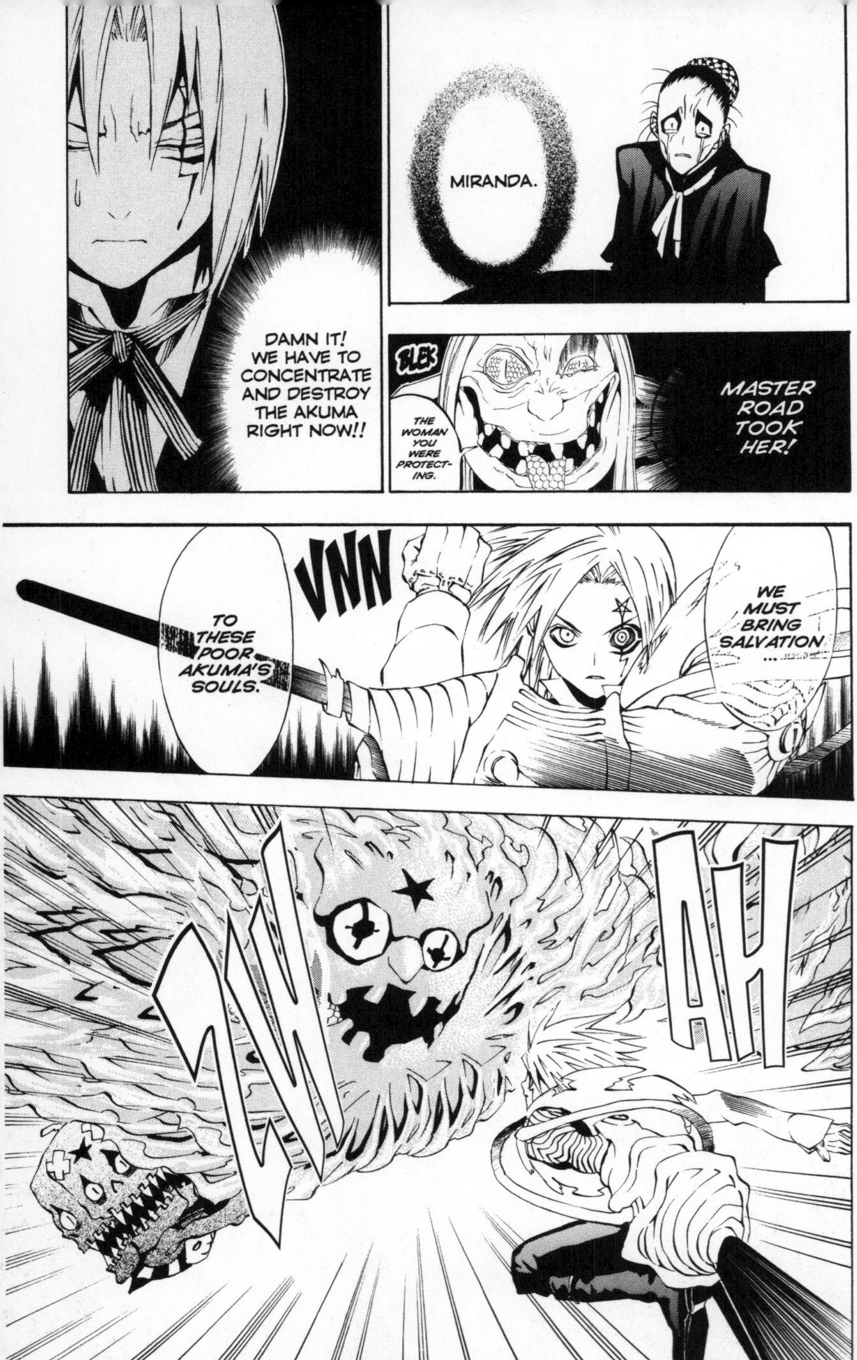
MIRANDA.
MASTER ROAD TOOK HER!
BLEK
THE WOMAN YOU WERE PROTECTING.
DAMN IT! WE HAVE TO CONCENTRATE AND DESTROY THE AKUMA RIGHT NOW!!
WE MUST BRING SALVATION...
VNN
TO THESE POOR AKUMA'S SOULS.
AH

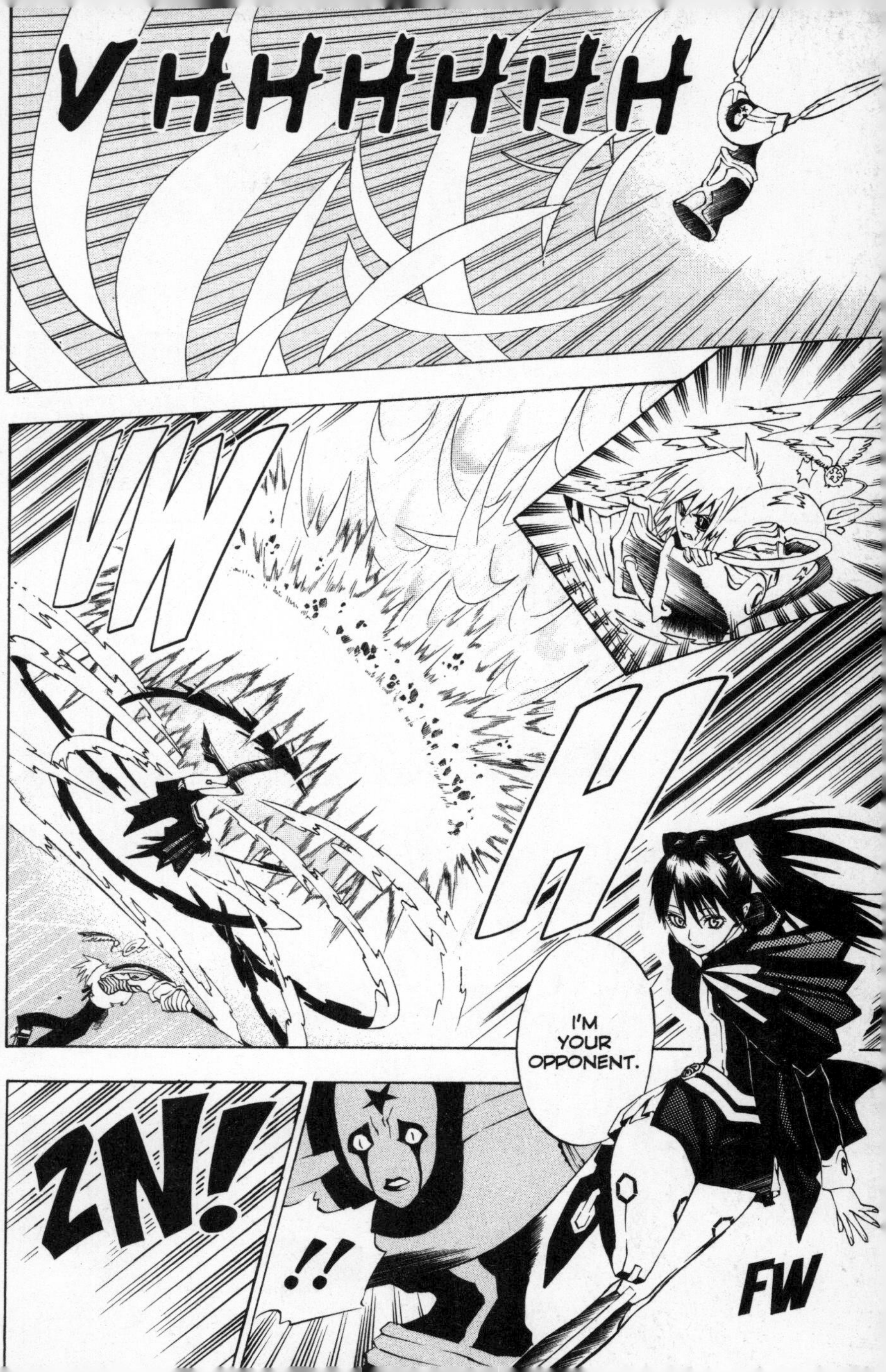
VHHHHHHH
VW
H
I'M YOUR OPPONENT.
FW
ZN!
!!

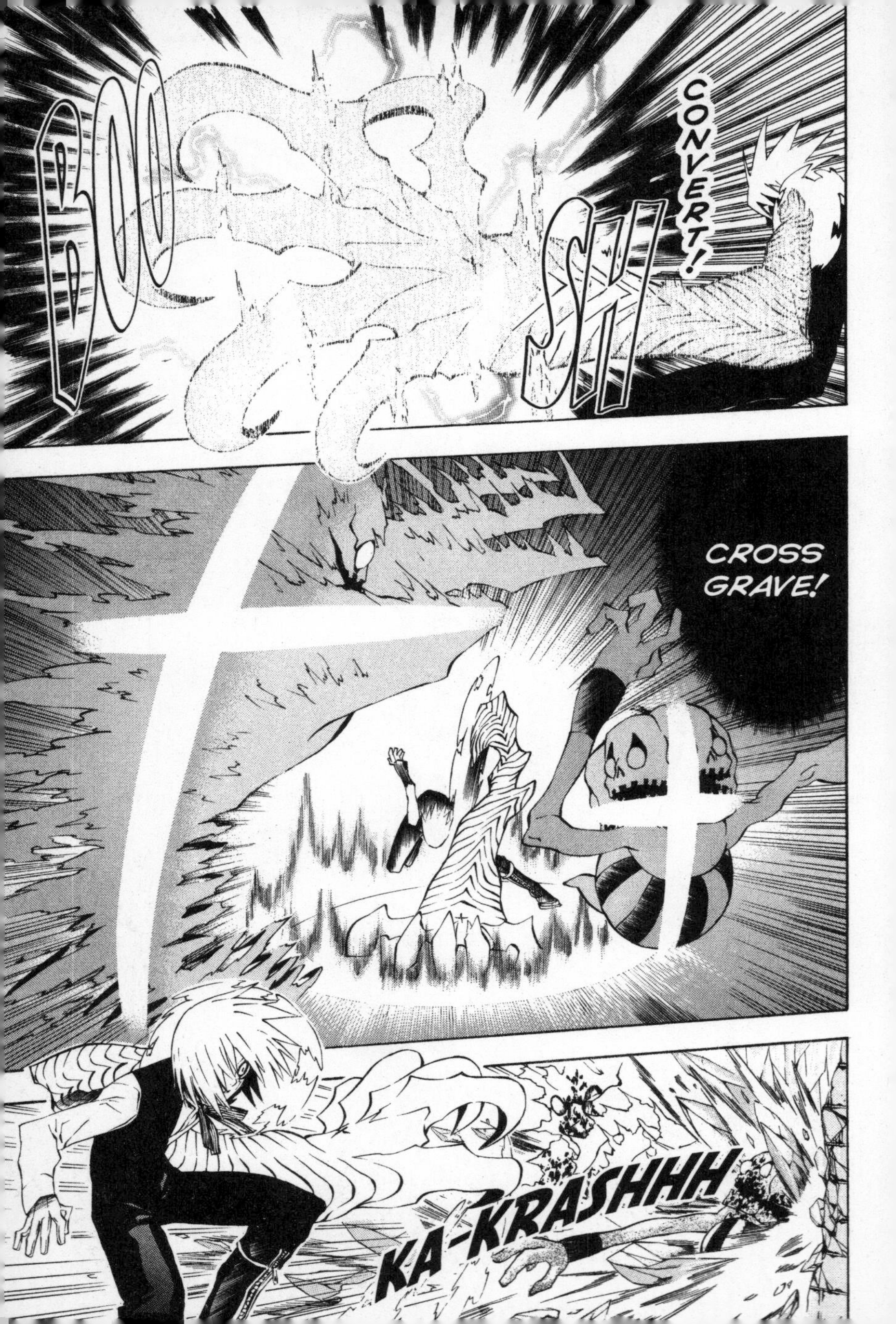
CONVERT!
SH
BOOO
CROSS GRAVE!
KA-KRASHHH

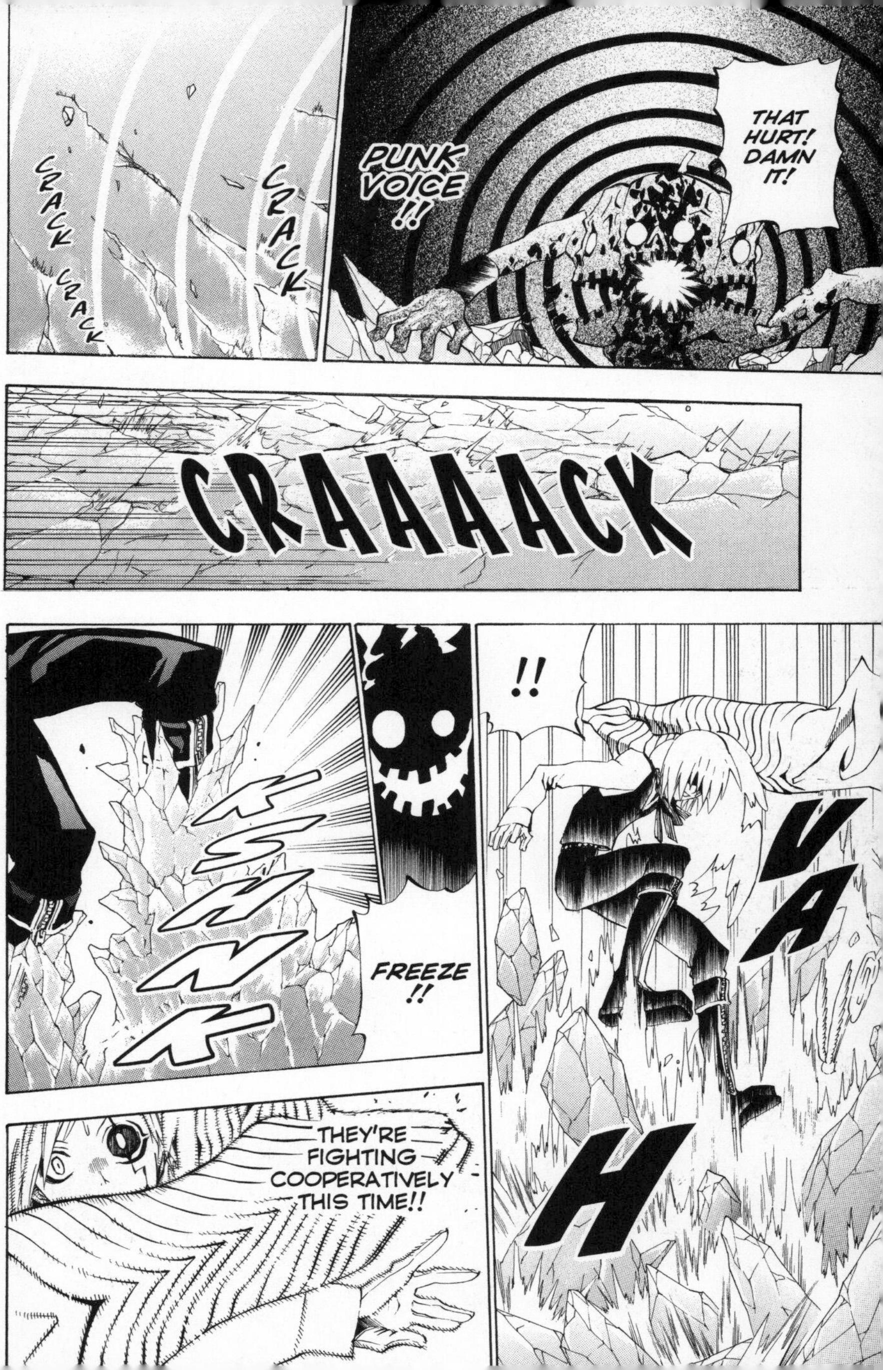
THAT HURT! DAMN IT!
PUNK VOICE!!
CRACK
CRACK CRACK
CRAAAACK
!!
VAH
KSHNK
FREEZE!!
THEY'RE FIGHTING COOPERATIVELY THIS TIME!!

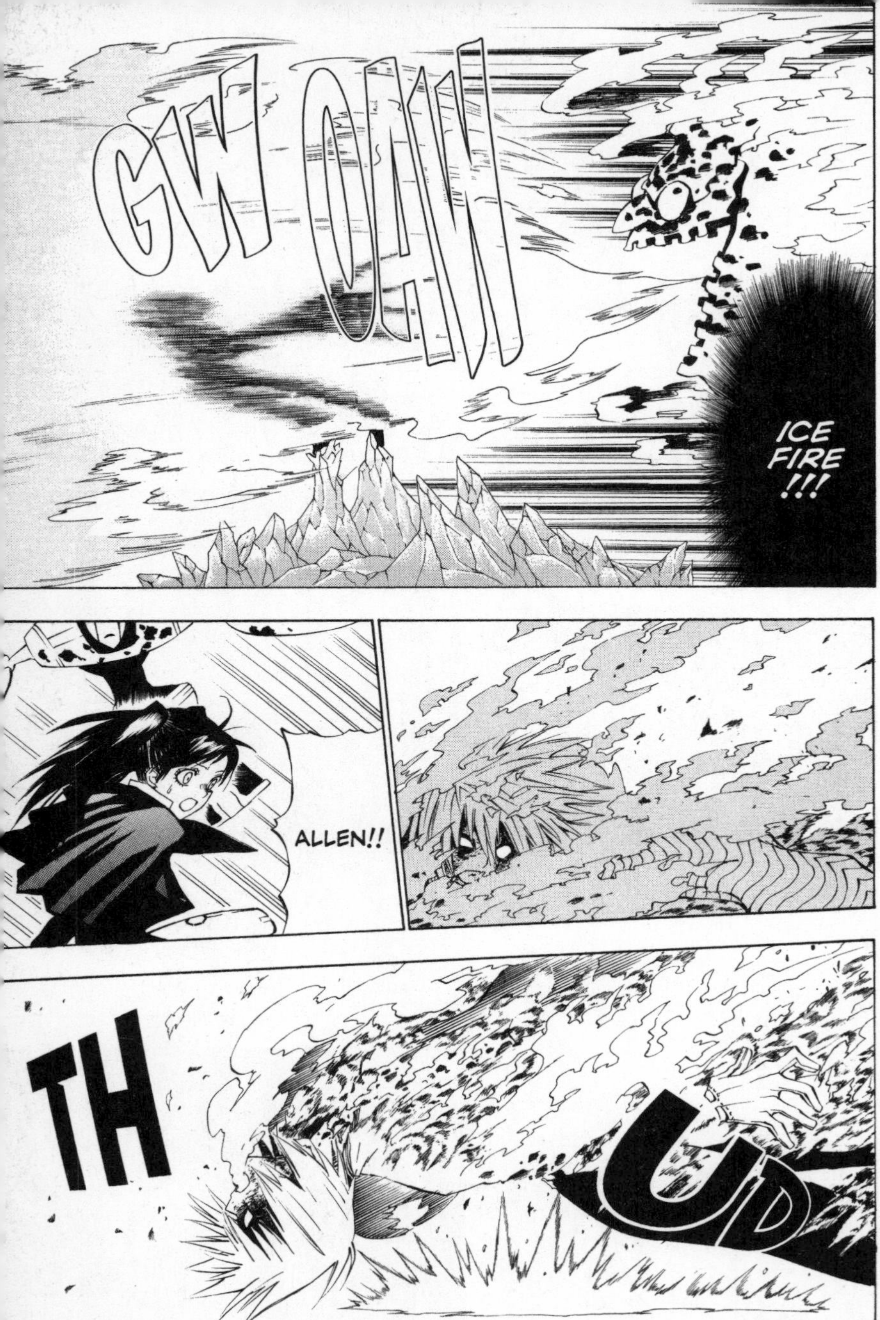
ICE FIRE !!!
GWOAN
ALLEN!!
THUD

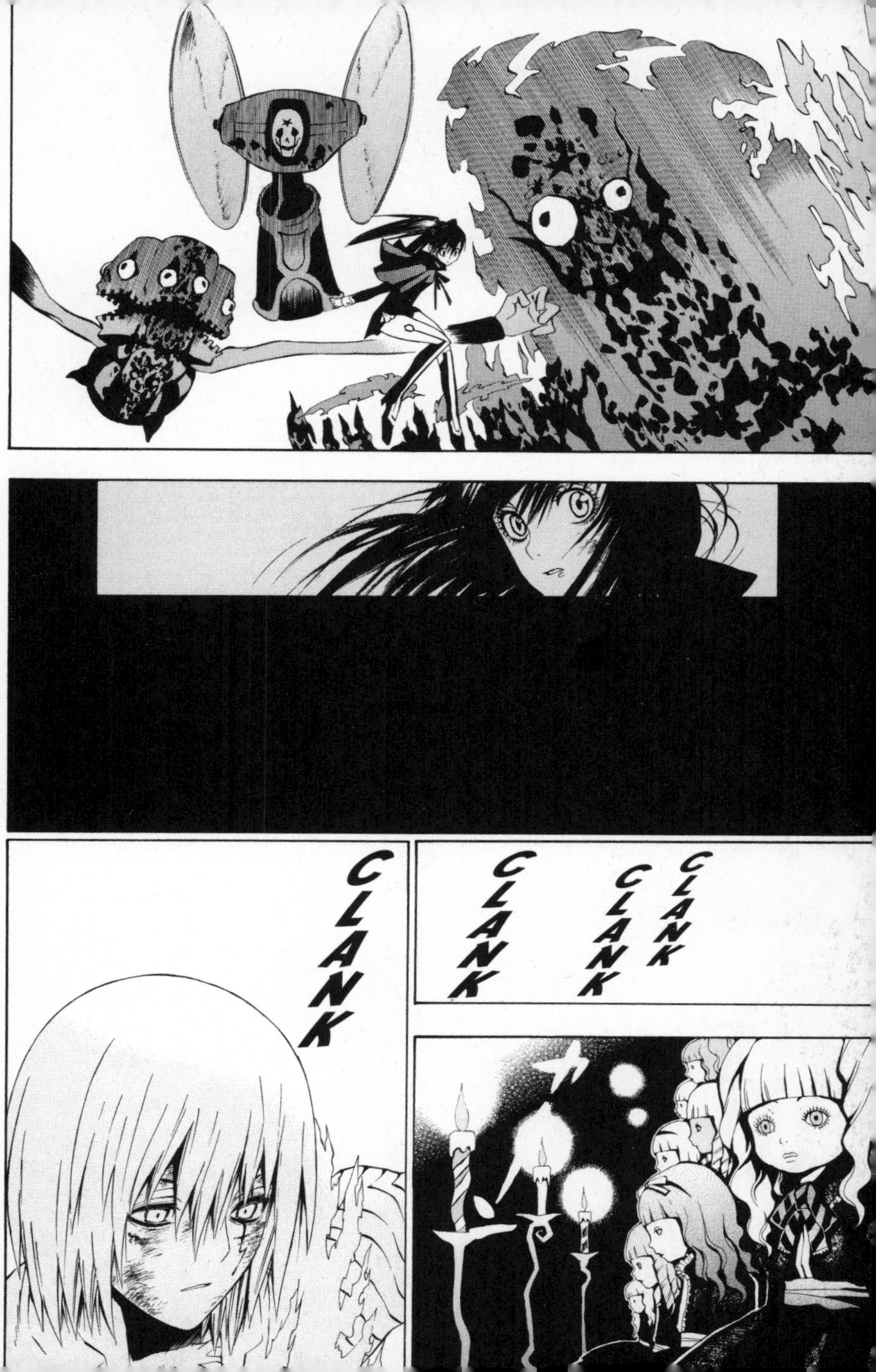
CLANK
CLANK
CLANK
CLANK

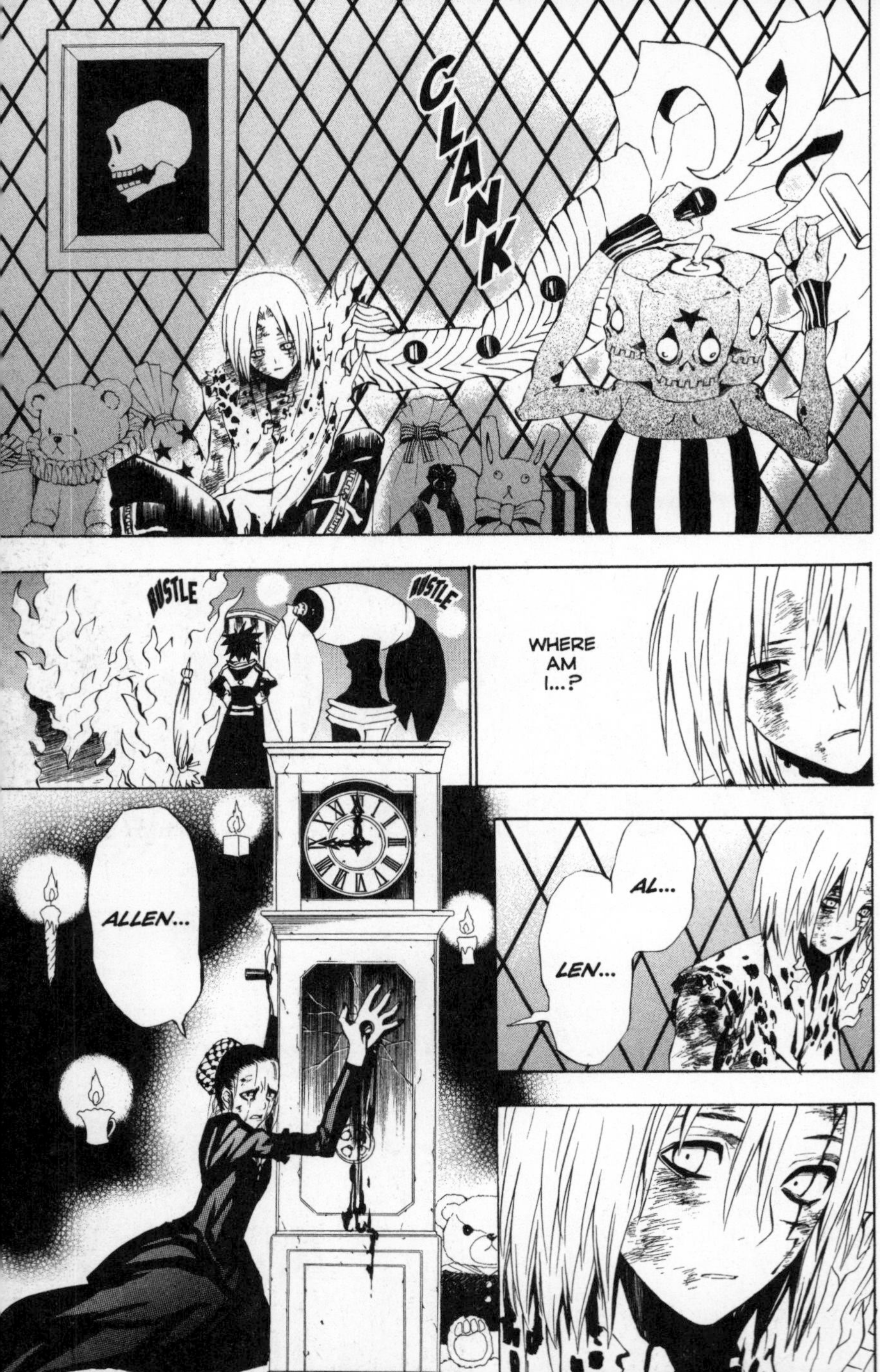
CLANK
WHERE AM I...?
BUSTLE
BUSTLE
AL... LEN...
ALLEN...

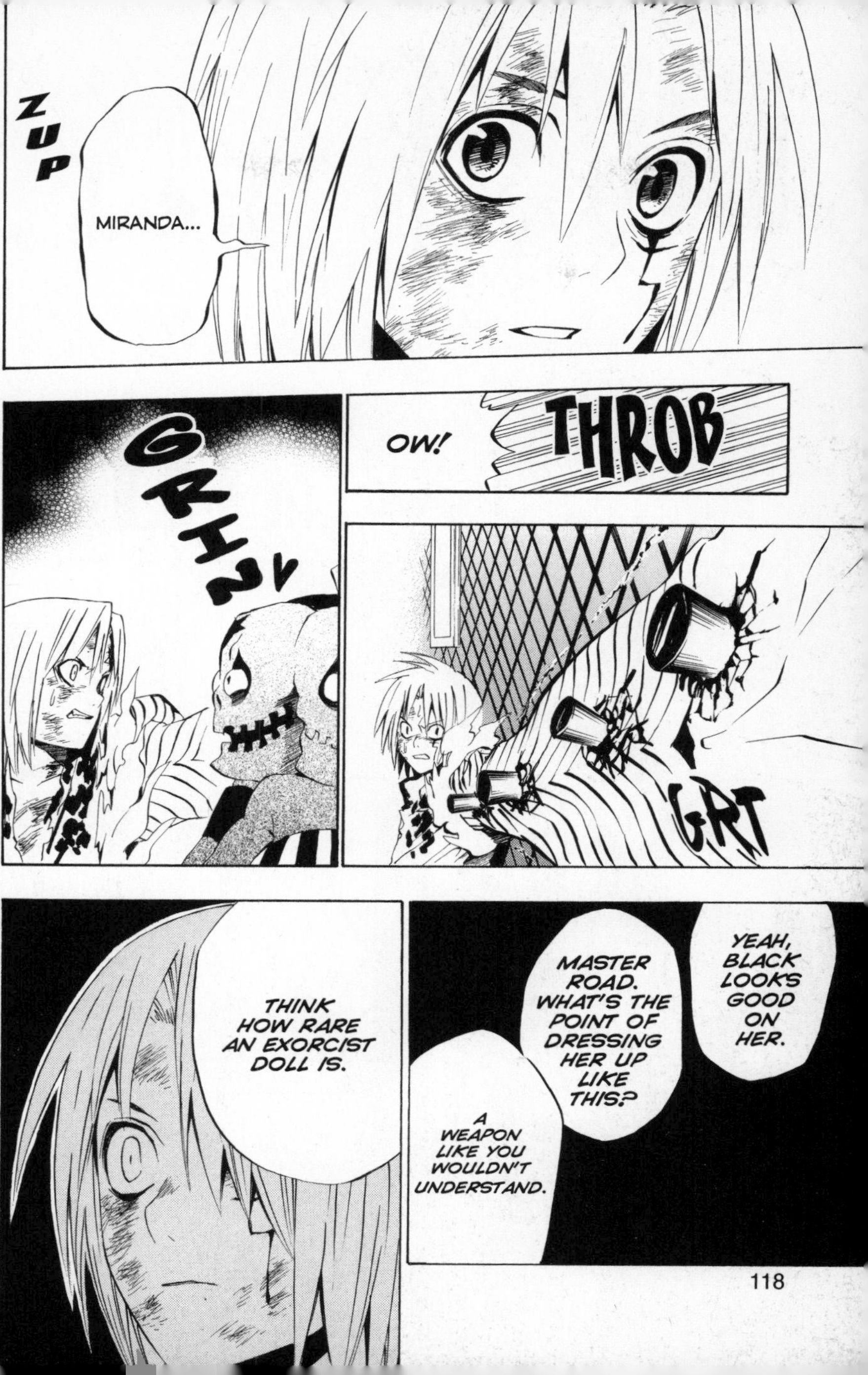
ZUP
MIRANDA...
THROB
OW!
GRT
GRIN
YEAH, BLACK LOOKS GOOD ON HER.
MASTER ROAD. WHAT'S THE POINT OF DRESSING HER UP LIKE THIS?
A WEAPON LIKE YOU WOULDN'T UNDERSTAND.
THINK HOW RARE AN EXORCIST DOLL IS.

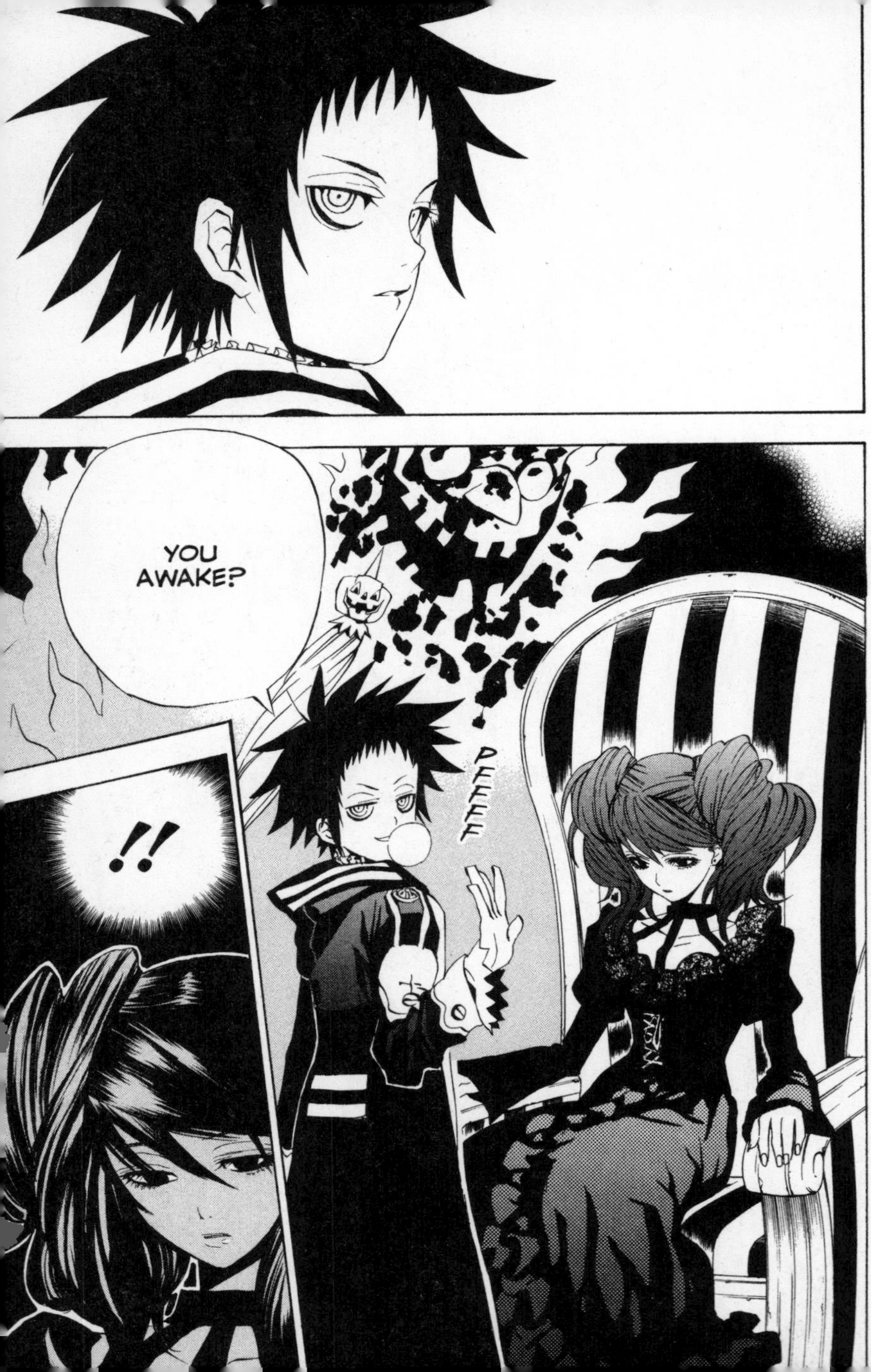
YOU AWAKE?
PFFFF
!!

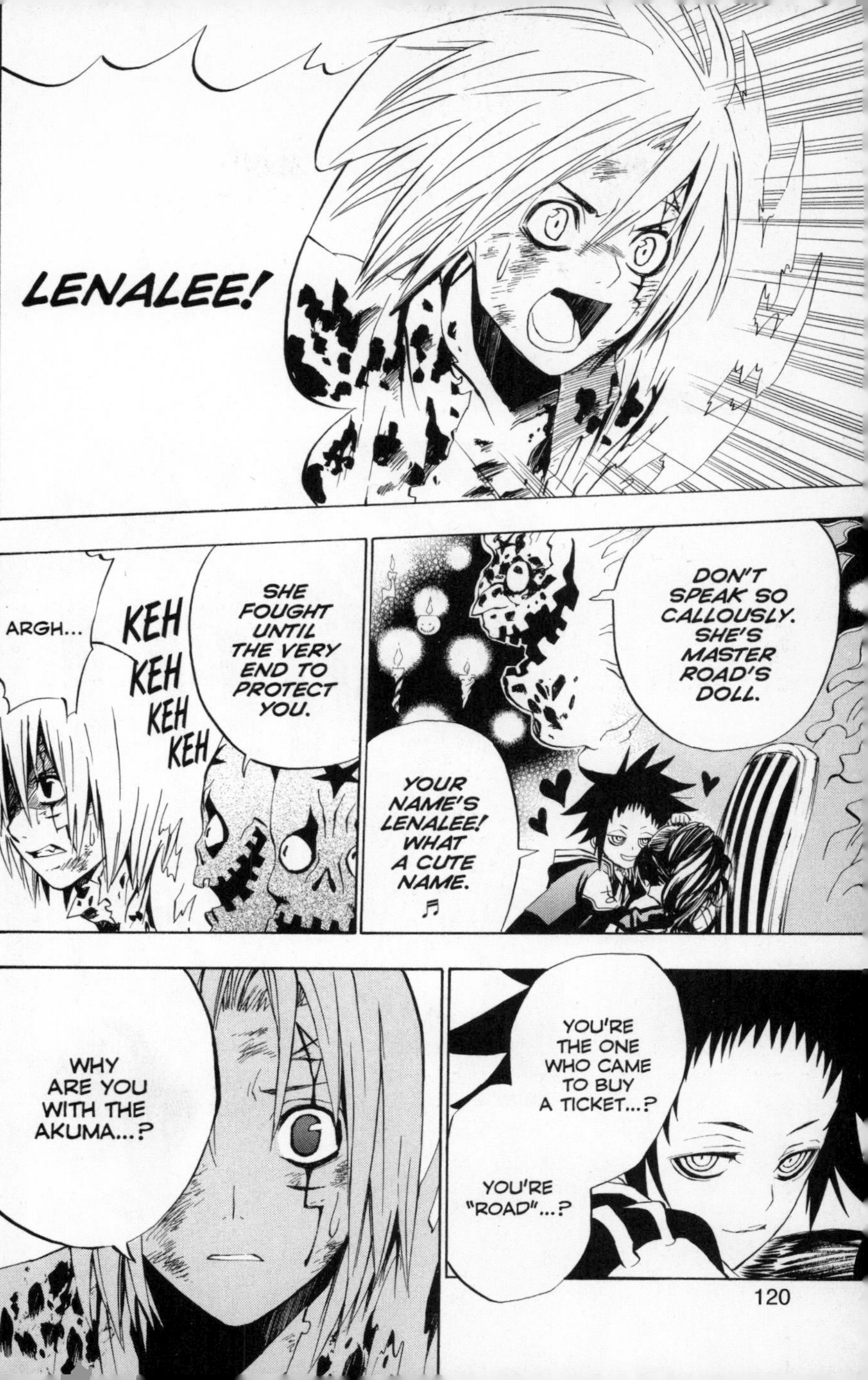
LENALEE!
DON'T SPEAK SO CALLOUSLY. SHE'S MASTER ROAD'S DOLL.
YOUR NAME'S LENALEE! WHAT A CUTE NAME. ♬
SHE FOUGHT UNTIL THE VERY END TO PROTECT YOU.
KEH KEH KEH KEH
ARGH...
YOU'RE THE ONE WHO CAME TO BUY A TICKET...?
YOU'RE "ROAD"...?
WHY ARE YOU WITH THE AKUMA...?

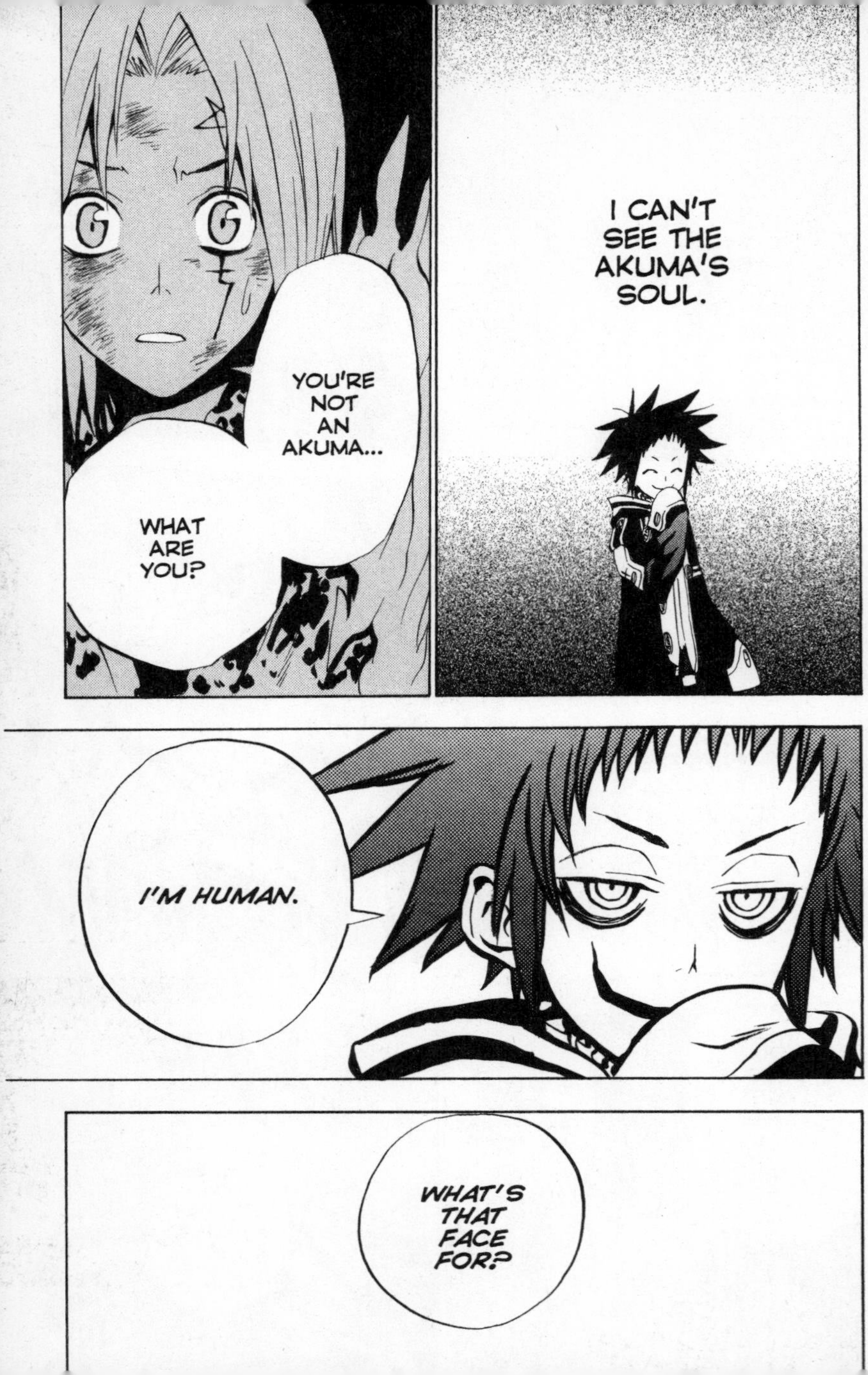
I CAN'T SEE THE AKUMA'S SOUL.
YOU'RE NOT AN AKUMA...
WHAT ARE YOU?
I'M HUMAN.
WHAT'S THAT FACE FOR?

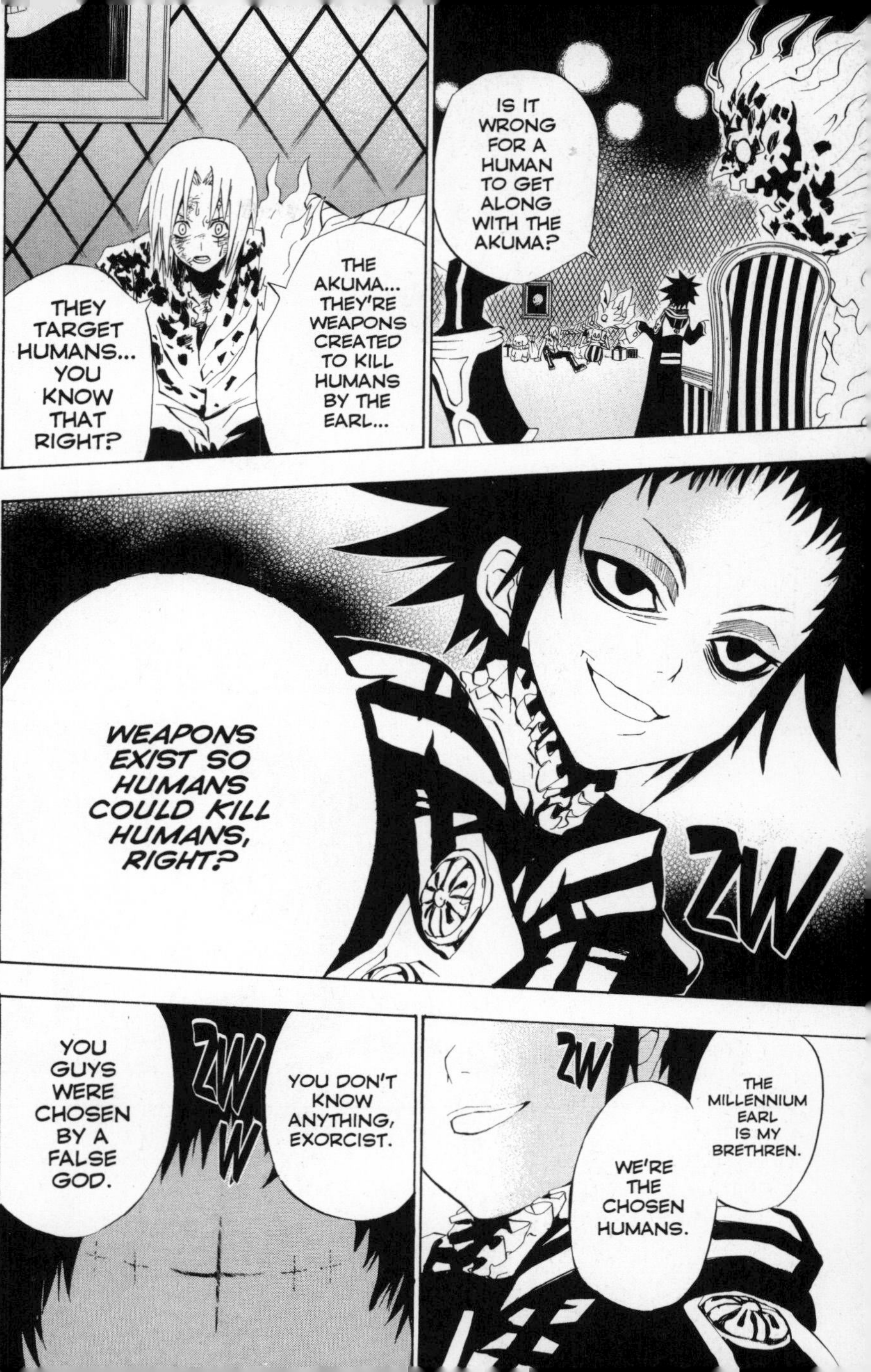
IS IT WRONG FOR A HUMAN TO GET ALONG WITH THE AKUMA?
THE AKUMA... THEY'RE WEAPONS CREATED TO KILL HUMANS BY THE EARL...
THEY TARGET HUMANS... YOU KNOW THAT RIGHT?
WEAPONS EXIST SO HUMANS COULD KILL HUMANS, RIGHT?
ZW
ZW
THE MILLENNIUM EARL IS MY BRETHREN.
WE'RE THE CHOSEN HUMANS.
ZW
W
YOU DON'T KNOW ANYTHING, EXORCIST.
YOU GUYS WERE CHOSEN BY A FALSE GOD.

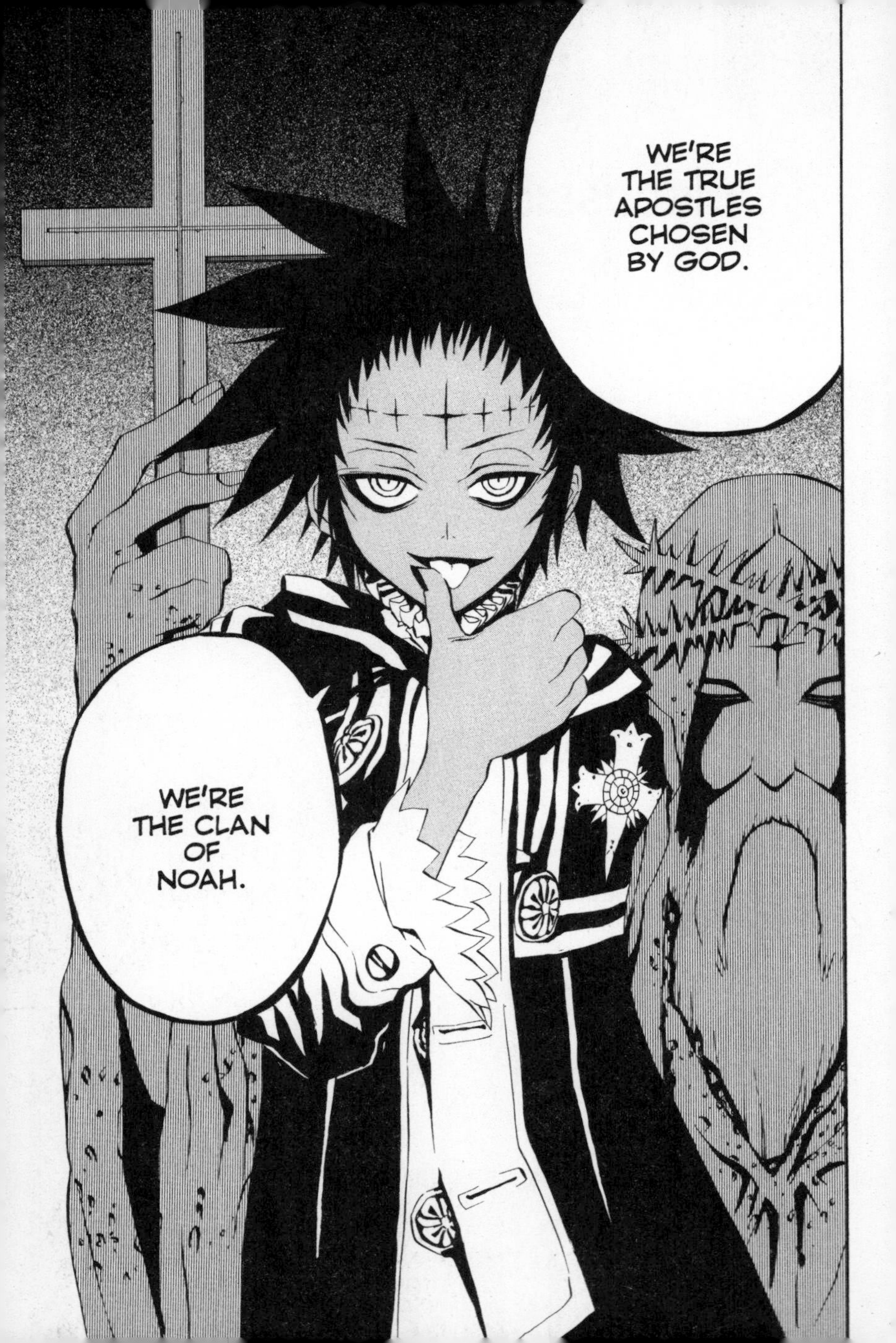
WE'RE THE TRUE APOSTLES CHOSEN BY GOD.
WE'RE THE CLAN OF NOAH.

DISCUSSION ROOM VOL. 6

Q 1.   WHERE DID YOU GET TIMCANPY'S NAME FROM?

A.   IT'S THE NAME OF A SILVER ACCESSORY BRAND NAME. I REALLY
     LIKE THEIR STUFF SO I'VE TAKEN SOME OTHER CHARACTER
     NAMES FROM THEM TOO.

Q 2.   IF SECTION LEADER RIBA WERE TO MAKE A CAREER CHANGE
       WHAT WOULD HE DO?

A.   HE'D BE A PRIVATE DETECTIVE OR A SCHOOL TEACHER.

Q 3.   WHAT KIND OF SHAMPOO DOES KANDA USE?

A.   HE USES SOAP.

Q 4.   DID ALLEN REALLY EAT ALL THAT FOOD IN TEN MINUTES IN
       VOLUME TWO?

A.   YES HE DID.

Q 5.   WHAT IS LOVE?

A.   ...I HOPE TO DRAW THAT IN THIS MANGA.

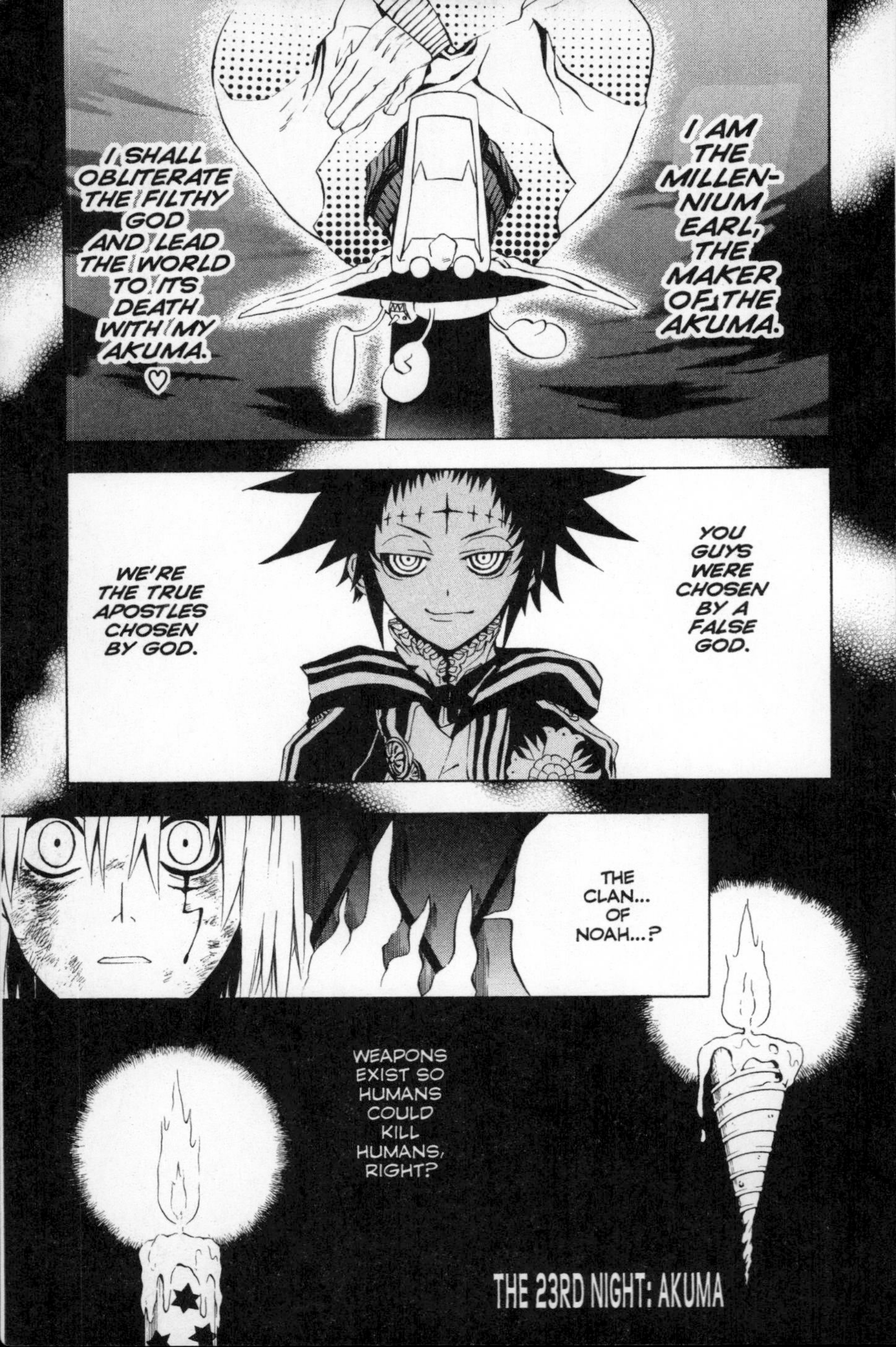
I AM THE MILLENNIUM EARL, THE MAKER OF THE AKUMA.
I SHALL OBLITERATE THE FILTHY GOD AND LEAD THE WORLD TO ITS DEATH WITH MY AKUMA. ♡
YOU GUYS WERE CHOSEN BY A FALSE GOD.
WE'RE THE TRUE APOSTLES CHOSEN BY GOD.
THE CLAN... OF NOAH...?
WEAPONS EXIST SO HUMANS COULD KILL HUMANS, RIGHT?
THE 23RD NIGHT: AKUMA

THE 23RD NIGHT: AKUMA

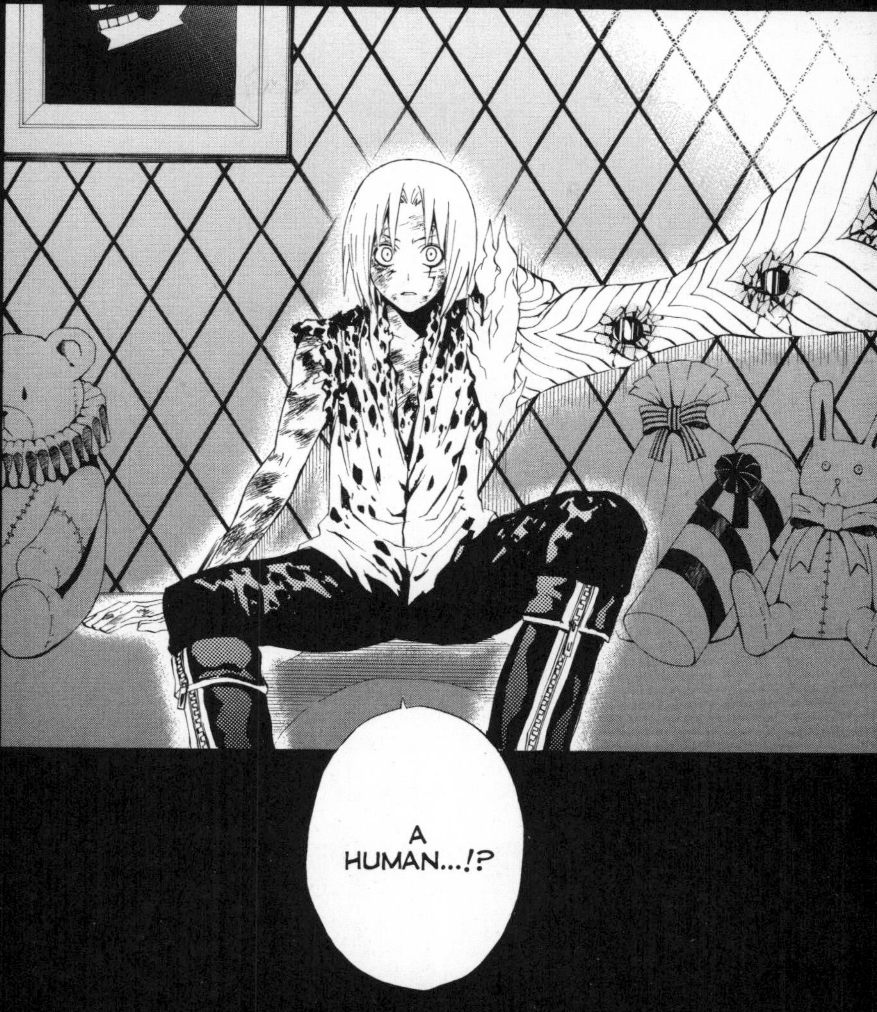
A HUMAN...!?

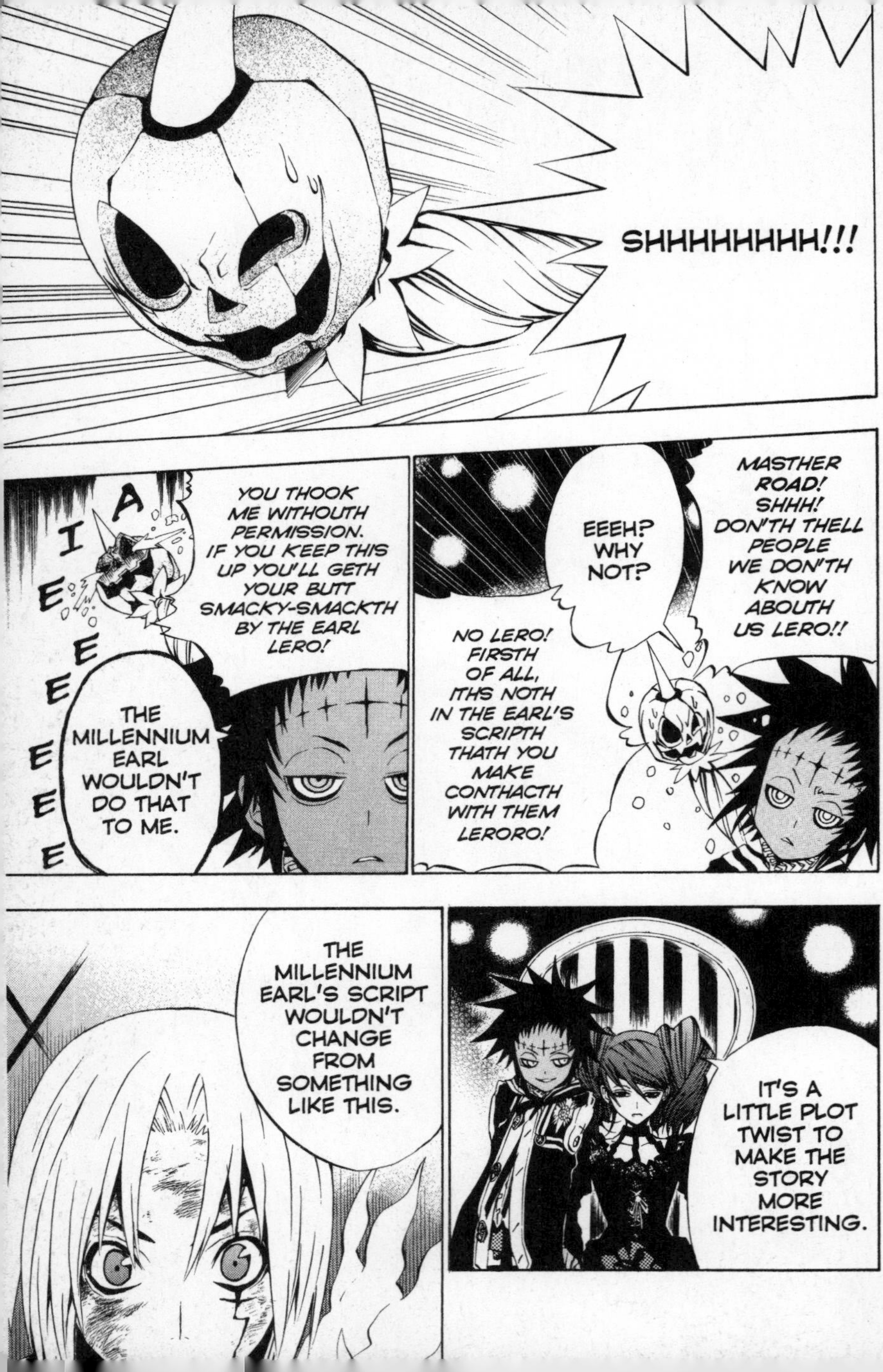
SHHHHHHHH!!!
MASTHER ROAD! SHHH! DON'TH THELL PEOPLE WE DON'TH KNOW ABOUTH US LERO!!
EEEH? WHY NOT?
NO LERO! FIRSTH OF ALL, ITHS NOTH IN THE EARL'S SCRIPTH THATH YOU MAKE CONTHACTH WITH THEM LERORO!
YOU THOOK ME WITHOUTH PERMISSION. IF YOU KEEP THIS UP YOU'LL GETH YOUR BUTT SMACKY-SMACKTH BY THE EARL LERO!
AIEEEEEE
THE MILLENNIUM EARL WOULDN'T DO THAT TO ME.
IT'S A LITTLE PLOT TWIST TO MAKE THE STORY MORE INTERESTING.
THE MILLENNIUM EARL'S SCRIPT WOULDN'T CHANGE FROM SOMETHING LIKE THIS.

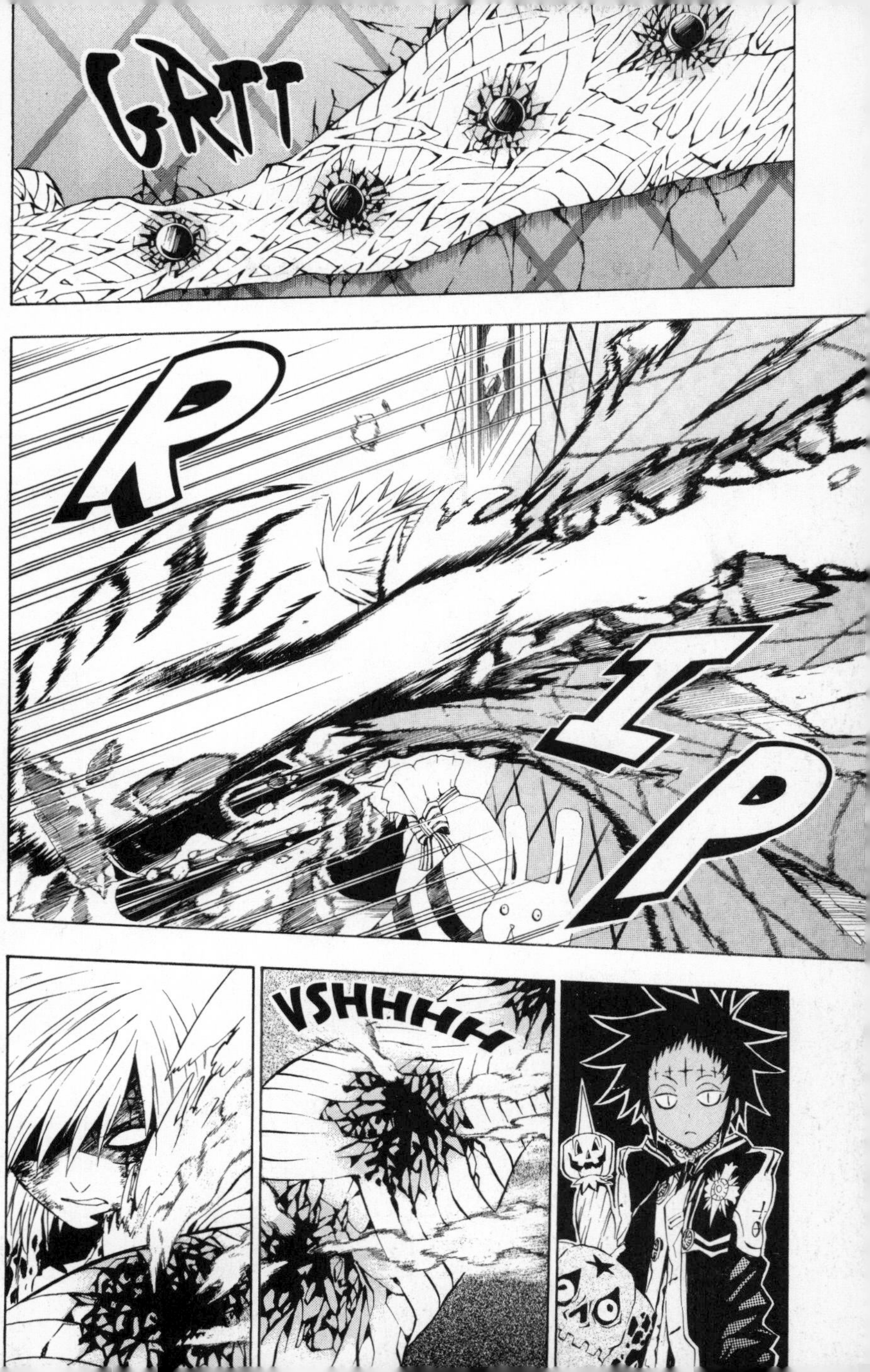
GRTT
RIP
VSHHHH

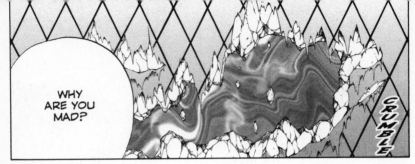

WHY ARE YOU MAD?

CRUMBLE

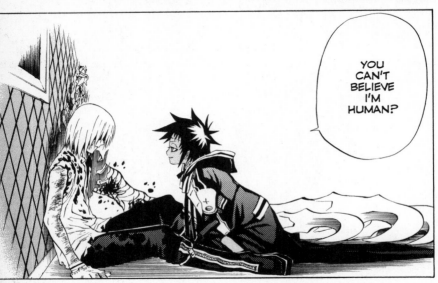

YOU CAN'T BELIEVE I'M HUMAN?

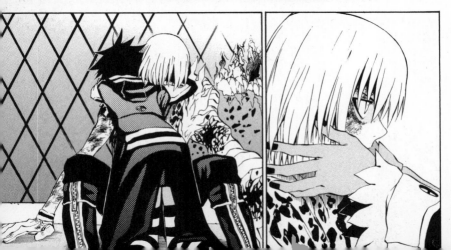

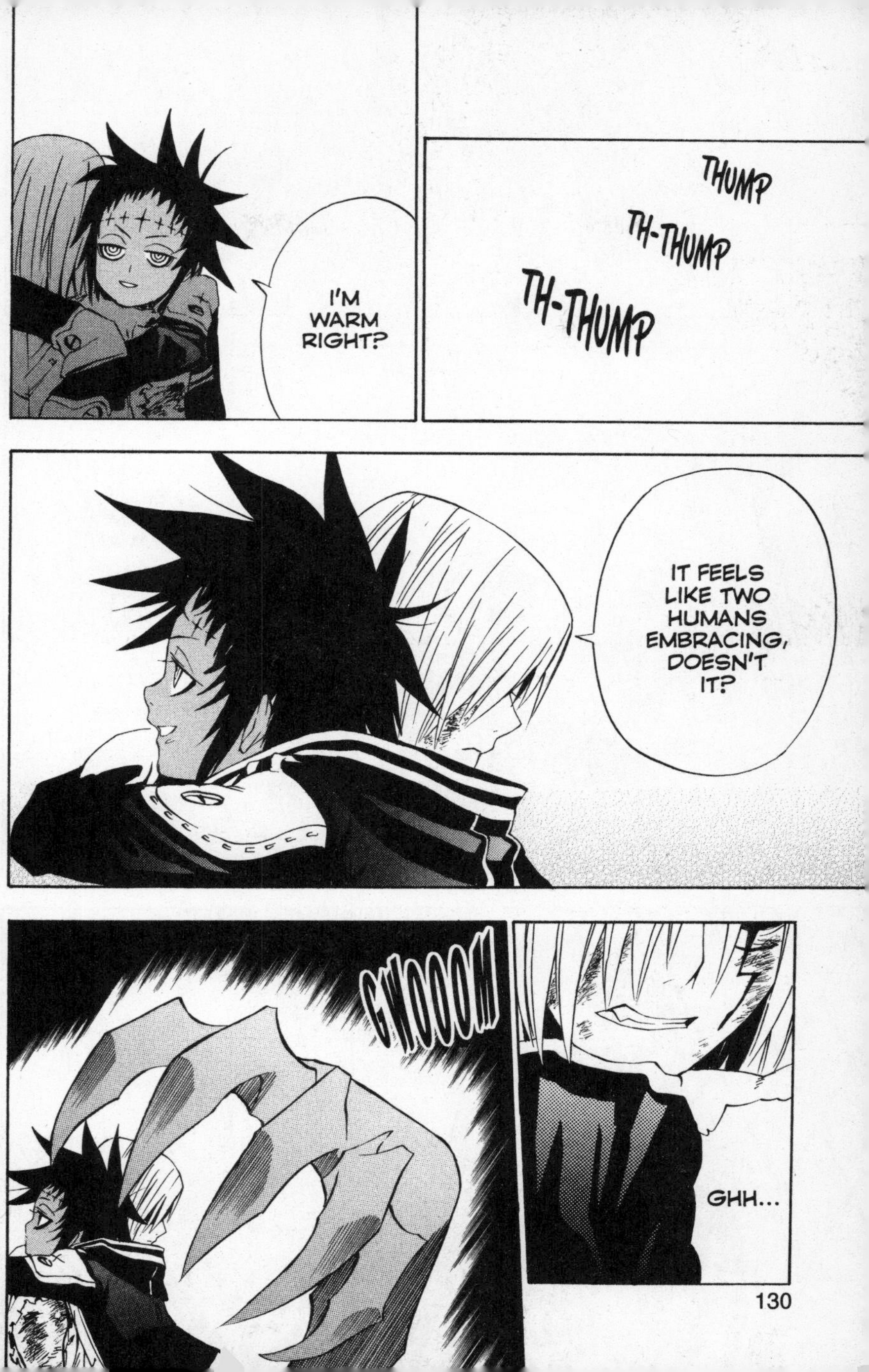
THUMP
TH-THUMP
TH-THUMP
I'M WARM RIGHT?
IT FEELS LIKE TWO HUMANS EMBRACING, DOESN'T IT?
GHH...
GWOOOM

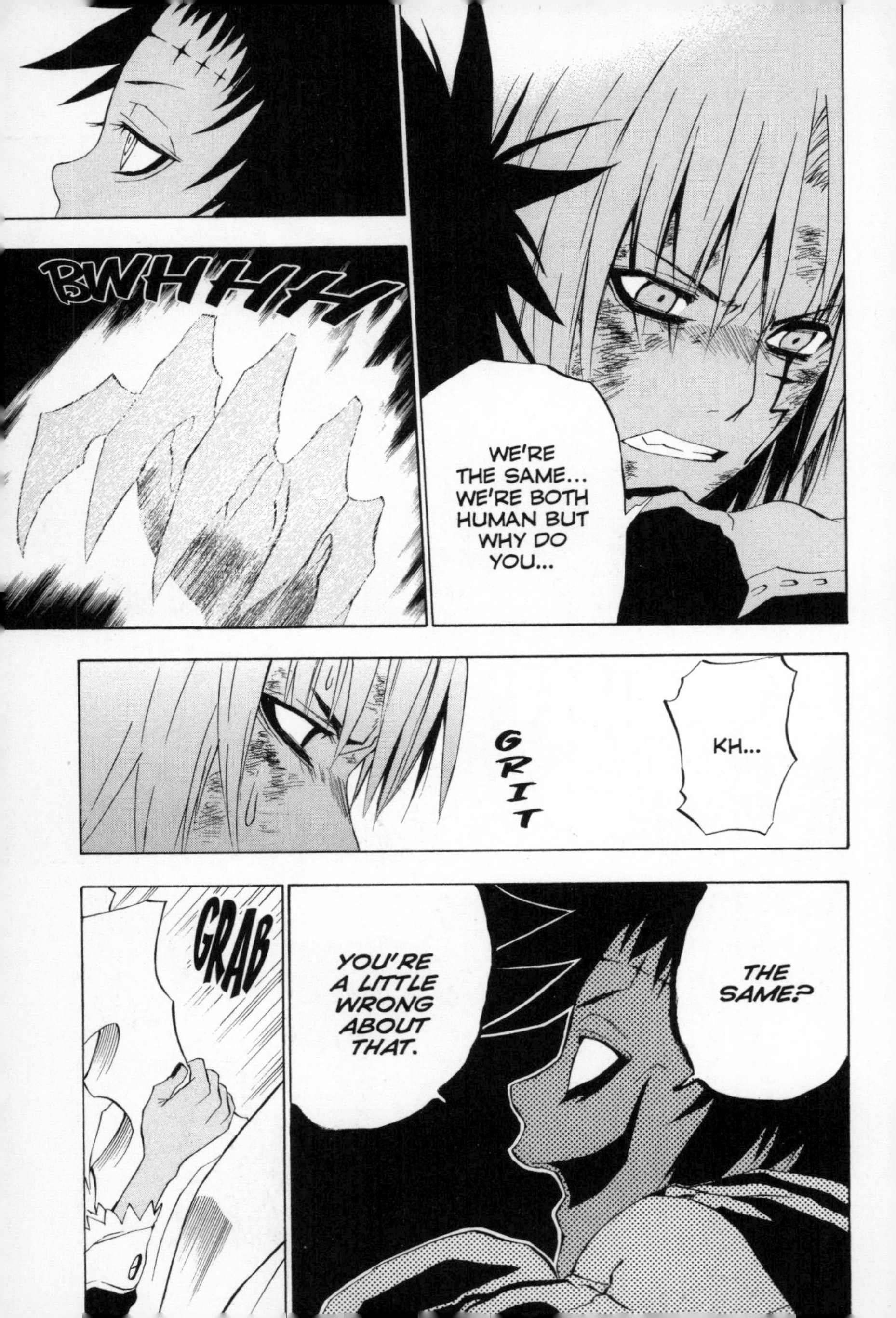
WE'RE THE SAME... WE'RE BOTH HUMAN BUT WHY DO YOU...
BWHHH
KH...
GRIT
THE SAME?
YOU'RE A LITTLE WRONG ABOUT THAT.
GRAB

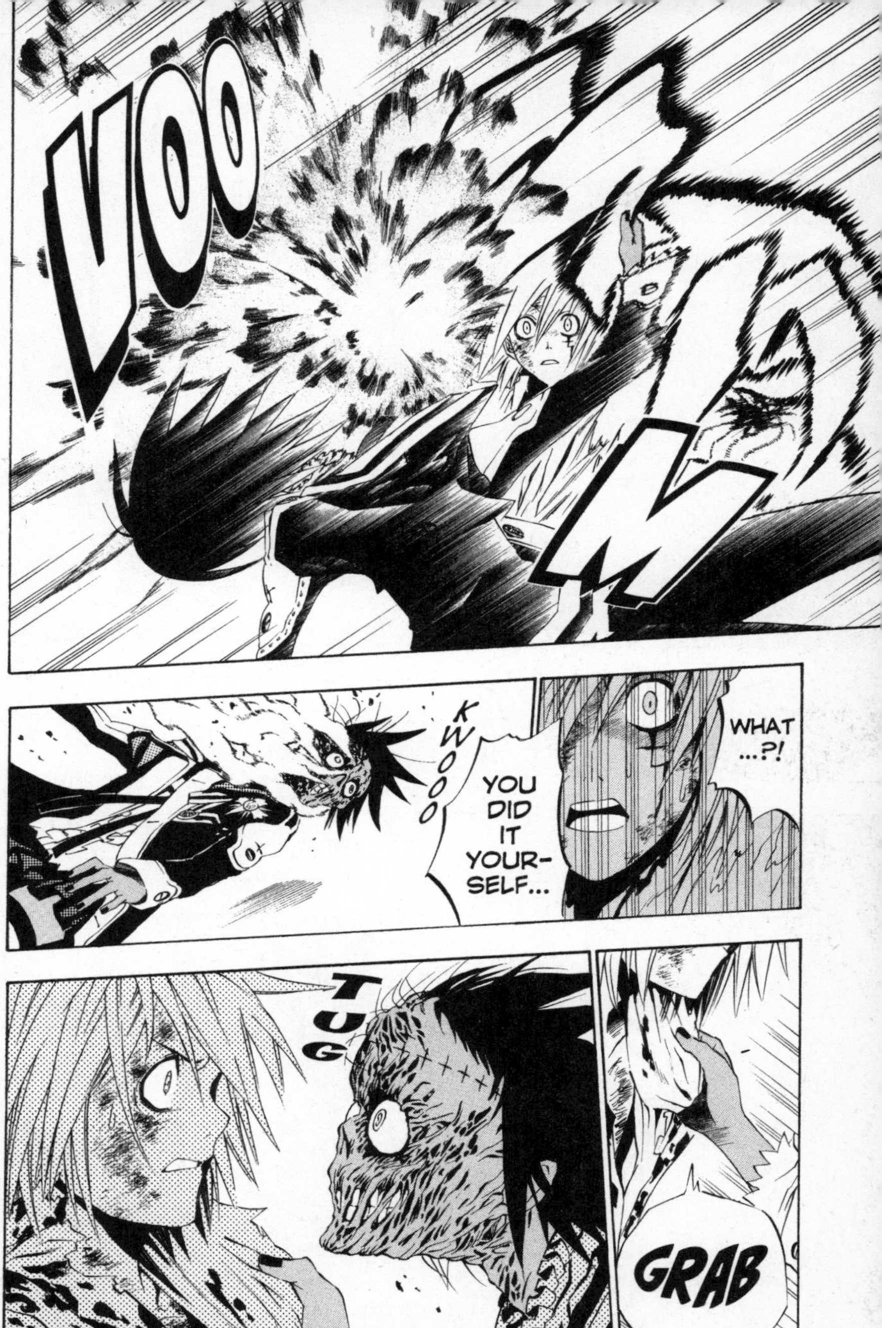
VOOM
WHAT ...?!
KWOOOO
YOU DID IT YOURSELF...
GRAB
TUG

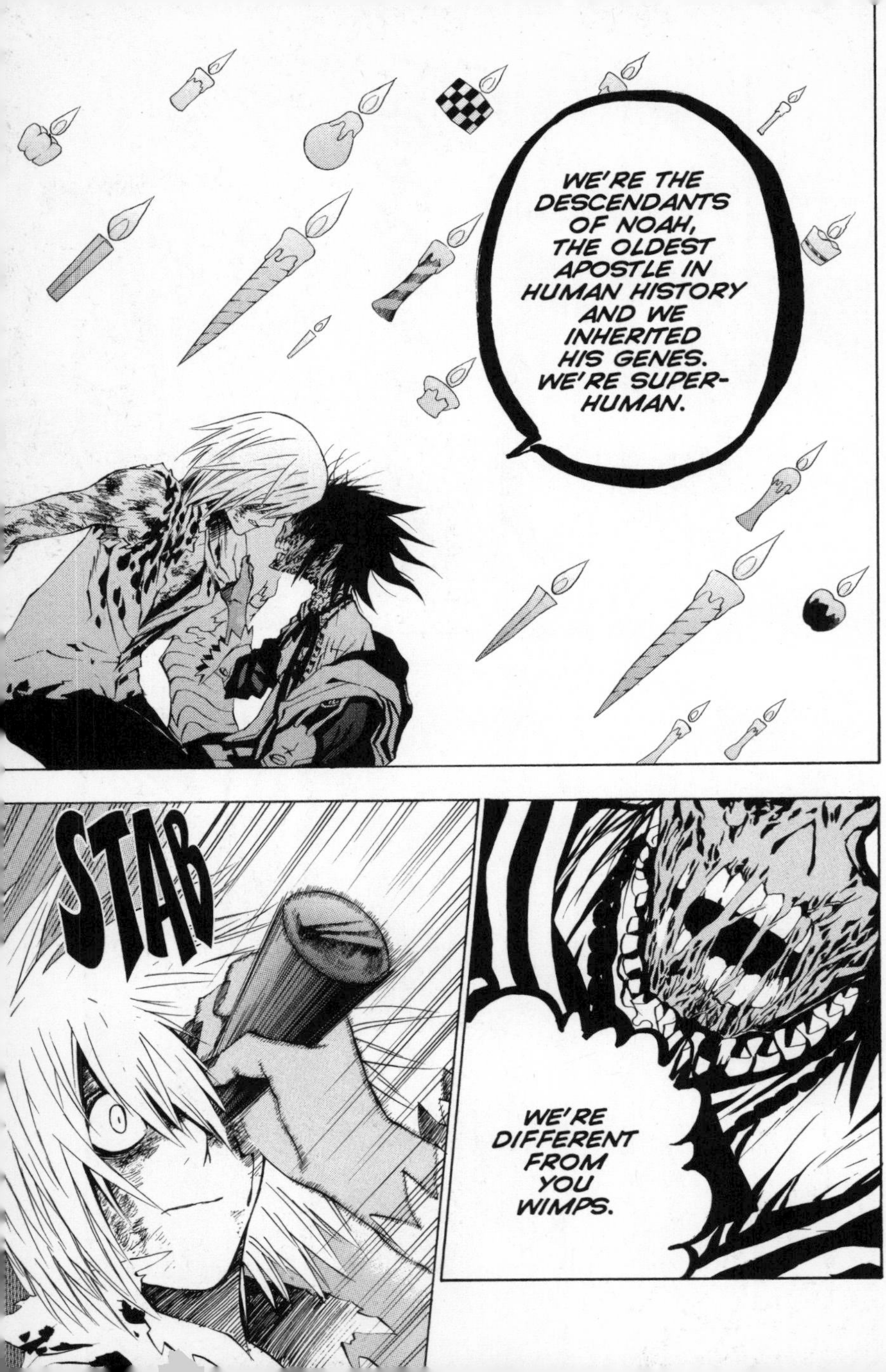
WE'RE THE DESCENDANTS OF NOAH, THE OLDEST APOSTLE IN HUMAN HISTORY AND WE INHERITED HIS GENES. WE'RE SUPER-HUMAN.
WE'RE DIFFERENT FROM YOU WIMPS.
STAB

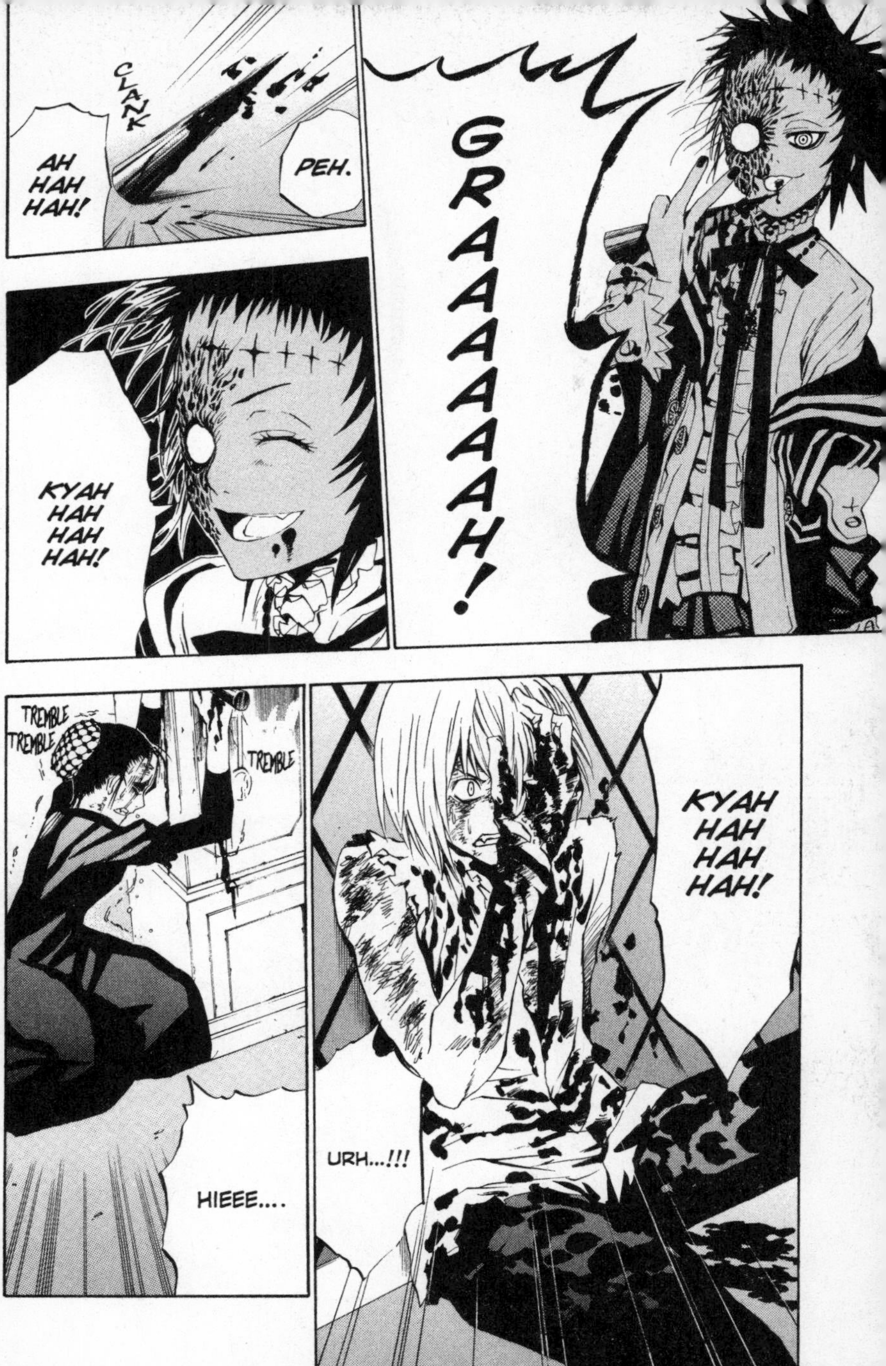
GRAAAAAAH!
CLANK
PEH.
AH HAH HAH!
KYAH HAH HAH HAH!
KYAH HAH HAH HAH!
URH...!!!
TREMBLE TREMBLE
TREMBLE
HIEEE....

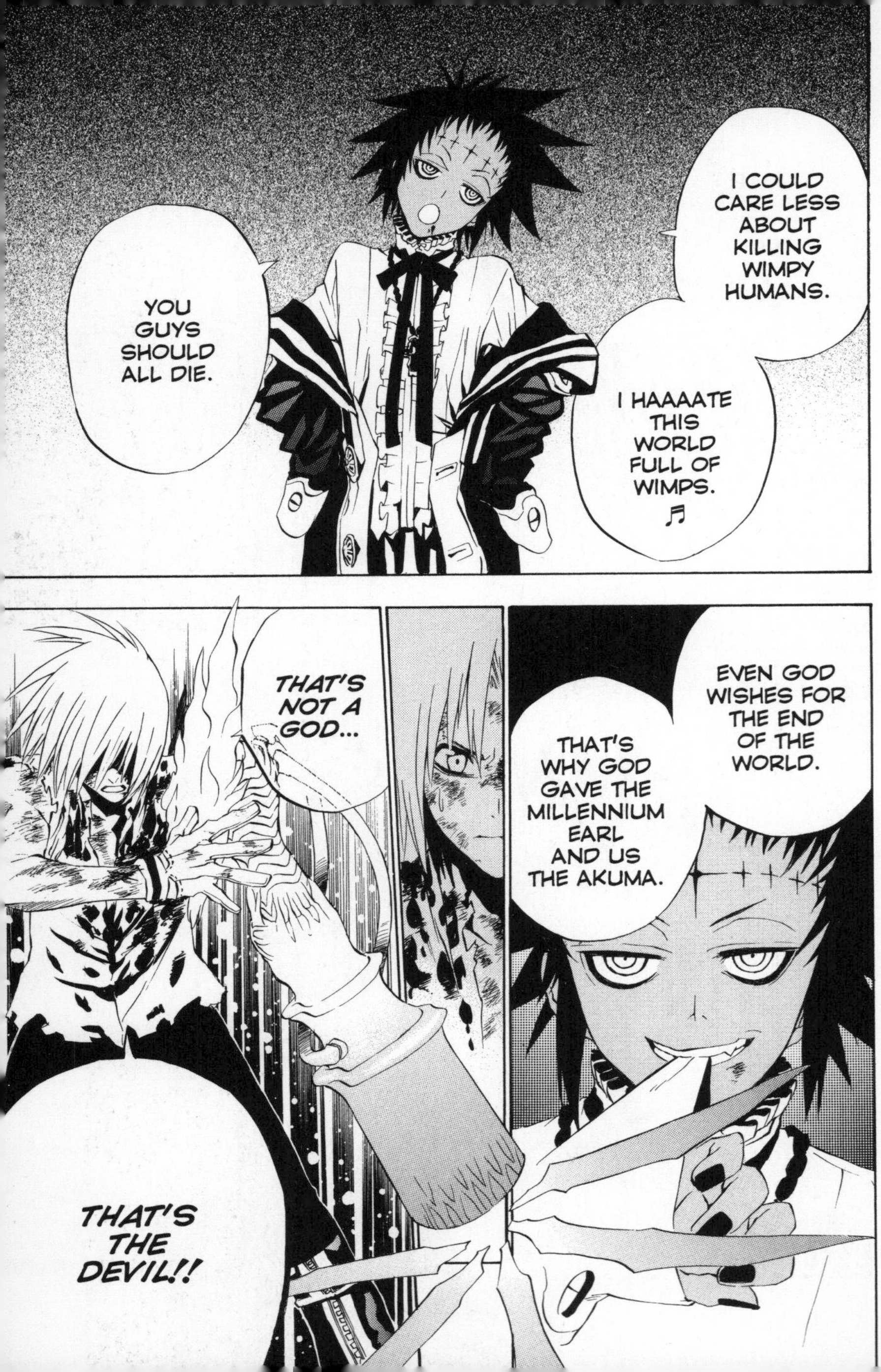
I COULD CARE LESS ABOUT KILLING WIMPY HUMANS.
I HAAAATE THIS WORLD FULL OF WIMPS. ♬
YOU GUYS SHOULD ALL DIE.
EVEN GOD WISHES FOR THE END OF THE WORLD.
THAT'S WHY GOD GAVE THE MILLENNIUM EARL AND US THE AKUMA.
THAT'S NOT A GOD...
THAT'S THE DEVIL!!

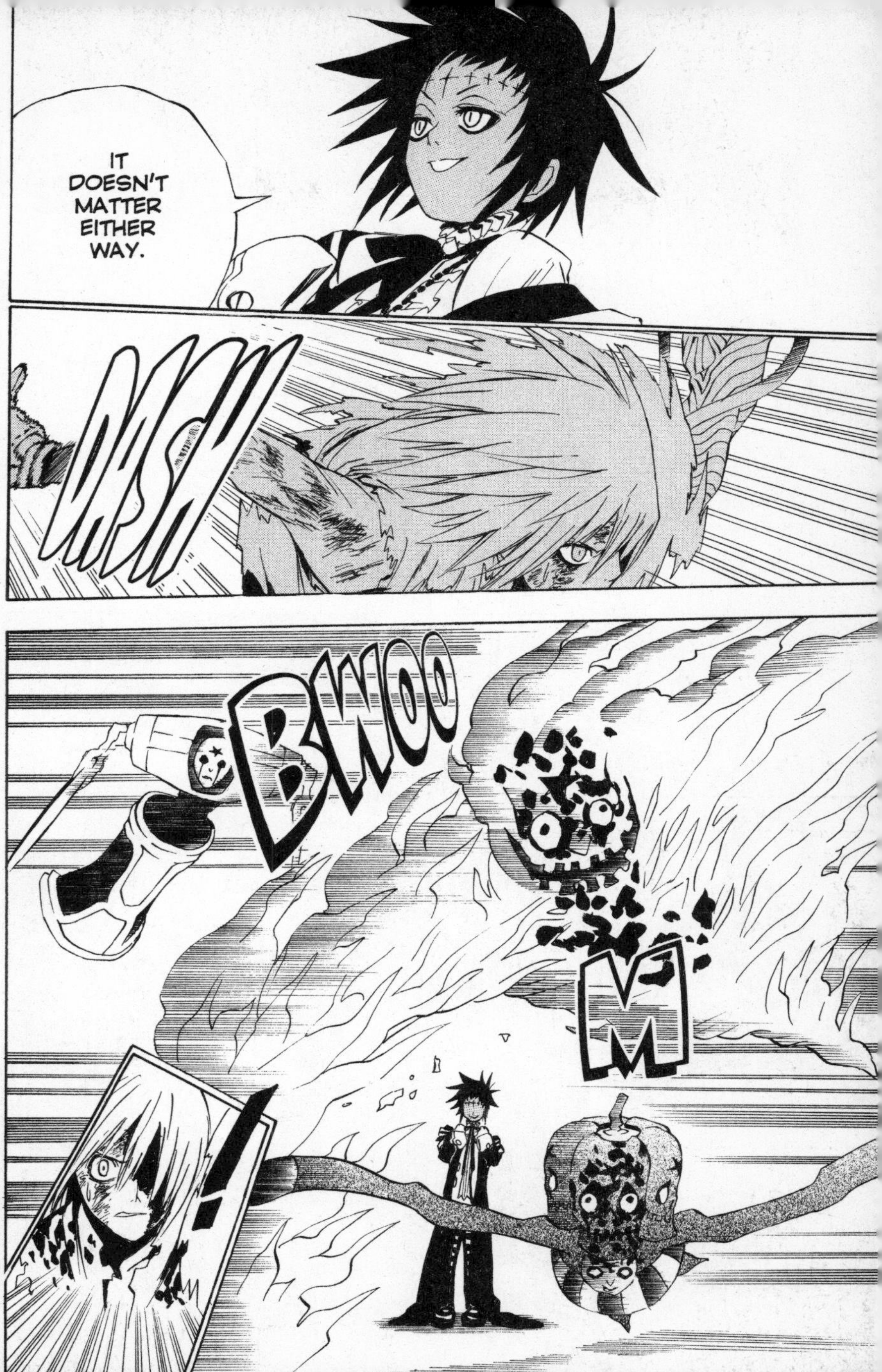
IT DOESN'T MATTER EITHER WAY.
DASH
BWOOM

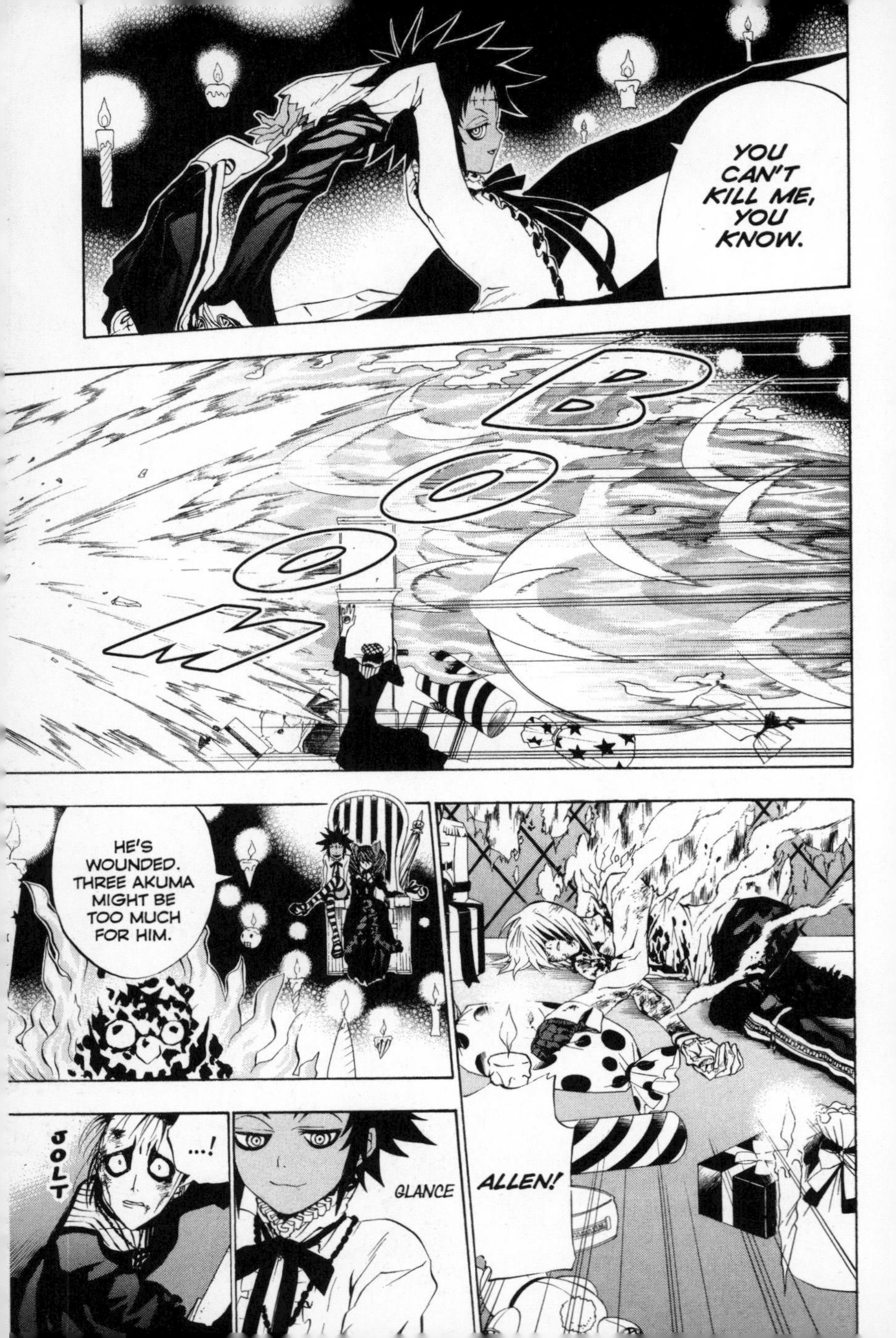
YOU CAN'T KILL ME, YOU KNOW.
BOOM
HE'S WOUNDED. THREE AKUMA MIGHT BE TOO MUCH FOR HIM.
ALLEN!
GLANCE
...!
JOLT

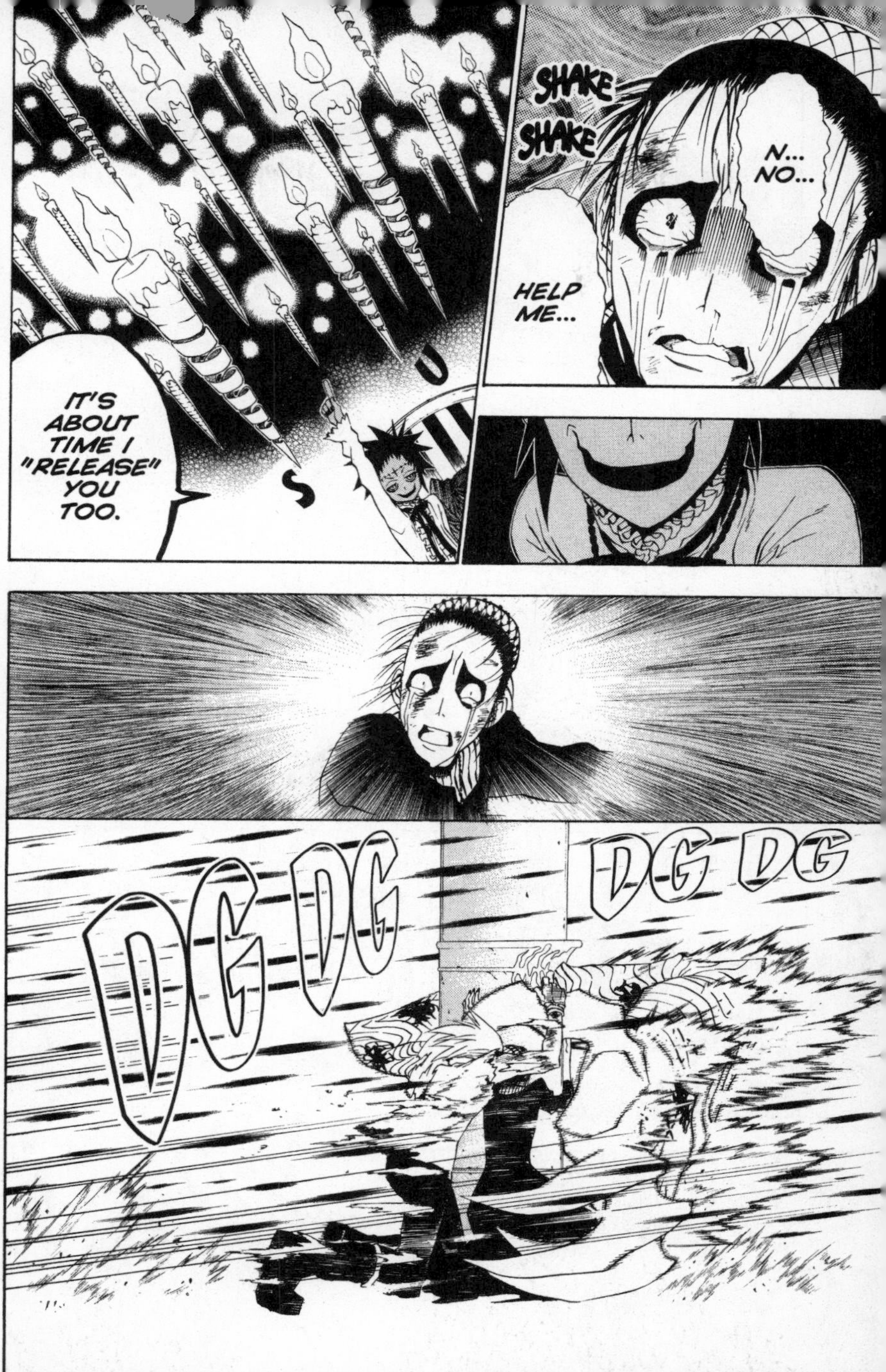
SHAKE
SHAKE
N... NO...
HELP ME...
IT'S ABOUT TIME I "RELEASE" YOU TOO.
DG DG
DG DG

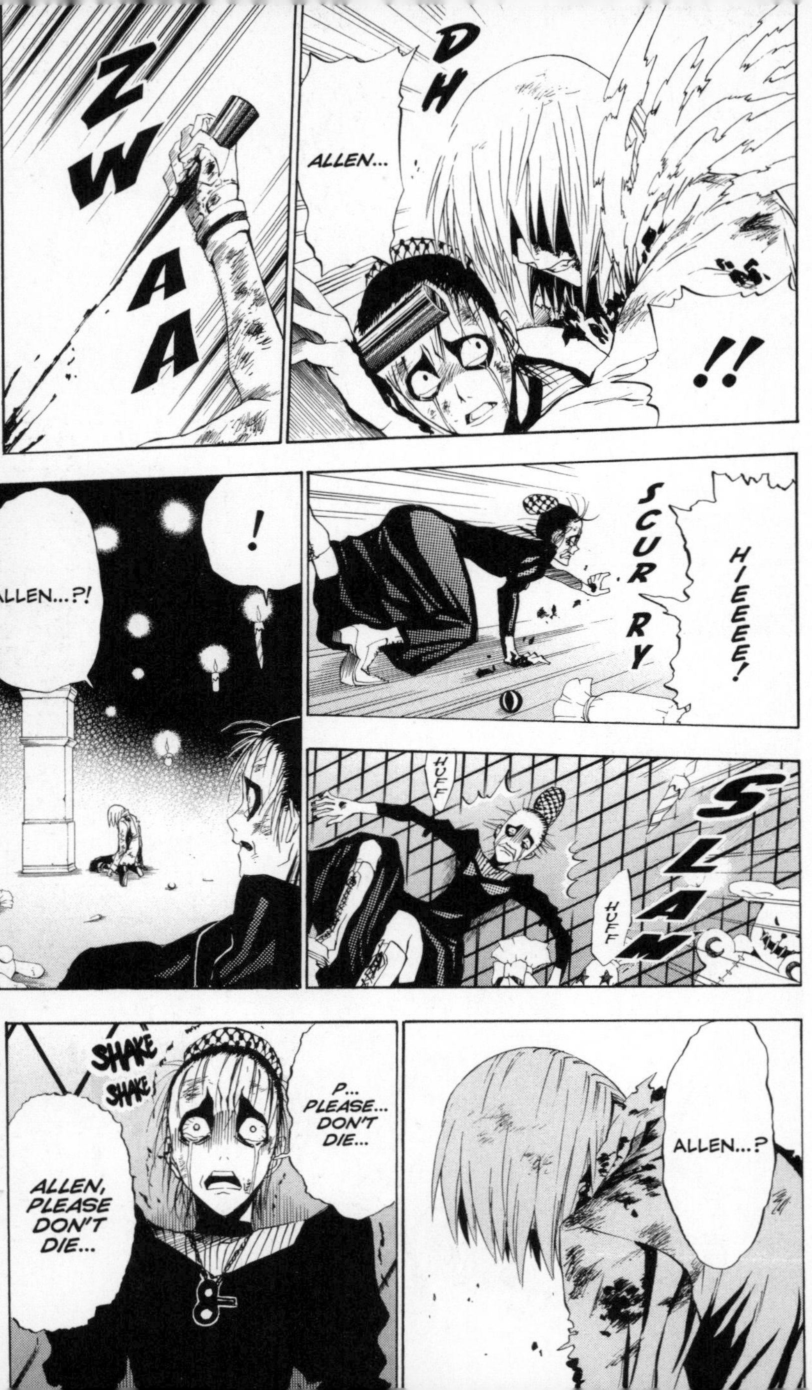
DH
ALLEN...
!!
ZWAA
HIEEEE!
SCURRY
SLAM
HUFF
HUFF
!
ALLEN...?!
ALLEN...?
SHAKE
SHAKE
P... PLEASE... DON'T DIE...
ALLEN, PLEASE DON'T DIE...

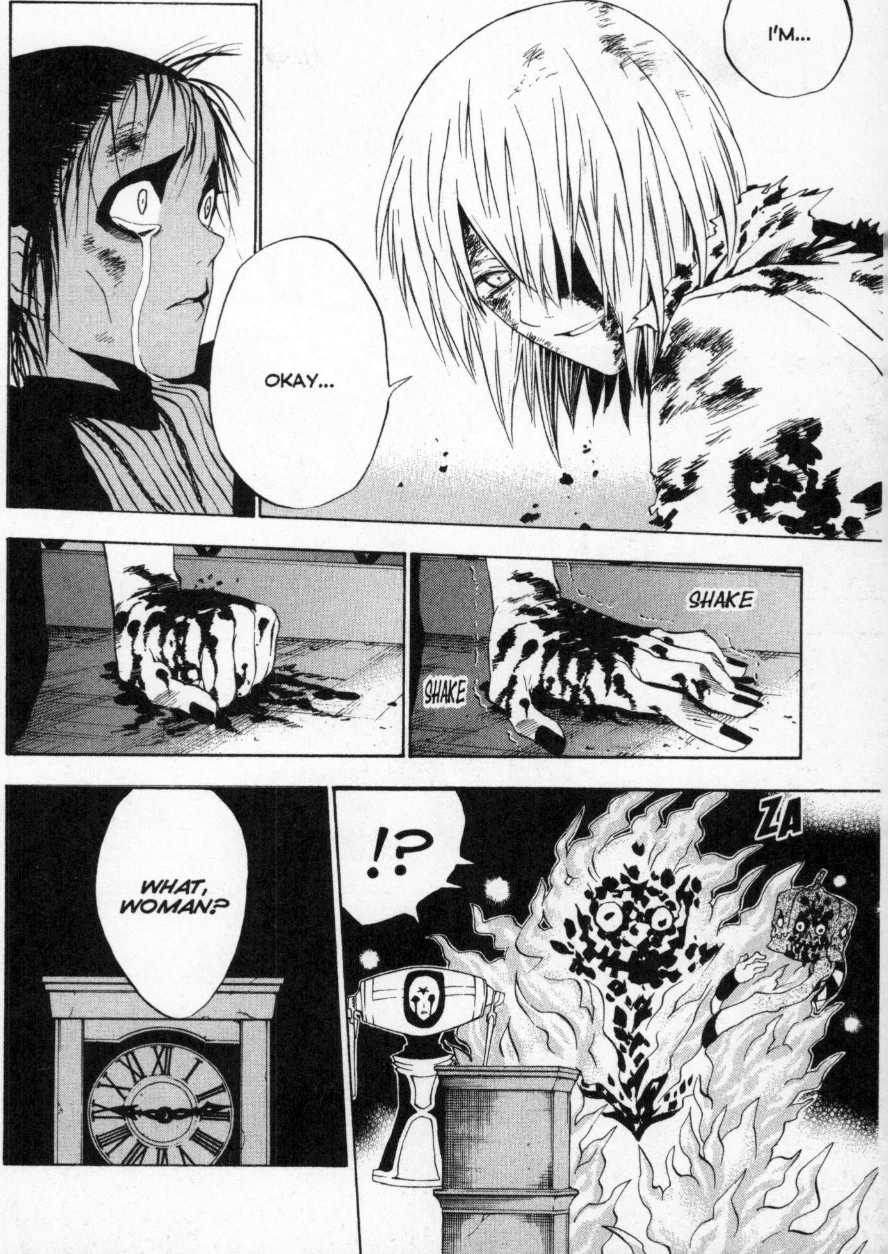
I'M...
OKAY...
SHAKE
SHAKE
!?
ZA
WHAT, WOMAN?

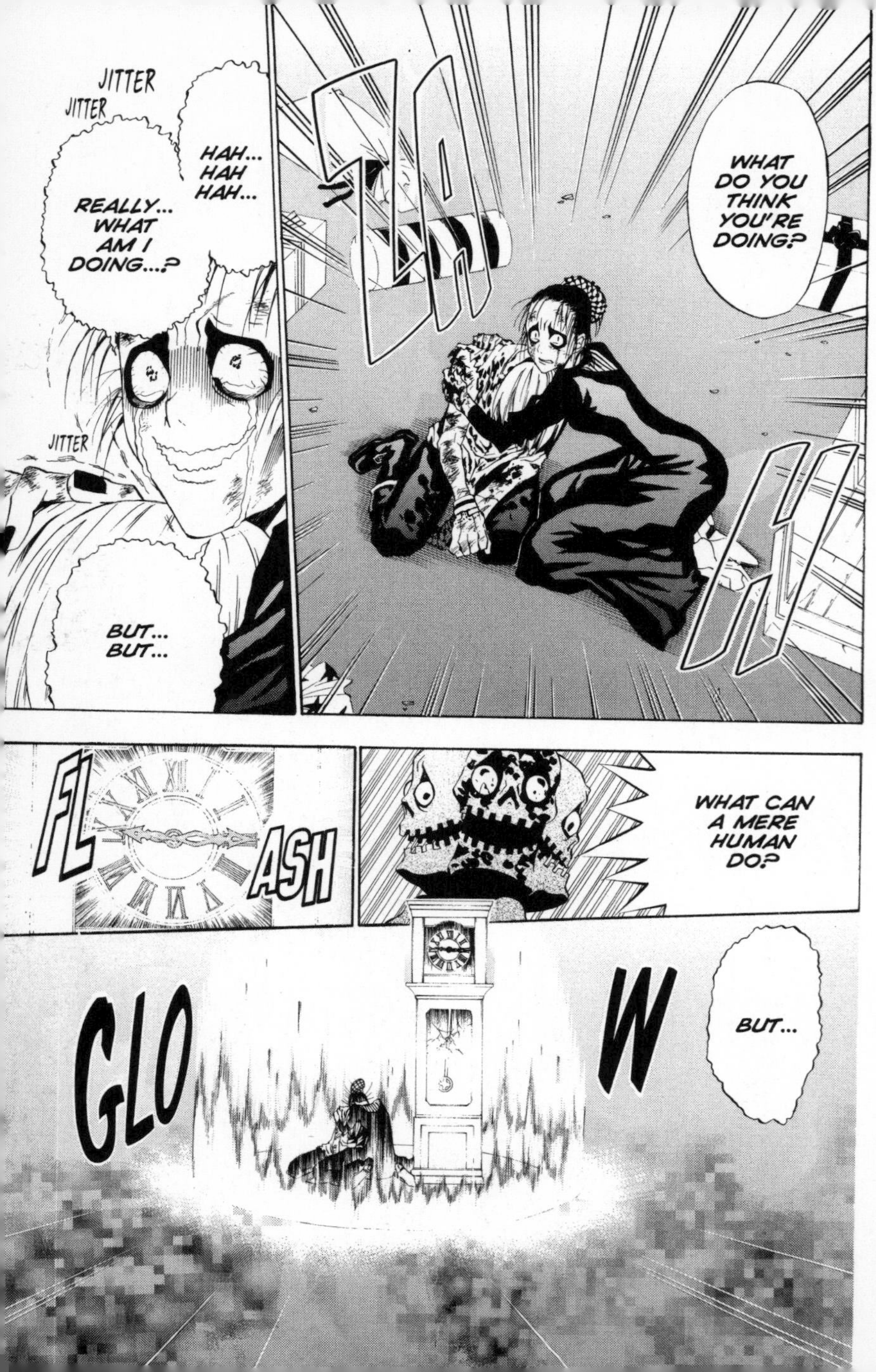
ZA
WHAT DO YOU THINK YOU'RE DOING?
JITTER
JITTER
HAH... HAH HAH...
REALLY... WHAT AM I DOING...?
JITTER
BUT... BUT...
WHAT CAN A MERE HUMAN DO?
FLASH
GLOW
BUT...

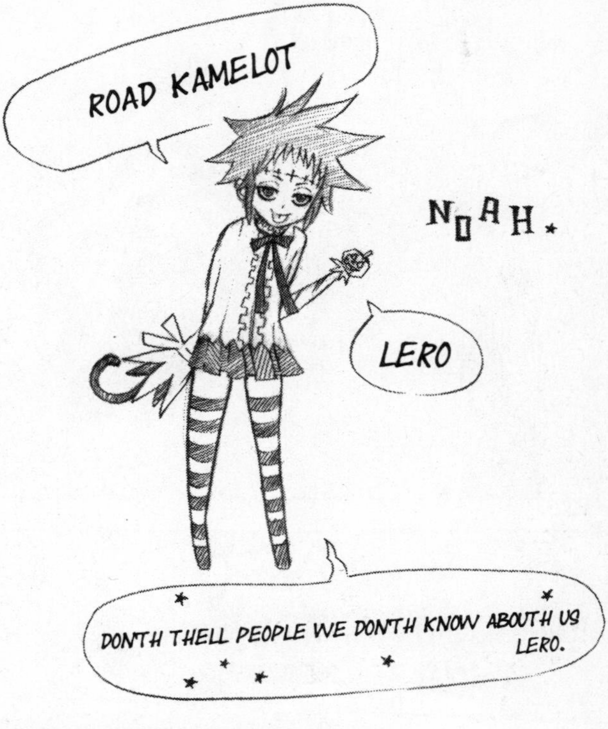
ROAD KAMELOT
NOAH.
LERO
DONTH THELL PEOPLE WE DONTH KNOW ABOUTH US LERO.

MY PROFILE DETAILS ARE STILL A SECRET.

THE QUESTION I GOT THE MOST ABOUT ROAD WAS IF SHE IS A BOY OR A GIRL. SHE'S A FEMALE, A GIRL. HER FAVORITE THINGS ARE CANDY AND THE EARL. SHE HATES HUMANS. SHE LIKES TO BE MEAN TO THE AKUMA AND LIKES TO PLAY JOKES ON PEOPLE, ESPECIALLY THE EARL. SHE TAKES LERO ALL THE TIME WHILE THE EARL TAKES A NAP.

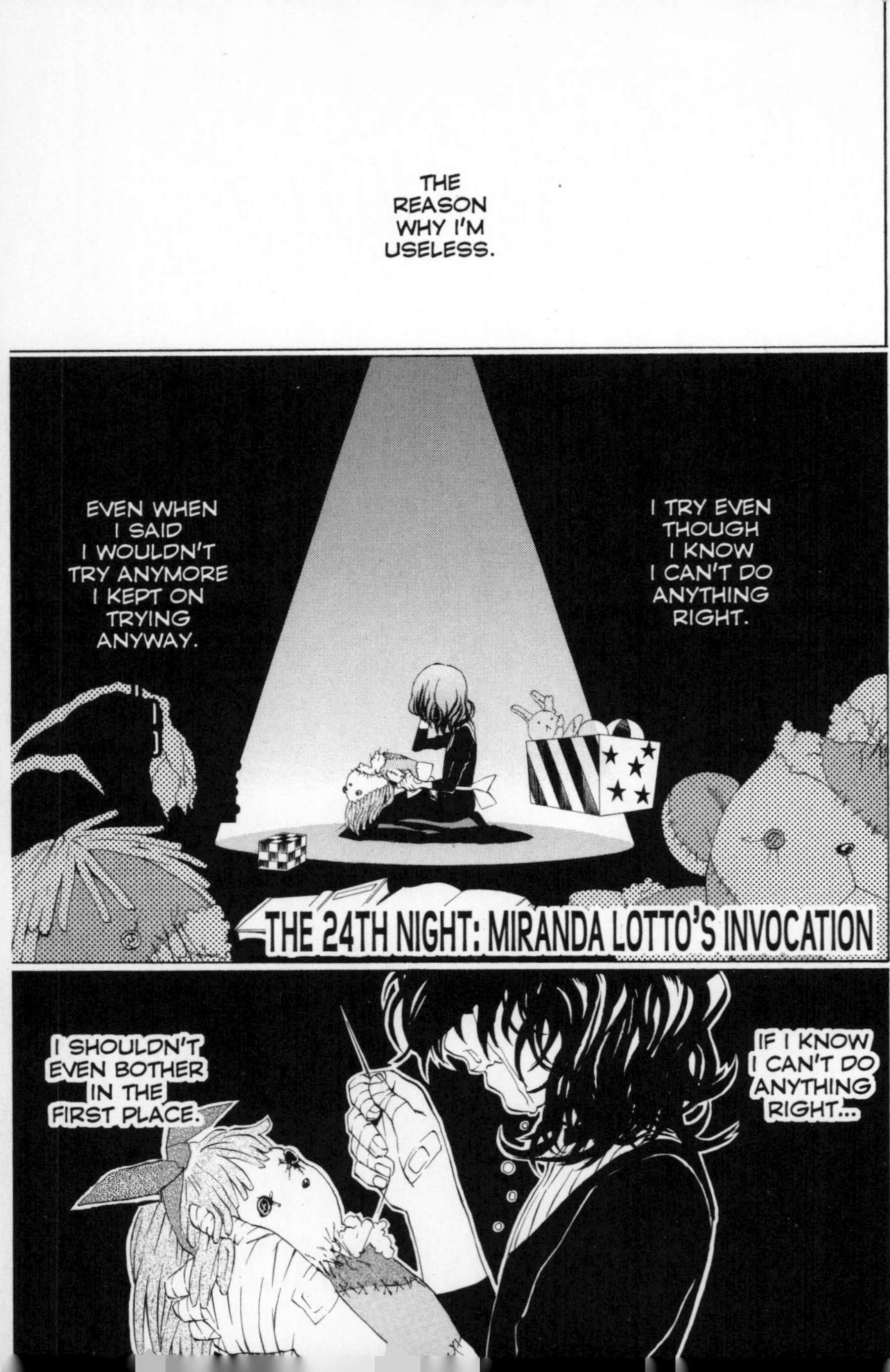
THE REASON WHY I'M USELESS.
I TRY EVEN THOUGH I KNOW I CAN'T DO ANYTHING RIGHT.
EVEN WHEN I SAID I WOULDN'T TRY ANYMORE I KEPT ON TRYING ANYWAY.
THE 24TH NIGHT: MIRANDA LOTTO'S INVOCATION
IF I KNOW I CAN'T DO ANYTHING RIGHT...
I SHOULDN'T EVEN BOTHER IN THE FIRST PLACE.

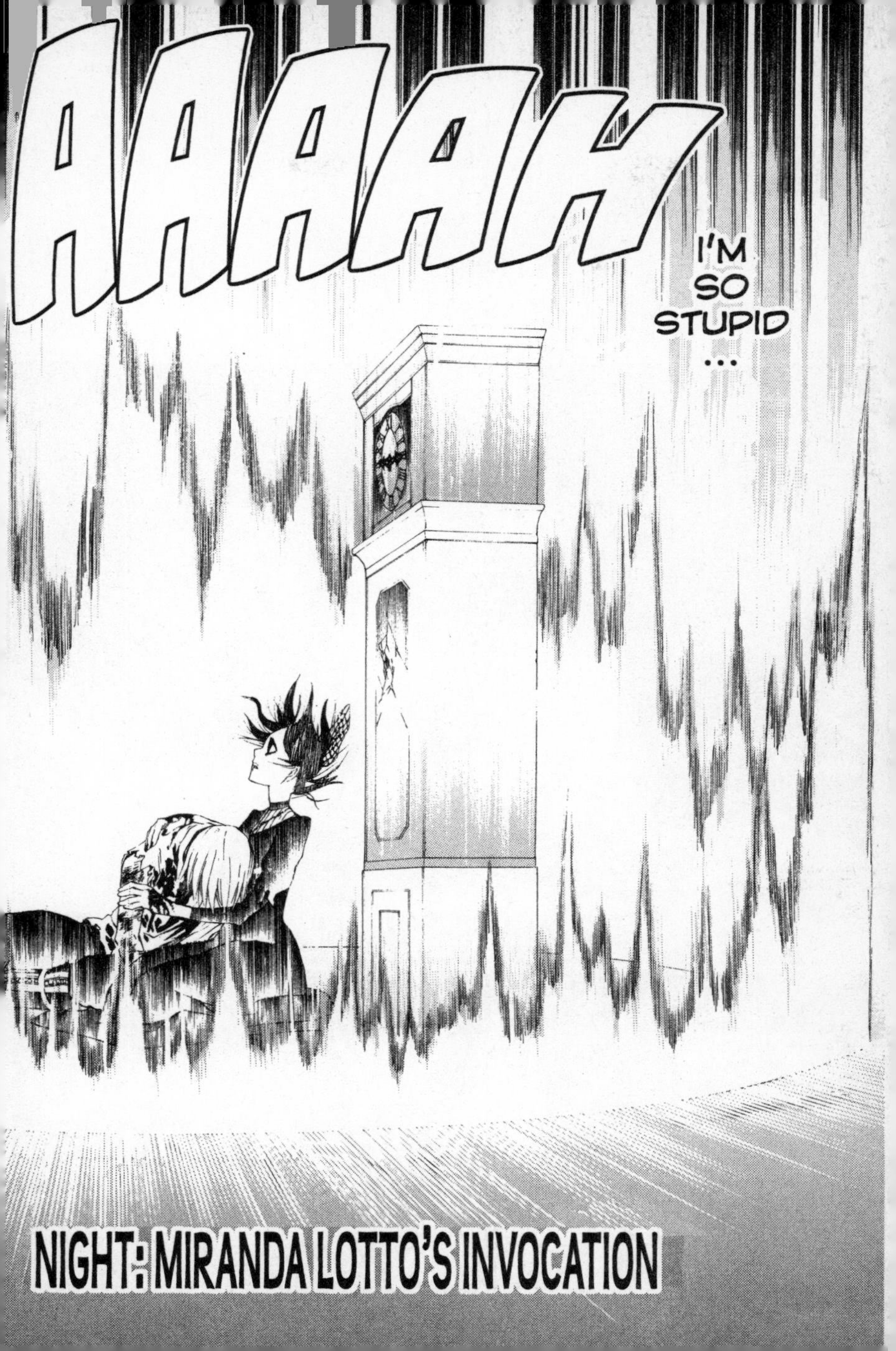
AAAAH
I'M SO STUPID ...
NIGHT: MIRANDA LOTTO'S INVOCATION

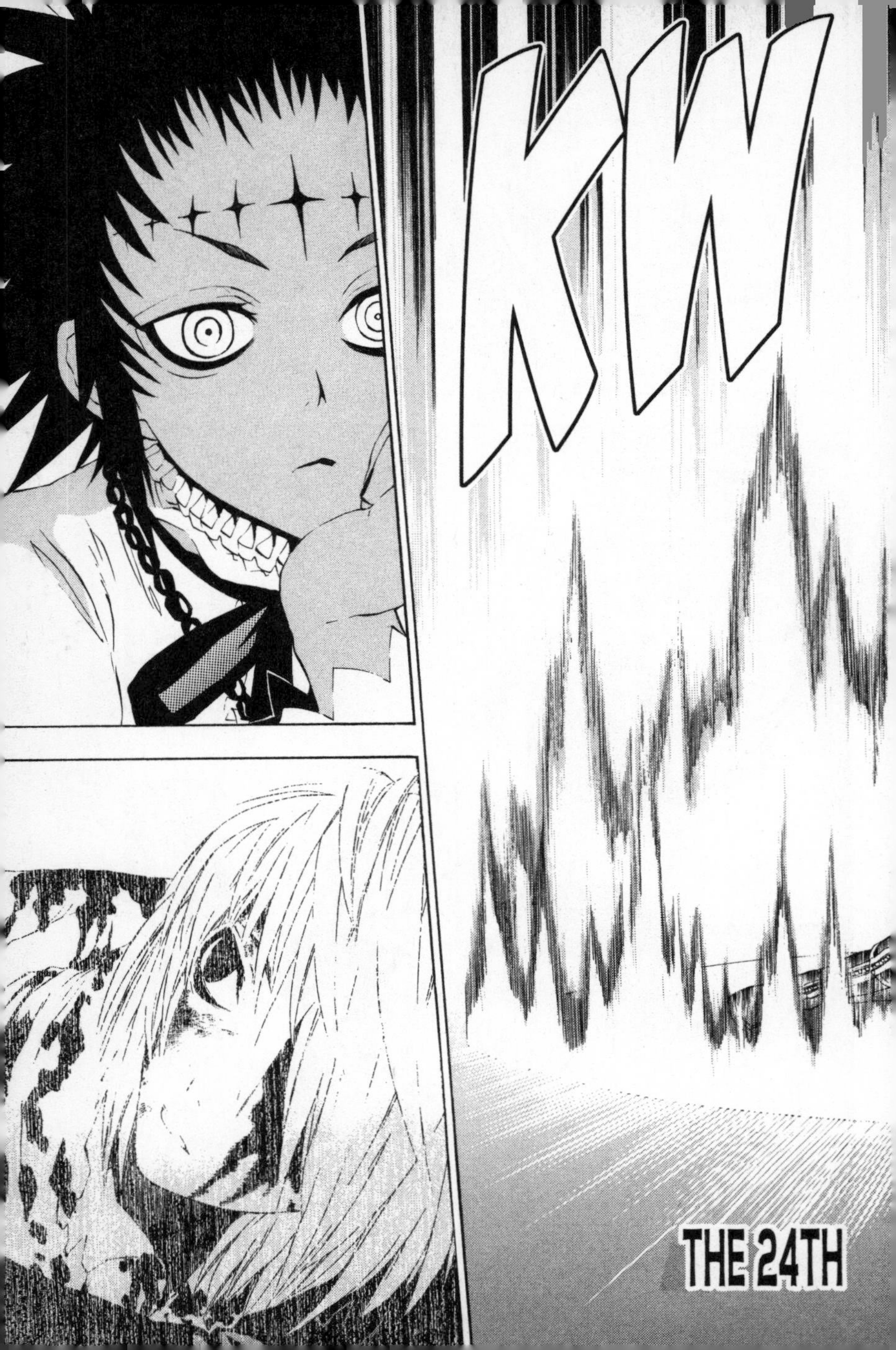
KIN
THE 24TH

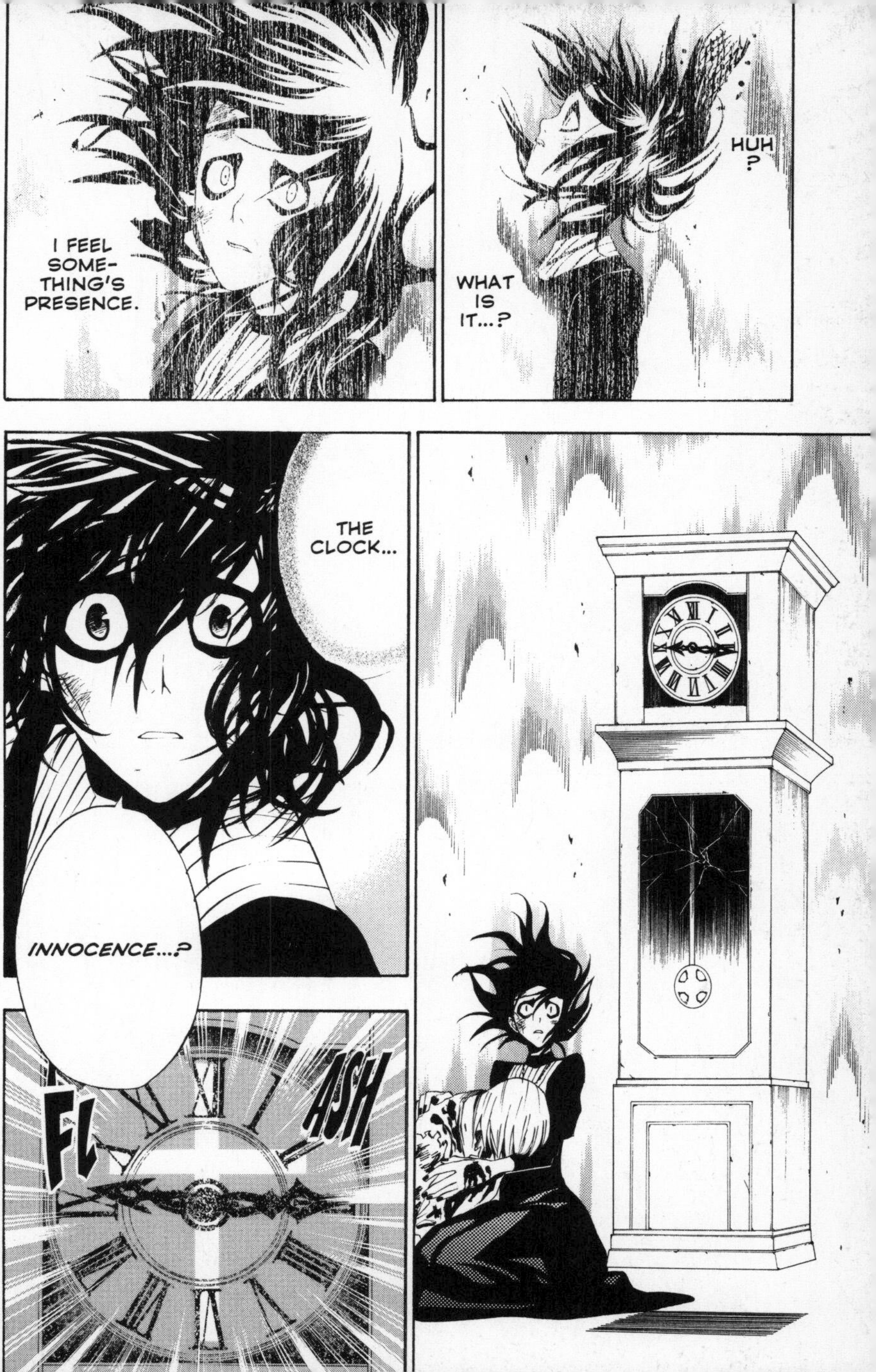
HUH?
WHAT IS IT...?
I FEEL SOMETHING'S PRESENCE.
THE CLOCK...
INNOCENCE...?
FLASH

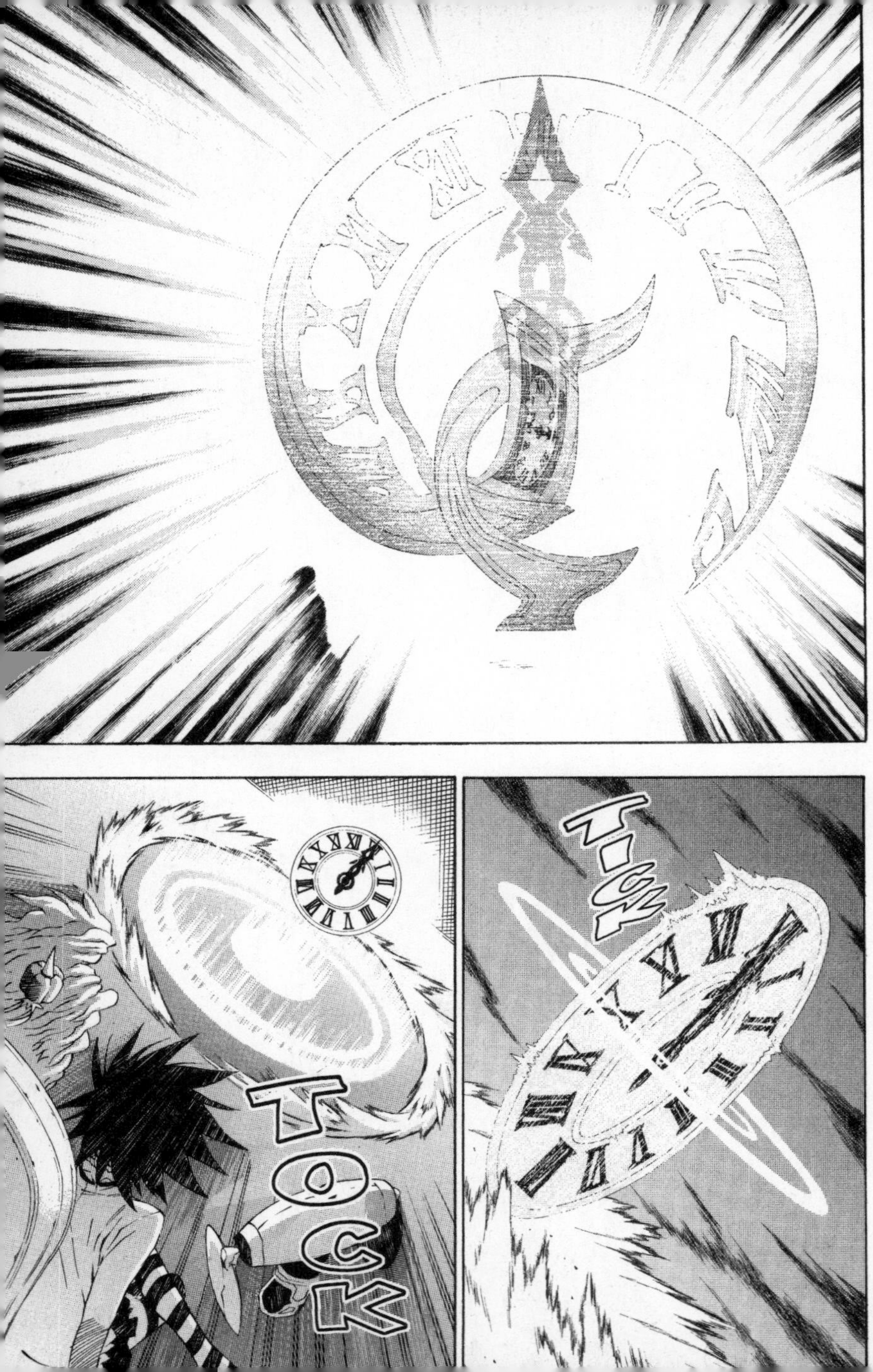
TICK
TOCK

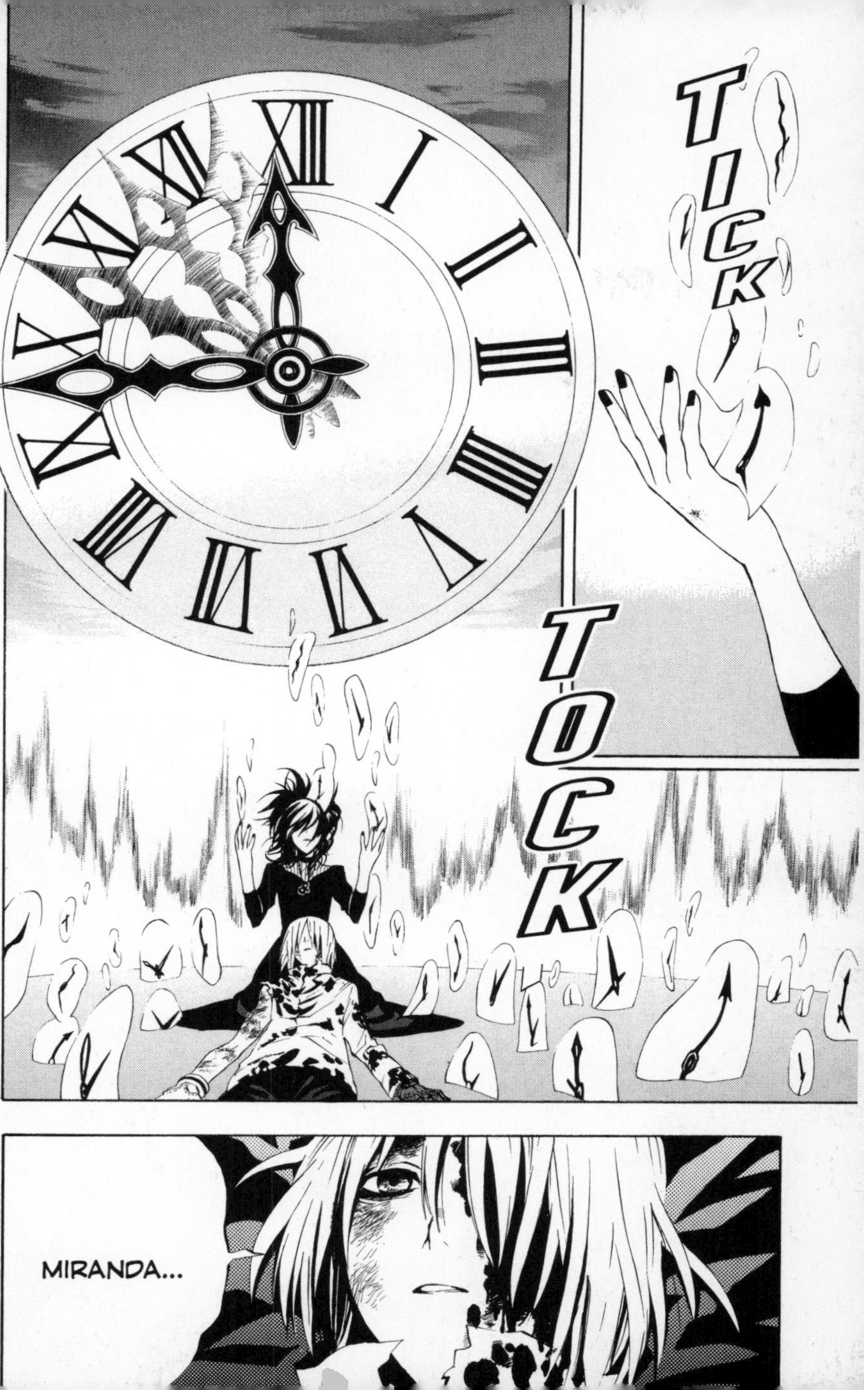
TICK
TOCK
MIRANDA...

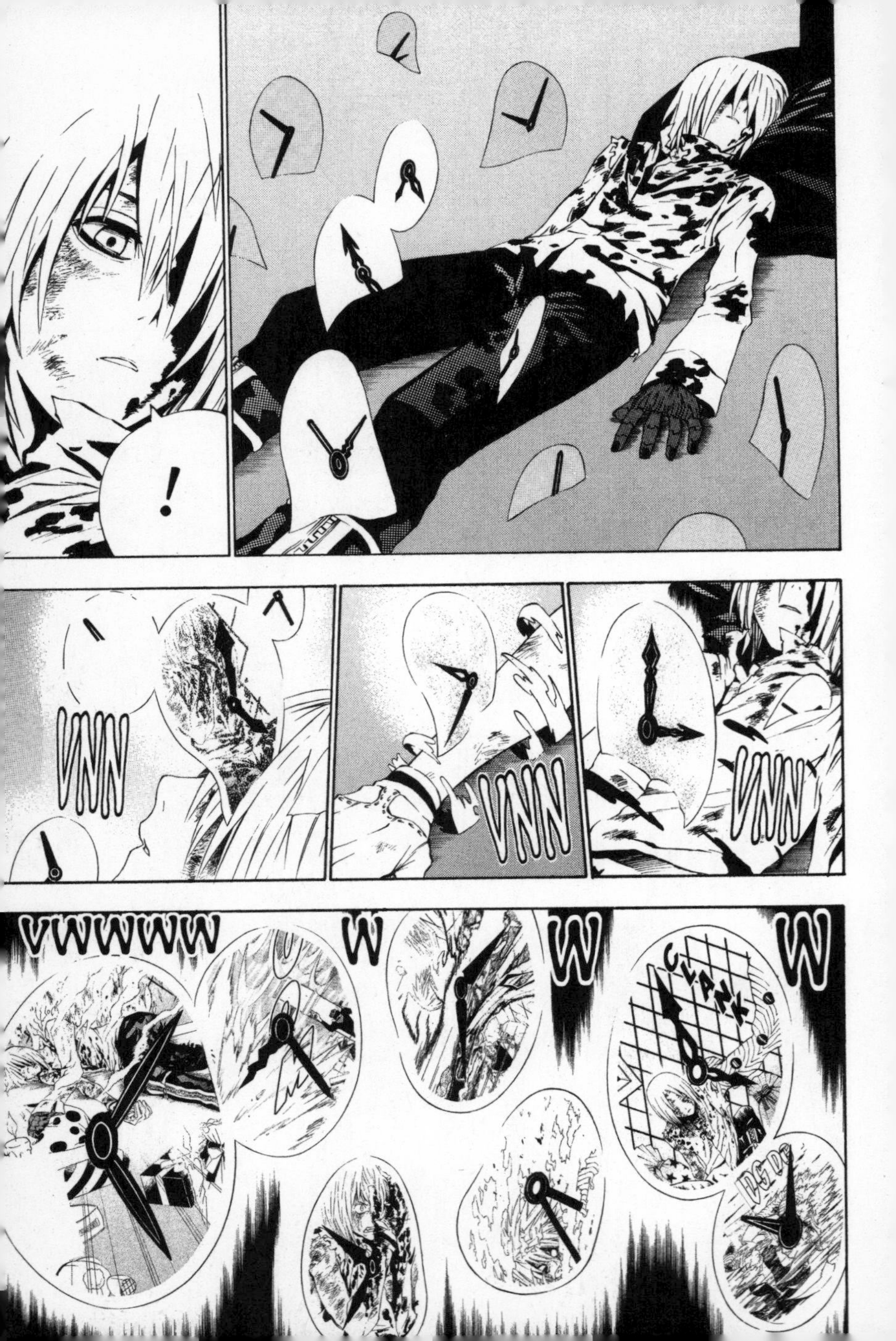
!
VNN
VNN
VNN
VWWWWW W W W
CLANK

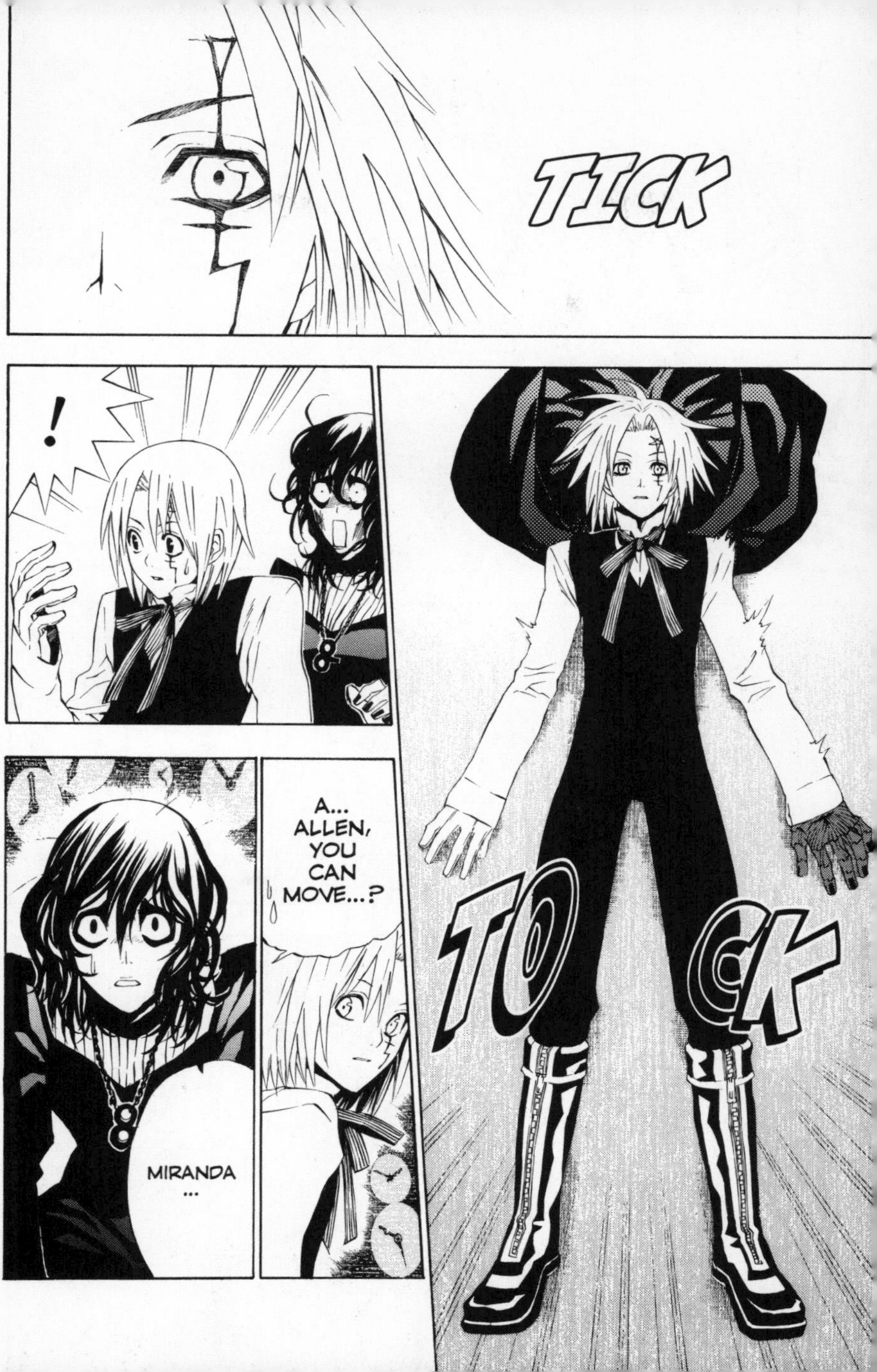
TICK
TOCK
!
A... ALLEN, YOU CAN MOVE...?
MIRANDA ...

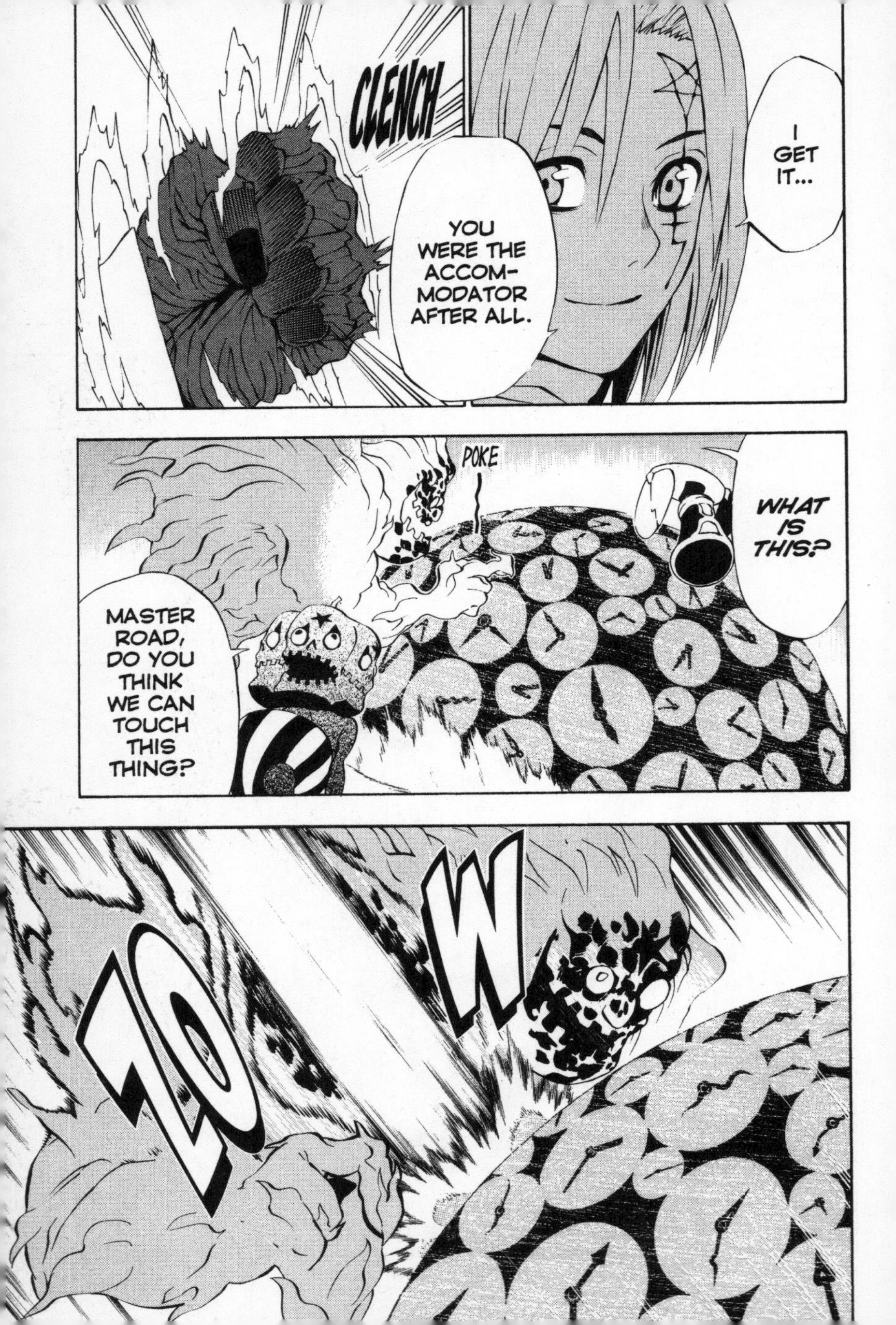
I GET IT...
YOU WERE THE ACCOM-MODATOR AFTER ALL.
CLENCH
WHAT IS THIS?
POKE
MASTER ROAD, DO YOU THINK WE CAN TOUCH THIS THING?
ZOOM

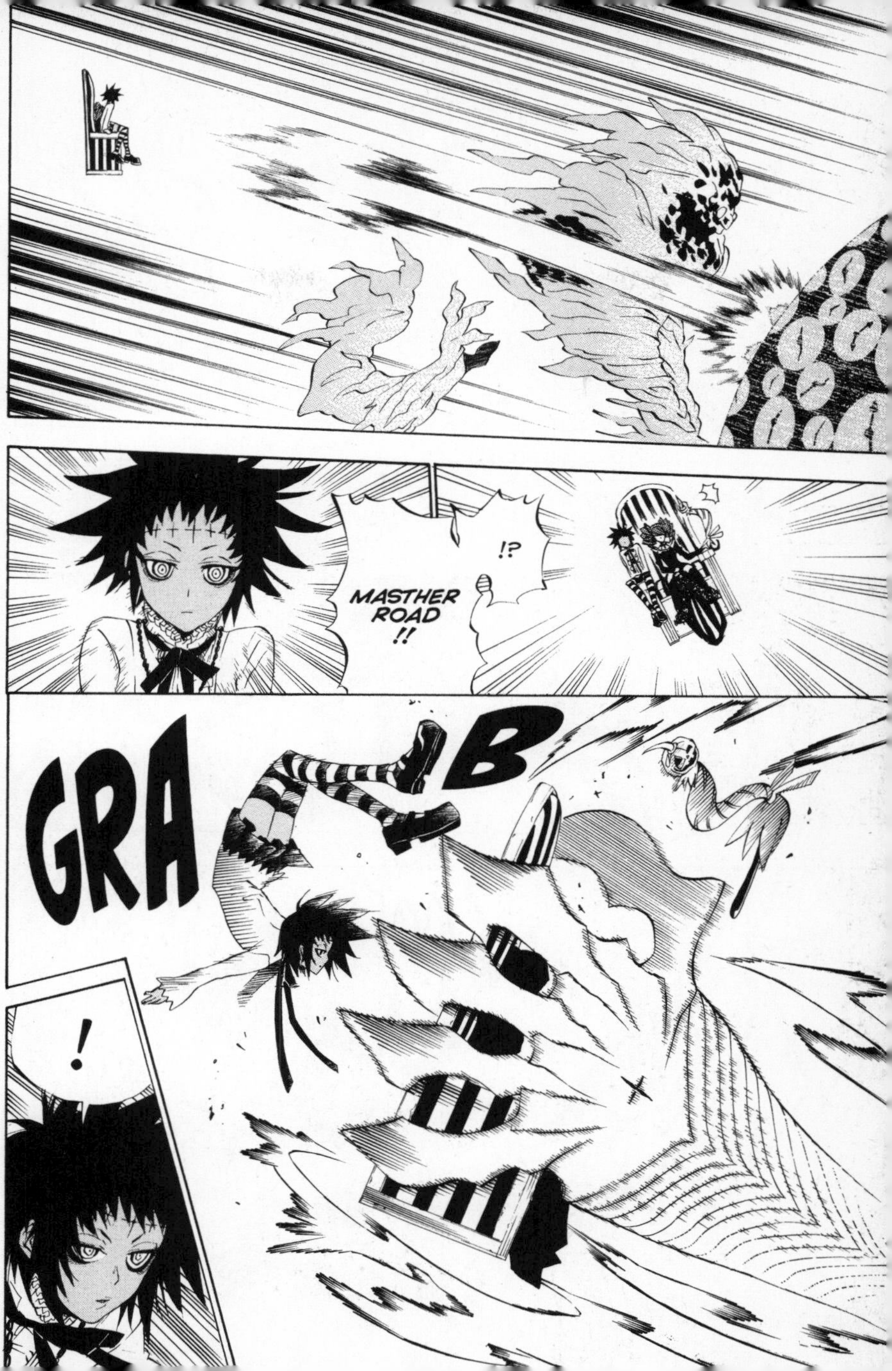
!?
MASTHER ROAD !!
GRAB
!

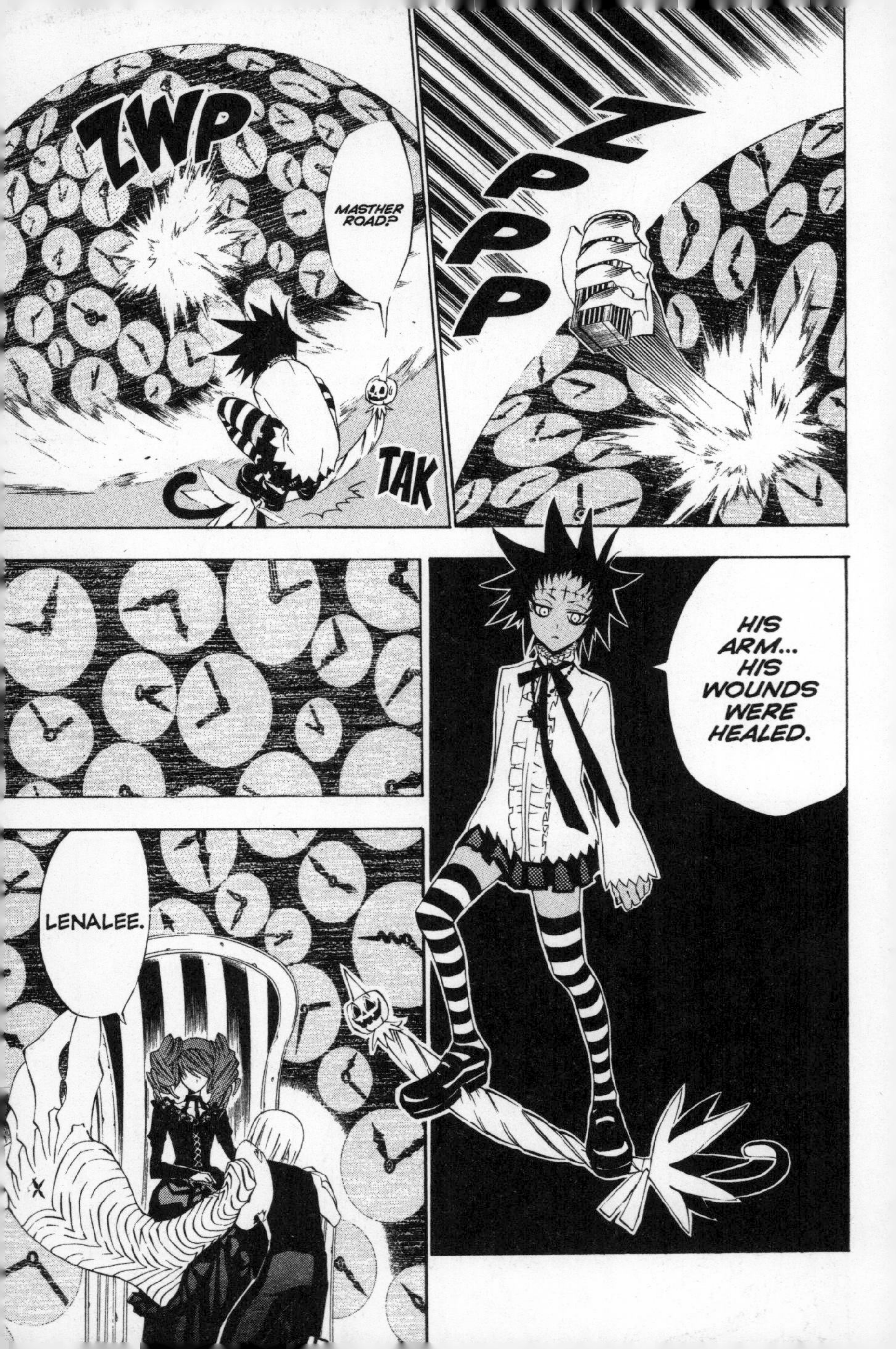
ZPPP
ZWP
MASTHER ROAD?
TAK
HIS ARM... HIS WOUNDS WERE HEALED.
LENALEE.

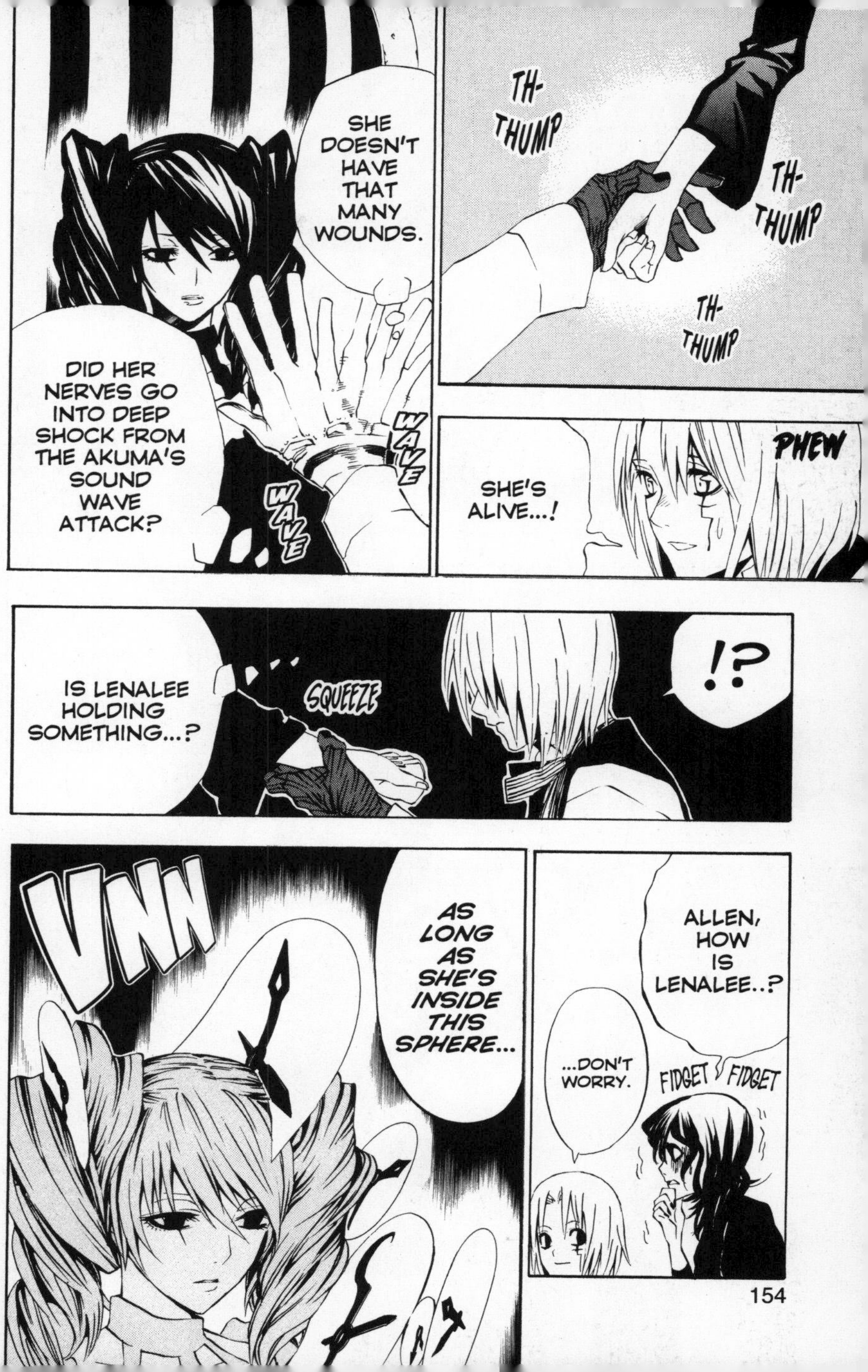
TH-THUMP
TH-THUMP
TH-THUMP
PHEW
SHE'S ALIVE...!
SHE DOESN'T HAVE THAT MANY WOUNDS.
DID HER NERVES GO INTO DEEP SHOCK FROM THE AKUMA'S SOUND WAVE ATTACK?
WAVE
WAVE
!?
SQUEEZE
IS LENALEE HOLDING SOMETHING...?
ALLEN, HOW IS LENALEE..?
FIDGET FIDGET
...DON'T WORRY.
UNN
AS LONG AS SHE'S INSIDE THIS SPHERE...

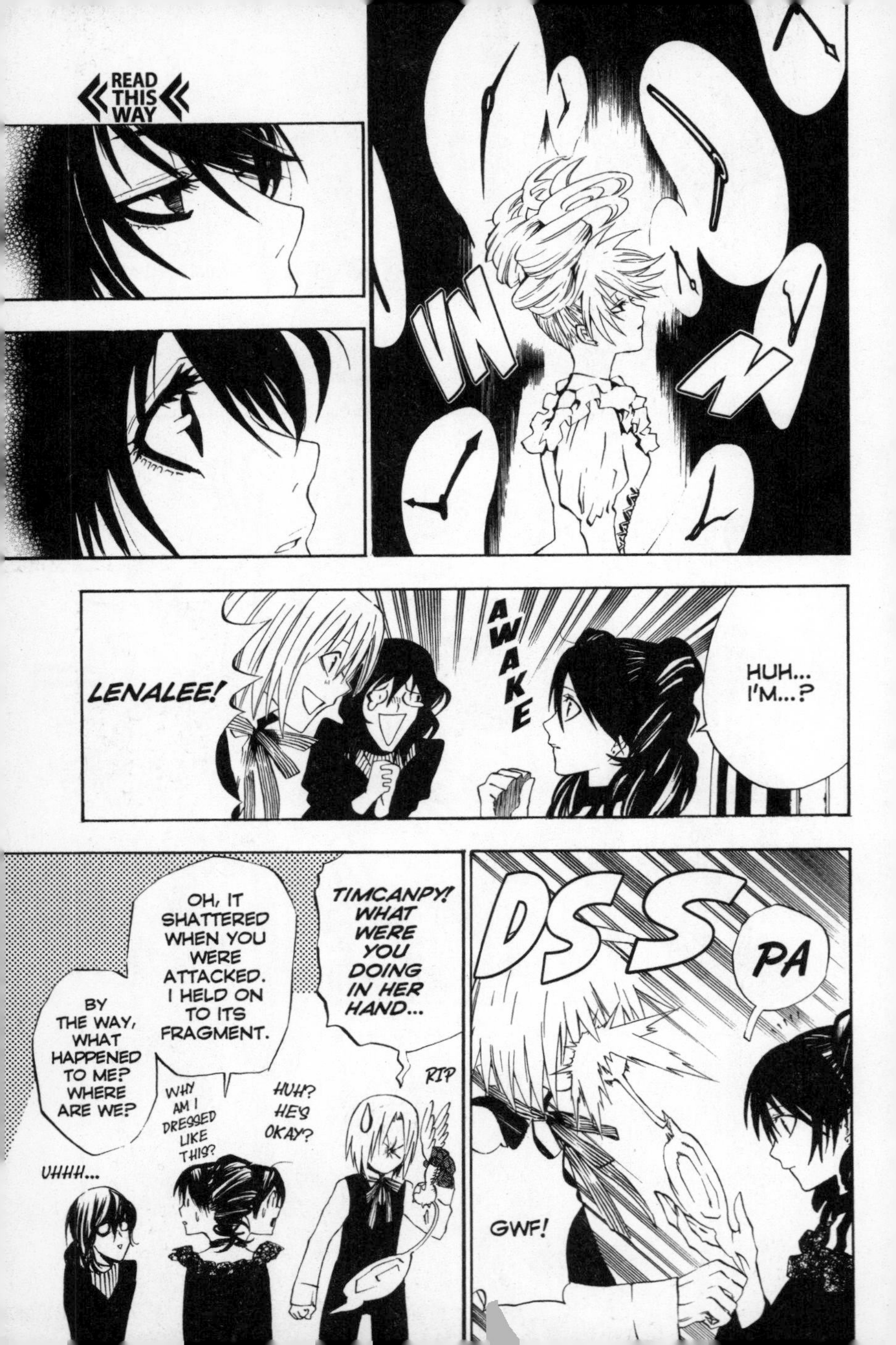
READ THIS WAY
VNN
HUH... I'M...?
AWAKE
LENALEE!
DS-S
PA
GWF!
TIMCANPY! WHAT WERE YOU DOING IN HER HAND...
RIP
HUH? HE'S OKAY?
OH, IT SHATTERED WHEN YOU WERE ATTACKED. I HELD ON TO ITS FRAGMENT.
WHY AM I DRESSED LIKE THIS?
BY THE WAY, WHAT HAPPENED TO ME? WHERE ARE WE?
UHHH...

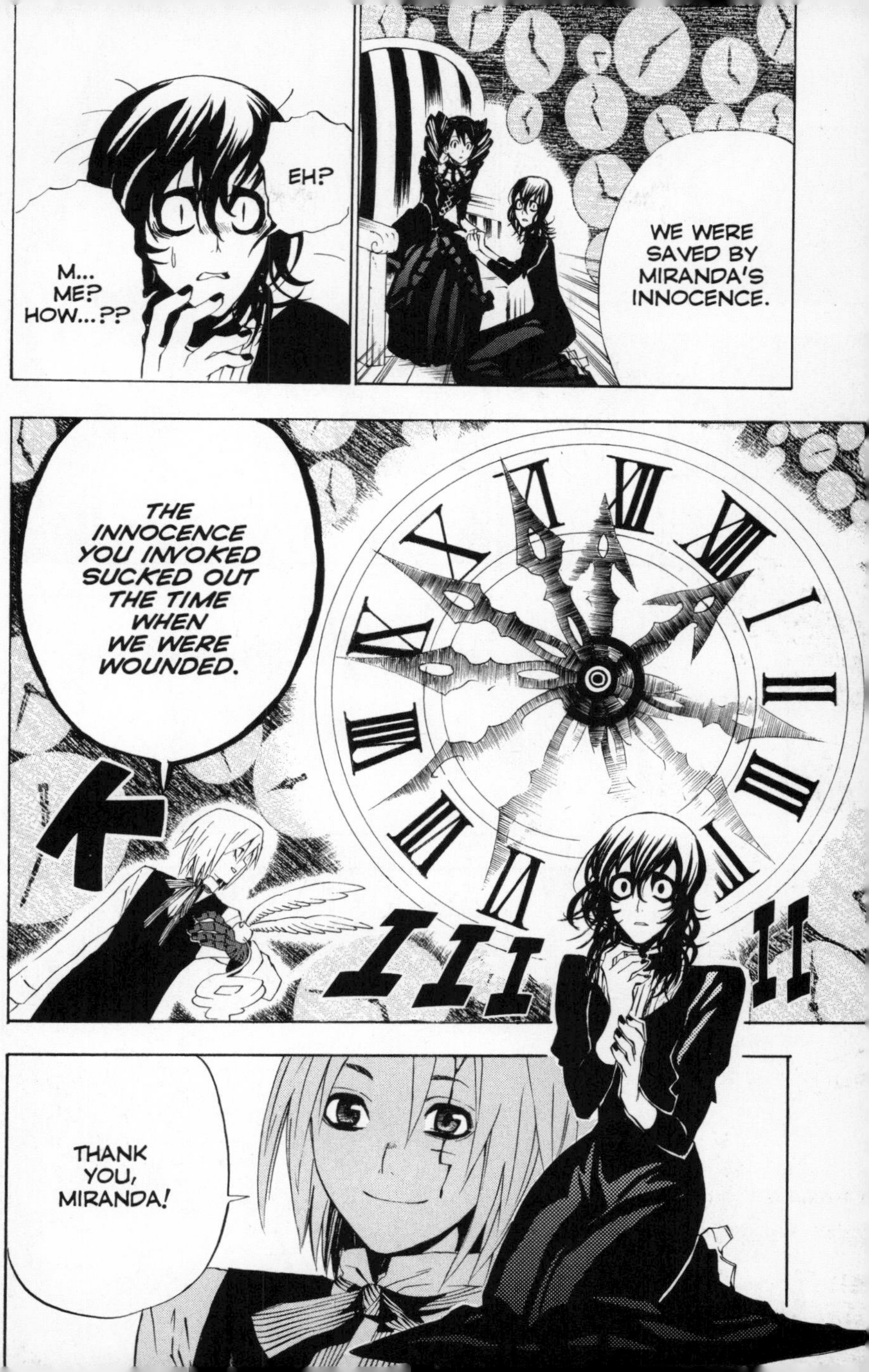
WE WERE SAVED BY MIRANDA'S INNOCENCE.
EH?
M... ME? HOW...??
THE INNOCENCE YOU INVOKED SUCKED OUT THE TIME WHEN WE WERE WOUNDED.
THANK YOU, MIRANDA!

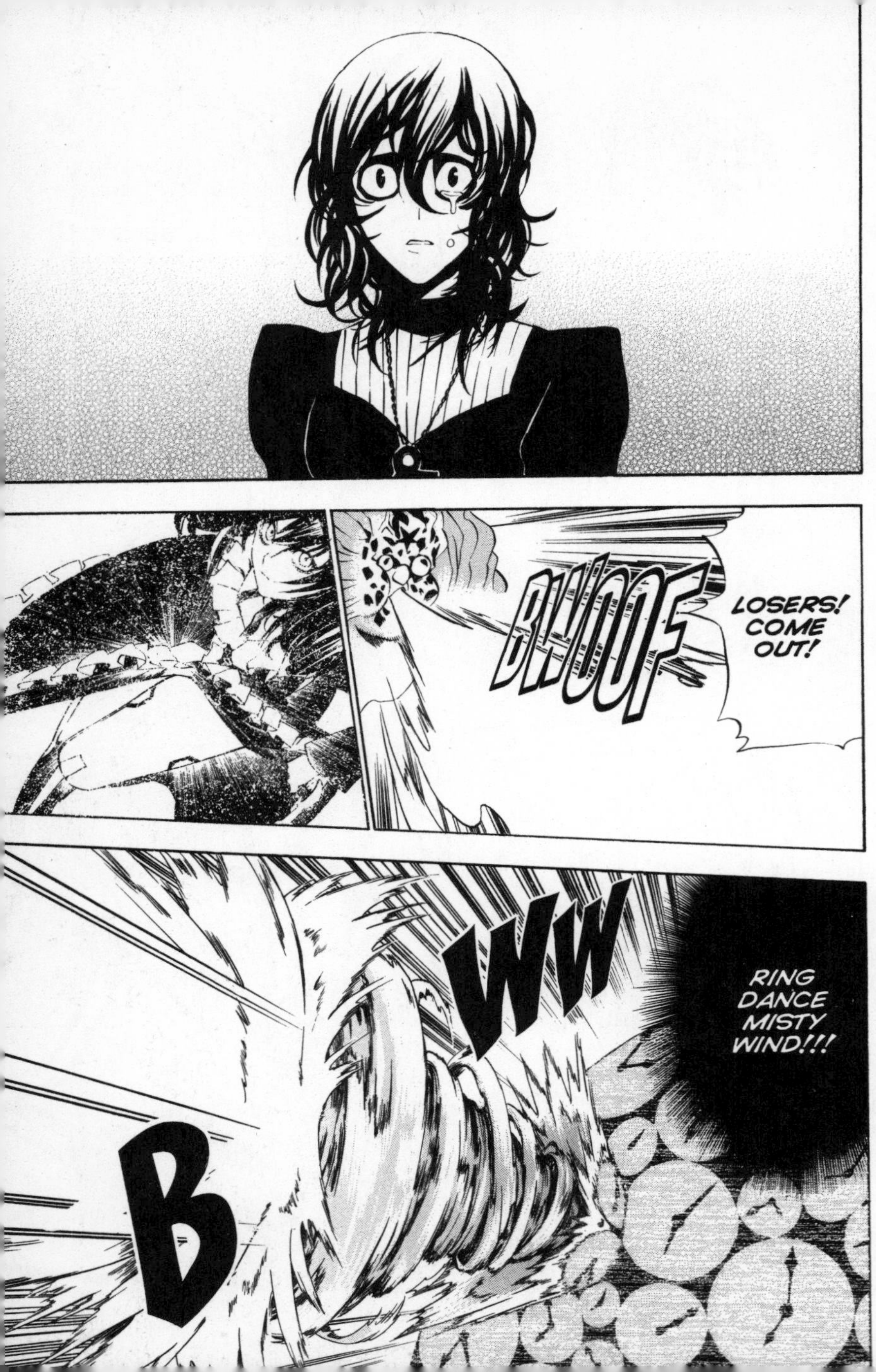
BWOOF
LOSERS! COME OUT!
RING DANCE MISTY WIND!!!
WW
B

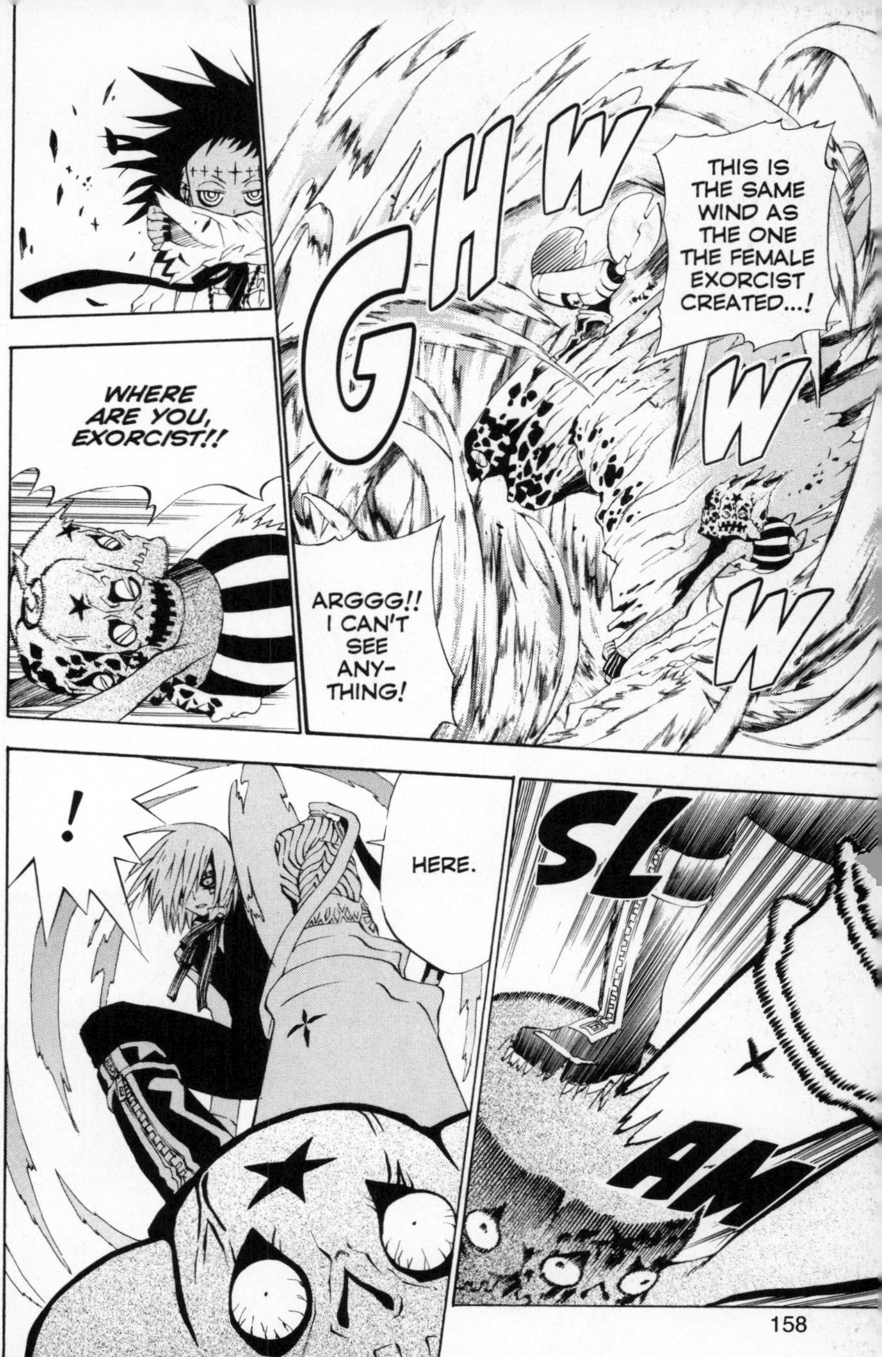
THIS IS THE SAME WIND AS THE ONE THE FEMALE EXORCIST CREATED...!
GHWWWW
ARGGG!! I CAN'T SEE ANY-THING!
WHERE ARE YOU, EXORCIST!!
SLAM
HERE.
!

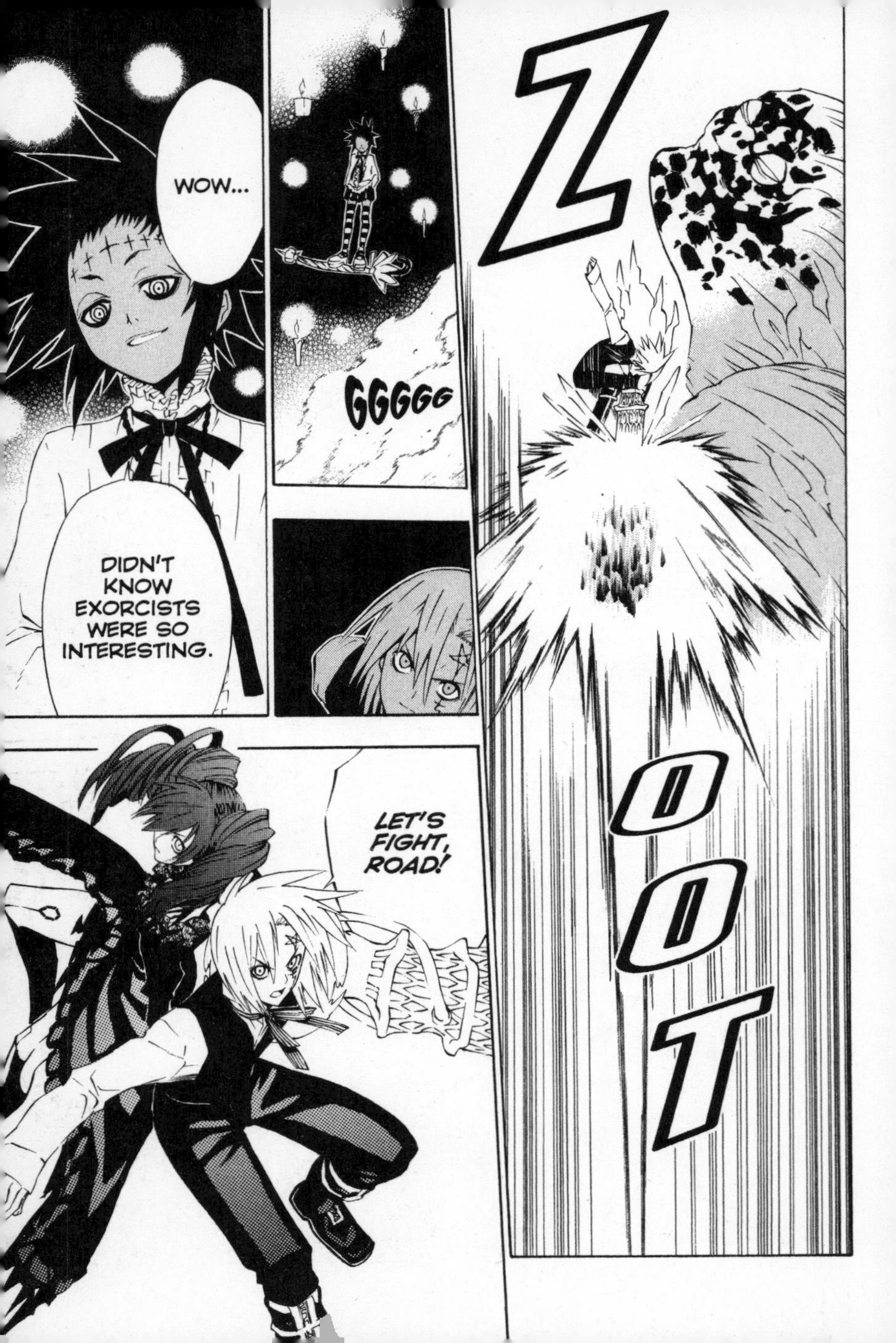
ZOOT
GGGGG
WOW...
DIDN'T KNOW EXORCISTS WERE SO INTERESTING.
LET'S FIGHT, ROAD!

MIRANDA LOTTO

GERMAN 25 YEARS OLD
HEIGHT 168 CM
WEIGHT 45KG
BIRTHDAY JANUARY 1ST
ARIES BLOOD TYPE O

I HAD NO INTENTION OF
MAKING MIRANDA AN EXORCIST
AT THE TIME I DREW THE
FIRST CHAPTER OF THE
REWINDING CITY. AFTER I
DREW HER I STARTED TO SEE
THAT WE'RE SIMILAR INSIDE
AND SHE GREW ON ME. I'M
LOOKING FORWARD TO DRAWING
MIRANDA IN THE ORDER'S
UNIFORM IN A BATTLE. I'M
LOOKING FORWARD TO
SEEING YOU SOON,
MIRANDA.

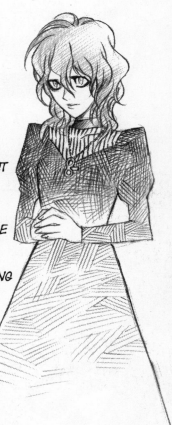

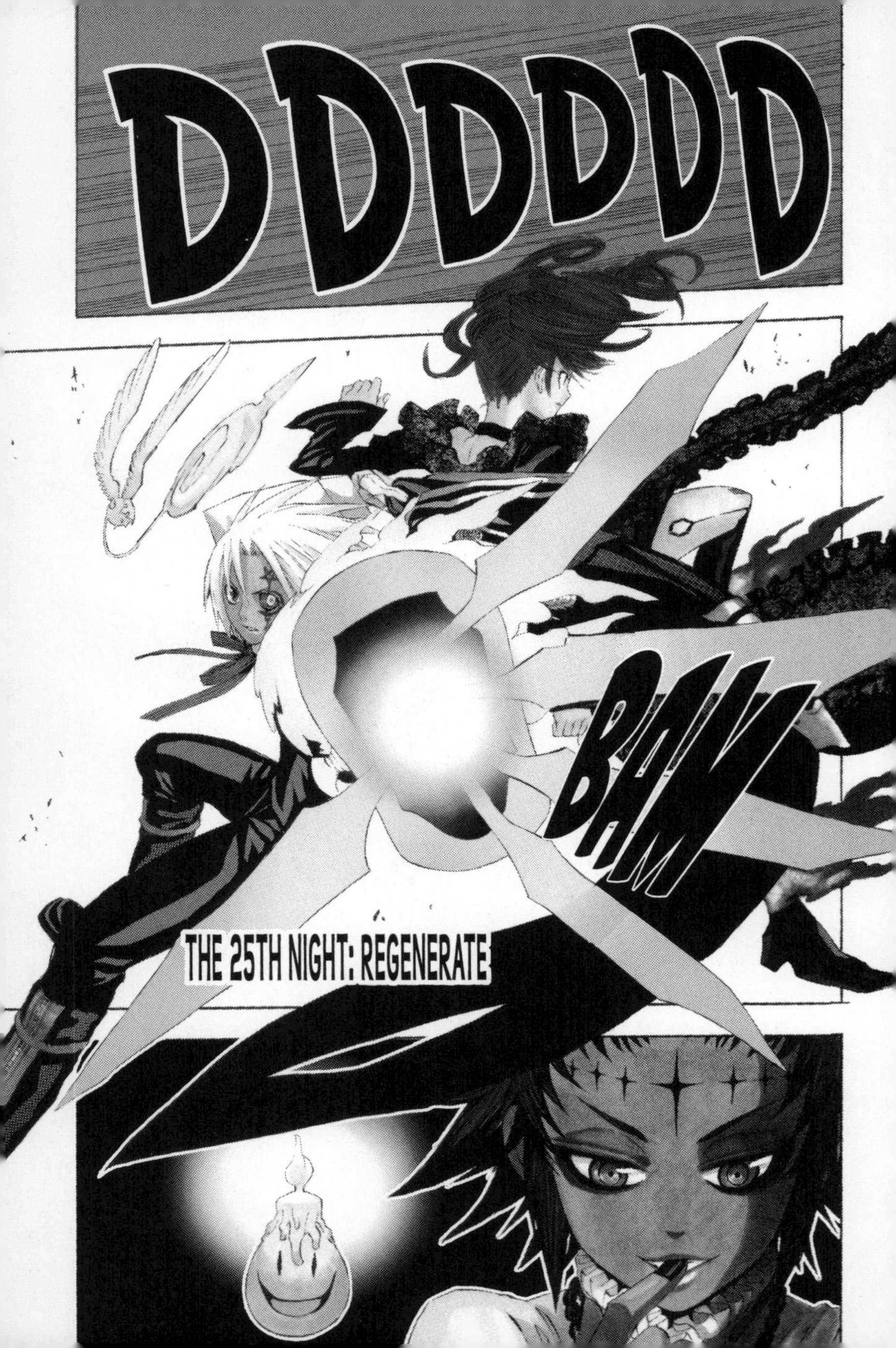
DDDDDD
BAM
THE 25TH NIGHT: REGENERATE

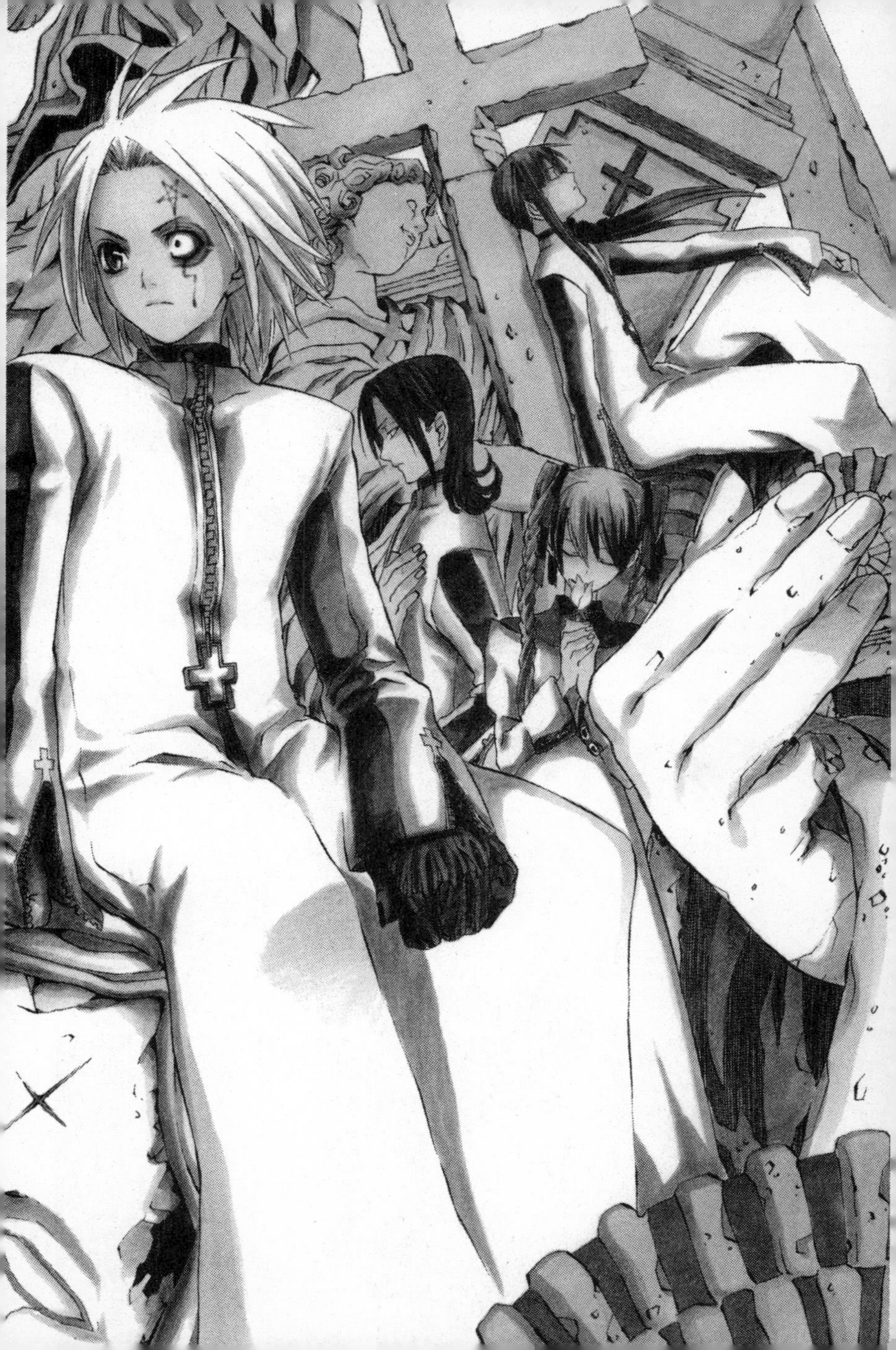

THE 25TH NIGHT: REGENERATE

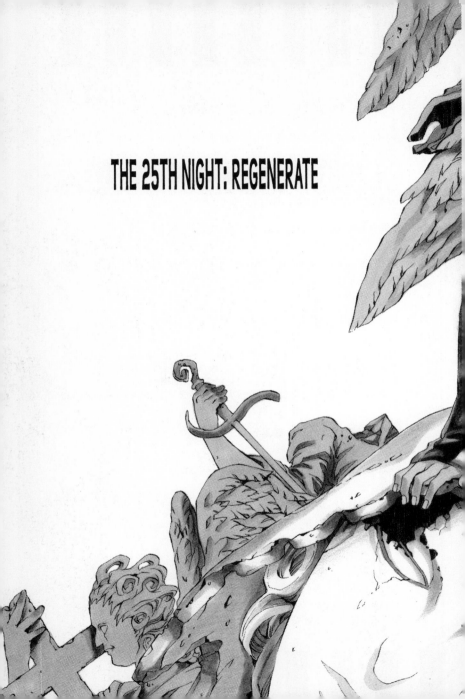

DISCUSSION ROOM VOL. 7

Q 1. WHY IS KOMUI ALWAYS WEARING SLIPPERS?

A. HE WEARS THEM BECAUSE THEY'RE COMFORTABLE. HE ALSO WEARS THEM BECAUSE HIS FEET START TO STINK IF HE WEARS SHOES FOR LONG PERIODS OF TIME AND LENALEE WON'T COME NEAR HIM WHEN THEY DO.

Q 2. DOES THE EARL WASH HIS FAVORITE COAT?

A. YES, HE WASHES IT. EARL TAKES GOOD CARE OF HIS THINGS SO HE TAKES GOOD CARE OF HIS COAT TOO.

Q 3. WHY DOES ALLEN EAT SO MUCH?

A. IN FACT, ALL PARASITE-TYPE EXORCISTS HAVE A BIG APPETITE. THEY REQUIRE A LOT MORE ENERGY AS THEY HAVE AN INNOCENCE LODGED WITHIN THEM, COMPARED TO THE EXORCISTS WHO EQUIP THEIR INNOCENCE, SUCH AS KANDA.

Q 4. IS KANDA A GUY OR A GIRL?

A. NO DOUBT ABOUT THAT ONE. HE'S A GUY.

Q 5. IS ALLEN LEFT-HANDED?

A. HE'S BOTH-HANDED.

Q 6. IS THERE SOME CONTRAPTION IN KOMUI'S BERET?

A. THAT'S A SECRET. APPARENTLY ONE OF HIS ASSISTANTS HEARD SOMETHING COMING FROM AROUND THAT AREA BUT WHO KNOWS...

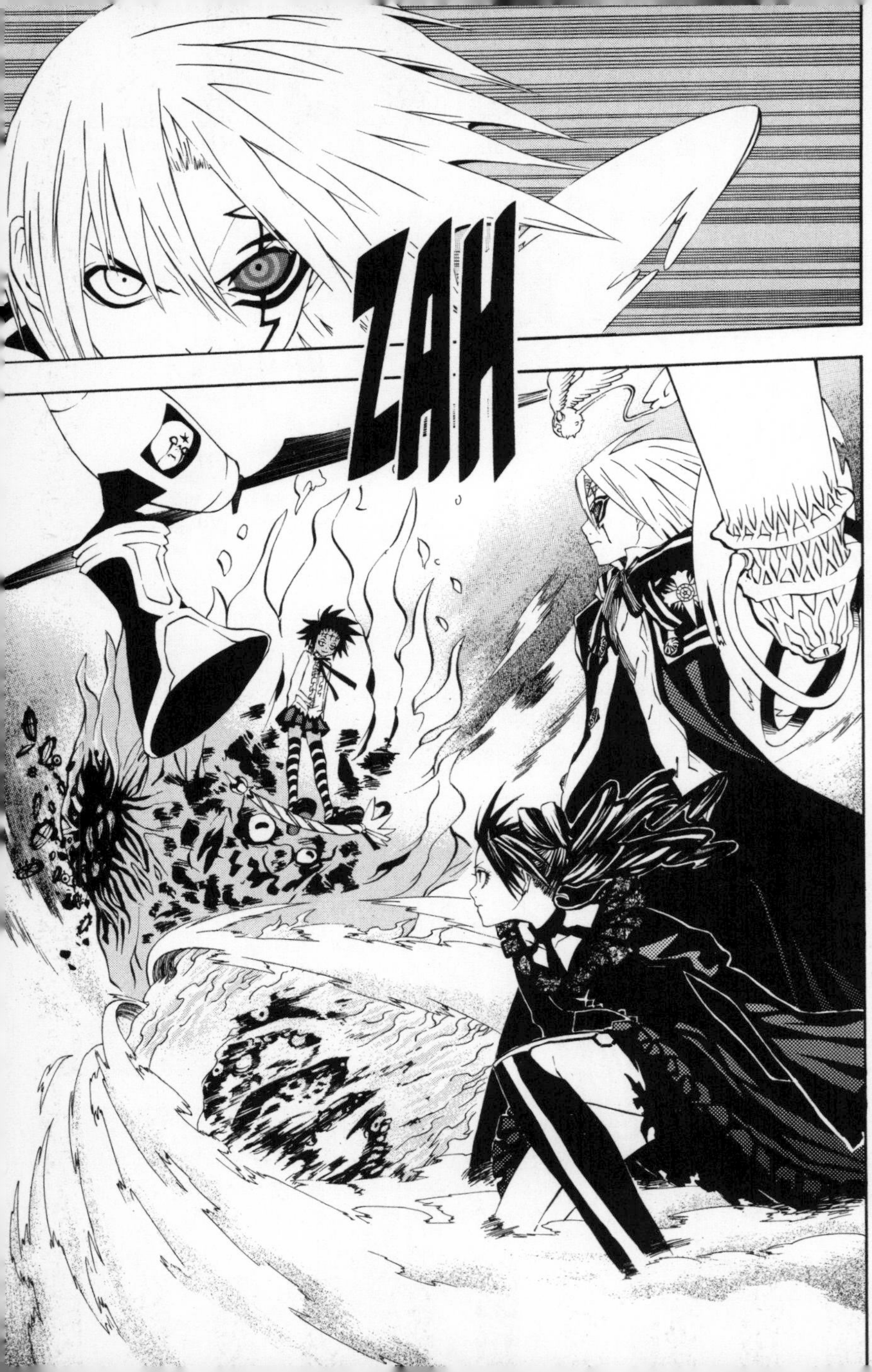
ZAH

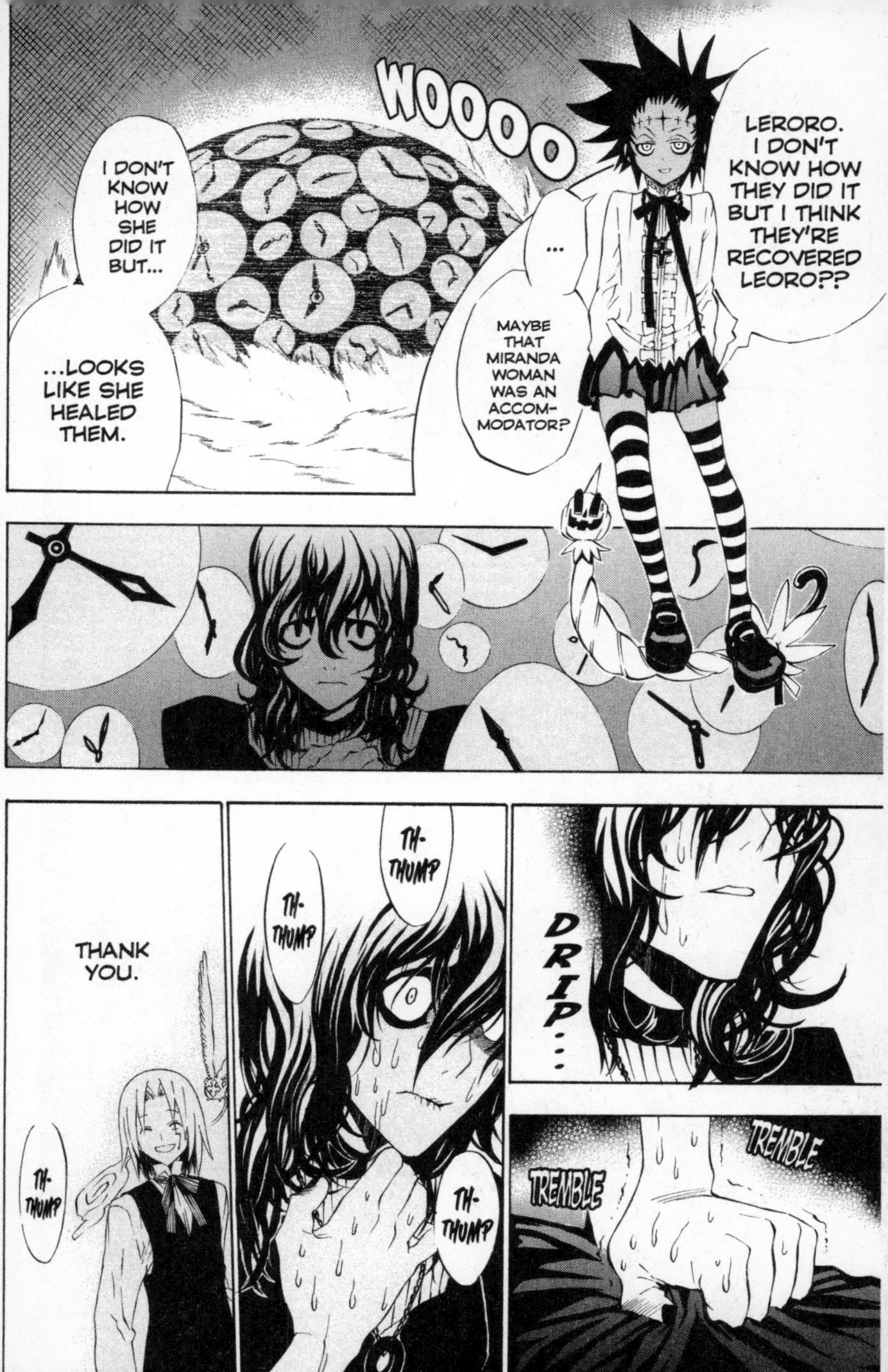
WOOOO
LERORO. I DON'T KNOW HOW THEY DID IT BUT I THINK THEY'RE RECOVERED LEORO??
...
MAYBE THAT MIRANDA WOMAN WAS AN ACCOM-MODATOR?
I DON'T KNOW HOW SHE DID IT BUT...
...LOOKS LIKE SHE HEALED THEM.
DRIP...
TREMBLE
TREMBLE
TH-THUMP
TH-THUMP
TH-THUMP
THANK YOU.
TH-THUMP

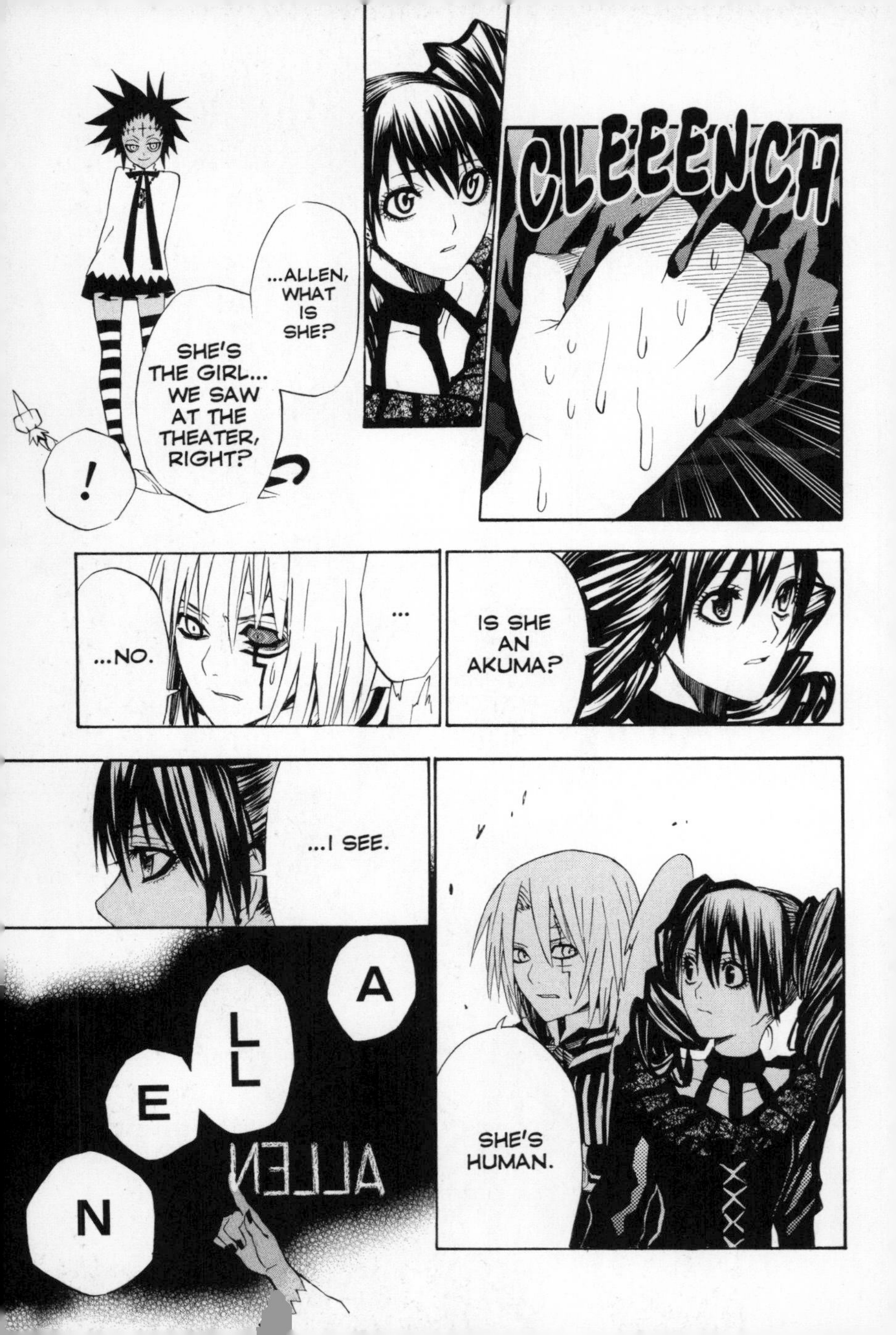
CLEEENCH
...ALLEN, WHAT IS SHE?
SHE'S THE GIRL... WE SAW AT THE THEATER, RIGHT?
!
IS SHE AN AKUMA?
...
...NO.
SHE'S HUMAN.
...I SEE.
A L L E N
ALLEN

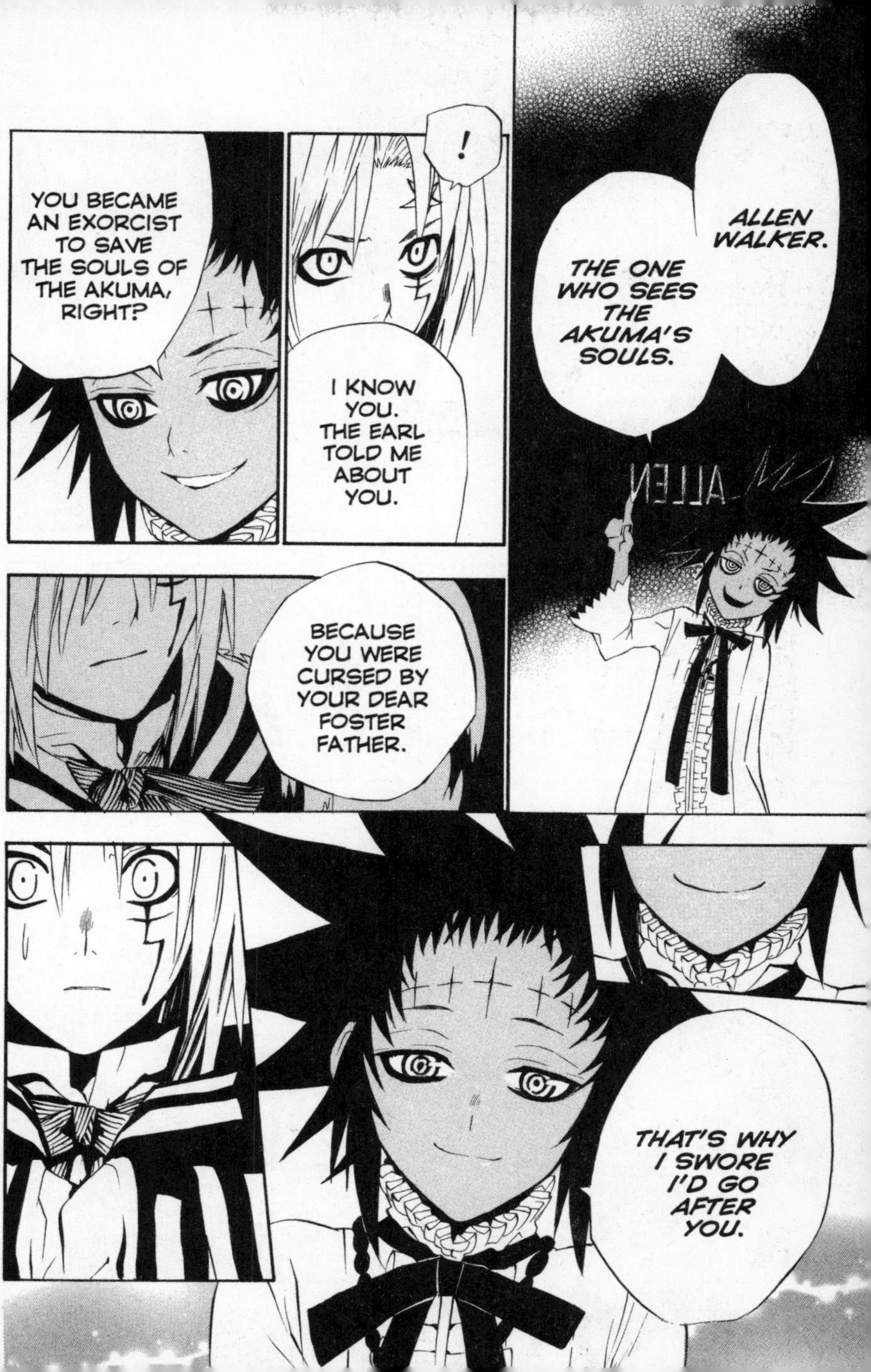
ALLEN WALKER.
THE ONE WHO SEES THE AKUMA'S SOULS.
!
I KNOW YOU. THE EARL TOLD ME ABOUT YOU.
YOU BECAME AN EXORCIST TO SAVE THE SOULS OF THE AKUMA, RIGHT?
BECAUSE YOU WERE CURSED BY YOUR DEAR FOSTER FATHER.
THAT'S WHY I SWORE I'D GO AFTER YOU.

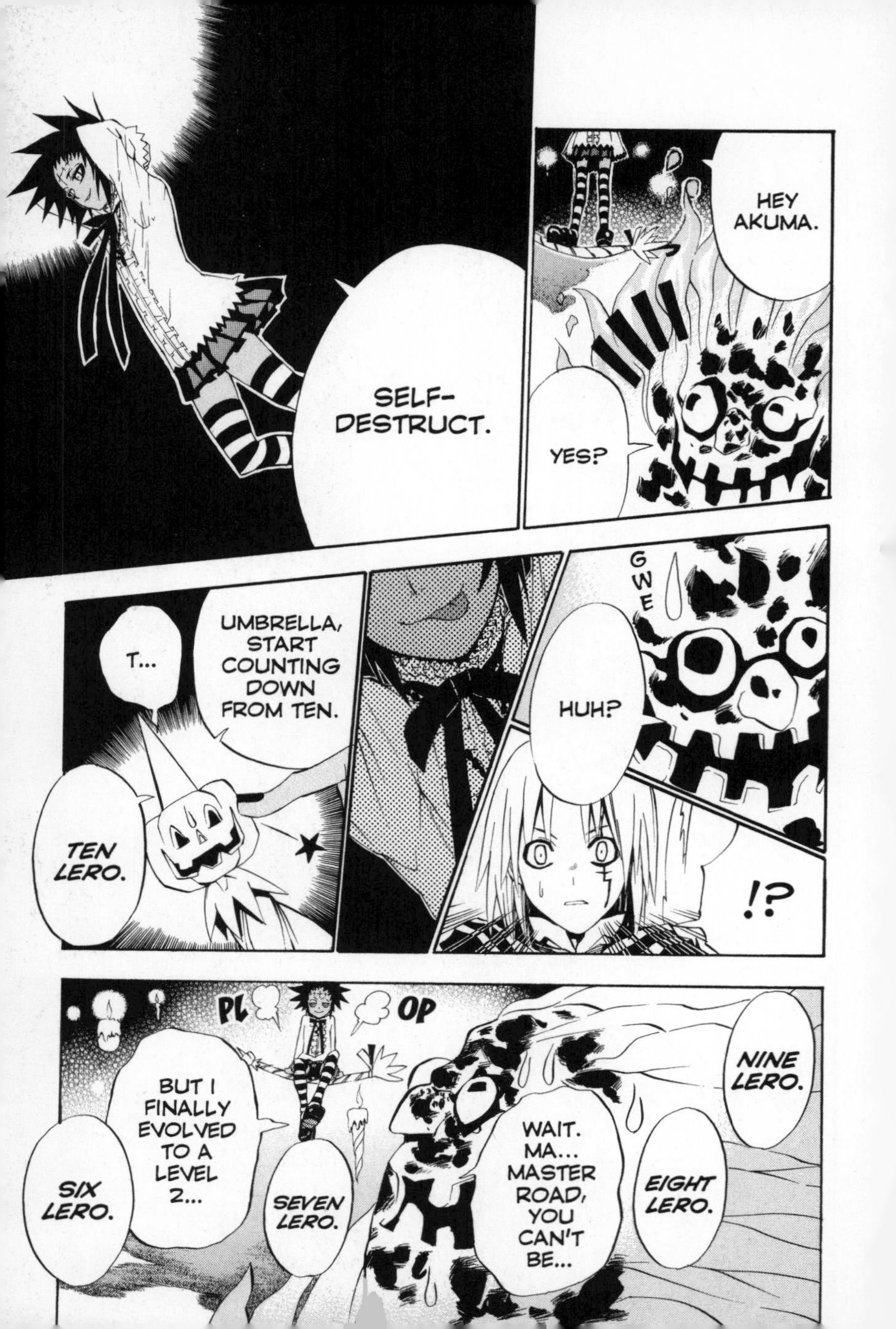
HEY AKUMA.
YES?
SELF-DESTRUCT.
GWE
HUH?
!?
UMBRELLA, START COUNTING DOWN FROM TEN.
T...
TEN LERO.
NINE LERO.
PL OP
EIGHT LERO.
WAIT. MA... MASTER ROAD, YOU CAN'T BE...
BUT I FINALLY EVOLVED TO A LEVEL 2...
SEVEN LERO.
SIX LERO.

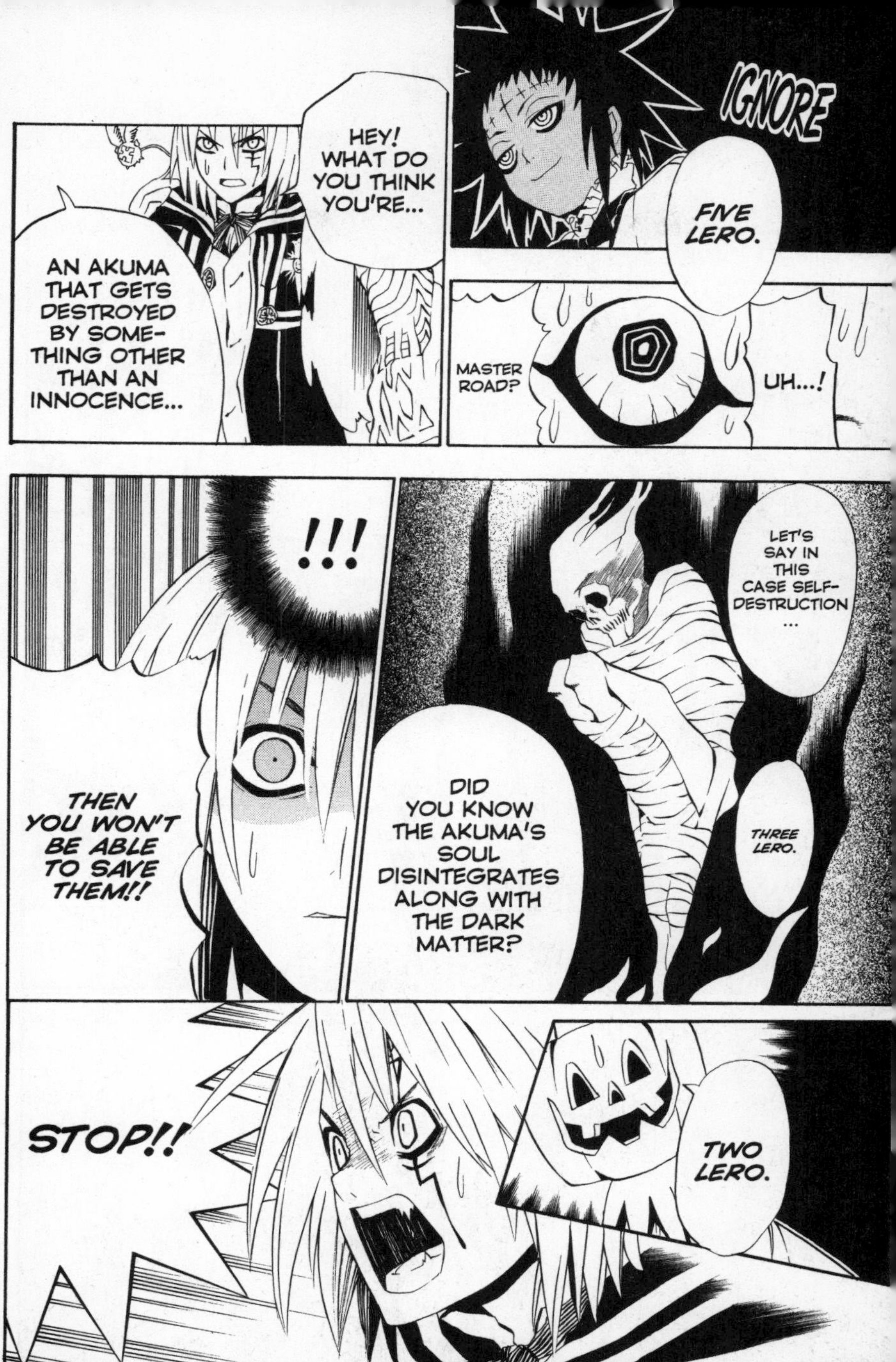
IGNORE
FIVE LERO.
UH...!
MASTER ROAD?
HEY! WHAT DO YOU THINK YOU'RE...
AN AKUMA THAT GETS DESTROYED BY SOME-THING OTHER THAN AN INNOCENCE...
LET'S SAY IN THIS CASE SELF-DESTRUCTION ...
DID YOU KNOW THE AKUMA'S SOUL DISINTEGRATES ALONG WITH THE DARK MATTER?
THREE LERO.
!!!
THEN YOU WON'T BE ABLE TO SAVE THEM!!
TWO LERO.
STOP!!

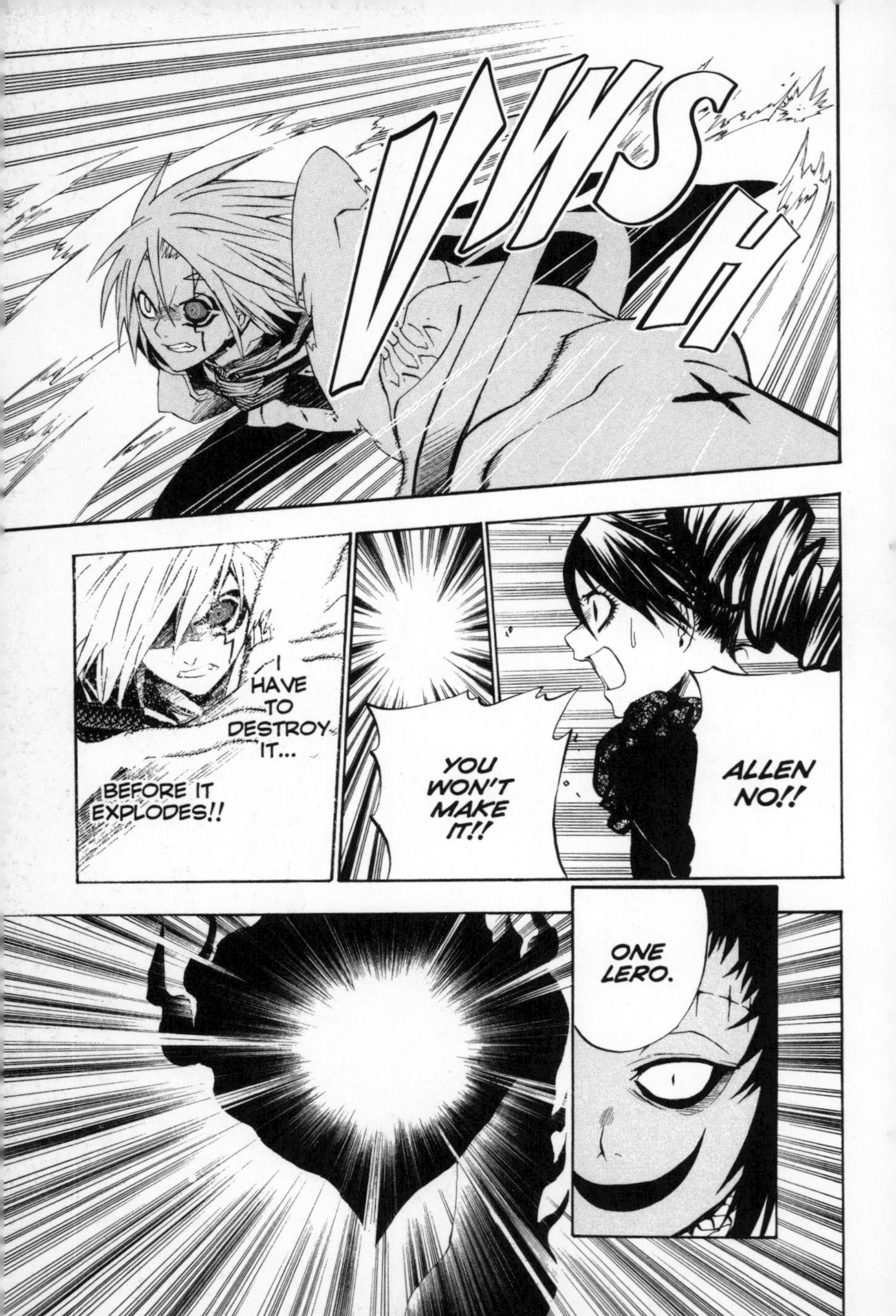
VWSH
ALLEN NO!!
YOU WON'T MAKE IT!!
I HAVE TO DESTROY IT...
BEFORE IT EXPLODES!!
ONE LERO.

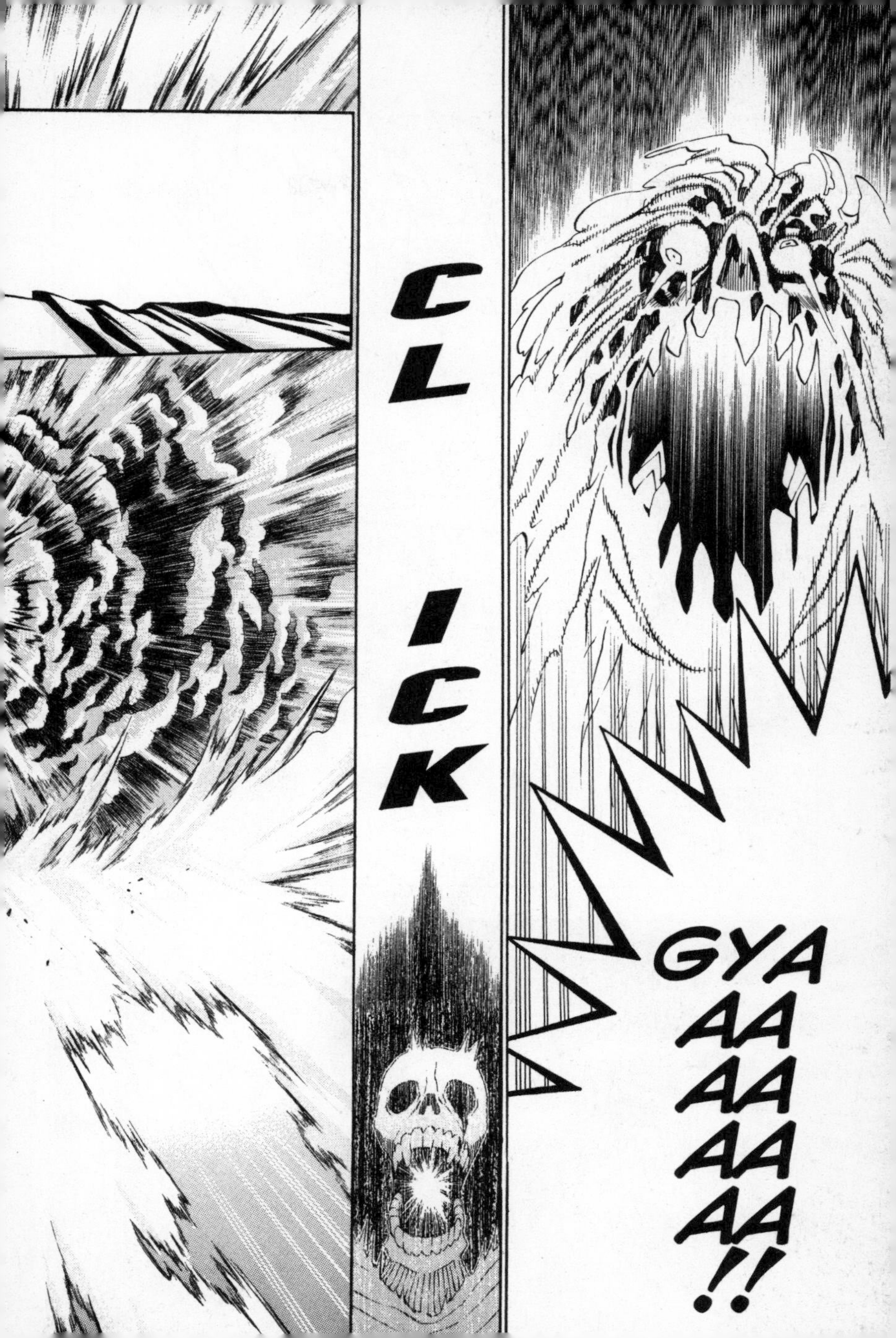
GYAAAAAAAAAA!!
CLICK

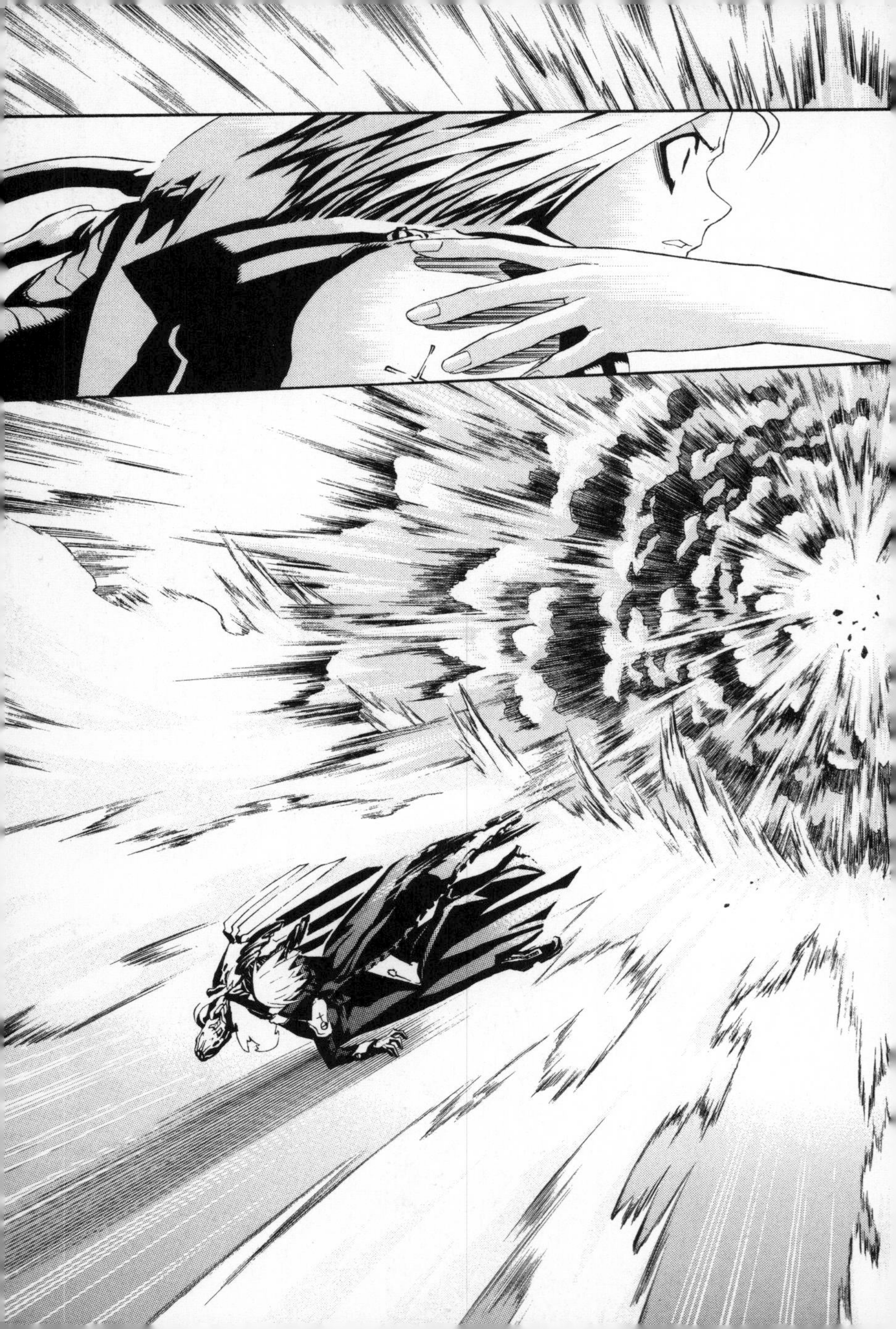

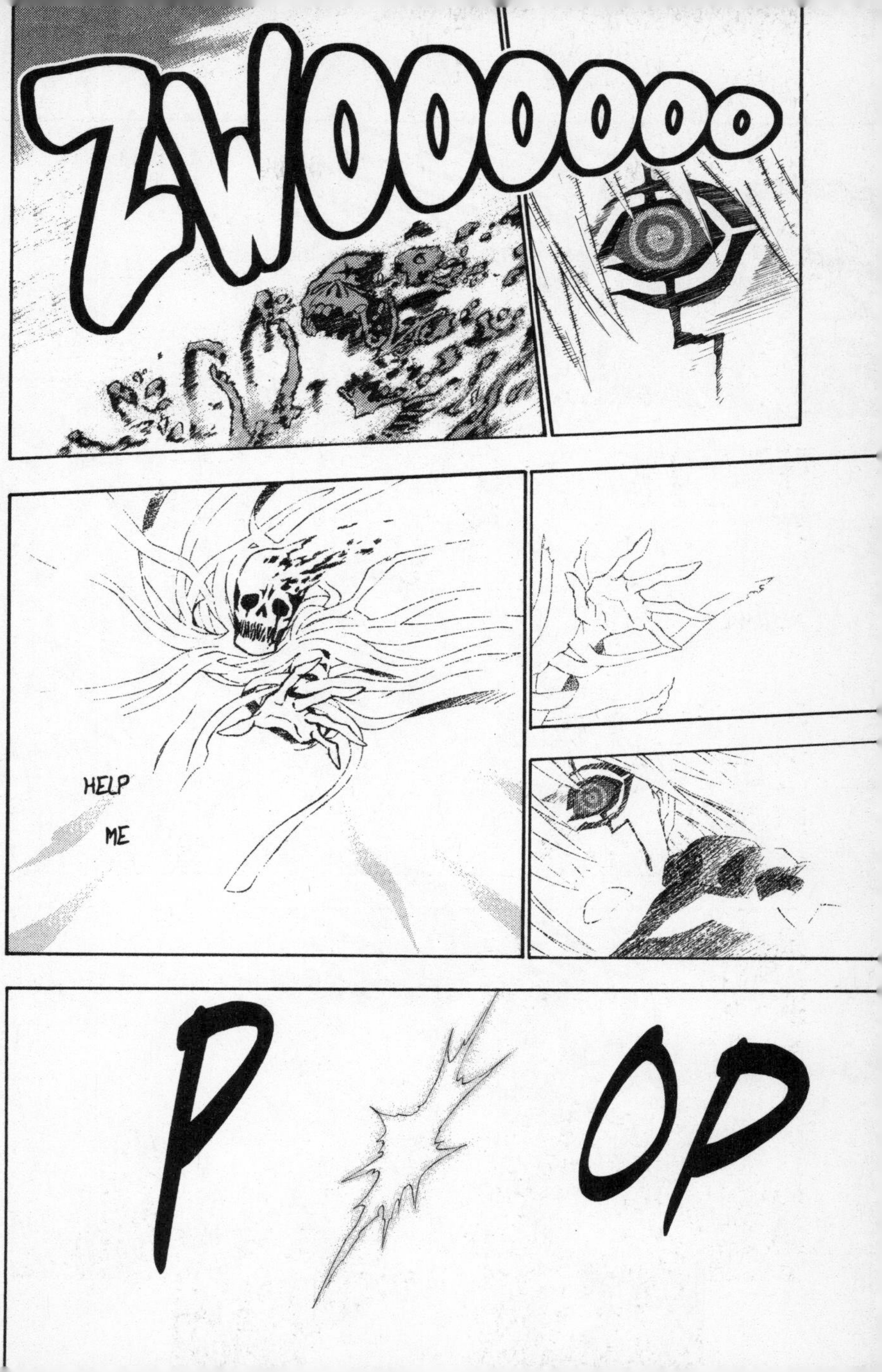
ZWOOOOOO
HELP
ME
P OP

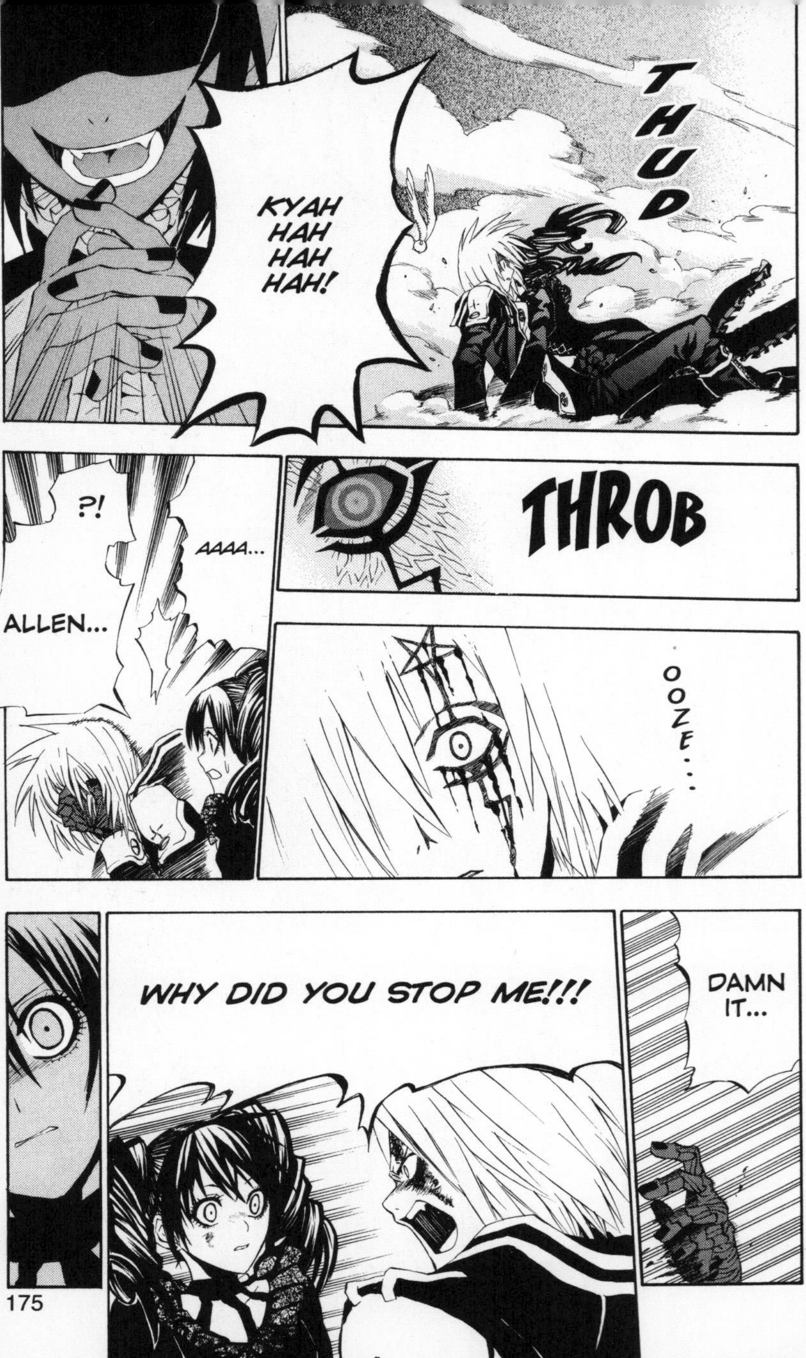
THUD
KYAH HAH HAH HAH!
THROB
OOZE...
?!
AAAA...
ALLEN...
DAMN IT...
WHY DID YOU STOP ME!!!

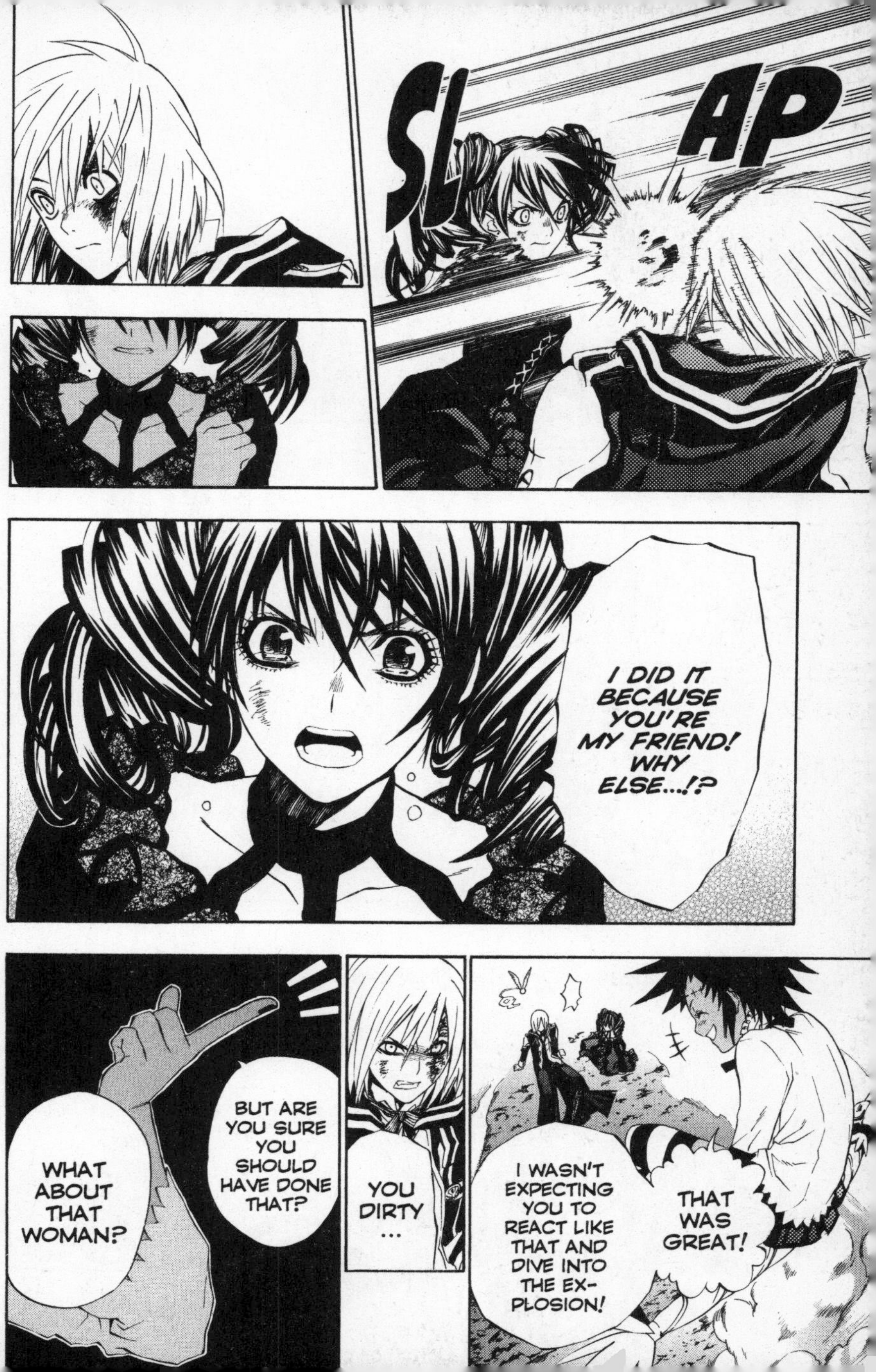
SLAP
I DID IT BECAUSE YOU'RE MY FRIEND! WHY ELSE...!?
THAT WAS GREAT!
I WASN'T EXPECTING YOU TO REACT LIKE THAT AND DIVE INTO THE EX-PLOSION!
YOU DIRTY ...
BUT ARE YOU SURE YOU SHOULD HAVE DONE THAT?
WHAT ABOUT THAT WOMAN?

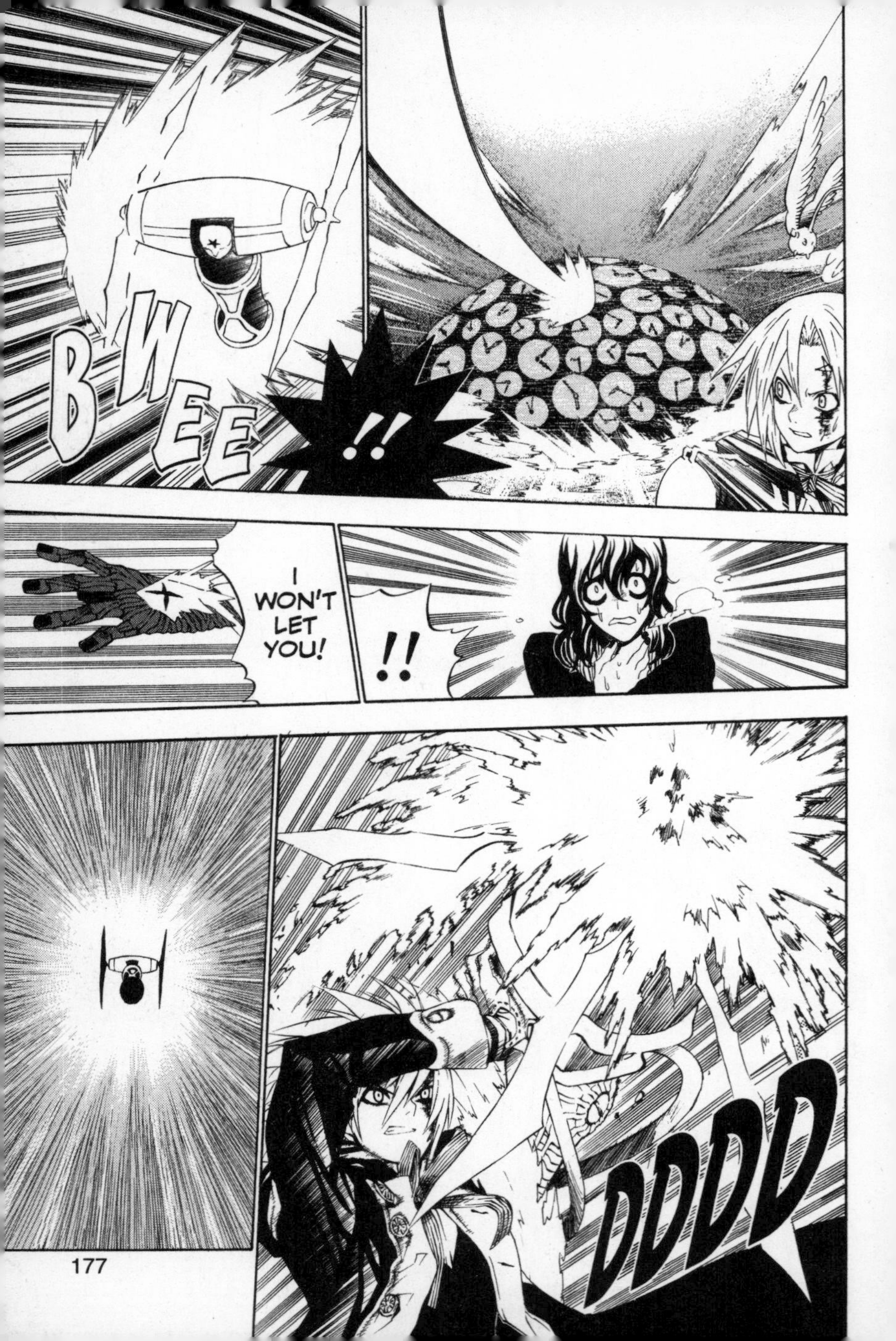
!!
BWEE
!!
I WON'T LET YOU!
DDDD

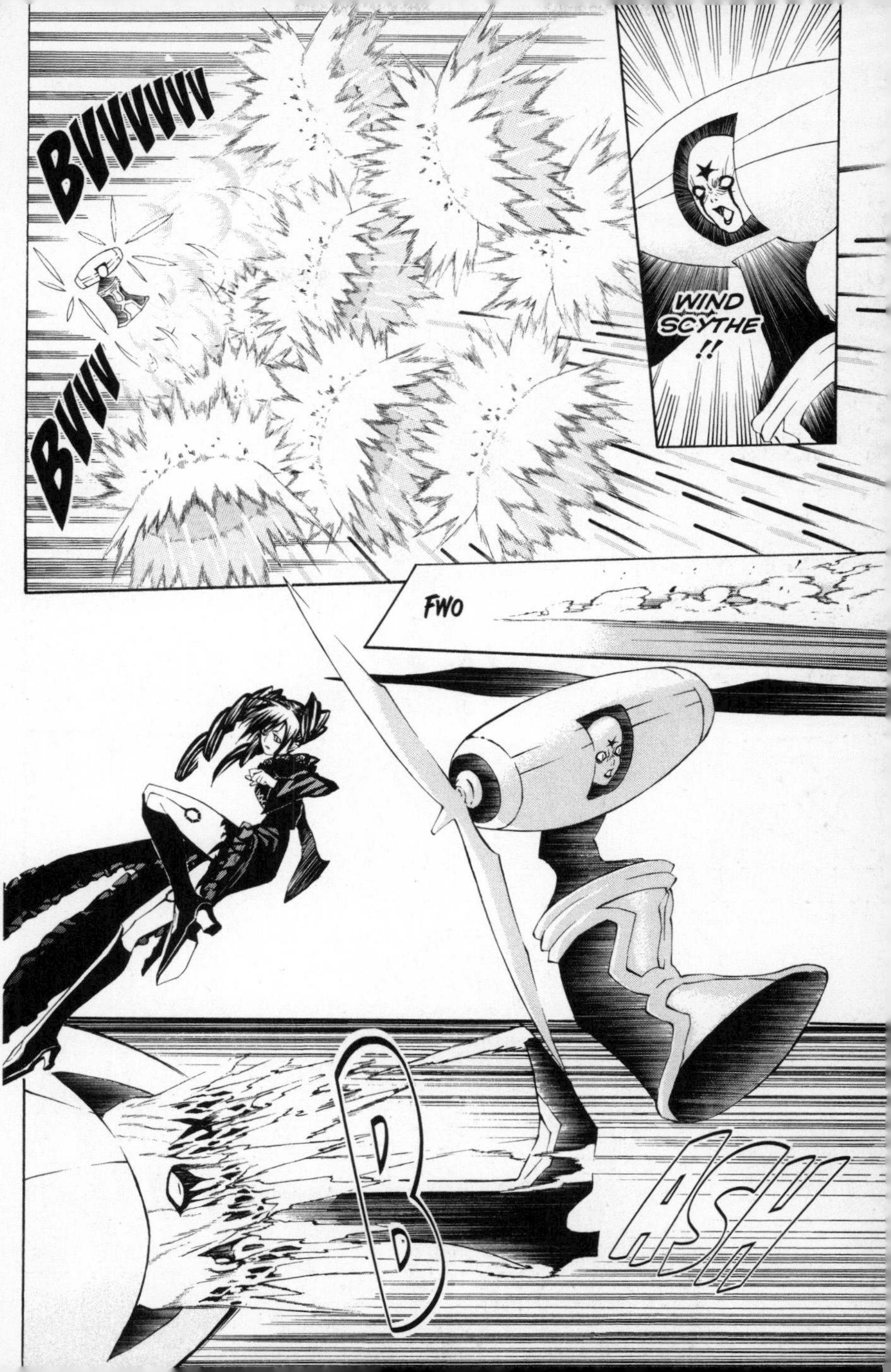
WIND SCYTHE !!
BVVVVVV
BVVV
FWO
BASH

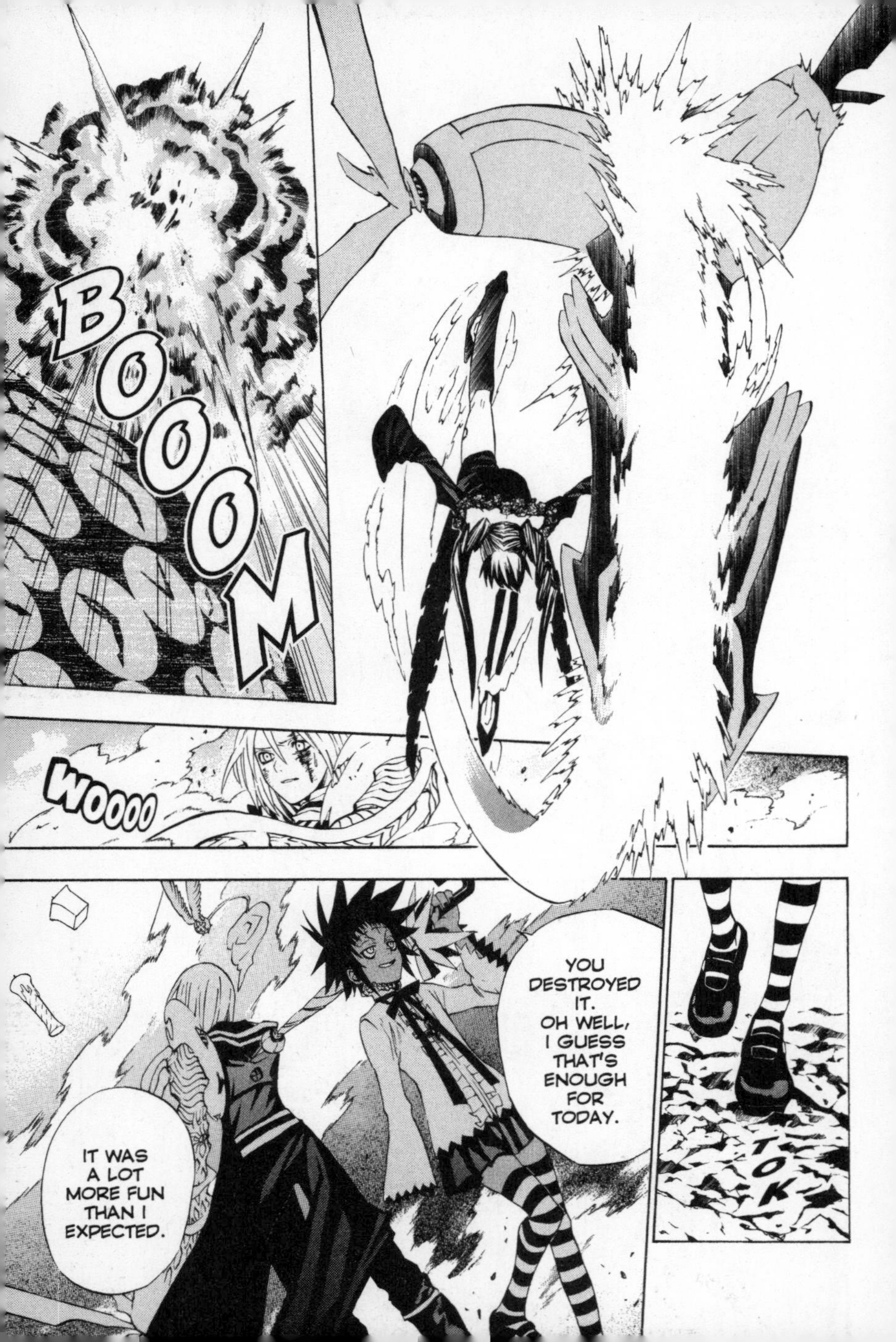
BOOOM
WOOOO
TOK
YOU DESTROYED IT. OH WELL, I GUESS THAT'S ENOUGH FOR TODAY.
IT WAS A LOT MORE FUN THAN I EXPECTED.

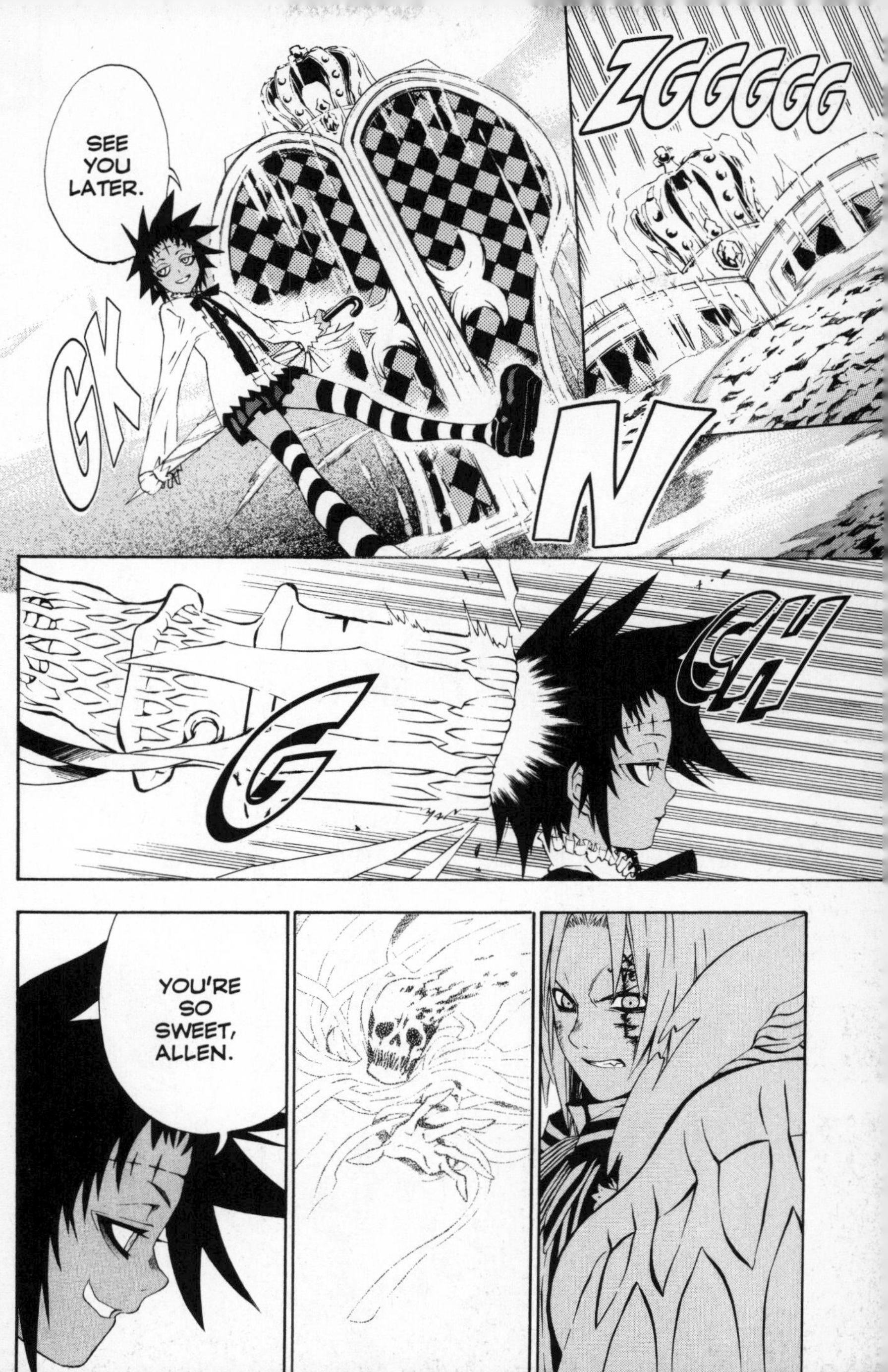
ZGGGGG
SEE YOU LATER.
GK
N
CH
G
YOU'RE SO SWEET, ALLEN.

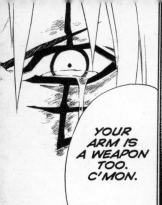

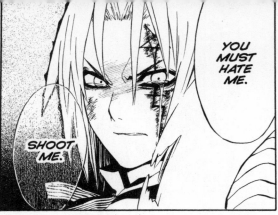

YOU MUST HATE ME.
SHOOT ME.
YOUR ARM IS A WEAPON TOO. C'MON.
GRIT
BUT AN EXORCIST SHOULDN'T CRY OVER A BROKEN AKUMA.
KLCK
YOU'RE GOING TO END UP ON YOUR OWN AT THAT RATE.
ALLEN...
LET'S PLAY AGAIN SOON.

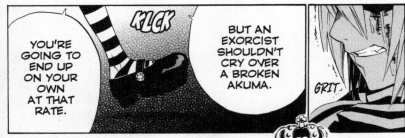

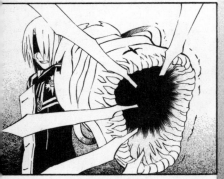

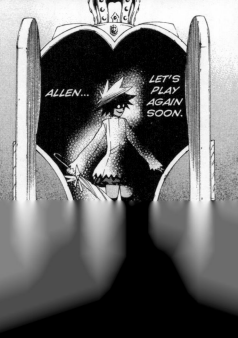

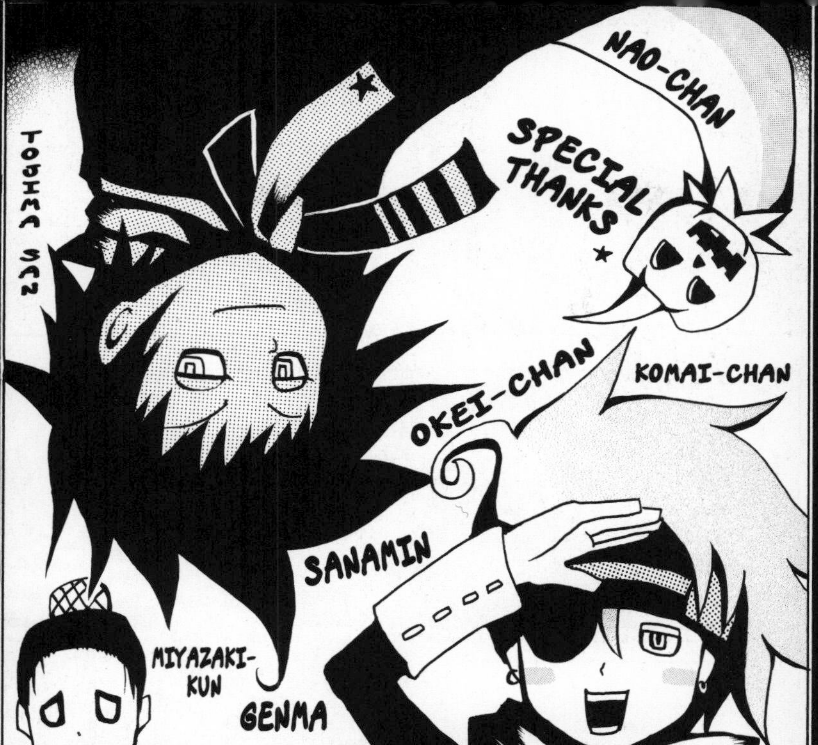
SPECIAL THANKS ★
NAO-CHAN
KOMAI-CHAN
OKEI-CHAN
TOJIMA SAN
SANAMIN
HOKA CHAN
GENMA
MIYAZAKI-KUN
OI-CHAN
YOSHIDA-SAN, AKIYAMA-SAN
YUBUU
KORO
HEY

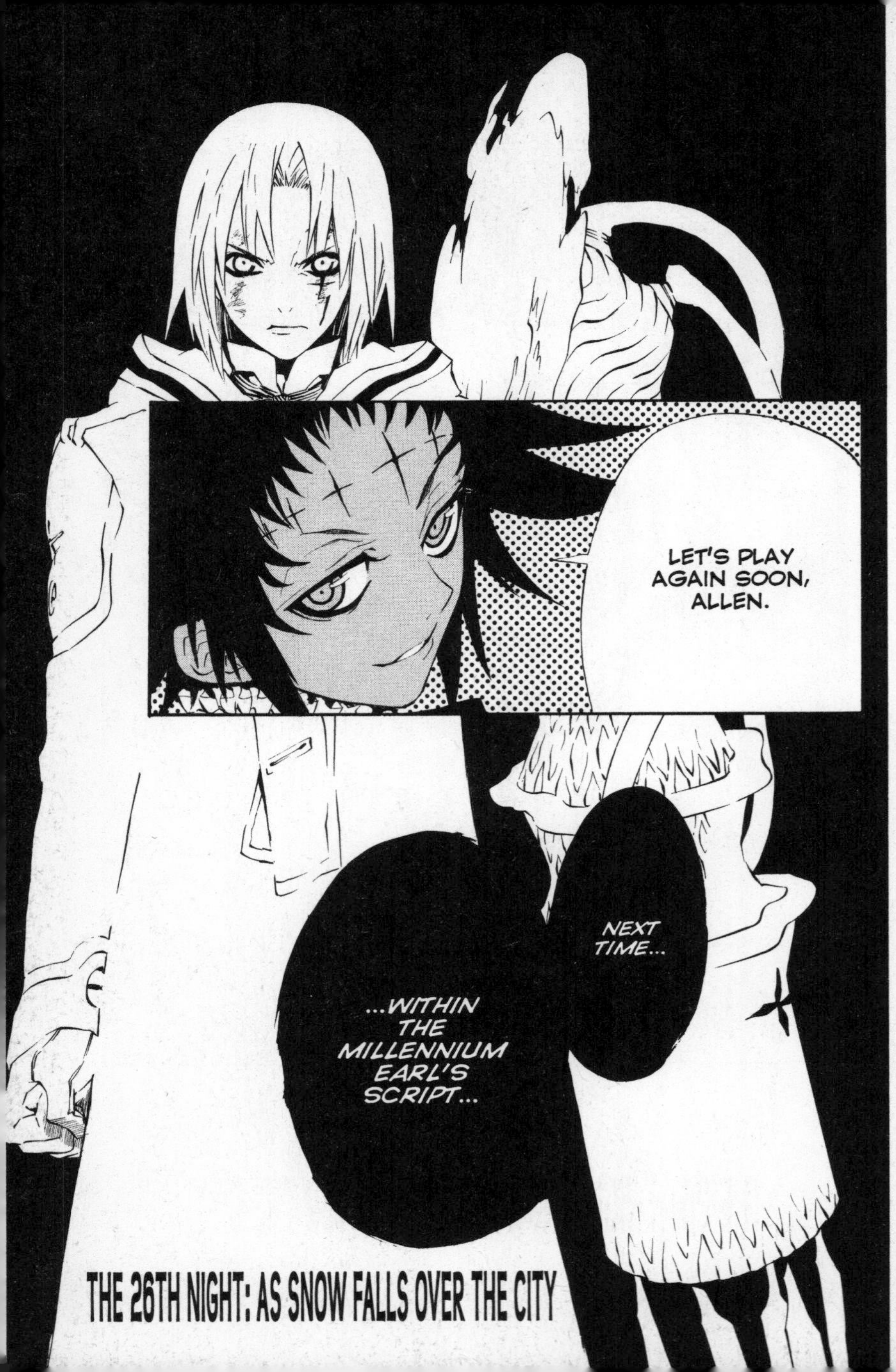
LET'S PLAY AGAIN SOON, ALLEN.
NEXT TIME...
...WITHIN THE MILLENNIUM EARL'S SCRIPT...

THE 26TH NIGHT: AS SNOW FALLS OVER THE CITY

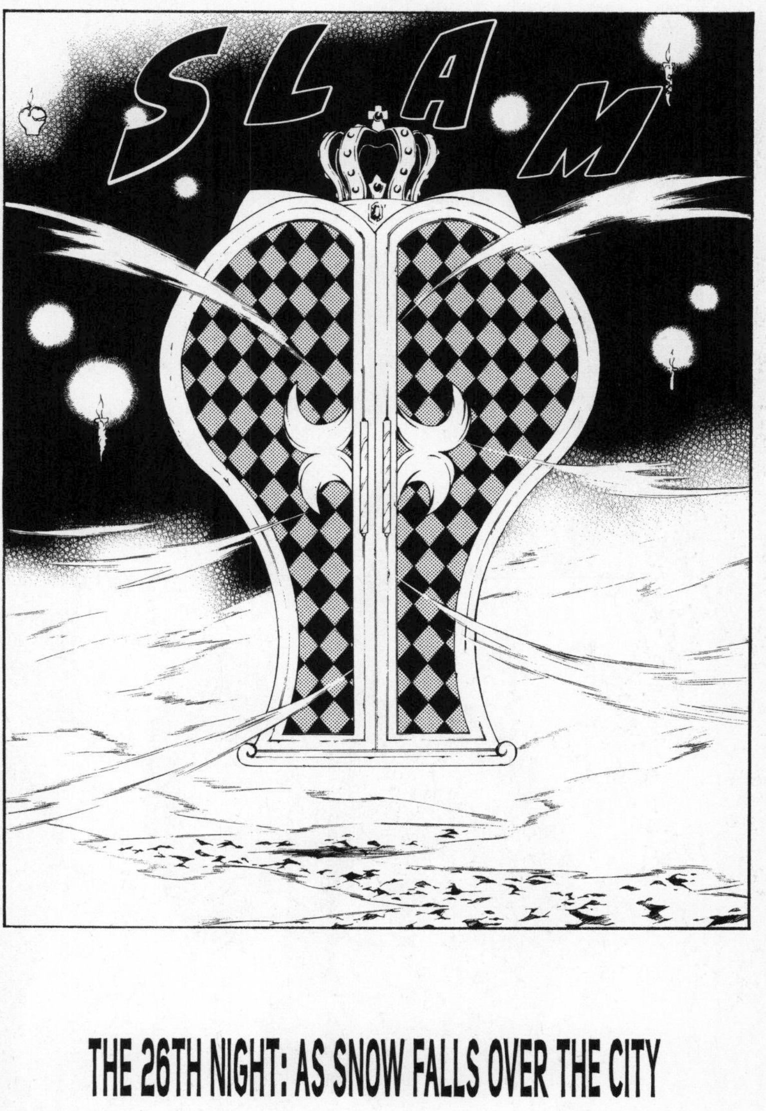
SLAM

THE 26TH NIGHT: AS SNOW FALLS OVER THE CITY

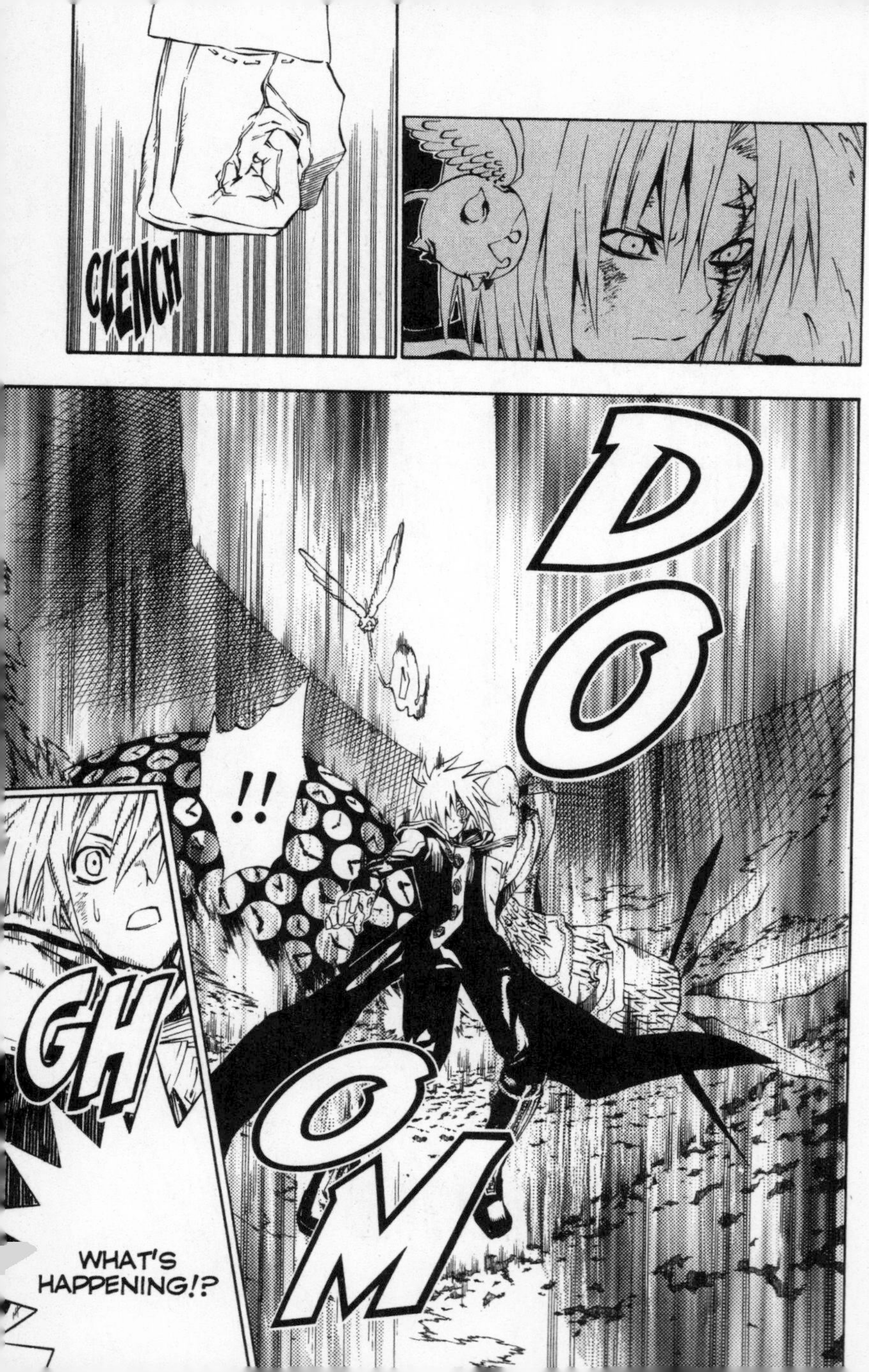
CLENCH
DOOM
!!
GH
WHAT'S HAPPENING!?

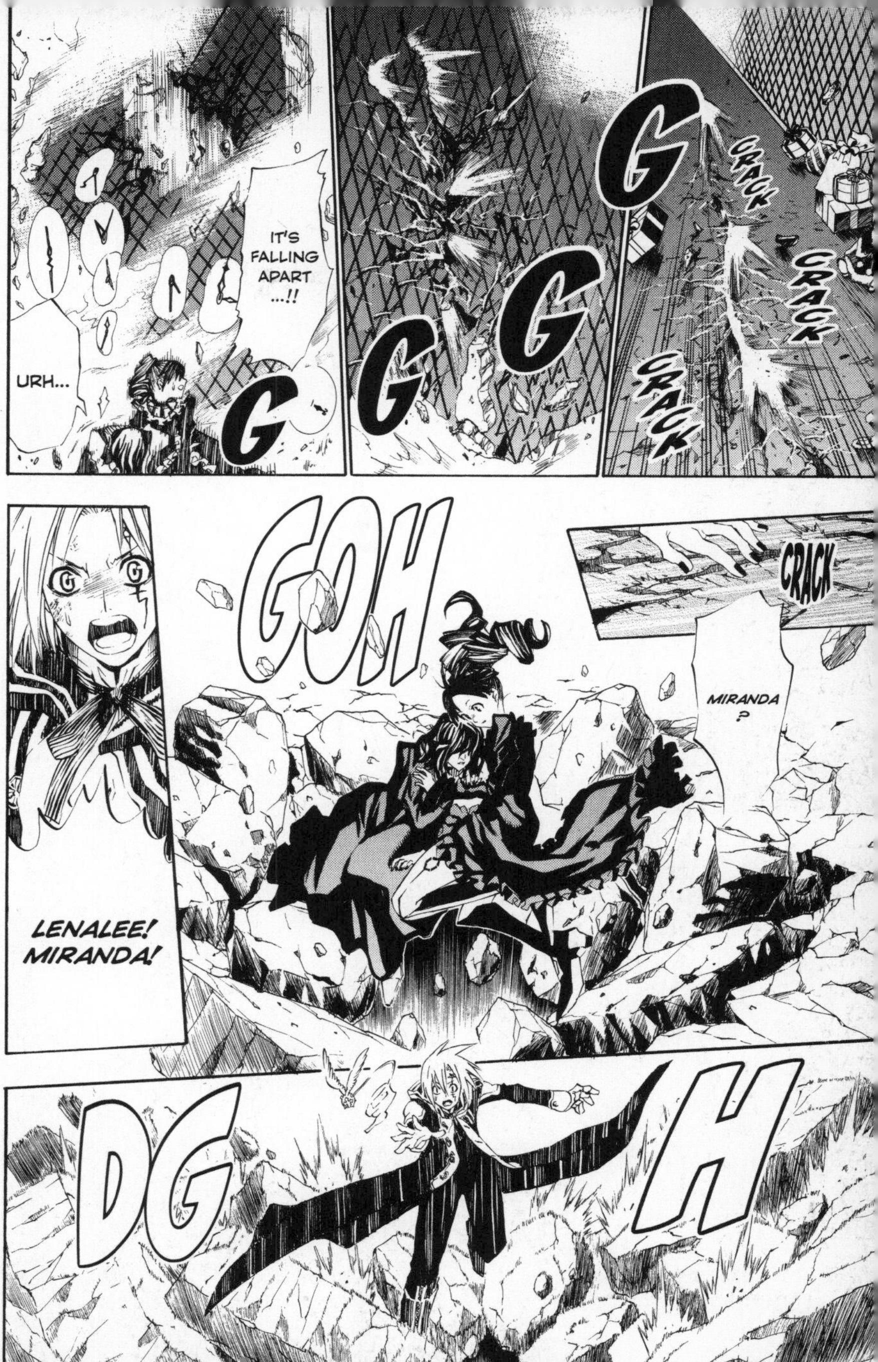
G
CRACK
CRACK
CRACK
G
G
G
IT'S FALLING APART ...!!
URH...
CRACK
MIRANDA ?
GOH
LENALEE! MIRANDA!
DG
H

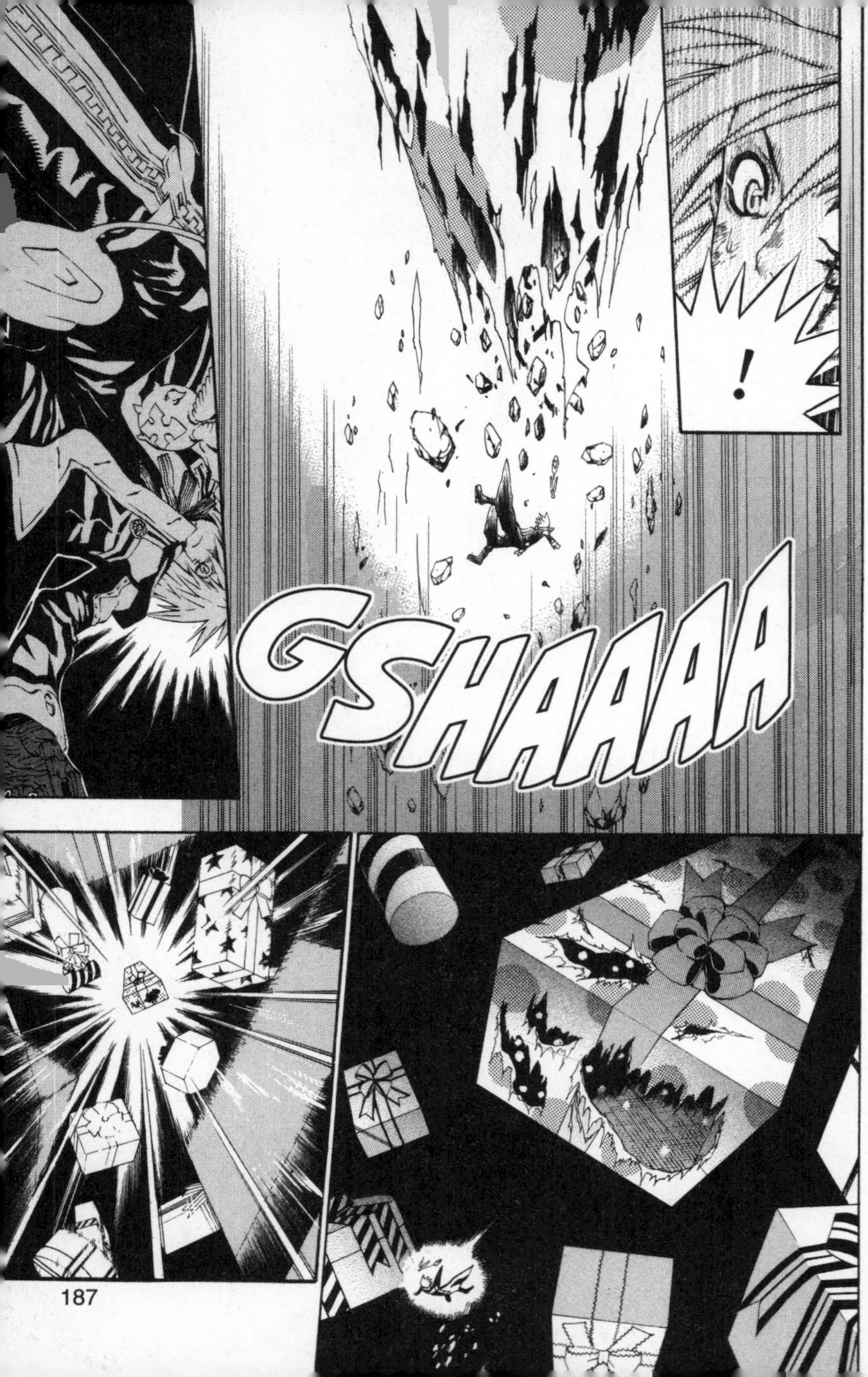
!
GSHAAAA

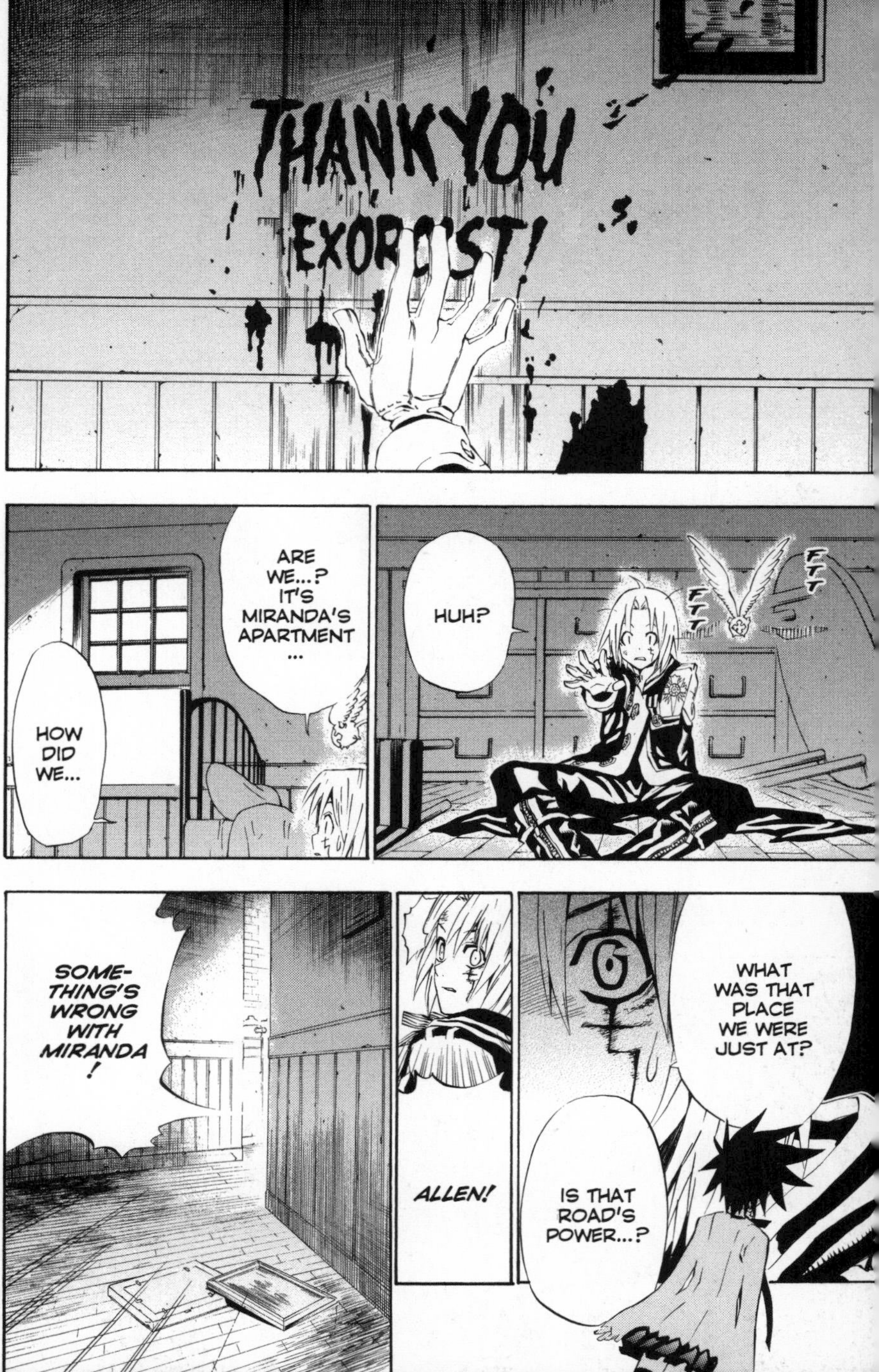
THANK YOU EXORCIST!
HUH?
FTT
FTT
ARE WE...? IT'S MIRANDA'S APARTMENT...
HOW DID WE...
WHAT WAS THAT PLACE WE WERE JUST AT?
IS THAT ROAD'S POWER...?
ALLEN!
SOME-THING'S WRONG WITH MIRANDA!

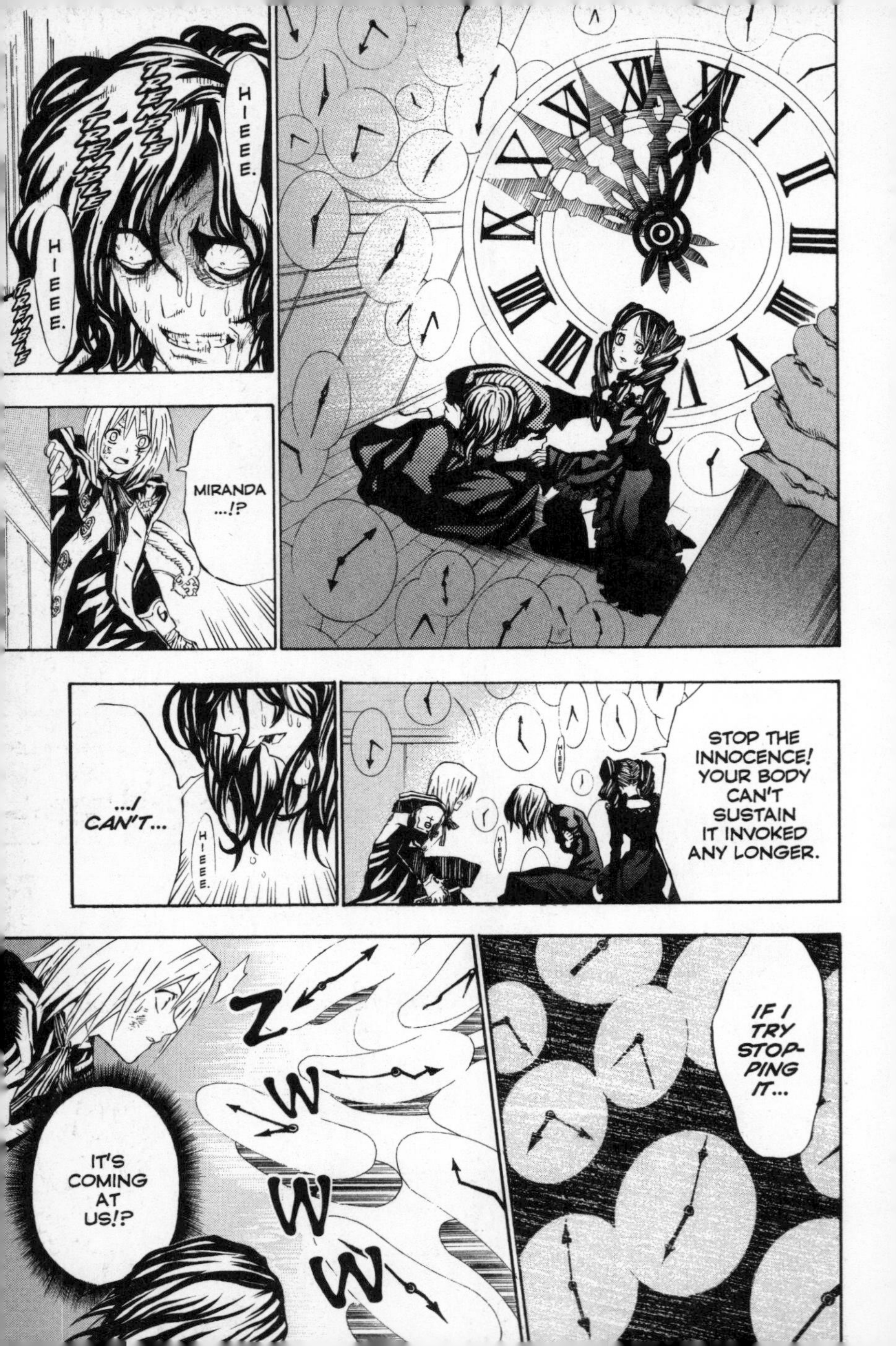

HIEEE.
HIEEE.
TREMBLE TREMBLE TREMBLE
MIRANDA ...!?
STOP THE INNOCENCE! YOUR BODY CAN'T SUSTAIN IT INVOKED ANY LONGER.
...I CAN'T...
HIEEE.
IF I TRY STOPPING IT...
IT'S COMING AT US!?
ZWWW

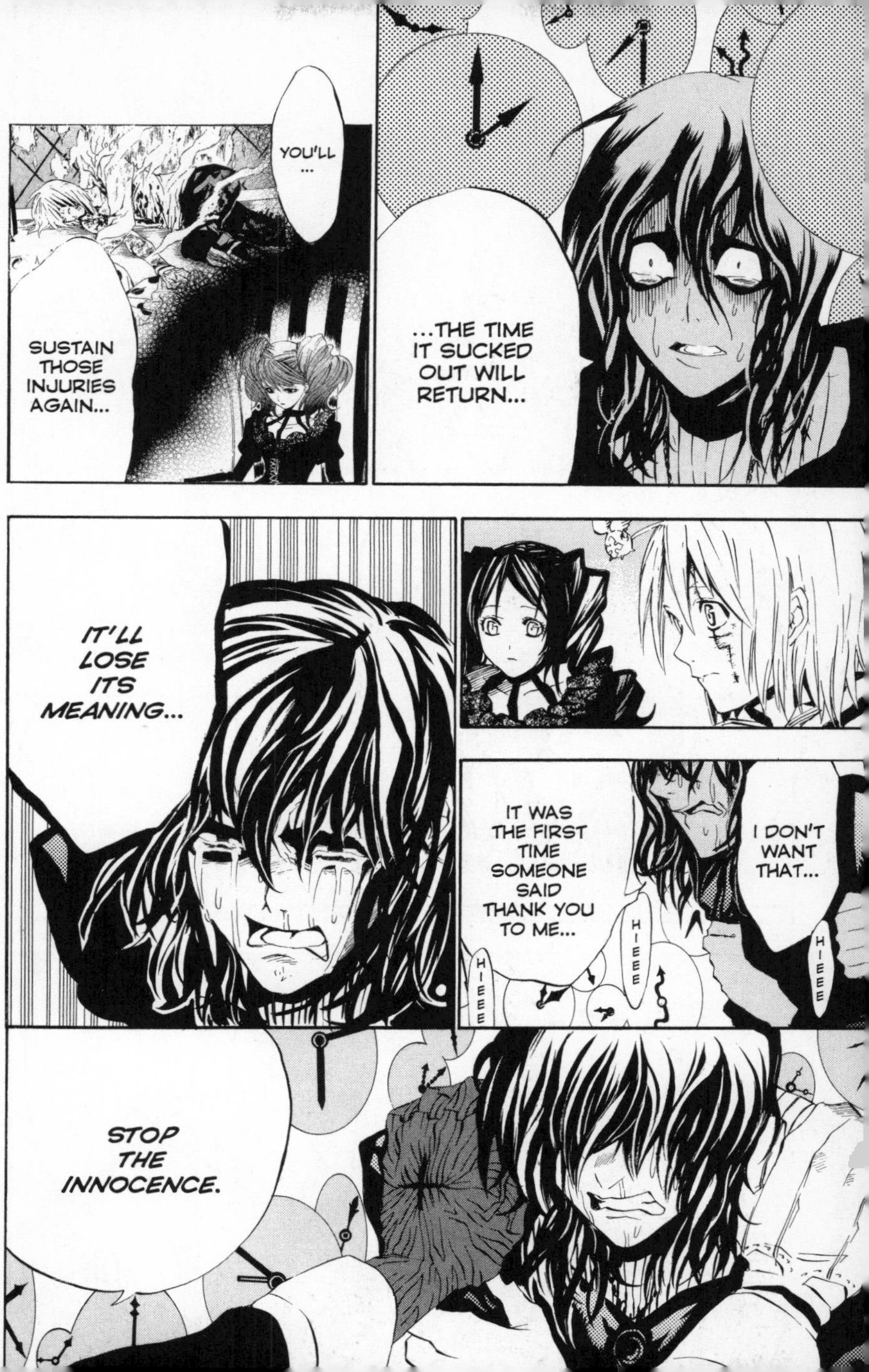
...THE TIME IT SUCKED OUT WILL RETURN...
YOU'LL ...
SUSTAIN THOSE INJURIES AGAIN...
I DON'T WANT THAT...
IT WAS THE FIRST TIME SOMEONE SAID THANK YOU TO ME...
HIEEE
HIEEE
HIEEE
IT'LL LOSE ITS MEANING...
STOP THE INNOCENCE.

READ THIS WAY

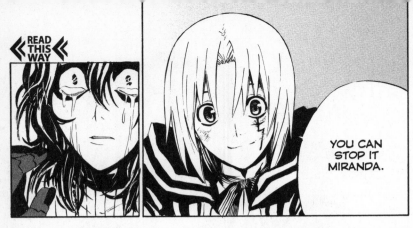

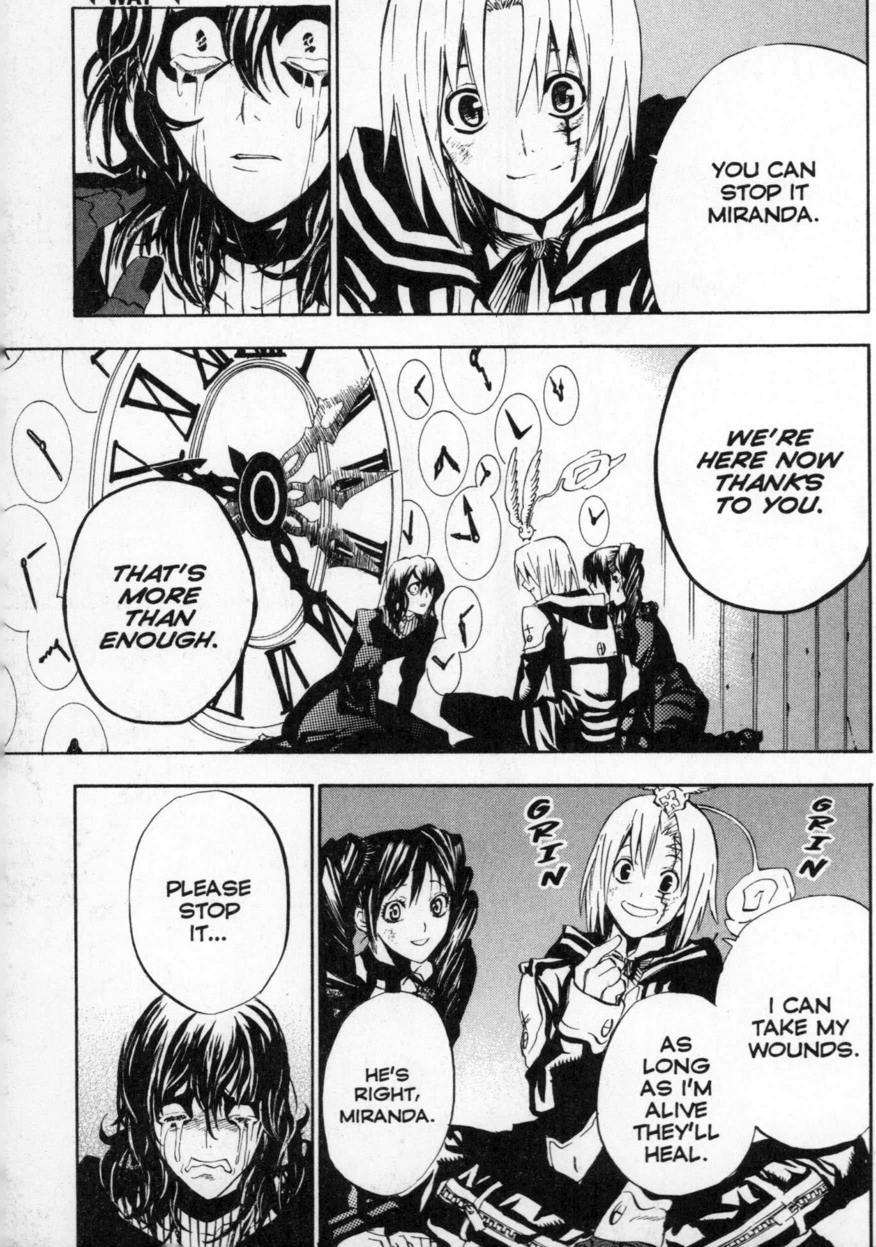
YOU CAN STOP IT MIRANDA.
WE'RE HERE NOW THANKS TO YOU.
THAT'S MORE THAN ENOUGH.
GRIN
GRIN
I CAN TAKE MY WOUNDS.
AS LONG AS I'M ALIVE THEY'LL HEAL.
HE'S RIGHT, MIRANDA.
PLEASE STOP IT...

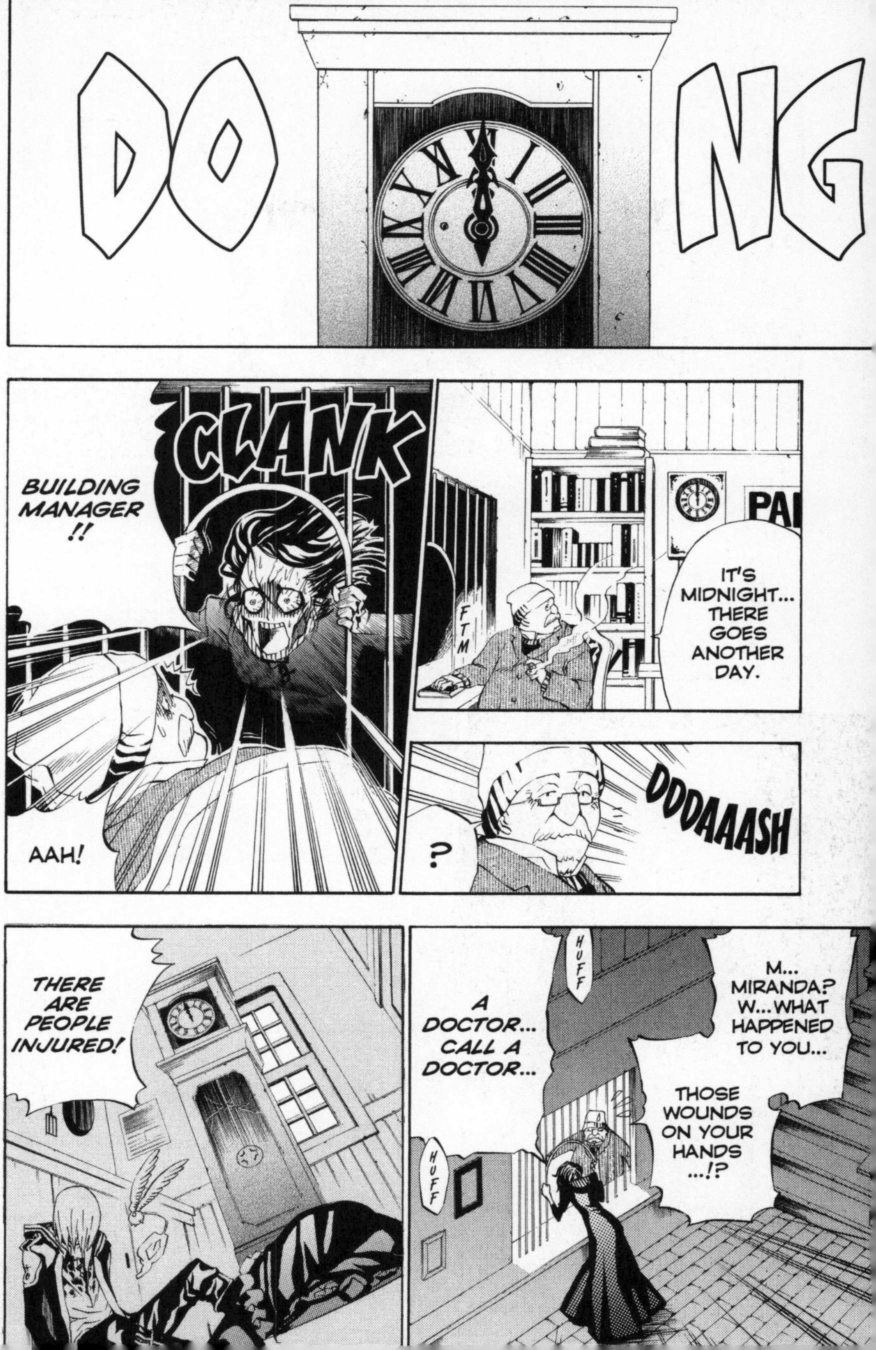
DONG
IT'S MIDNIGHT... THERE GOES ANOTHER DAY.
FTM
DDDAAASH
?
CLANK
BUILDING MANAGER !!
AAH!
M... MIRANDA? W...WHAT HAPPENED TO YOU...
HUFF
A DOCTOR... CALL A DOCTOR...
THOSE WOUNDS ON YOUR HANDS ...!?
HUFF
THERE ARE PEOPLE INJURED!

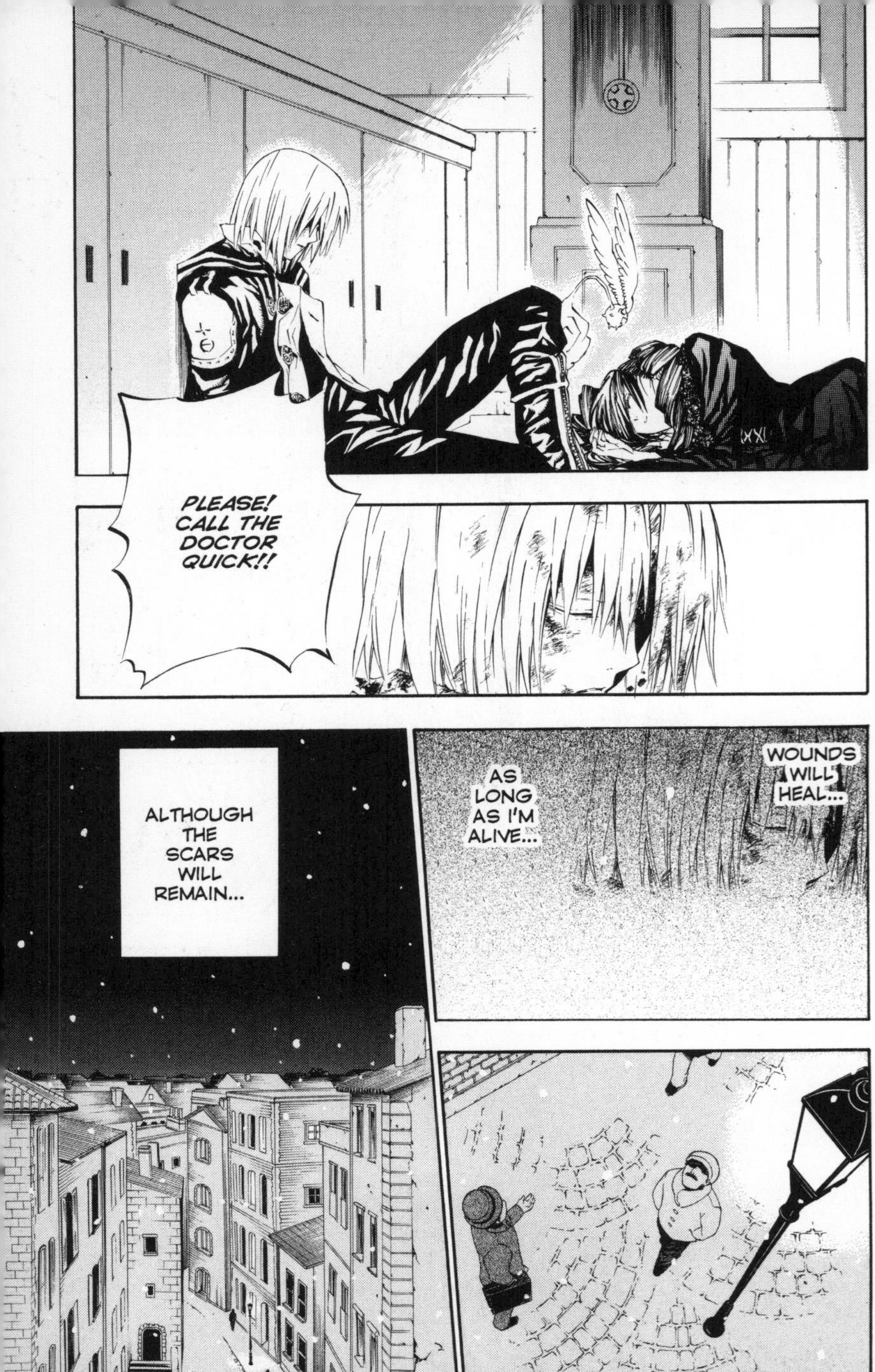
PLEASE! CALL THE DOCTOR QUICK!!
WOUNDS WILL HEAL...
AS LONG AS I'M ALIVE...
ALTHOUGH THE SCARS WILL REMAIN...

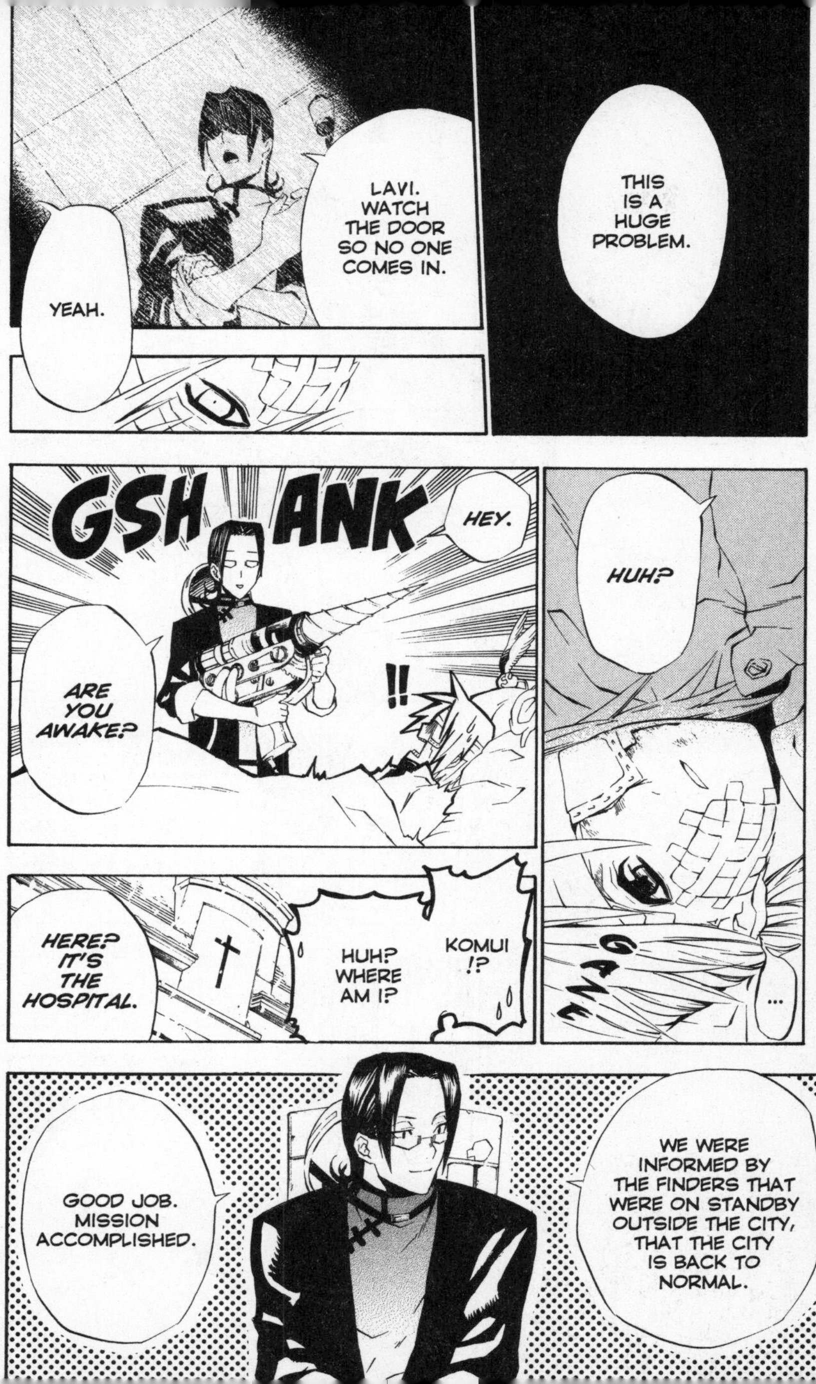
THIS IS A HUGE PROBLEM.
LAVI. WATCH THE DOOR SO NO ONE COMES IN.
YEAH.
HUH?
GAZE
...
GSH ANK
HEY.
ARE YOU AWAKE?
!!
KOMUI !?
HUH? WHERE AM I?
HERE? IT'S THE HOSPITAL.
WE WERE INFORMED BY THE FINDERS THAT WERE ON STANDBY OUTSIDE THE CITY, THAT THE CITY IS BACK TO NORMAL.
GOOD JOB. MISSION ACCOMPLISHED.

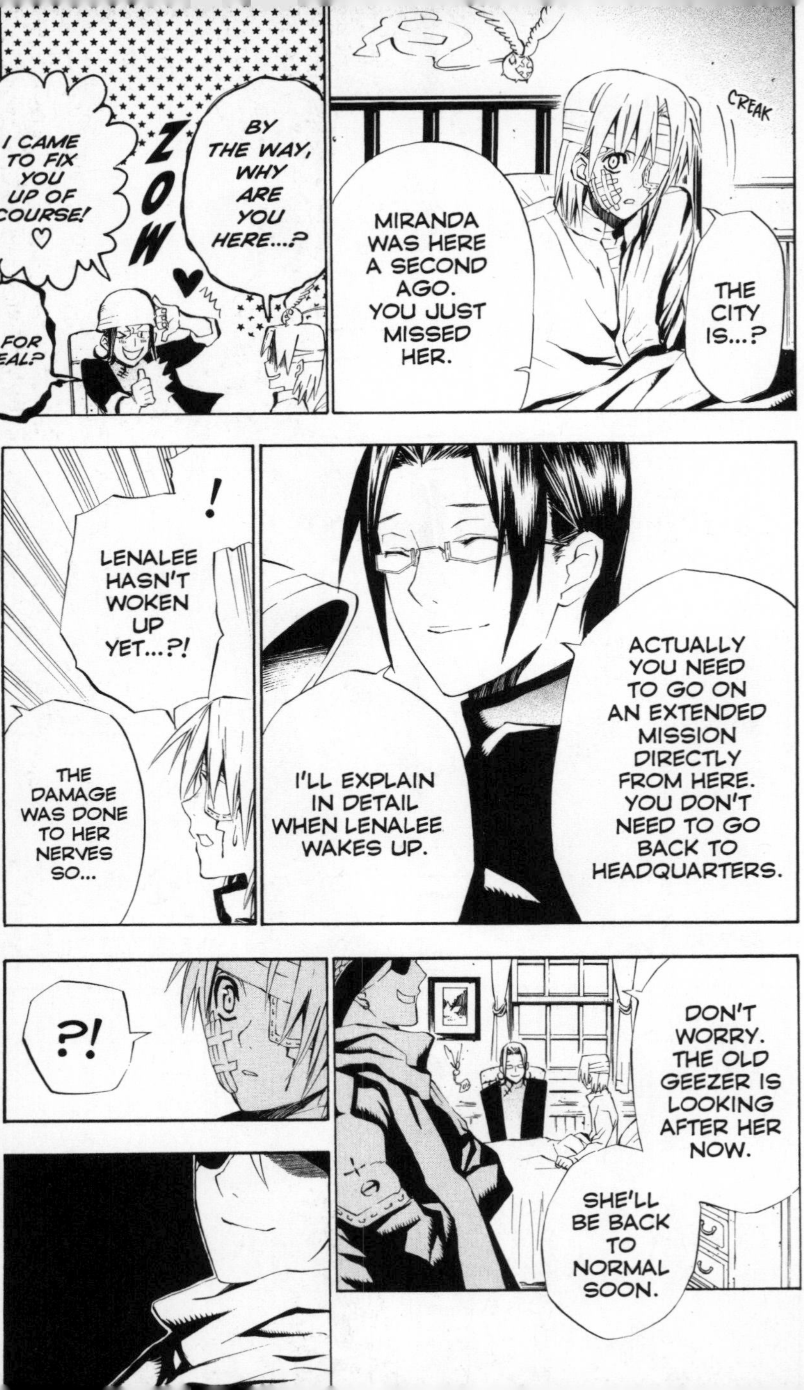
CREAK
THE CITY IS...?
MIRANDA WAS HERE A SECOND AGO. YOU JUST MISSED HER.
BY THE WAY, WHY ARE YOU HERE...?
ZOW
I CAME TO FIX YOU UP OF COURSE! ♡
...FOR REAL?
ACTUALLY YOU NEED TO GO ON AN EXTENDED MISSION DIRECTLY FROM HERE. YOU DON'T NEED TO GO BACK TO HEADQUARTERS.
I'LL EXPLAIN IN DETAIL WHEN LENALEE WAKES UP.
!
LENALEE HASN'T WOKEN UP YET...?!
THE DAMAGE WAS DONE TO HER NERVES SO...
DON'T WORRY. THE OLD GEEZER IS LOOKING AFTER HER NOW.
SHE'LL BE BACK TO NORMAL SOON.
?!

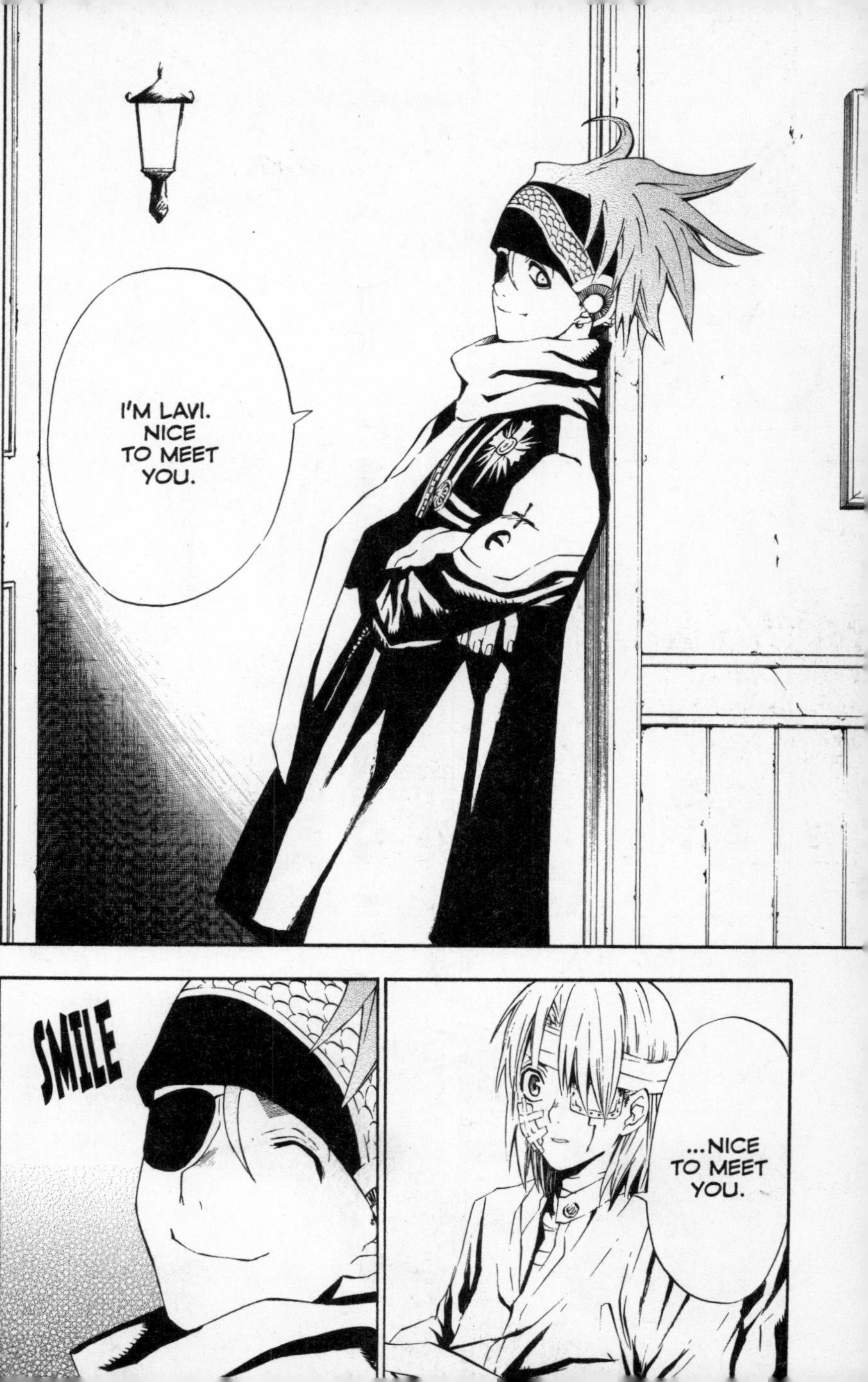
I'M LAVI. NICE TO MEET YOU.
...NICE TO MEET YOU.
SMILE

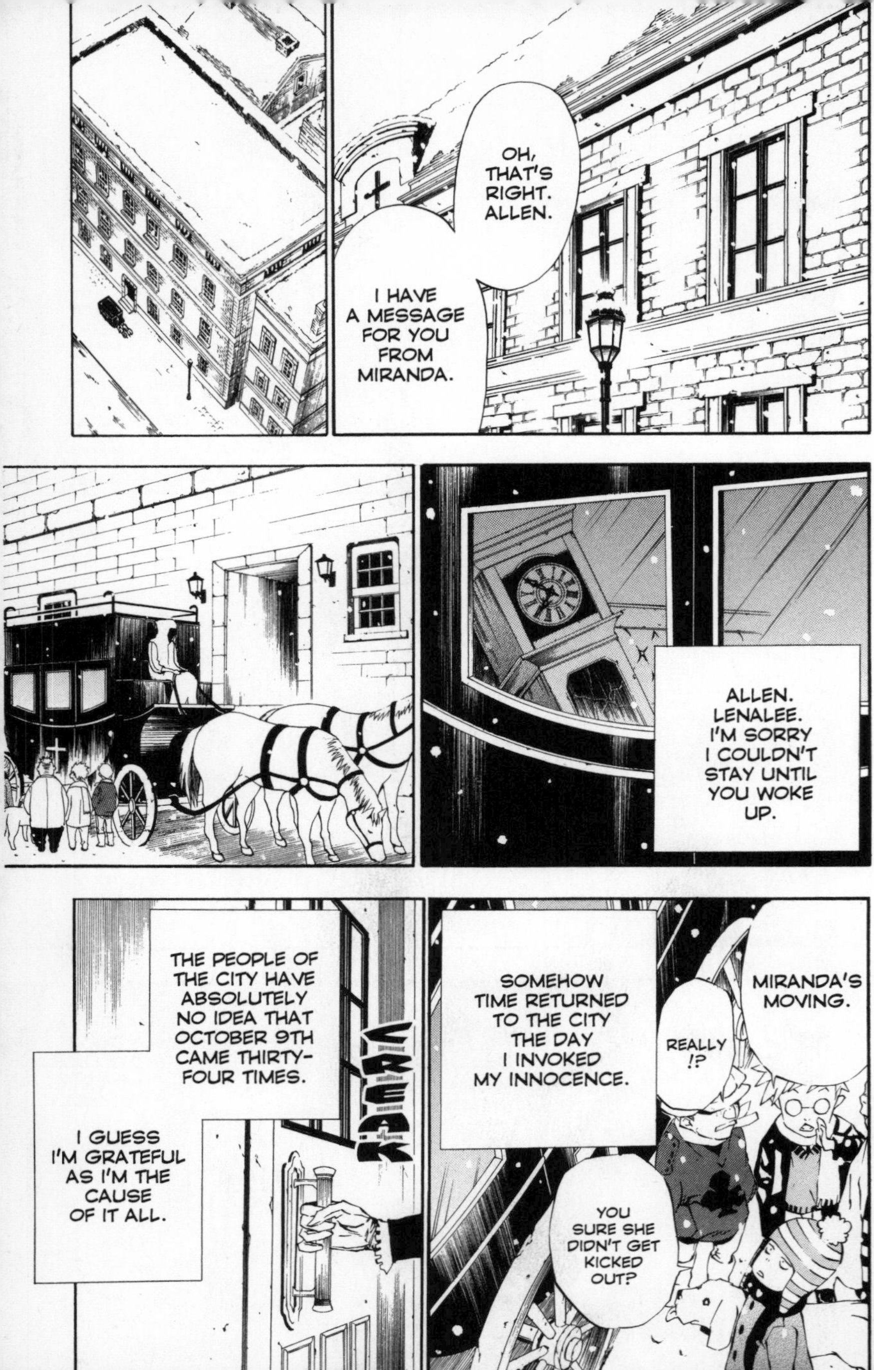
OH, THAT'S RIGHT. ALLEN.
I HAVE A MESSAGE FOR YOU FROM MIRANDA.
ALLEN. LENALEE. I'M SORRY I COULDN'T STAY UNTIL YOU WOKE UP.
MIRANDA'S MOVING.
SOMEHOW TIME RETURNED TO THE CITY THE DAY I INVOKED MY INNOCENCE.
REALLY!?
YOU SURE SHE DIDN'T GET KICKED OUT?
THE PEOPLE OF THE CITY HAVE ABSOLUTELY NO IDEA THAT OCTOBER 9TH CAME THIRTY-FOUR TIMES.
CREAK
I GUESS I'M GRATEFUL AS I'M THE CAUSE OF IT ALL.

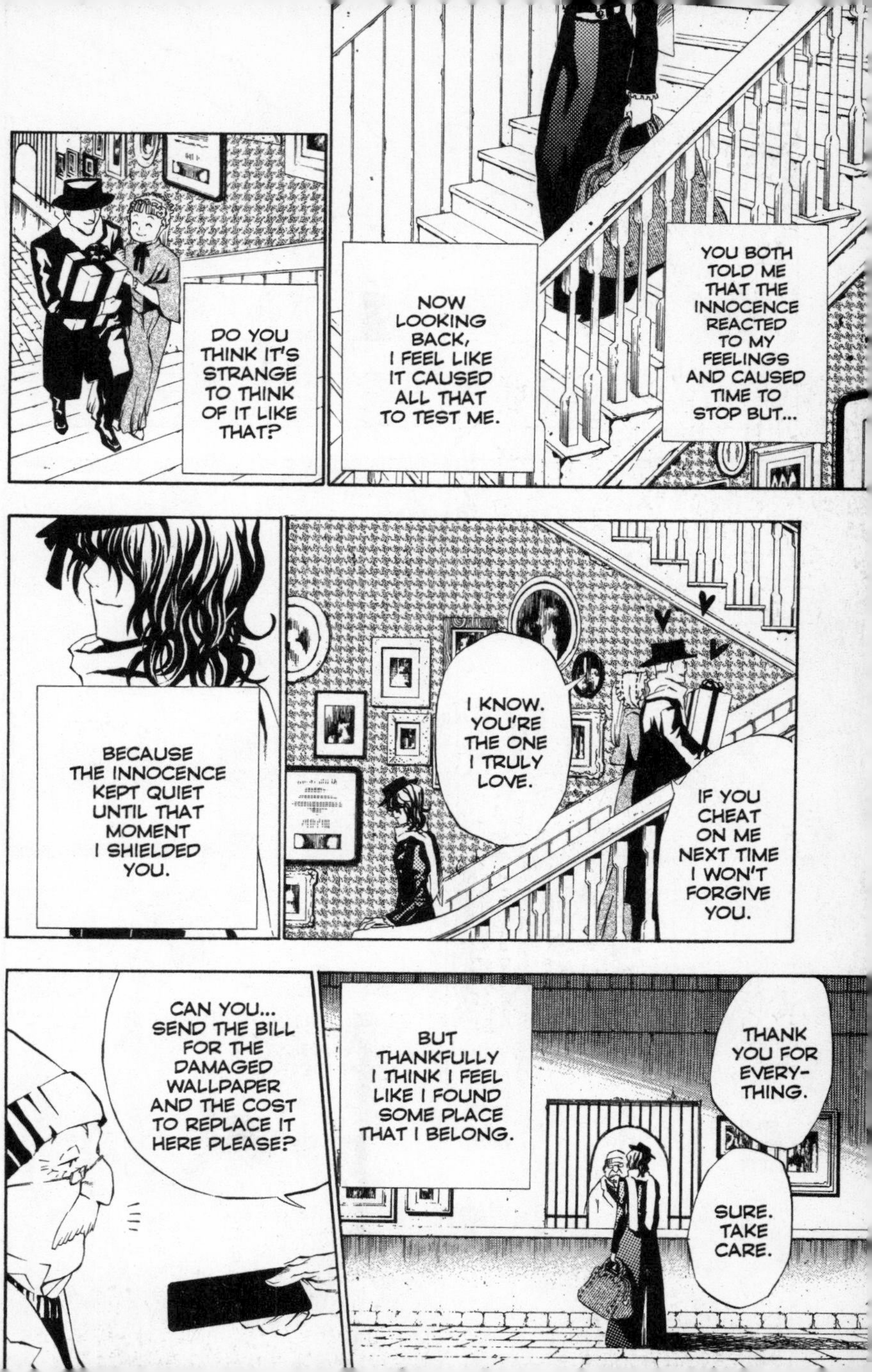
YOU BOTH TOLD ME THAT THE INNOCENCE REACTED TO MY FEELINGS AND CAUSED TIME TO STOP BUT...
NOW LOOKING BACK, I FEEL LIKE IT CAUSED ALL THAT TO TEST ME.
DO YOU THINK IT'S STRANGE TO THINK OF IT LIKE THAT?
I KNOW. YOU'RE THE ONE I TRULY LOVE.
IF YOU CHEAT ON ME NEXT TIME I WON'T FORGIVE YOU.
BECAUSE THE INNOCENCE KEPT QUIET UNTIL THAT MOMENT I SHIELDED YOU.
THANK YOU FOR EVERY-THING.
SURE. TAKE CARE.
BUT THANKFULLY I THINK I FEEL LIKE I FOUND SOME PLACE THAT I BELONG.
CAN YOU... SEND THE BILL FOR THE DAMAGED WALLPAPER AND THE COST TO REPLACE IT HERE PLEASE?

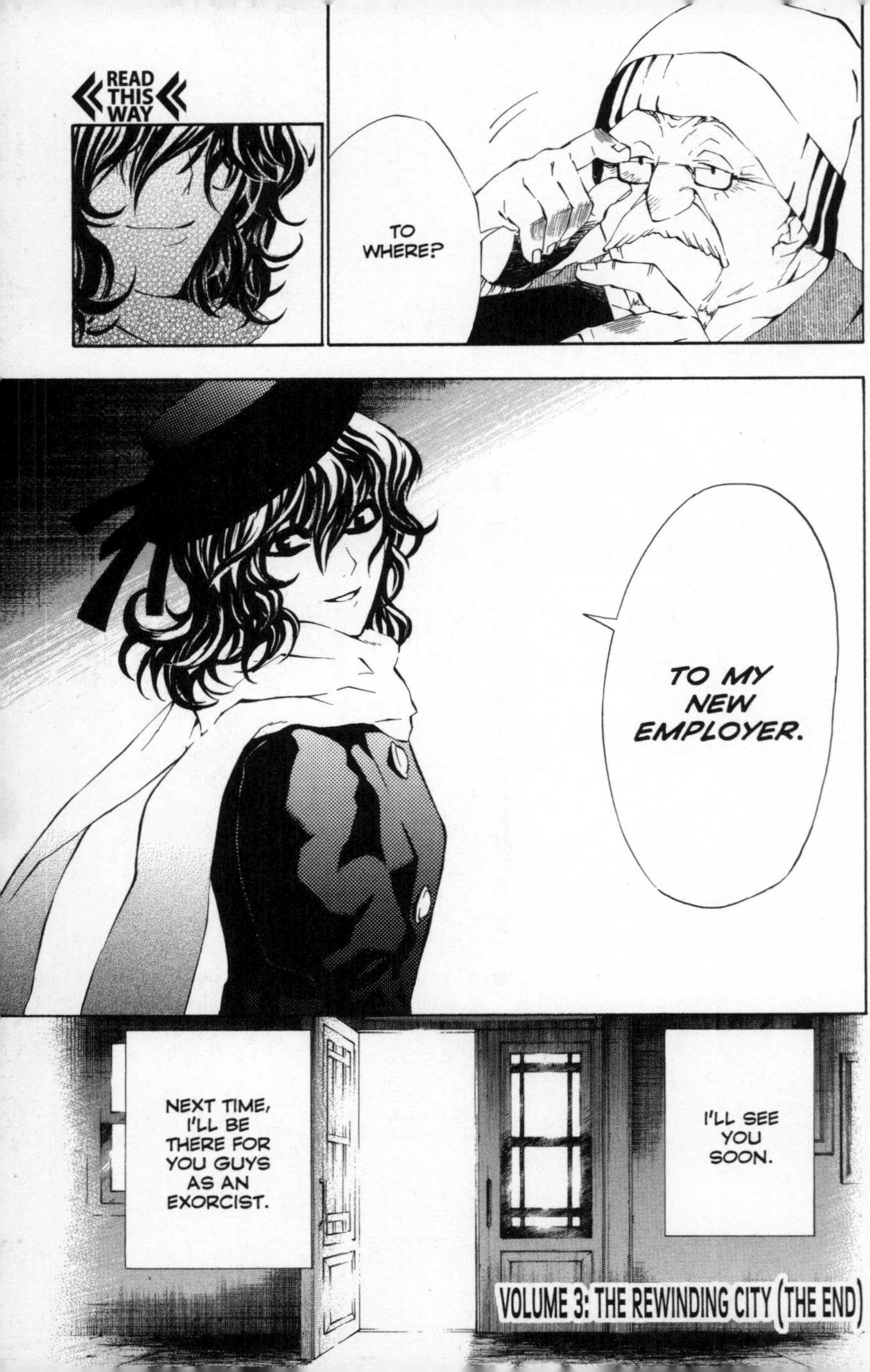
READ THIS WAY
TO WHERE?
TO MY NEW EMPLOYER.
I'LL SEE YOU SOON.
NEXT TIME, I'LL BE THERE FOR YOU GUYS AS AN EXORCIST.
VOLUME 3: THE REWINDING CITY (THE END)

IN THE NEXT VOLUME...

The Akuma have been attacking the leaders of the Black Ministry, searching for something called the "Heart" of the Innocence. Allen is sent to investigate and find his master, Cross, deep in the heart of Germany. En Route he finds himself detoured when he winds up helping a small town with a little Vampire problem.

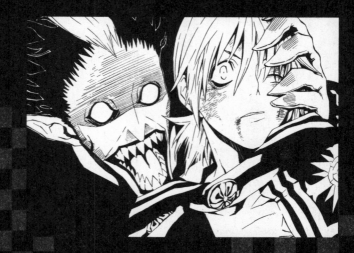

Available Now!

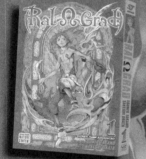
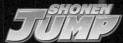

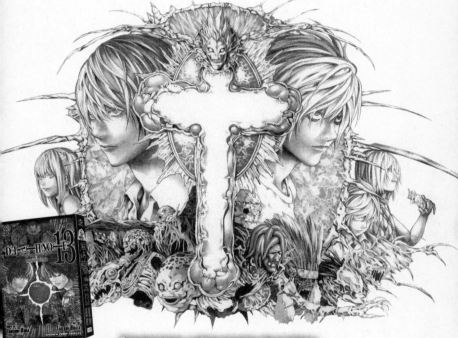

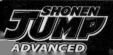

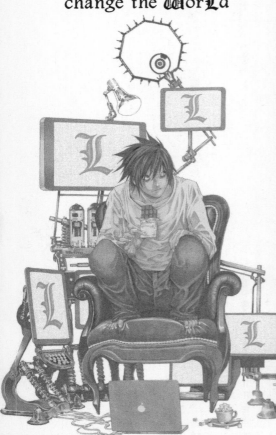
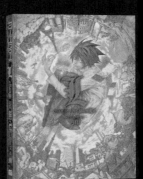

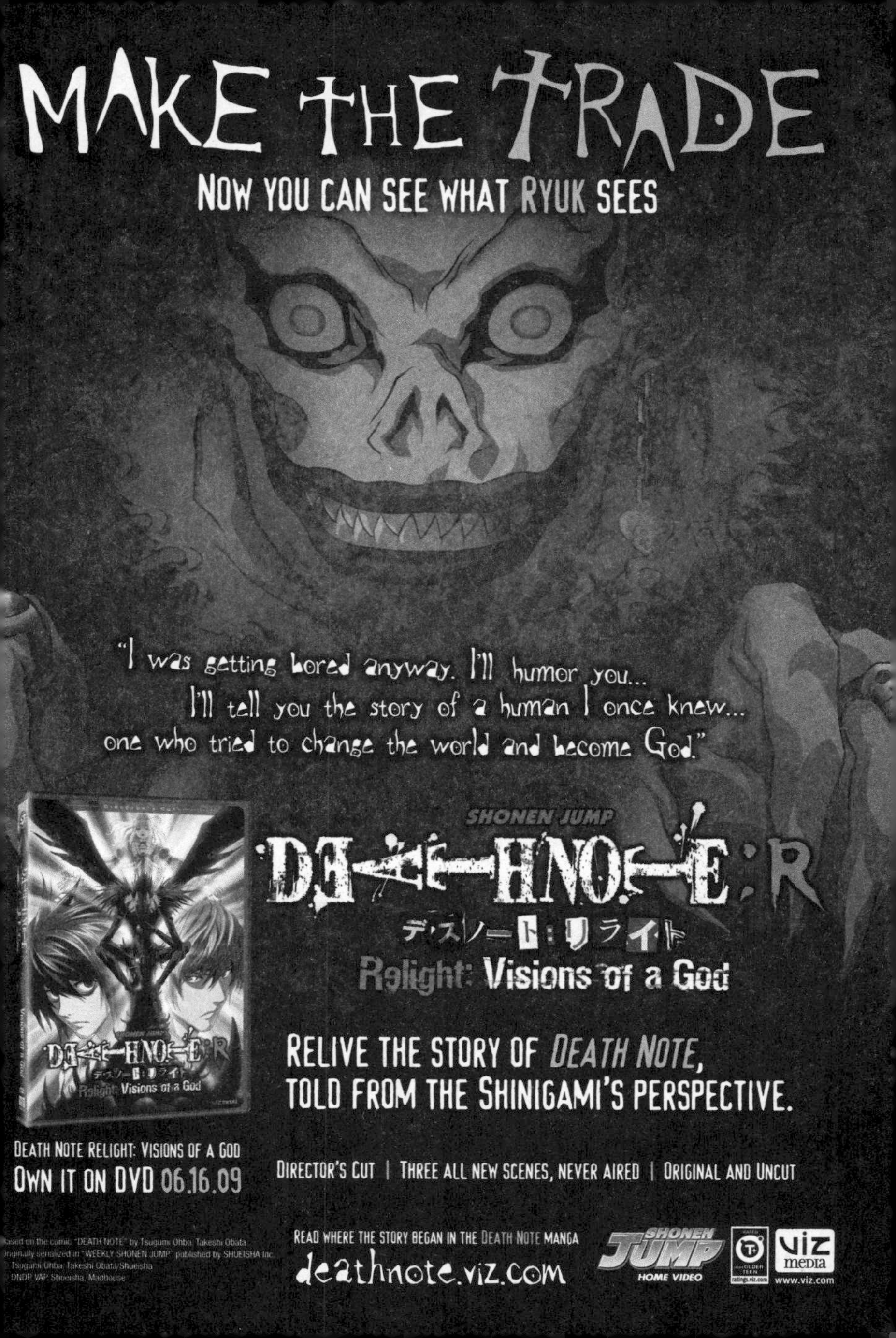

MAKE THE TRADE
NOW YOU CAN SEE WHAT RYUK SEES
"I was getting bored anyway. I'll humor you... I'll tell you the story of a human I once knew... one who tried to change the world and become God."
SHONEN JUMP
DEATH NOTE:R
デスノート:リライト
Relight: Visions of a God
RELIVE THE STORY OF DEATH NOTE, TOLD FROM THE SHINIGAMI'S PERSPECTIVE.
DEATH NOTE RELIGHT: VISIONS OF A GOD
OWN IT ON DVD 06.16.09
DIRECTOR'S CUT | THREE ALL NEW SCENES, NEVER AIRED | ORIGINAL AND UNCUT
READ WHERE THE STORY BEGAN IN THE DEATH NOTE MANGA
deathnote.viz.com
SHONEN JUMP HOME VIDEO
viz media
www.viz.com
Based on the comic "DEATH NOTE" by Tsugumi Ohba, Takeshi Obata
Originally serialized in "WEEKLY SHONEN JUMP" published by SHUEISHA Inc.
© Tsugumi Ohba, Takeshi Obata/Shueisha
© DNDP, VAP, Shueisha, Madhouse

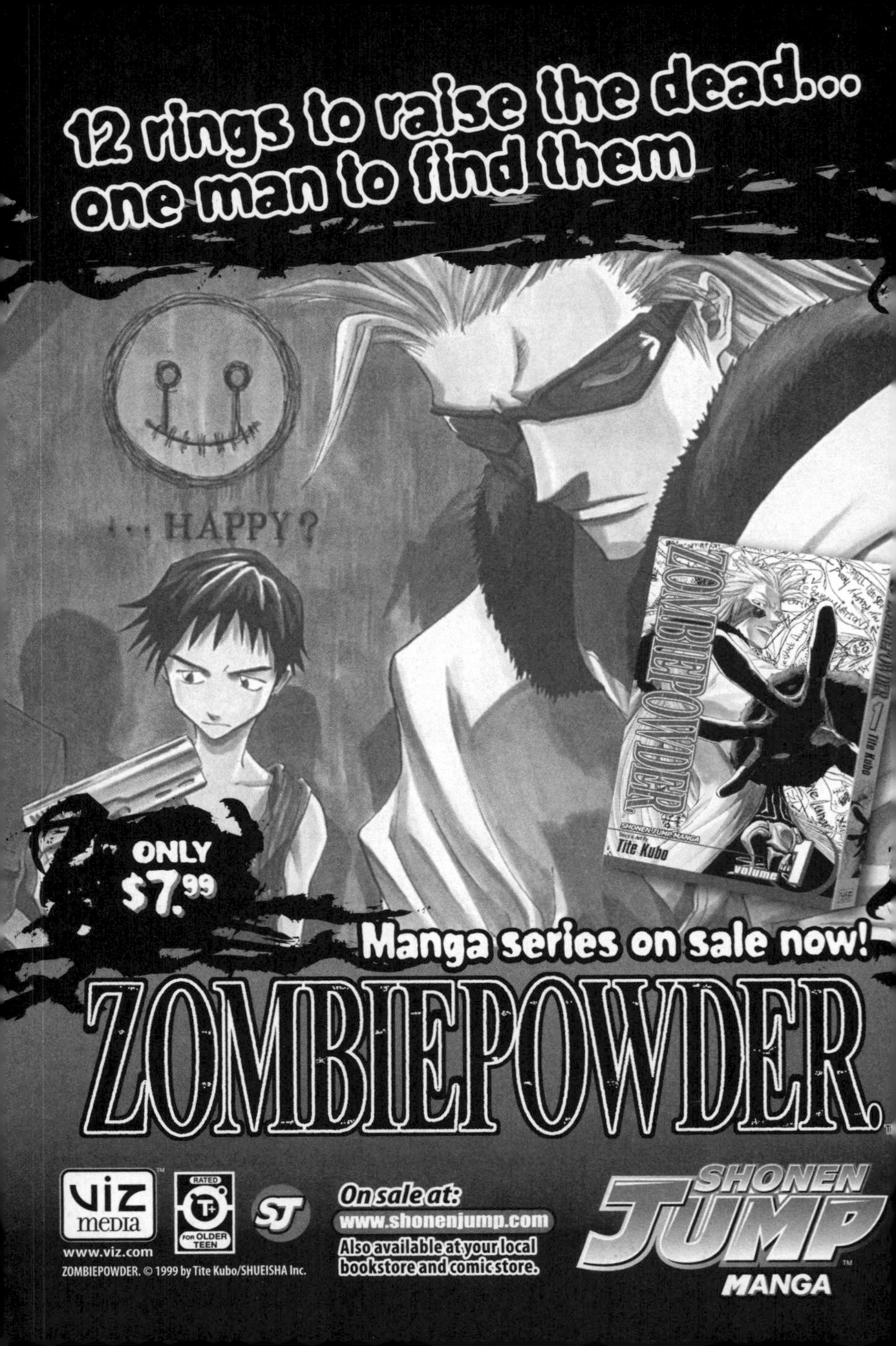

12 rings to raise the dead...
one man to find them
...HAPPY?
ZOMBIEPOWDER 1
Tite Kubo
SHONEN JUMP MANGA
Tite Kubo
volume 1
ONLY $7.99
Manga series on sale now!
ZOMBIEPOWDER.
viz media
RATED T+ FOR OLDER TEEN
SJ
On sale at:
www.shonenjump.com
Also available at your local bookstore and comic store.
www.viz.com
ZOMBIEPOWDER. © 1999 by Tite Kubo/SHUEISHA Inc.
SHONEN JUMP MANGA

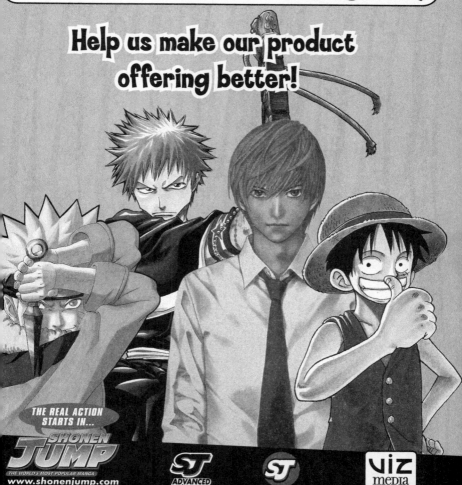

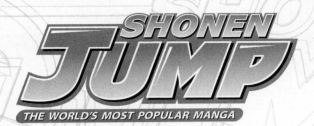
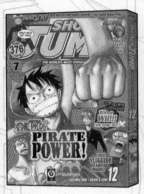
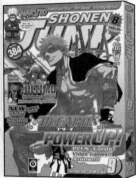
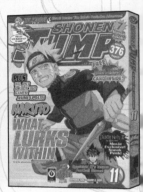

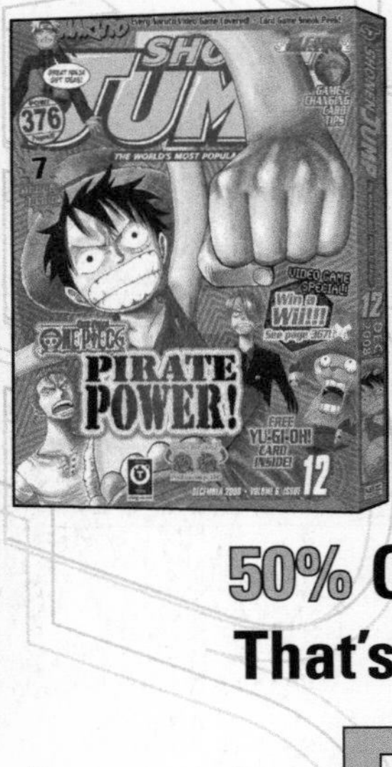

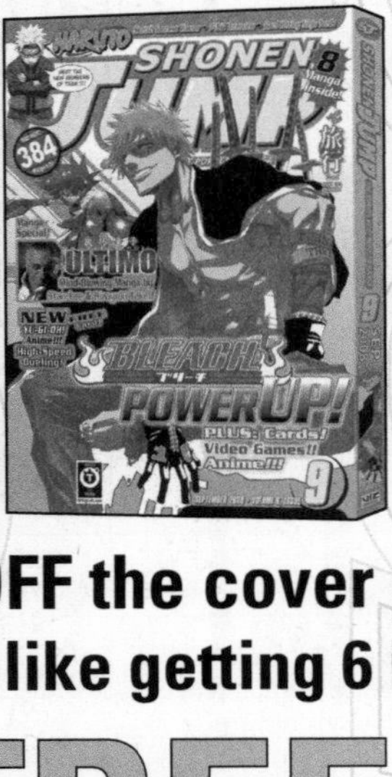

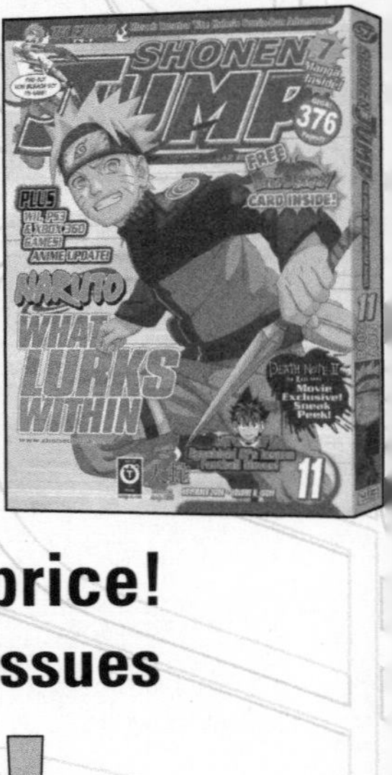

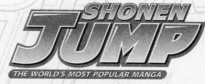